ROSICRUCIANISM RENEWED

The Unity of Art, Science, and Religion

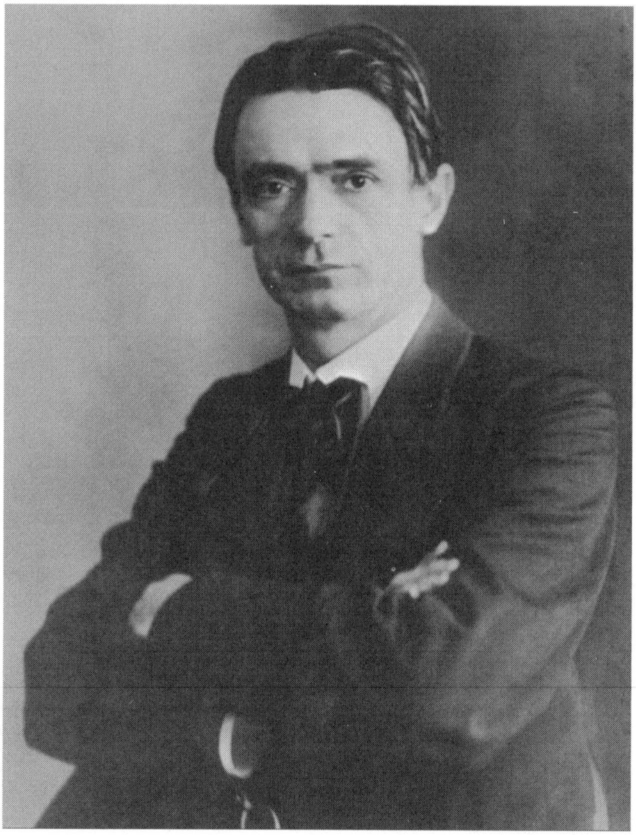

RUDOLF STEINER (1905)

ROSICRUCIANISM RENEWED

The Unity of Art, Science, and Religion

The Theosophical Congress of Whitsun 1907

Essays and Lectures from 1907, 1909, and 1911
with Reports by Marie Steiner, Mathilde Scholl,
Ludwig Kleeberg, and E.A. Karl Stockmeyer

Translated by Marsha Post
Edited by Joan deRis Allen
Introduction by Christopher Bamford

RUDOLF STEINER

SteinerBooks

CW 284

SteinerBooks
Anthroposophic Press

610 Main Street
Great Barrington, Massachusetts 01230
www.steinerbooks.org

Original translation from the German by Marsha Post.

This book is volume 284 in the Collected Works (CW) of Rudolf Steiner, published by SteinerBooks, 2007. It is a translation of the German *Bilder Okkulter Siegel und Säulen. Der Münchner Kongress Pfingsten 1907 und Seine Auswirkungen,* published by Rudolf Steiner Verlag, Dornach, Switzerland, 1997.

Library of Congress Cataloging-in-Publication Data

10 9 8 7 6 5 4 3 2 1

Printed in the United States

CONTENTS

The Theosophical Congress in Munich

Report in the magazine *Lucifer-Gnosis,* No. 34 (Summer 1907)

RUDOLF STEINER

Ideas of worldviews made visible in surroundings of the human being. Spiritual-scientific striving in outer arrangements of the Congress. Description of the décor of the congress space. Red the primary color of the walls. Apocalyptic seals and their meaning. The columns correspond to seven columns of the true Rosicrucian initiation temple. Capitals depict planetary evolution of our Earth system.

The Rosicrucian Initiation

First Congress Lecture, Munich, May 19, 1907

RUDOLF STEINER

Hegel's view of evolution: not a repetition but a steady progress. Mentality on physical plane forms no idea of differences from epoch to epoch. Intellect descended most deeply onto physical plane and is at the point of ascending again. Ptolemaic system a projection of astral knowledge onto physical plane. Difference between what Chaldean-Babylonian wisdom saw and what modern science sees. Everything below as above. Truth universal but paths to truth varied. Seven stages of Christian initiation. Rosicrucian intiation born out of necessity of the time. Seven stages of Rosicrucian initiation.

Planetary Evolution and the Evolution of Humanity

Second Congress Lecture, Munich, May 20, 1907

RUDOLF STEINER

Contemplate evolution of cosmos by beginning with the human being. Seven members of the human being. Our planet must alter its form for us to evolve. Seven planetary conditions of Earth. Seven kingdoms or rounds of each planetary stage. Seven conditions of revelation of each kingdom: arupa, rupa, astral, physical, plastic, intellectual, and spiritual (archetypal). Earlier conditions always repeat in later ones. Earth repeated Saturn, Sun, and Moon and now in Earth condition. Cosmic and human evolution intimately connected.

Explanations of the Arrangement and Décor of the Congress Hall

Lecture, Munich, May 21, 1907

RUDOLF STEINER

Explanation of the use of the color red in the lecture hall. The two pillars. The Golden Legend. Producing the philosopher's stone. The Tree of Knowledge and the Tree of Life. The Tree of Death. The Apocalyptic seals. The symbols of the Rosicrucian school: E.D.N. I.C.M. P.S.S.R.

Report of the Congress in the Berlin Branch

Given before the lecture in Berlin, June 12, 1907

RUDOLF STEINER

Theosophy should engage practical life, be a matter of culture. A unity between what we behold and what we feel inwardly. In earlier times every structure was a construction of the soul. Entire village arranged around the church and all etheric streams collected there. Materialistic age has split the unity apart. Healthy outer world can come about through expression of inner soul moods. Theosophical worldview brought to expression in the congress space. Deeper significance of red not to be misjudged. Seven motifs of the columns. Theosophy will be able to offer new column motifs to architecture. Seven Apocalyptic seals between the columns. Principle of Rosicrucianism. Theosophy to raise art to mystery art. Rosicrucianism takes what Christianity has imparted and leads it into the future. Intention of the Congress.

The Apocalyptic Seals

Lecture, Stuttgart, September 16, 1907

RUDOLF STEINER

The human being is a microcosm. Seven Apocalyptic seals. Larynx as reproductive organ of the future. Planet to end in fire matter and human being to speak in the fire matter. Group souls. Apocalyptic animals portray earlier evolutionary condition of the human being. In future human beings will be portrayed with the form of the cosmos, instead of the human form. Sun-face that rests on the cloud-body on the rock and the pillars. Sun will again unite with Earth. The human being to become a Sun-being. The Sun-woman, the beast with seven heads and ten horns. Human being risen to high level like the form of Michael. Whole being of the world revealed in the symbol of the Holy Grail. E.D.N. I.C.M. P.S.S.R.

Symbols and Signs as Effects of Chaos

Lecture, Berlin, October 19, 1907

RUDOLF STEINER

An examination of chaos. Our words today are attached to materialistic meaning of material objects, no longer for spiritual meaning. Theosophical Movement had to come precisely when it did. Rosicrucianism once totally secret, but today may impart some secrets. Gotthold Lessing. Comenius. Johann Baptist van Helmont. Gas a relatively young word coined by Helmont. Chaos and creation. Chaos still there all around us and is the foundation of further-working fertility or fruitfulness. Chaos versus cosmos. None could exist if only cosmos worked upon them. Cosmos as that which was formed out of preceding causes and forces. Seven seals are pictures of the astral world. In the seven columns are the concepts coming into the universe when we examine devachan. The spiritual Music or Harmony of the Spheres that is devachan. A caution concerning the proper use of the seals. All future art will be crystallized esoteric teaching.

pages 95-108

Report on the Congress at the Sixth General Meeting of the German Section of the Theosophical Society

Berlin, October 20, 1907

RUDOLF STEINER

Our intentions visible through the arrangement of the congress space. No deficit due to contribution. Work done in devoted manner. Unity and harmony among workers. Management circumspect. Gratitude for Edouard Schuré and Bernhard Stavenhagen.

pages 109-111

Pictures of the Apocalyptic Seals and Columns: An Introduction to the Portfolio of the Fourteen Plates

October 1907

RUDOLF STEINER

Seals portray facts of astral world, spiritual seeing. Columns depict facts of spiritual world, a spiritual "hearing." Things have archetype in astral world and their primordial forces in spiritual world. Our pictures of Apocalyptic seals based on spiritual-scientific method corresponding to modern spiritual needs. General pictures of encompassing secrets of evolution of humanity. Meaning of Apocalyptic seals. Mystery of creative word. Group souls and Apocalyptic animals: lion, bull,eagle, and "human being." Harmony of the

Spheres. Astral afterimages of spirit land. Apocalyptic riders main points of evolution of human being. Two pillars. Oxygen-rich blood and carbon dioxide-rich blood in human evolution. Tree of Knowledge and Tree of Life. Earth will unite with Sun again. Woman who bears the Sun. Beast with seven heads and ten horns. Sun-human. Cleansed human being, not only spiritual but becomes strong in spirituality. Mystery of the Holy Grail. All evolution based on advancement through seven stages. Description of the metamorphoses of forces in the seven columns: Saturn, Sun, Moon, Mars, Mercury, Jupiter, and Venus columns.

pages 112-120

"The History of Our Society: Four-Times-Seven Years Ago"

Essay from *What's Happening in the Anthroposophical Society: News for Its Members*

(1935)

MARIE STEINER

Rudolf Steiner as bringer of a new element. The attempt to awaken understanding of art in the spiritual life of humanity. The color red has an enlivening effect for some and is divine wrath for others. Dr. Steiner as president of Congress instead of Mrs. Besant. The seals unlocked secrets that ignited the desire for knowledge, or they offended. Greek history spoke in Schuré's Eleusinian drama. The column motifs as the primordial story of the evolution of humanity. The pillar wisdom. E.D.N. I.C.M. P.S.S.R. The Congress as germ for the festival plays. The Congress led to the separation and the later founding of the Anthroposophical Society.

pages 121-123

The Congress in Munich

From *Mitteilungen für die Mitglieder der Deutschen Sektion die Theosopischen Gesellschaft* [News for the members of the German Section of the Theosophical Society]

August 1907

MATHILDE SCHOLL

Description of the daily events of the Congress: music and artistic contributions, greetings, remembering Colonel Olcott, lectures. Décor and arrangement of hall. Two pillars and the Golden Legend. Apocalyptic seals and their meaning.

pages 124-136

Concerning Forerunners of the Goetheanum

Written for [News out of the Anthroposophical work in Germany], Christmas 1949

E. A. KARL STOCKMEYER

Impression of décor of the congress space. Effect of columns and capitals and question of appropriate space with ceiling for them to carry. Process of designing model building in Malsch from indications by Rudolf Steiner. Elliptical room with cupola in form of ellipsoid with three axes. Light source and relation to spring equinox. Overcoming difficulties of design a matter of artistic question translated into the realm of mathematics. Malsch building not finished but the beginning point for another building. The building should be the center for work of the human being. Designing Stuttgart building. Adapting design of Malsch building for space available. Hall served its purpose until WWI. Hall became storeroom, then editorial offices. Column room rediscovered and made into memorial room. 1935 column room torn out. Columns moved to Wiesneck. Excerpt from *Architecture as a Synthesis of the Arts.* First Goetheanum combined two functions; second Goetheanum took over second function. It was also a commemoration building. Anthroposophical Society to accomplish reverse ritual. Floor plan and cross-sections of the model building by Erich Zimmer of Dornach.

pages 146-155

The Architectural Problem of the Munich Congress Hall of 1907 and the Design for the Malsch Model Building of 1908

(Unfinished Essay from the Last Year of His Life)

E. A. KARL STOCKMEYER

Ellipsoid as an abstract concept that must be clearly determined in building plan if it is to become concrete building element. Dimensions and proportions for Malsch model building. Floor plan for Stuttgart building a bulbous ellipse due to unfavorable size and orientation. Cupola, flat and almost circular, on two-times seven columns. Ellipsoid vaults. Load and support.

pages 156-158

The Roof Vault Resting on Two-Times-Seven Columns

(Notes Out of the Estate of E.A. Karl Stockmeyer)

Form motif of ellipsoid vault with three axes resting on two-times-seven columns stands between Greek temple and the cupola building. Cupola construction makes ancient temple into Christian structure. Rudolf Steiner's temple building merges the tendencies of older temple buildings and cupola buildings.

page 159

The Esoteric Aspects of the Stuttgart Building

Stuttgart, October 15, 1911 (Evening)

RUDOLF STEINER

Mood and atmosphere in this space. Not immaterial which color works upon the human being or how long. Red and blue colors. Transparent color versus color on opaque wall. Effect and significance of signs and symbols in this space. The musical element. Two pictures by Stockmeyer. Two motifs in two pictures. Two motifs in one picture. Raphael's *Sistine Madonna.* Significance of Theosophical work having its own home.

In What Sense Are We Theosophists, and in What Sense Are We Rosicrucians?

Stuttgart, October 16, 1911

RUDOLF STEINER

Harm of one-sidedness. Importance of worthy surroundings for spiritual knowledge. Discipline to wait for answers to questions. Develop sense for what particular time can provide out of spiritual world. Theosophy creates foundation where most varied findings can flourish. A strict law. The Christ-name. Rosicrucianism has flowed into our stream. Difficulties. Blavatsky and Rosicrucianism. Blavatsky concerning Christ. We are Rosicrucians of the twentieth century. We are Theosophists in accordance with first principle of the Theosophical Movement: "No religion is higher than the truth." Christ. Buddha. Practicing tolerance.

Report on the Dedication of the Stuttgart House

From *Mitteilungen für die Mitglieder der Deutschen Sektion der Theosophischen Gesellschaft*, No. 12, November 1911 [News for the Members of the German section of the Theosophical Society]

[AUTHOR UNKNOWN]

Temple built for the spirit. Space worked beautifully and harmoniously upon the spectators; all suitable to produce the right mood and true soul reflection. Brief description of the décor and arrangement of the space. Triangle form, two pictures by Stockmeyer, visibility, Rose Cross. Marie von Sivers. An institute of Theosophical striving is a necessity of life.

Appendix

List of Facsimile Reproductions, Photographs, and Plates

Facsimile Reproductions

Photographs

Plates

INTRODUCTION

CHRISTOPHER BAMFORD

From several perspectives, the present volume, which contains the core proceedings and some important consequences of the Congress of the Federation of the European Sections of the Theosophical Societies (Munich, Whitsun, 1907), records a—perhaps even *the*—pivotal moment in the progressive manifestation of Rudolf Steiner's spiritual mission: to establish Anthroposophy as the mystery teaching of our time. In addition and more generally, the Congress and its documents mark a watershed in the emergence of Western esotericism into the outer, public sphere as a vehicle for cultural and social renewal. The volume therefore has an exoteric historical significance beyond its undoubtedly far-reaching esoteric consequences for the Anthroposophical Movement.

In terms of Steiner's biography, the Congress marked the completion of the seventh year since providence (and karma) had first brought him into the Theosophical orbit in 1900. Having realized during the first half of his life the inner and outer Christian-gnostic and Rosicrucian initiatory stages necessary to step onto the world stage as a teacher, Steiner recognized in the Theosophical Society the right conditions and forces for the realization of his mission. Understanding this, he strove with his entire being to realize the opportunity the moment offered. In 1902, he assumed the mantle of spiritual teacher and accepted the position of the General Secretary of the German Section. Five years of full Theosophical activity followed, during which interest and participation in the Movement expanded exponentially.

However, despite the appropriateness and congeniality of the Theosophical Movement and his dedication to it, Steiner's relationship with the Adyar (India)-based leadership was always ambiguous. From the beginning, he had stated explicitly that, while he recognized the Society's world-historical context and the authenticity of its dispensation, he understood that his own unique spiritual vocation left him free to follow a course based on his experience and mission. While he fully accepted, made his own, and taught with complete sincerity the Theosophical canon (including the Esoteric Section), he did so under the proviso (as he put it) that he would teach nothing that he had not experienced himself and that his own spiritual calling did not determine.

Therefore, since his calling was Western and Christian, and his experience had been given predominantly by intense, extended meditative engagement with his own central-European, German-language tradition, Steiner not so subtly began to change the nature of "Theosophy." He did so covertly by including his own "masters" (Meister Eckhart, Angelus Silesius, Paracelsus, Basil Valentine, Jacob Boehme, the Rosicrucians, Goethe and the great Romantic philosophers and poets (Fichte, Novalis, Hegel, and Schelling) as "Theosophists" in the lineage of Theosophical teachers. In doing so, of course, he affirmed that, just as there was no need to look beyond one's own experience for spiritual insight, so there was no need to turn to the East to discover wisdom, for wisdom existed equally in the West and indeed in a form more appropriate to Western consciousness. More controversially still, by drawing on his German tradition in which Christ and the Christ event in human evolution was implicit, Steiner at the same time placed—and began to elucidate—the "Mystery of Golgotha" as the heart of the Theosophical (Anthroposophical) worldview. In a word, with hindsight, it may be said (as he himself stated on many occasions) that, in fact, Steiner never taught anything other than Anthroposophy.

That something new was entering the world through Rudolf Steiner's teaching did not go unnoticed in Theosophical circles in London and elsewhere. His colleagues in the Theosophical Movement realized that Steiner's approach was different. On the whole, however, they accepted it. They concluded rightly and honestly that Steiner's increasingly Christ-centered, Western, evolutionary approach was compatible with Theosophy, as Madame Blavatsky had envisaged it. Accepting Steiner's brilliance and self-evidently enormous spiritual gifts, they explained what was happening by characterizing him as a "Christian mystic."

As Steiner's sense of his own mission deepened, perhaps providentially again, problems arose within the Theosophical Society, culminating in

1906 with sexual scandals surrounding C.W. Leadbeater, the Society's leading spiritual researcher. Circumstances thus put Rudolf Steiner into an influential position. Without assigning blame or making a judgment in the case, he made it clear that in his view such lapses were inevitable given the "methods" of research Leadbeater employed. For Western human beings, Steiner declared, one sole method was safe and recommended, the Christic-Rosicrucian one.

In this context the historic Munich Theosophical Congress unfolded with far-reaching consequences.

On one hand, realizing discretion was the better part of valor, Annie Besant had the political wisdom to acknowledge Steiner's unique spiritual calling and give him her permission to pursue his own course and teach his own way. He would in turn endorse her for President on the death of Colonel Olcott. Besant's blessing had important consequences (such as the establishment of an independent Western-Rosicrucian Esoteric Section), but it would have meant much less had the Congress of which Steiner was the host, organizer, and impresario, not been about to take place. For, with and through the Congress, Steiner was given, and took, the opportunity at last to unveil the full meaning of his "course"—in other words, his mission and the mission of "Anthroposophy"—as effectively as he could at that moment. It is this that constitutes the revolutionary nature of the event.

None of this should suggest that Rudolf Steiner did not wholly honor and respect H. P. Blavatsky and the Theosophical lineage or the aspirations and accomplishments of the Theosophical Society. On the contrary, he embraced the spirit of Theosophy, if not its letter. Rather, he transformed the letter, spiritualizing and incarnating it according to the triple imperative of his own spiritual experience, his Christic-Rosicrucian initiation, and what we might call his deep karmic responsibility. More accurately, however, perhaps he only "seemed" to transform it, for according to his own intuitions, he was doing no more than actualize—out of his own initiate-consciousness—the deep, implicit purpose of its founding.

Put another way, perhaps the best way to describe Rudolf Steiner's relationship to H.P. Blavatsky and the Theosophical stream is to say that, as he saw it, his primary allegiance, as Blavatsky's, was to the Mahatmas or "Masters of Wisdom and the Harmony of Feelings." From this perspective, Steiner always saw himself as a coworker, on the same "team" as Blavatsky, and drew from the same source of inspiration.

As Steiner understood it, this purpose—as indeed his own purpose—was no less than the creation of a new, global spiritual culture: a culture of light. Millennia of the progressive darkening of consciousness had reached a cosmic low-point in the night of mid-nineteenth century materialism. But no sooner had the nadir been reached than, with the turn of the twentieth century, humanity had emerged from the "little" Kali Yuga—the recent Age of Darkness—and stood poised to cross the threshold of the spiritual world. The archangel Michael, mediator of the Christ and cosmic wisdom, and since 1879, the "Regent of the Age," stood ready to help. Potentially then, humanity was ready for an epochal and necessary transformation: from a sense-based, materialist culture to a culture thoroughly permeated on every level by the supersensible worlds. Human activity, and the world itself, could now—if human beings only awoke from the sleep of matter—realize its full sacramental nature once again.

The import of this cosmic-historical understanding was fundamental and global. It asserted that Anthroposophical (Theosophical) teaching, and more importantly Anthroposophical (Theosophical) *practice*, was for the sake of the world, not just a few privileged souls. It was intended for everyone. While there were of course exceptions, the older esoteric societies had become largely elite, exclusive spiritual clubs. Something different was needed now—something that could become, as it were, a seed for the transformation of culture as a whole. Steiner in fact had never taught simply for the enlightenment or redemption of a few. He had always taught that spiritual work, if it was not dedicated to the further evolution of humanity and the cosmos, was an illusion, even a kind of black magic. The early publication of *How to Know Higher Worlds*—addressed to everyone and based on the assumption that spiritual capacities lie dormant in everyone—makes this clear. He saw those who undertook serious spiritual work under his guidance—those who developed their own meditative practices, joined the "Esoteric Section," and took part in the ritual work of the Misraim Service (the "Cognitive Cultic Section")—not as elite, but only as forming a nucleus, a powerful cultural seed or embryonic Temple, whose function was to grow, to expand, until ideally its manifestation was coextensive with human culture itself and no clear line could be drawn between spiritual work and culture.

Such was the mighty vision, which first manifested publicly with the Congress of 1907. From it, the impulse leads through the construction of the first Goetheanum directly to the Christmas Conference of 1923/24, when the Foundation Stone of what was intended to become the new Temple, the "General Anthroposophical Society," was laid in human hearts. Anthroposophy begins here.

The global, underlying idea is that the primary task of Anthroposophy (Theosophy) is the renewal or rebirth of the Mysteries. In other words, the task of Anthroposophy is to create a new and different kind of "Mystery Center," appropriate to the present moment, from which a new kind of "mystery culture" could radiate.

In ancient times, from the fall of Atlantis onward, Mystery Centers had guided humanity in its spiritual and evolutionary development. Such Mystery Centers deriving directly from the Oracles of Atlantis, were the source of all wisdom, transmitted not just horizontally on the plane of history, but vertically as well in the form of the always-available wellspring or grace of new inspirations. From the beginning of the post-Atlantean age to the present, the gift of Atlantis could be received and communicated. Thus, for Rudolf Steiner, the Rosicrucian stream welled directly from Atlantis:

> Atlantis is the source of all Eastern and Western Wisdom...
>
> The wisdom of Atlantis was embodied in water, in a drop of dew. And the word "dew" [German, *Tau*] is nothing other than the ancient Atlantean sound...The [the Egyptian] Tau symbol, the ancient sign of the Cross, is *Crux* in Latin. And what is the name for dew in Latin? *Ros. Ros-Crux* is our Rose-Cross. Now we recognize its true significance. It is the Tao of Atlantis, the wisdom of Atlantis...

During the long pre-historic ages flowing from Atlantis no distinction had been made at first between sacred and profane. Everything heavenly and earthly—divinity, cosmos, nature, and all human activity—was holy. Science, art, and religion were one. All human cognitive activity was experienced as a unity. Even so "late" a manifestation as the historical culture of Egypt, in fact, cannot begin to be understood without recognizing that science, art, and religion are so unified in it that they cannot be taken apart or separated. Over the course of time, however, the Mystery Centers and Mystery Temples slowly declined until with the beginning of Hellenism, around the time of the Mystery of Golgotha, they died away. Without their support, the unity of science, art, and religion gradually separated to become what they are today: namely, as Hella Wiesberger puts it, "an agnostic science, an a-cosmic art, and an atheistic religion." Renewing ancient mystery wisdom in a new way, the 1907 Congress therefore sought to regain that lost unity under a new ideal: science as cognition of the supersensible; art as "seeing" of the supersensible; religion as experience of the supersensible—three in one, one in three, three as one, one as three.

The groundwork for a new science had already been laid both in the epistemological works (*Truth and Knowledge* and *The Philosophy of Freedom*) and in the elucidations of Goethe's Hermetic, participatory approach to nature. The Congress itself, as well as the *Mystery Dramas* and the art of eurythmy that would follow in the years to come, would establish the foundations for a "supersensible aesthetic." The ground for a new religious sensibility, based on the experience of the supersensible, would have to wait for the Foundation Stone Meditation and the Christmas Conference of 1923/24—where it would be prefaced, naturally enough, by the magisterial lectures on *Mystery Knowledge and Mystery Centers* and followed, again naturally enough, by the coda on *Rosicrucianism and Modern Initiation*.

Two more points underlie the deeper, historical meaning of the Congress and so determine Steiner's ideal for the future unfolding of Anthroposophy. First, such a project, while naturally depending upon individuals, is above all *social* and *cultural* and requires people working together. Emerging from the decline of the ancient Mystery cultures, the essentially materialistic tendency had arisen to consider enlightenment or redemption as an individual or personal matter. Though, of course, such a view was in direct contradiction to Christ's sacrifice on Golgotha—

whose inner and outer meaning was primarily the unity of all human beings in the "mystical body"—esoteric societies in the centuries following Golgotha had increasingly become focused on individual illumination. Esoteric societies had become permeated, so to speak, with a kind of egotism. They had become, in contemporary terminology, narcissistic. To create a culture, however, requires the opposite: a selflessness and an understanding that humanity is truly a single organism, a single being, of which we are all members, interdependent, and responsible for and to each other. True spiritual work therefore requires that nothing be undertaken that is not done within, through, and for the single being that we all co-constitute. Of this organism, the group—in this case, the Theosophical (Anthroposophical) Society should be a microcosm.

Bluntly stated, the "rebirth" of the Mysteries is a collective responsibility, requiring the almost magical coinherence of interrelationship of a true social organism in which individuals live for each other—and all "others"—and not for themselves. It is a communal reality. One of the things, in fact, that drew Rudolf Steiner to unite his mission with that of the Theosophical Society was that he recognized in it the coming together of souls—in Theosophical "brotherhood"—capable of the social forces necessary to accomplish it, that is, capable of becoming a microcosmic catalyst for global cultural transformation.

The second point concerns the Rosicrucian element. Rosicrucianism was central in Steiner's life, any close reading of which makes it clear that the spiritual school radiating from the being and personality of Christian Rosenkreutz provided the substance and guiding principles of his teaching and mission. Furthermore, between-the-lines evidence suggests that Rudolf Steiner was actually "initiated" into this school and given the task of revealing it publicly by Christian Rosenkreutz himself. None of this can be explicitly spelled out, but the following may be said. Steiner entered his present incarnation with certain capacities and tasks, which led him in the first place to seek for a contemporary basis, consonant with modern scientific consciousness, for the conscious, distinct, and detailed cognition of supersensible phenomena within the world of experience. His guides in this were the German idealistic philosophers (especially Fichte, Hegel, and Schelling) and above all Goethe, who situated Steiner's effort explicitly in a broadly Hermetic-Rosicrucian context, the tradition which Goethe had assimilated and transformed.

Steiner's project of translating ancient, once and future Rosicrucianism into modern consciousness (implicit in his Goethe work) was blessed by a meeting with a living heir to that tradition, the "old herb gatherer" Felix Kogutski, who in turn introduced Steiner to the "Master," most likely Christian Rosenkreutz himself. This "initiation experience" made it possible for Steiner to complete the inner and outer work—including his cognitive experience of the reality of the Mystery of Golgotha—that allowed him to enter the world-stage with spiritual maturity. It is also the case that, as far as Steiner was concerned, Theosophy in its origins in Blavatsky's *Isis Unveiled* was inspired "by the great initiates of the West who also inspired the Rosicrucian wisdom." Though Blavatsky then came under the influence of "Eastern Initiates"—at first beneficially, then less so—it remained paradigmatic for Steiner that the opening of consciousness represented by Theosophy was destined to be Rosicrucian and to represent its first full, public emergence onto the plane of history.

None of this, and hence Steiner's relationship to Theosophy itself, is without its ambiguities. "Rosicrucian" meant for Steiner, among other things, Christocentric and evolutionary. While *The Secret Doctrine*, Blavatsky's "Eastern" book, was among the first to publicly introduce the idea of a primordial revelation of ancient wisdom (transmitted, in Steiner's account, from Atlantis to form the teaching of the Mystery Centers), it ignored the Christ event and tended to be cyclical, not evolutionary, in its cosmology. That is to say, Theosophy already contained the seeds of the "rebirth of the Mysteries," yet it did so from a perspective that, emphasizing Indian (Hindu and Buddhist) tradition, ignored and even disparaged Judeo-Christian tradition and the Mystery of Golgotha. For Steiner, Rosicrucianism healed and overcame the split and was therefore truly global and hence true Theosophy. Therefore, in his Esoteric Lessons, in addition to the two Theosophical Eastern "Masters" or "Mahatmas," Kuthumi and Morya, Steiner recognized two Western Masters, the Master Jesus and the "fourth Master," Christian Rosenkreutz. But the extent to which Steiner's "Rosicrucian" (Anthroposophical) revolution remained a revolution within Theosophy or whether it was a birth from it of another, different stream must remain moot.

Ultimately, however, the historical event of the Munich Congress, understood as the unveiling of Theosophy in its true Rosicrucian (Anthroposophical) nature, may be seen as a new "Renaissance," the culmination of a series of Renaissances, through which the Rosicrucian impulse unfolded as human consciousness evolved.

According to this "likely story," as Plato would call it, human spiritual history was initially guided (in Steiner's view) by mystery wisdom emanating from Mystery Centers. Approaching the Mystery of Golgotha, as humanity sank deeper into matter, the Mystery Centers slowly declined. Though Greek Mystery Centers such as Eleusis, Ephesus, and Samothrace continued to have an importance into the historical period (Eleusis was not "closed" until the purge of Justinian in the sixth century after Christ), they gradually lost their cultural influence: they went underground. Orphists and others like the Pythagoreans played at best a transitional role, but, as Steiner showed in *Christianity as Mystical Fact*, most of what remained of the Mysteries was transmitted by philosophy.

Most importantly, as all this was occurring, the love of Christ deepened in the hearts of the earliest Christian communities, and Christian "theosophists"—like Clement of Alexandria and Origen—sought to create a new Christian "mystery culture." Overtly, these different elements never cohered sufficiently to form the new impulse of Christianized perennial wisdom in an inclusive culture uniting science, religion, and art. The time was not yet ripe for that. It is true that the monasteries—"schools of love"—were a kind of Mystery School and undoubtedly created a superb, enduring vessel for the transmission of much important wisdom and practice. Yet the overriding reality remains that what had been a unity split into separate and opposing streams, such as Christianity, Rabbinic Judaism, Hermetism, and Platonism, to name only a few, all of whom defined "heresy" and "orthodoxy" relative to their own limited positions. Politics, sectarianism, exclusivity, and spiritual bigotry seemed triumphant. Nevertheless, covertly, much of this great flowering went underground, passing into Celtic Ireland, to resurface at a more opportune moment. The first manifestation that the wisdom of the Mysteries would remain part of human life and not be lost entirely—in other words, the first incipient "Renaissance" (or proto-Renaissance) of mystery wisdom—occurred during Hellenist times in the centuries surrounding Christ's incarnation. This was the time of the so-called Gnostics—spiritual researchers, who, understanding something unique had happened, sought to make experiential, cognitive-mythological sense of it. Paralleling them, Middle and neo-Platonic (and Stoic) philosophers (like Plotinus and Proclus) created esoteric Schools of life, meditation, and sometimes ritual (as in the case of Iamblichus) in which they sought to understand and experience the "divine play" of unity in the multiplicity of the beings and consciousnesses constituting divine and cosmic reality. The deep wisdom of the Mysteries flowed into this situation in the form of the mystery teachings of Homer and the Greek pre-Socratic philosophers, but the historically most important source was Egypt. From that "image of Heaven on Earth," in the form of Hermetism and, above all, alchemy, the ancient and primordial non-dualistic sacred science of the cosmos, nature, and the human being impregnated the new Christian vessel with the seeds of the new culture that was to be born. At the same time, important esoteric elements, such as the secrets of the Eleusinian Mysteries, the Seven Liberal Arts, and the soul's journey through the planetary spheres after death, were also preserved and transmitted by Latin writers such as Apuleius (*The Golden Ass*), Martianus Capella (*The Marriage of Philology and Mercury*), and Boethius (*The Consolation of Philosophy*). Ptolemy and Firmicus Maternus, among others, transmitted astrology. Some of these individuals and groups of so-called Gnostics, philosophers, alchemists, and Hermetists could be said to have formed embryonic Mystery Schools, which, had history been otherwise, would have had an important role to play. But that was not to be, despite the prophetic but doomed attempt by the Emperor Julian (the "Apostate") to unite all the elements in a new proto-Rosicrucian and proto-Anthroposophic solar cult of the Threefold Sun. Nevertheless, even if fragmented and disorganized, everything that had come down from ancient times was present.

That moment, loosely speaking, may be called the "twelfth century Renaissance." Rudolf Steiner speaks of it as a meeting of the "inner"

Christianity of the South and East with the cosmic Christianity of the North. He also indicated it to be the first fruit of the work of the archangel or "folk soul" of esoteric Christianity, who had been the guiding spirit of the Celtic peoples, but had sacrificed that task to become the guide of esoteric Christianity itself. (To guide exoteric Christianity, the "folk soul" of the Greeks had performed a similar sacrifice.)

Like the moment of Hellenism, the twelfth century, was a complex, multifaceted event—necessarily so because one of the meanings of Renaissance is that it is a global event encompassing all human activity from religion, philosophy, and art to psychology, science, and social organization. This makes it difficult to know where to start with a description.

The twelfth and thirteenth centuries witnessed, for instance, both what has been called "the discovery of the individual," traceable in the movement of consciousness from Abelard's discovery of the inner voice of moral responsibility to Aquinas's unfolding of the personality in pure thinking and the appearance of the great Grail cycles (from Robert de Boron's first Cistercian account to Chrétien de Troye's *Perceval* and Wolfram von Eschenbach's *Parzival*, key texts for Steiner) as well as similarly initiatory works like the *Tale of Flor and Blanchflor*, and the *Romant de la Rose*. Echoing these, new preaching and mendicant Orders—preeminently Dominicans and Franciscans—arose with a new sense of Christ and his meaning in the world. Others, like the Carthusians, intensified inner work.

Outwardly, the culture saw the dawning of Sophia, the divine feminine, as evidenced in the new understanding of Mary and the humanity of Jesus as the extension or prolongation of Mary, as in "Jesus our mother." A "Sophianic," soul element runs through the whole period from St. Bernard to Hildegard of Bingen and the School of Chartres, where Hermetic Platonists sought to reopen the Book of Nature and renew the sacred science of the Goddess *Natura* (Steiner speaks of a rebirth of Persephone). From Chartres, too, Alain de Lille (Alanus ab Insulis, as Steiner refers to him), by then a Cistercian, laid down the Seven Liberal Arts as moral-cognitive therapy—initiation—for both the soul of nature and the human soul. At the same time, the first translations of alchemical texts from Arabic into Latin, beginning with

Morienus around 1182, began to appear and groups arose to transform and Christianize it. Steiner, holding them in greatest esteem, calls them "the old philosophers." For him, they are the true seed of the return of the Rosy Cross. Meanwhile, in Provence, where Troubadours and Cathars were drawing together Christian, Ismaili, Manichaean, and Sufi teachings to create a unique vernacular culture of love, which sought to transform the world in the human soul, Moses de Leon compiled the *Zohar*, the high point of Kabbalah. Elsewhere, especially among the Beguines (lay women mystics dedicated to a communal life of service and contemplation) as well as in the new monasteries inspired by St. Bernard, women mystics were creating a sophisticated non-dualistic path of knowing and being—a path of the heart. Everywhere popular devotion to the Eucharist flourished: the blood and body—the Sacred Heart—available to all.

Underlying all these manifestations was the centrality of the heart, the purified soul, and the feminine, along with a sense of the unity of the individual soul with the world soul, the *Anima Mundi*. In this way, the path to a thinking heart was sown in human consciousness with the promise of something new. Perhaps sensing this, Joachim of Fiore, a Franciscan monk from Calabria, received an illumination regarding the Trinitarian structure of history. He saw history unfolding through thee ages: the Age of the Father, the Age of the Son, and the Age of the Holy Spirit:

> The first age [he wrote] was that of knowledge, the second that of understanding, and the third will be the period of complete intelligence. The first was servile obedience, the second filial servitude, and the third will be freedom. The first was affliction, the second action, and the third will be contemplation. The first was fear, the second faith, and the third will be love. The first was the age of slaves; the second the age of sons; and the third will be the age of friends.

Thus, the twelfth century looked forward with anticipation for "The Age of the Spirit"—the Third Kingdom. And accompanying and midwifing all was the near miraculous and historically difficult to explain artistic accomplishments of Romanesque and Gothic art, as well as the emergence of new art forms in painting and sculpture.

Again carried by small, fragmented "mystery groups," all this would form a new experiential, vernacular spirituality, carried for instance by the *Devotion Moderna* and the Brethren of the Common Life and taught by the mysterious "Friend of God from the Highlands" (according to Steiner the "Master Jesus") who influenced mystics like Johannes Tauler, Heinrich Suso, and Rulman Merswin. From this vernacular, experiential spirituality of the heart would arise the next and explicitly "Rosicrucian" Renaissance. This is the exoteric side.

Esoterically, what is important from our point of view is the relationship with Christian Rosenkreutz, for Rudolf Steiner speaks of the Rosicrucian stream as also beginning around 1250. He tells us that this period, while giving birth to a new culture, was at the same time from a certain point of view a period of spiritual darkness—"a spiritual eclipse." Innate, intuitive access to the spiritual world was in decline; initiates rarely had direct knowledge of it. The ancient pre-Christian mysteries had by now definitively passed. There was no longer any temple. The gods, the divine part of the natural world, had withdrawn. What remained was mostly memory. Nature, rather than manifesting divine activity directly, was experienced only as a "picture" of it—a picture that at the same time could be found within the human being. This meant that there was nevertheless still a kind of ethical dimension to knowledge. Only those of great inner purity and goodness could begin to lift the veil. Yet their knowledge had a certain tragic dimension: while the spirits at work in natural phenomena could be known, the cosmic intelligences—the cosmic divinities whose distant prolongation they were—remained inaccessible.

It was then that a circle of twelve initiates—including the "seven Holy Rishis," who could look back into the seven ancient Atlantean wisdom streams, together with four others who carried the wisdom of the four post-Atlantean epochs, and one whose province was natural science—gathered together. They were joined by a thirteenth, a youth of extraordinary piety and devotion. According to Steiner, he was born about 1250. Educated by them, kept apart from the world, they taught him all they knew. The youth, who was the individuality that would become Christian Rosenkreutz (in a previous incarnation, according to Steiner's research, he had been Lazarus-John), took in all that they gave him. But, in proportion as his spiritual forces increased, his physical being drained away, until he lay there as if dead. The twelve then gathered around him and ineffably allowed all their wisdom—fully enchristed—to flow into him in short, prayer-like formulae. The thirteenth then felt something new entering him and returned to life: initiated, just as Paul had been initiated on the road to Damascus. He then revealed to the twelve all that they had given him, but now transformed into "a new form, as if given by Christ himself." Soon after, he died. The twelve then devoted themselves to recording what he had taught in the form of symbolic pictures or diagrams, which then passed into esoteric tradition.

The story continues into, and as, the next "Renaissance." On the one hand, exoterically, this begins with the visit to Italy as part of the Orthodox delegation to the last great Ecumenical Council of Florence-Ferrara in 1438/39 of the octogenarian Greek sage, philosopher, and initiate George Gemistos, known as "Plethon" to indicate his close affinity to Plato, whose reincarnation he was reputed to be. While in Florence, Plethon had met with and inspired Cosimo de Medici with the idea of a lineage of ancient theologians—Hermes, Zoroaster, Orpheus, and others—reaching back into primordial times, to a primordial revelation. Cosimo accordingly "conceived in his noble mind a kind of Academy"—or "Mystery School"—and, about 1450, asked the son of his favorite doctor to organize it and start translating the texts of the ancient masters that Plethon had provided. Thus the Platonic Academy of Florence came into being, and Marsilio Ficino began his epoch-making translations, including those of Plato, Plotinus, Iamblichus, Porphyry, Proclus, the *Corpus Hermeticum*, and the *Chaldean Oracles*.

Plethon, too, Rosicrucian in this, publicly introduced the project of the Christianization of ancient wisdom. To what extent Plethon himself believed in the project, or whether he would have preferred a return of the most ancient solar cosmic religion, must remain a moot point. Certainly, his influence was enormous. He did much more than inspire Ficino's translations and Cusa's philosophy and Columbus' journey to the New World (for which he provided the map!): he brought the symbol of "fire" to the center of what would become the Rosicrucian tradition and pushed the idea of ecumenicism to the bounds of heresy by upholding the universality of all forms (again, a Rosicrucian tenet). His position, to adapt a slogan current today, was "to think religion globally and embody it locally."

The consequences of Plethon's initiation, as transmitted by Ficino's translations, were culturally far-reaching: essentially, they created what we call the Renaissance. In Italy, the teaching of the Academies of Florence and Rome became culture in the work of the great painters and architects like Botticelli, Raphael, Leonardo, Michelangelo, and Alberti. Pico Della Mirandola and others created the philosophy of Renaissance Humanism. From Italy, their influence spread across Europe through France, Germany, and England, where the effect, in the person of John Dee (according to some, like Frances Yates, an inspirer of Rosicrucianism) was especially significant. Esoterically, perhaps the most important consequence was the effect on Paracelsus, the great and acknowledged precursor of Rosicrucianism and perhaps the "new Elias" who would usher in the Age of the Spirit. Whatever the case, from the influx of ancient wisdom Paracelsus—a precursor likewise of Anthroposophy—was able to forge in the crucible of his own experience a vocabulary of ideas and practices to transform our ideas of the world and human nature.

Paracelsus returns us to the story of Christian Rosenkreutz, who, according to the published documents, as confirmed by Rudolf Steiner, was born (reincarnated) in 1378, under the name we know him by, in Germany, perhaps into a Cathar household on the border of Hess and Thuringia.

Placed in a monastery at the age of five, as soon as he was able, Christian Rosenkreutz set off on a pilgrimage to the Holy Sepulcher in Jerusalem. His was a journey to the East in search of initiation. It would take him to Syria, Arabia, Egypt, and North Africa. Wherever he went he sought out the Wise and sat at their feet. After a stop in Cyprus, he traveled to Damascus, where he found so great a wisdom that he gave up the idea of continuing to Jerusalem and decided instead to learn Arabic. This he did, imbibing as he did so all the wisdom of that place. After three years, he moved further east, to "Damcar," perhaps Basra, where he met scientists, astrologers, alchemists, theologians, and mathematicians (perhaps members of the *Ikhwan al'Safa* or *Brethren of Purity*) and translated into Latin their great "Summa" of the sacred sciences, the *Liber M(undi)* or "Book of the World," perhaps the fifty-two *Epistles* of the Brethren. Thereafter he went to Egypt and Fez, whence he returned to Europe, where he sought to create a new culture based on what he had learned.

Rosenkreutz first tried to interest scholars and scientists in Spain in his ideas, "but to them it was a laughing matter." A similar reception greeted him as he moved northward. Disappointed, he returned to Germany, where, after five years of intense study and inner work, he formed a small group for the purpose of inseminating a "general reformation."

Such was the beginning of the Rosicrucian Brotherhood, the Fraternity of the Rose Cross. Together the group—first four, then eight—studied the *Book M*, created a "magical language," a series of *Axiomata* [Sayings], a mysterious *Rota* [or Wheel], a secret dictionary, and built a house, a Temple, called *Sancti Spiritus* or Holy Spirit.

Determining to disperse into the world to spread the word, the group then created a Rule for themselves:

> *First,* To profess no other thing than to heal the sick, and that *gratis*
> *Second,* To wear no kind of special habit, but to follow always the custom of the country in their dress
> *Third,* To meet together at the house *Sancti Spiritus* every year at Christmas
> *Fourth,* To seek for a worthy person to succeed them after they die
> *Fifth,* To make R.C. "their seal, mark, and character."
> *Sixth,* To remain secret one hundred years

In other words: to love; to be oriented toward the world and work selflessly and compassionately for its sake; to be anonymous, attached to no form; to have the "gift of tongues" and be able to address each person in his own or her own language; thus, to be a true cosmopolitan or citizen of the world; to meet in unity in the spirit; to create no institution but a lineage of friends; to have the Rose Cross, the union of love and knowledge inscribed in their hearts; and to "remain secret for a hundred years"—more precisely, a hundred-and-twenty years after Christian Rosenkreutz's death, when his tomb would be opened and all in it revealed.

Thus, in due course, Rosicrucianism erupted into the light of history (ten years after the tomb was opened) with the sequential publication of three texts in 1614, 1615, and 1616: *The Fama Fraternitatis* ("Announcement of the Brotherhood"), the *Confessio Fraternitatis* ("Confession of the Brotherhood"), and *The Chemical Wedding.*

The first text, the Fama, addressed "to the learned in general and the governors of Europe," begins by announcing the possibility of a universal reformation:

> Seeing the only Wise and Merciful God in these latter days hath poured out so richly his mercy and goodness to Humankind, whereby we do attain more and more to the perfect knowledge of his Son Jesus Christ and of Nature, that justly we may boast of the happy time wherein there is not only discovered unto us the half part of the world, which was hitherto unknown and hidden, but He hath also made manifest unto us many wonderful and never-before seen works and creatures of Nature, and, moreover, hath raised human beings, endued with great wisdom, which might partly renew and reduce all arts (in this our spotted and imperfect age) to perfection, so that we might thereby understand our own nobleness and worth, and why we are called *microcosmos,* and how far our knowledge extends in Nature.

It then goes on to recount the story (as told above) of how Christian Rosenkreutz dedicated his life to this project, how he had died in 1484 at the age of 106, and how his tomb had been opened, as he instructed on an inscription on the vault, a hundred-and-twenty years later in 1604.

Within the vault, instead of a tomb, was an altar, on which was engraved: *This compendium of the universe I made in my lifetime to be my tomb.*

Around the rim was engraved: *Jesus all to me*

In the middle, four figures were engraved, surrounded by further sayings: *Nowhere a vacuum; The yoke of the law; The liberty of the Gospel; The whole glory of God*

All over the vault secret figures and further sayings were inscribed. There were chests, containing books, especially the works of Paracelsus, and much else. Moving the altar, they discovered beneath it the uncorrupted body of Christian Rosenkreutz himself. In his hand he held a parchment describing his mission, which the first Brothers had also signed. Beneath this was written:

> *Ex Deo Nascimur, in Christo Morimur, per Spiritum Sanctum Reviviscimus*
> (From God we are born, in Christ we die, through the Holy Spirit we are reborn.)

The *Fama* concludes by returning to the idea of "a general reformation of things human and divine" and calls for "all the learned in Europe" to ponder the announcement and, if in agreement, to introduce themselves and come together in the great Rosicrucian project of creating a new culture. The *Confessio*, appearing a year later, repeats the offer (and the story), while *The Chemical Wedding* provides the initiatory teaching of the Brotherhood in alchemical and allegorical form.

As a result, a *"furor"* erupted: Rosicrucians and those aspiring to join the Brotherhood suddenly appeared everywhere, publishing manifestos and texts. It must be said, however, that amazing proto-Rosicrucian texts and manuscripts (by John Dee, Heinrich Khunrath, Simon Studion, and others) had already begun to proliferate during the previous fifty years. Clearly, the situation was desperate and stakes were high. The possibility of a true Renaissance, whose first note had been sounded in Italy, was at risk. In Anthroposophical terms, the "consciousness soul" was faced with a moment of decision: to go the way of Ficino, Pico, Paracelsus, the alchemists, and Christian Rosenkreutz or the way of Galileo and Descartes—the way of modern science. With the outbreak of the Thirty Years War in 1619, historical spiritual forces determined the outcome. For the next three centuries, culture would be determined by reason, science, and materialism. The stream of the Mysteries we have been following would have to go more or less underground. The Age of the Spirit would have to wait.

Underground, many aspects of the Rosicrucian Mystery stream—alchemical-scientific, initiatory universal-spiritual, and social-political—were transmitted from its disappearance around 1620 into the eighteenth century by certain branches of Freemasonry, which as if providentially had arisen to carry it. At the same time, various smaller esoteric Christian groups (followers of Jacob Boehme, Pietists, and others), as well as illuminated and unaffiliated individuals, also ensured the transmission of the spirit and meaning of Christian Rosenkreutz's mission. However, no attempt to actually create a new culture was undertaken.

Usually thought of as a purely literary movement, encompassing virtually the whole of Europe—England (Blake, Shelley, Keats, Wordsworth, Coleridge, Byron), Germany (Goethe, Schiller, Novalis, Hölderlin, Kleist, the Schlegel brothers, Fichte, Hegel, and Schelling), France (Chateaubriand, Victor Hugo), and even Poland (Mickiewicz), Russia (Pushkin), and the United States (the Transcendentalists)—Romanticism was much more than literary: it was revolutionary, esoteric, Rosicrucian, and Michaelic.That would not happen until the Renaissance we call Romanticism.

It was revolutionary because the Romantics were the first to foresee the full consequences of the turn taken with the rise of modern science. They experienced prophetically what fragmentation and alienation, what fear of freedom and responsibility, what destruction, death, sleep and loss of will lay ahead if the course of human evolution were not changed and materialism overcome. Their response, furthermore, was fully conscious and informed—for they were the first to reap the full fruits of the previous Renaissances. They were the first, since the waning of the Mysteries, to be able to-imagine the fullness of Mystery Wisdom. What had entered into history sequentially was now present simultaneously and enchristed. Thus, they were given fullness of vision—Heraclitus and Plato, Aristotle and St. Paul, St. John and Plotinus, Bruno and Leibniz, the Hermetic, alchemical, and Rosicrucian texts, as well as Augustine, Thomas Aquinas, Meister Eckhart, and Jacob Boehme. The result was a renewed understanding of the primacy, unity, and universality of human beings and nature as consciousness and imagination, not matter, together with a profound sense of the selfishness and egotism unleashed by the powers of abstract, calculating rationality. They could see that the development of rational abstraction had caused an apparently irresoluble separation (and objectification) between the knower and the known, subject and object, and that this would result in utter materialism, whose consequences, applied technologically, could well destroy humanity and nature. Therefore they sought to oppose the Cartesian-Newtonian turn with a new culture based on the Mysteries and sought to transform art (poetry, painting, drama, philosophy), science (chemistry, physics, biology, medicine, psychology), religion (a new kind of truly universal, non-exclusive Christianity), and society (education, law).

As for Romanticism's "Michaelic" quality, Rudolf Steiner indicates that, in the years immediately preceding the archangel Michael's victorious struggle with the dragon in 1879, as the culmination of the preparation of a Michael School (which Rudolf Steiner a century later would seek to gather together on earth), Michael convened a meeting of his School in the spiritual world. The implication is that Romanticism was the earthly reflection of that School. Certainly, all the Romantics were explicitly connected to, and consciously sought to experience and transform into contemporary language the wisdom and accomplishments of the previous Renaisssances, thus linking back to the ancient Mystery Schools.

In this regard, the timing was again providential for, as Steiner points out in *Cosmic and Human Metamorphoses*, esoteric texts flowing from the previous Renaissance—in his example those of Jacob Boehme and Louis-Claude de Saint Martin—were still quite understandable before 1800, but seemed more or less incomprehensible after. One need only compare Paracelsus or Basil Valentine with Goethe's scientific writings to see what he means. The first are written in a dense, cryptic language of their own, while the last is clear and modern, though the teaching is the same. The same is true of Blake, Novalis, Keats, Coleridge, Hegel, and Schelling. All drew on esoteric and Rosicrucian wisdom, but transformed it into a cultural mission, thus effectively "rending the veil" between esoteric and exoteric.

While it cannot be said that Romanticism "failed"—Owen Barfield, after all, calls Anthroposophy "Romanticism come of age"—it lost the moment of being able to determine culture to materialism. For Steiner, the end of that possibility was marked by the death of Kaspar Hauser, the "child of Europe, who had he lived might have inaugurated a new "Romantic" epoch of peace and harmony. Materialism triumphed. By the mid-nineteenth century, it was in full control.

Such was the background of the Congress of 1907. Such was the situation that Rudolf Steiner was called to address and the history he was called to fulfill: to renew, under the aegis of the archangel Michael, the promise of the Rosicrucian ideal—that is, the creation of a new spiritual culture for humanity, permeated from the spiritual world with the fully enchristed content of the ancient Mysteries, both directly and through the historical lineages discussed above. It is important to recognize that, while in principle, all the wisdom is always available directly from the spiritual world, as earthly beings it is important to commune also with the earthly reflections of that wisdom. Throughout his life, while always confirming everything inwardly, Rudolf Steiner immersed himself in the traces of those who had gone before, reading and meditating the entire corpus of the Mystery tradition. Precisely this allowed him, more successfully than anything else, to grasp the significance of that tradition and understand, out of its inner necessity, how it is to be understood today.

It was always important for Rudolf Steiner to make a lineal connection with those who had carried the esoteric traditions through time; hence his affiliations with Spiritism, Theosophy, Freemasonry, and various carriers of the Rosicrucian impulse. At the same time, he knew what he was to bring was new, a new culture, appropriate to the new "Age of Light."

The key word here, of course, is *culture*. The time was no more when esoteric or occult societies could work exclusively and invisibly behind the scenes of ordinary life. The task—as each of the previous Renaissances had realized with increasing self-consciousness— was to create something like a new, contemporary Mystery Center, a manifestation of the ever-growing point of civilization and consciousness from which powerful impulses of spiritual-cultural transformation could radiate until Center and culture were one. The Center would epitomize the whole wisdom tradition, drawing upon it in multiple, interdependent ways—textual, akashic, and directly from the spirit. It would transform it in the crucible of the consciousness now seeking a human home into a new way or path of sacramentalizing all of earthly life. Ideally, too, it would provide a home for all human striving, where all traditions could flow together to unite in the common goal: that the Earth might become a Sun. Whatever one may think of it, the audacity and confidence such a project demanded of Rudolf Steiner cannot but take one's breath away.

The 1907 Congress marked the first stage in this process; building the first Goetheanum, the second; re-founding the Anthroposophical Society, the third. In this process, against all odds, the inspiration for the unified re-spiritualization of art, science, and religion was progressively unveiled throughout the remainder of Steiner's life through practical programs for painting, sculpture, movement, architecture, education, social organization, medicine, agriculture, and religion.

At the Congress, true to the founding principles of Rosicrucianism as a call to a "general reformation," Rudolf Steiner unveiled the inner principles of an artistic renewal. He treated the space of the hall, in which the meeting was held, as a garden. In it he planted the seeds—the archetypal or spiritual prototypes—that he hoped would become the forms of the new culture. It has been said that, in a movement of cultural transformation, after the "coffee house stage" when a "thousand flowers bloom" has been passed, it is time to focus on essentials and manifest them physically. Steiner transformed the entire hall so that the whole became a living symbol and mediator of the spirit: a blueprint for a new Temple in the world and in human hearts. As the first seed, it was necessarily esoteric, primordial. It was his hope that the seed—which would grow into the Goetheanum—would resonate and proliferate into the culture as a whole to create a new cultural vessel in which humanity could once again, and in a new way, assume its true function as uniting Heaven and Earth. He knew, as the Temple and Cathedral builders (and all those anonymous craftspeople and artists throughout the millennia dedicated to sacramentalizing matter through image) had always known, that art determines, and expresses, the consciousness of a society.

As to the success of the mission that Rudolf Steiner set for himself and worked with great ardor to accomplish until the end of his earthly life, the work goes on. The task remains and it is up to those who understand and are called to it to carry it out today. The seeds have been planted.

Further Reading

RUDOLF STEINER:

Alchemy: The Evolution of the Mysteries (ed. Andrew Welburn) (London: Sophia Books, 2001)
Cosmic and Human Metamorphoses (Blauvelt: Spiritual Research Editions, 1989)
An Outline of Esoteric Science (Great Barrington: SteinerBooks, 1996)
Autobiography: The Course of My Life (Great Barrington: SteinerBooks, 2006)
Christianity as Mystical Fact and the Mysteries of Antiquity (Great Barrington: SteinerBooks, 2006)
Esoteric Lessons (1902-1908) (Great Barrington: SteinerBooks, 1998)
"Freemasonry" and Ritual Work: Misraim Service, From the History and Contents of the Cognitive Cultic Section (Great Barrington: SteinerBooks, 1998)
From the History and Contents of the First Section of the Esoteric School 1904-1914 (Great Barrington: SteinerBooks, 1998)
Mystery Knowledge and Mystery Centers (London: Rudolf Steiner Press, 1997)
Mystics After Modernism (Great Barrington: SteinerBooks, 2003)
Rosicrucian Wisdom (London: Rudolf Steiner Press, 2004)
Rosicrucianism and Modern Initiation (London: Rudolf Steiner Press, 1965)
Spiritualism, Madame Blavatsky and Theosophy: A Bird's Eye View of Esoteric History (Great Barrington: SteinerBooks 2000)
The Archangel Michael: His Mission and Ours (Great Barrington: SteinerBooks, 1994)
The Redemption of Thinking: A Study in the Philosophy of Thomas Aquinas (Great Barrington: SteinerBooks, 1980)
The Secret Stream: Christian Rosenkreutz and Rosicrucianism (Great Barrington: SteinerBooks, 2000)
The Spiritual Foundations of Morality: Francis of Assisi and the Christ Impulse (Great Barrington: SteinerBooks, 1998)
The Sun Mystery in the Course of Human History (London: Rudolf Steiner Press, 1955)
The Temple Legend (London: Rudolf Steiner Press, 1985)

OTHER AUTHORS:

Paul M. Allen (ed), *A Christian Rosenkreutz Anthology* (Blauvelt: Rudolf Steiner Publications, 1968)
Christopher Bamford, *An Endless Trace: The Passionate Pursuit of Wisdom in the West* (Codhill Press, 2004)
Paul Foster Case, *The True and Invisible Rosicrucian Order* (York Beach: Samuel Weiser, 1985)
Christopher McIntosh, *The Rose Cross and the Age of Reason: Eighteenth Century Rosicrucianism and its Relationship to the Enlightenment* (Leiden: E. J. Brill, 1992)

———*The Rosy Cross Unveiled: The History, Mythology, and Rituals of an Occult Order* (Wellingborough: The Aquarian Press, 1980)

Wilhelm Rath, *The Friend of God from the Highlands* ((Stroud: Hawthorne Press,1991)

Frances Yates, *The Rosicrucian Enlightenment* (London: Routledge, 2001)

Andrew Welburn, *The Mysteries: Rudolf Steiner's Writings on Spiritual Initiation* (Edinburgh: Floris Books, 1998)

Ralph White (ed), *The Rosicrucian Enlightenment Revisited* (Great Barrington: Lindisfarne Books, 1997)

C.M. Woodhouse, *George Gemistos Plethon: The Last of the Hellenes* (Oxford: Oxford University Press, 1986)

INTRODUCTION TO THE 1977 GERMAN EDITION

HELLA WIESBERGER

In 1902 Rudolf Steiner took on the role of General Secretary of the German Section of the newly founded Theosophical Society and, together with his closest colleague, Marie von Sivers (later Marie Steiner), built up a wide-reaching Central European spiritual-scientific movement. This they established from the start as an independent section for his Anthroposophically oriented spiritual science, until this became the autonomous Anthroposophical Society in 1912-1913.

At the time of the Munich Congress in 1907, Steiner still taught within the Theosophical Society and, for that reason, continued to use the expressions *Theosophy* and *Theosophical.* He also employed the conventional terminology of Theosophical literature for the names of the members of the human being and other things as well, terminology with which his audience of the time was accustomed. However, in his public writings, he had begun to use expressions "borrowed for certain reasons from an esoteric language that somewhat differs from conventional Theosophical writings but which are naturally in full agreement in the matter." Later, also in his lectures, he replaced Indian Theosophical expressions more and more with those adapted to European culture.

Berlin and Munich were the main centers for Steiner's work until World War I broke out in 1914. The spiritual orientation of these two cities resulted in Berlin's developing more the scientific pole and Munich more the artistic one. For that reason, the first Theosophical congress in Germany took place in Munich. Through the arrangement of this congress by Steiner, the first step in the history of the Anthroposophical Movement was taken toward the realization of the building-idea. The building as an all-encompassing work of art, in the sense of a renewal of the mysteries, was to reunite knowledge, art, and religious life.

Because Steiner could see how spiritual forces find expression in forms, colors, and tones, he was fully conscious of the significance placed on the way surroundings are fashioned. For this reason, at the laying of the foundation stone of the first house designed following his esoteric-artistic viewpoint, he said on January 3, 1911, in Stuttgart:

> We should be clear that as long as we are forced to come together in halls whose forms belong to a dying culture, our work must more or less suffer the destiny ordained to destruction. The spiritual stream will be able to bring forth the new culture that it is called to bring forth only when it can work rightly into purely physical forms, even the walls that surround us. Spiritual life will work differently when it flows out of spaces whose proportions are determined by spiritual science, whose forms proceed out of spiritual science.

That this in no way needed to remain an ideal goal and that Steiner possessed the artistic ability to realize it and to bring about a necessary union of science, art, and religious experience for the progress of humanity was demonstrated through the Munich Congress. Marie Steiner-von Sivers, herself a significant artist, thought of Rudolf Steiner as a born artist. However, this born artist became productive unusually late. Rudolf Steiner, who was a recognized interpreter of Goethe at age twenty-two and who founded Anthroposophy and the international movement connected with it, was forty-six years old when, in 1907, he began his artistically creative phase. He stood on the threshold of his fifth decade as he wrote his first Mystery Drama, laid the seeds for the plans of the first Goetheanum, developed the art of eurythmy, and painted his first painting. However, the sources of his artistic activity reach back much further.

As a boy of about nine or ten, he drew with charcoal in the village school he attended. Under the direction of the assistant teacher of the school, he copied pictures and even portraits. In order to attend high school, he had to pass a preliminary examination, which he did splendidly, on the basis of all the drawings he had done in the village school. Geometric drawing was a favorite subject for him during his high school years. During his years of study at the Technical College in Vienna, he immersed himself intensively in art history, especially the development of architecture, in addition to his scientific studies.

Steiner was particularly stimulated by the prevalent architectural atmosphere of Vienna. It was just at that time that the great buildings of Vienna were completed: the parliament buildings, the Town Hall, the Votive Church, and the palace theater. He became personally acquainted with the architects Theophil Hansen, Friedrich Schmidt and Heinrich Ferstel at the Technical College. Ferstel, the builder of the Votive Church, became headmaster of the Technical College in 1879, just as Steiner began his studies there. Steiner said once that the statement in Ferstel's inaugural speech concerning the fact that "architectural styles are not invented but are born out of the ages," resounded in him throughout his whole life. He also had personal connections with the aesthetic philosopher Josef Bayer, a follower of Gottfried Semper and a teacher at the Technical College, and with Robert Zimmerman, a lecturer on aesthetics at Vienna University. Yet, despite all the ingenuity in the sphere of art, the materialistic trend that was asserting itself ever more strongly brought him to an inner despair. In looking back, after he had created the forms of the new capitals of the columns for the Munich Congress and the Goetheanum, Steiner remembered how many "sleepless nights" the Corinthian capital had cost him.

Steiner worked not only with architecture but also with painting in his early years in Vienna. The impulse for him to do this arose from the first exhibit in Vienna, in 1882, of the work of the Swiss symbolist painter Arnold Böcklin. Böcklin's paintings appeared to him to be a lively protest against the materialistic painting models of that time. He sensed that in Böcklin there was a quality that could lead art away from naturalism.

At the same time, he was wrestling with aesthetics, the science of beauty. In contrast to German aesthetics, which had proclaimed that beauty was to be thought of as "idea" in the form of sense appearance, Steiner demanded a complete reversal of aesthetic thinking. In about 1881 or 1882, he wrote to a friend: "Art is the divine, not as such, but in the sense perceptible. And as such, the divine does not have to please." Seven years later, in 1888–1889, he established this view philosophically as an aesthetic of the future: "The aesthetics then, which proceeds from the definition that 'beauty is a sense-perceptible reality that appears as if it were an idea' does not exist yet. It must be created. It can be characterized as *'the aesthetics of the Goethean world-view'*. And this is *the aesthetics of the future*."

During his Weimar years, from 1890 to 1897, Steiner continued to seek a spiritual conception of the artistic element in discussions with the artists he met there. However, his actual artistic study took place during his many travels from the turn of the century onward, the fruits of which one finds in his lantern-slide lecture on art history entitled "Art History as Image of Inner Spiritual Impulses." Drawing on this background, Steiner could unite, little by little, the development of new art forms with Anthroposophy as a science. What he wrote on November 25, 1905, to Marie von Sivers, who stood energetically by his side in her deeply artistic understanding, can count as a kind of prelude:

> It shall be our ideal to create forms as an expression of the inner life. For in a time that cannot behold forms—and, in the beholding, cannot create them—the spirit must of necessity evaporate into shadowy abstraction, and the reality must confront this merely abstract spirit as an aggregate of matter without spirit.
>
> If human beings are able to understand real forms—for instance, the birth of soul-substance out of the cloud-ether of the Sistine Madonna—then for them, there is soon no longer any matter without spirit. And because we can show large groups of people spiritual forms only through the medium of religion, the work for the future must be to shape religious spirit in a sense-perceptible and beautiful form.
>
> For this, a deepening in content is needed. At first, Theosophy must bring about this deepening. Until human beings sense that spirits live in fire, air, water, and earth, we will not have an art that renders this wisdom in outer forms.

By 1906 it was decided that the next Theosophical Congress of the Federation of the European Sections of the Theosophical Society would take place under Steiner's leadership. Soon after he wrote this letter, Steiner characterized this ideal for Berlin friends as the cultural mission of spiritual science. He said:

> We live in a barbaric time, in a chaotic time without style. All great art epochs were created out of the deepest spiritual life.... Through the spread of spiritual-scientific teachings, the world will again be filled with a spiritual content.... That which lives in spiritual science must reveal itself in outer forms, [and] then we will have a style that expresses this spiritual life. Thus, we must consider the mission of spiritual science to be a cultural mission.

The Munich Congress offered the first possibility for the realization of this cultural mission. In Munich in 1907 the threefold unity appeared mightily for the first time: the nurturing of supersensible knowledge in connection with a mystery drama as a ritual element in an artistic space, designed and decorated in accordance with these three elements.

From the event of the Munich Congress there is a straight line to the First Goetheanum in Dornach. At the unofficial opening, Steiner expressed the significance of the Goetheanum in these words: "The building shall be dedicated to what can proceed out of a triad for the life of humanity. This triad is visual art, science that grasps things spiritually, and religion that experiences the rebirth anew in the supersensible." That the idea for building a temple stood in the background of the Munich Congress, was not just implied by the capital forms of the columns that Steiner created. The connection is also explicit in a letter that Marie von Sivers wrote to Edouard Schuré, whose reconstruction of the *Sacred Drama of Eleusis* was premiered at the Munich Congress. She wrote: "With that, we can try to approach the idea of a temple."

It is worth noting how the inauguration of Steiner's new art impulse fits into the general evolution of art as an art-historical phenomenon. The year 1907 was of decisive significance for the whole development of European art in the twentieth century, as documented in the fiftieth jubilee exhibit in Amsterdam in 1957. For example, in 1907 Pablo

Picasso painted his world-famous *Le Demoiselles d'Avignon*, which introduced cubism. The avant-garde were the Fauves in France, and the Brücke group in Germany. Art moved ever more strongly from Impressionism to Expressionism and stood on the eve of abstract painting. In the year 1907, as in hardly any other year of our epoch, "so much ended and so much new was built out of it, so much old and new crossed".

In this year—the decisive year for art history in this century—Steiner laid the foundation stone for his building-idea, which is to be understood as a comprehensive work of art. This came to fruition through various initial stages—Malsch, Stuttgart, Munich—and found artistic completion in the first and second Goetheanum buildings on the Dornach hill near Basel, Switzerland. Steiner, who never worked for the sake of art as such but always in a social connection, took the impossible and made it possible. He gave the directions, created the models, sketched the motifs, and carved and painted examples, and many artists, technicians, and scientists worked together enthusiastically for ten years toward the realization of the [first Goetheanum]. Much of this took place during World War I, at a time when Europeans were fighting one another. In this way, Steiner's building-idea gave rise not only to a new spiritual and artistic life but also to a new social life.

In this volume are collected all the materials from Rudolf Steiner's Complete Works pertaining to the preliminary stages of the building of the Goetheanum: the Munich Congress and its effects in Malsch, Berlin, and Stuttgart. The imperfection of the artistic form of the apocalyptic seals by the painter Clara Rettich drew much criticism right from the beginning, but Steiner was fully conscious of it. His reason for publishing these seals after the Munich Congress, despite the controversy, becomes clear from his comment to a critic:

> You misunderstood the conversation in the Munich Congress hall in which you called the seals inartistic and I answered, "Yes, certainly." I agreed with you completely and would have been very glad if these things had been artistic. Nevertheless, the esotericist must think realistically, not fancifully, and must take what is to be

> had. "Yes, certainly" says everything. The point is that at present there is no artist who is able to recreate *real* life. And so we have only the choice of either the formal abstract intimation of inner life and content by inartistic means or the dead forms and phantoms that are often called artistic today and which have an effect similar to that of a corpse that would simulate life (Draft of a letter to a person unknown, April 12,1909).

It is with the draft of this letter that Rudolf Steiner confirms once again the foundational motif of his artistic work, as he had already expressed it in the letter to Marie von Sivers quoted in this volume: to bring life and form into true correspondence with each other. However, because life itself is not physically perceptible but can reveal itself only through form, new forms must be created for the new spiritual life, if it is to prove itself to be full of vitality and not evaporate into abstraction. And the first great historical prelude to the realization of Rudolf Steiner's ideal "to create forms as the expression of inner life" was the Munich Congress at Whitsun 1907.

ROSICRUCIANISM RENEWED

The Unity of Art, Science, and Religion

Rudolf Steiner

Statement from Rudolf Steiner

It should be anticipated that errors and or omissios could be found in the documents, which have not been reviewed by me.

Translator's Note

The quotations of Bible verses in this text were given by Rudolf Steiner from memory. The translation of those verses as given will, therefore, not coincide exactly with any particular version of the Bible. Quotations from Edouard Schuré's *Sacred Drama of Eleusis* are literal translations of renderings by Marie Steiner and Rudolf Steiner from the original French.

Also, various people have given reports of what Rudolf Steiner said or did in talks, dedications, and the various preparations and proceedings of the Munich Congress. Because these reports came from either memory or notes, there can be discrepancies between a given report and the actual words spoken or deeds performed by Rudolf Steiner.

PROLOGUE

Art and Its Future Task

Rudolf Steiner

Penmaenmawr, August 24, 1923

Remarks following a lecture by the painter Arild von Rosenkrantz

It was requested that I add something about art and its future task to the interesting presentation by Baron Rosenkrantz† and that I also should give a picture of the Goetheanum and what it will look like in the future.†

I would like to answer these questions with only a few indications that apply more to the fashioning of an artistic impulse or impulses in the future. I do not mean that this artistic impulse can be undertaken arbitrarily or intentionally by anyone. Rather, to a certain extent, we see this impulse—to which art in the near future must orient itself—only in preparation at present. We see in our present time the old impulses of human civilization in all domains, in the areas of science, art, and religious sensibilities. However, we also see, on the other side, that there are certain latent yearnings, under the surface, in a surprisingly large number of people, yearnings towards something indeterminate. People want to explore these longings in the area of Anthroposophy; they wish to understand them to a certain extent. And it seems to me that, indeed, a large part of that which wants to assert itself as Anthroposophy meets these indeterminate, more or less unconscious longings of numerous human beings in the present time.

It is precisely because in the past three to four centuries intellectuality has flooded everything—for intellectuality has sunk its roots far more deeply into the human soul than one thinks—that human beings have such difficulty finding the bridge from this indeterminate yearning to that which can give this yearning its manifestation in earthly work. We see this when we examine spiritual science itself.

I have had to mention often in my lectures here† how spiritual science must be drawn out of research into the supersensible worlds through Imagination, Inspiration, and Intuition but that the results of such research can be understood by the ordinary, healthy human intellect. We are only clinging to old judgments when we do not find enough strength in our souls to approach the results of spiritual science without bias. The objections that human beings today so often bring against these results of spiritual science arise out of an indeterminate fear deep in the soul. Basically, human beings are afraid of the results of spiritual science. Everything that the last few centuries have brought about in human civilization contradicts spiritual science so much that it appears as something completely unknown to most people. We always fear the unknown, but we clothe it in logical refutations, logical criticism. Those who understand these matters see how the logic of the opponents of spiritual science is basically nothing other than a pretext for the fear of it in their own souls.

Thus it is in artistic areas. We hear the following extremely often: Yes, spiritual science wants to penetrate into the higher worlds through ideas, through scientific findings, but science suppresses free artistic activity. Those who want to work artistically must be free from all ideas, from all judgment; they must create out of pure imagination. There are many poets, painters, and musicians—artists in all areas—who have pure fear that their imaginations will dry up if they come too close to spiritual science, that they would then no longer be able to let their imaginations unfold but would, to a certain extent, reproduce through color or tones only what occurs in spiritual science.

You see, ladies and gentlemen, with the old Goetheanum there was, to be sure, much conflict. It is true that those who do not possess a deep artistic impulse come to a kind of outer symbolism or outer allegory because of a certain misunderstanding of this spiritual direction. I can indeed admit that there were very many Anthroposophists and Theosophists who sought the artistic in ideas that are painted or even sometimes composed and the like. Those who came into such an Anthroposophical or Theosophical space and saw there these symbolic and allegorical straw pictures could despair! There the artistic was driven out, to be sure! I can say that as the old Goetheanum was under construction, there were friends who really meant well but who wanted to install all sorts of symbols. I have resisted this quite decisively. Every line, every form had to arise in such a way that the building could be looked at in a purely inward artistic way.

Thus, the forms of the Goetheanum were not meant to be interpreted but, strictly speaking, to be looked at. When friends or visitors from outside come to the Goetheanum, they always want a guided tour and to have someone explain how the columns are formed, the capitals are made, the architraves are shaped, and the images are painted. We are supposed to give them the inner meanings. As a rule, I have said as an introduction, even when I led friends: "That which I now have to say to friends or visitors is extremely disagreeable to me. I have never had more antipathy for anything I have ever said as when I have been asked to explain these forms of the Goetheanum. They were not there to be explained, to be put into concepts, but rather to be looked at, to be grasped artistically, aesthetically."

Why would that be? We can best see why by looking at human beings themselves. We can study the human being according to the findings of science of the past three to four centuries. We come, however, only to a certain point, at most only to the physical organism. In the moment when we want to approach the higher members, or aspects, of human nature, we cannot—unless we let the world enter into an artistic grasping of the human being, because the world itself creates artistically where it works spiritually. Those who do not allow the scientific to pass over into the artistic in their own inner view cannot comprehend the human being. Present-day science then says: "Yes, those who pass over from science to the artistic abandon the path of logic, the observation of logic, which must be part of science. They are no longer scientists."

Ladies and Gentlemen, we can speak such rhetoric for a long time, but when nature works in a different way from our rhetoric, when it begins at a certain point to be no longer so naturalistically logical but rather to be artistic, only those who themselves become artistic can approach nature. It is precisely so with true Anthroposophy. Anthroposophy does not want to be, nor can it be, something that is merely a lively ideal—this is anathema to it. Rather, at a certain point, that which is expressed scientifically in ideas in a living way passes over into the directly and immediately artistic, the picture-like. For this reason, every time we even begin to describe the human etheric body, the ordinary scientific description will transmute into an artistic form, into an artistic visualization.

As soon as we grasp this completely, we will find everywhere that Anthroposophy—true spiritual science—is not a stranger to art or even an enemy of art, but rather that it will lead into the truly artistic in the future. This showed itself in practice in the old Goetheanum. If one were to draw a median line through the floor plan of the old Goetheanum, one would see that both sides were symmetrical, but there was no other symmetry beyond the left-right symmetry. The columns of the spectators' space had capitals that were not all alike but which progressively developed. The capital on the first column was relatively simple on the right and left; the second column had a somewhat more complicated capital, and so on. The artistic work on these capitals was throughout such that in the inner sensing of the lines, in the curves, everything in the form of the second capital proceeded out of the first capital and the third out of the second, and so on. Thus, we gave ourselves over absolutely to life in lines, surfaces, and curves. This progression followed through to the seventh column. We then had a complete form created by these lines and curves. Beyond this it went no further; one had to stop.

People look at the seven columns and believe that seven is a deep mystical number. They think that the choice of seven is based on an old formula, on something that lives on in superstition, and the like. But that is not the way it is! When we work purely artistically, we have to stop with the seventh column. Just as the rainbow has seven colors and the music scale has seven tones from the prime to the octave—the octave is a repetition of the prime—so do we have seven columns. Still, something more becomes apparent in such a work. We let the second capital arise through metamorphosis out of the first, the third out of the second, and so on until we had seven. Then we look at that form. One looks at one's own creations and discovers all kinds of things in them that one had not planned. I discovered there, for example, as I compared the seventh column's capital with the first—naturally approached artistically—that all the forms that were concave in the first capital were convex in the last one and that all the forms that were convex in the first were concave in the last. If we were to place them somewhat differently, we could place the seventh one into the first one, the sixth into the second, and the fifth into the third. The fourth one remains by itself in the center. This came about quite without my planning it.

There we could be sure that we mixed nothing of human arbitrariness into the forms but worked out of the life of the forms themselves. We connected with the creative cosmic world itself, including the forces at work in the metamorphoses of the plants, and thus, all that works and weaves in nature on another level. We did not fashion human-made allegories but rather wove ourselves, to a certain extent, into the working of nature, and then we created as nature creates. That is true artistic work, and in the future all the arts will return to this truth more or less. That was the nature of artistic activity in all the great epochs. And that is what shone forth from all the examples of Baron Rosenkrantz's excellent lecture. It is what one can see most particularly wherever new artistic impulses arise in Earth evolution. From new impulses we receive the courage and the hope that new art forms can really proceed out of what can be experienced in spiritual science.

I

THE MUNICH CONGRESS OF WHITSUN 1907

FOREWORD

HELLA WIESBERGER

Rudolf Steiner gave the first spiritual-scientific lectures in Munich in November 1904 upon the invitation of Sophie Stinde (1853-1915) and her friend, Countess Pauline von Kalckreuth, both leaders of what later became the main branch of the society in Munich. Sophie Stinde, the sister of the author Julius Stinde† and herself a talented landscape painter, placed her energy in the service of Steiner's spiritual-scientific movement in a truly "exemplary" manner, to use Steiner's own words. He said at her cremation: "When a course of spiritual work is entered upon, there is so much that one must be able to place in the hands of others, of whom one can be sure that they will carry it out in a way that one could not begin to do oneself.... Sophie Stinde belongs among those people who most energetically participated" in this work.

Sophie Stinde not only built up the actual Munich work but also, after renouncing her own beloved artistic practice, became the main bearer of the organizational burden for the large Munich events: the Munich Congress of 1907, whose art exhibit included several of her landscape paintings, and the annual summer festivals that arose out of the Munich Congress and which were held from 1909 to 1913, with the premieres of Rudolf Steiner's Mystery Dramas. She was the first to conceive of the courageous idea, as Marie Steiner put it, to begin the realization of the central building. She produced the supporting documents to make possible the realization of the project and thus was the founder and first chairperson of the Munich and then the Dornach Building Association.

When Rudolf Steiner was in Dornach for the first time after Stinde's death and spoke at the building site, he said that it was because of her deep artistic sense, because she was so "intimately connected" with the building, that it was possible:

> to develop the will that then spread and took hold within others—that will for evolution that we find in our building. Stinde was among the very first in whom the idea of our building dawned. We would have found it possible only with much difficulty to take the path from our Munich mystery-imagination to this building, if her strong will had not stood at the starting point of the idea for this building.

He went on:

> Her place in the outer, physical world will be empty from this time forward. However, for those who have learned to understand her, there will spread among us the idea of exemplary, devoted, sacrificial work. And this idea must live, especially in the rooms over which the double cupola arches, in the rooms in which her soul worked in this earthly incarnation. When we come to truly realize our relationship to her, it will be impossible to look at our forms without feeling connected with her—the forms to which she was the first to turn her attention and to which she dedicated her own work and which will work further in Sophie Stinde's soul.

The following chronicle shows how Steiner, together with Marie von Sivers and the Munich friends, carefully prepared the Congress of 1907 long beforehand, as a way to inaugurate the renewal of the mysteries in the sense of modern Rosicrucianism, as a harmonizing of science, art, and religion. These dates mark only the most essential points in connection with the planning of the Congress. Rudolf Steiner traveled regularly throughout Germany in order to hold lectures in various places.

June 1906

The Congress for 1907 shall take place in Germany

The location was decided at the third Congress of the Federation of the European Sections in Paris, held on June 3-5, 1906.

June/July 1906

Marie von Sivers's initiative to connect a mystery play with the Congress

As can be seen from a letter to Schuré written on July 18, 1906 (quoted below), Marie von Sivers conceived, at the congress in Paris, the idea for a performance of a mystery play: the reconstruction of *The Sacred Drama of Eleusis,* by Edouard Schuré. Schuré had just met Rudolf Steiner and Marie von Sivers for the first time in Paris, after Marie von Sivers had corresponded with him for seven years. She was made aware of Theosophy through Schuré and then met Steiner in Berlin in 1900. Marie von Sivers wrote the letter from the town of Landin in the Mark Brandenburg region of Germany, where she, along with Steiner and several other friends, were staying for a short rest. Sophie Stinde, named as secretary of the Congress, and Countess Kalckreuth, named as treasurer, also came to meet "with Dr. Steiner and Miss von Sivers about the Munich Congress, as it seemed to be the best opportunity.... Winter would be full of strenuous work, and Whitsun would come very early that next year."[†]

Marie von Sivers to Edouard Schuré from Landin, on July 18, 1906:[†] "If the inn near your home still exists, it would be splendid to see you again and to get a little rest in your company. Then you could speak with Dr. Steiner, instead of posing questions in writing. We could discuss the arrangement of your mystery drama for the stage. For instance, the Persephone scene with the nymph choir in the chapter on Plato is a quite beautiful prelude for the Mystery of Eleusis. We have a member in Stuttgart who is very earnest and very musical.[†] Perhaps the Theosophy will inspire him to compose for the choirs. You deserve it."

September 1906

The Eleusis performance is discussed again with Schuré

Rudolf Steiner and Marie von Sivers stayed five days with Schuré in Barr in Elsass. Marie von Sivers reported: "Lively conversations were held during hikes to the ruins of old castles, to Odilienberg and to Heidenmauer. It was there that I, after looking back into the time from the Druid mysteries to the Greeks, dared to ask Schuré if we might venture to present the drama of

Eleusis at the Congress to be held next year in Munich. Steiner, insofar as he was concerned, had already answered in the affirmative. Schuré was joyfully surprised."†

October 1906

Place and time of the Congress and its form are officially communicated

At the annual meeting of the German Section in Berlin, on October 21, 1906, Rudolf Steiner made the recommendation that the Congress be held in Munich "purely out of practical motives," because "only there" would forces be available that were suitable for the "long work that would demand much devotion." Whitsun appeared to be the most appropriate time.

To a question about the form, he replied that all the congresses to this point were to be seen as experiments. The task of the German Section would be to bring everything into harmony, so that art, music, and speech would interweave and resound together, striving to remind us of the old mysteries, for which reason the performance of a mystery was planned.

October/November 1906

The exact plan of the Congress is drawn up, and the necessary rooms are rented. The mystery play is to be performed by members of the society under the direction of Rudolf Steiner

From October 27 to November 6, 1906, in Munich, Steiner held three public lectures and a cycle of eight lectures for members. Marie von Sivers reported on these to Edouard Schuré:

Berlin, November 10, 1906

We've just returned from Munich, where Dr. Steiner held a lecture cycle with the title *Cosmogony* [Theosophy in Light of the John Gospel].† It was magnificent. During the twelve days we were there, the plan for the Congress was designed, and the halls were rented. They are according to our taste: noble, spacious, well proportioned, and free of ornament, so that the decoration will be up to us. We can attempt to draw nearer to the idea of the temple. The stage is also large, and we will be far enough away from the audience to achieve the illusion of a mystery, which matters quite a lot to us. Now we would like to ask your permission to perform *The Sacred Drama of Eleusis*, but we will give the roles not to actors but to members of our society. Dr. Steiner does not want a theatrical routine. He will be the director and reveal to us the deeper meaning of our roles. Since he can do everything, he will be able to do that too. He will also use a sure eye to choose those who have special ability for specific roles. I believe that you will not risk much, especially since it will not be a public performance. There will be only members of the Theosophical Society there, and the newspapers will not interfere. Only in the case of a completely unexpected success could one think about a repeat performance for the public, if you agreed.

Of course, as you said yourself, we must make a few changes and then give the finished translation to the composer. We must begin to work immediately, as the Congress will take place at Whitsun (on May 19). Sometimes, if we take things in hand with energy and goodwill, the stars come to our assistance. They inspire us and send us the good guardian spirits. Who knows whether such an undertaking, carried out with courage and faith, could open the portal for greater successes? If we are not active ourselves, we cannot expect that others will take risks. Naturally, we must expect an enormous amount of work. If you refuse, Dr. Steiner will write something himself in the sense of the ancient mysteries, for we value the mystery. However, we would like very much to have yours.

It is true that Dr. Steiner wants to give me the role of Demeter, and that shocked me. I would sooner have chosen Persephone, the grandmother. But Dr. Steiner said that this mother must have something of the quality of a nun and that, indeed, my mouth is especially appropriate for this role but not for that of Persephone. Now I cannot be the one to resist this choice; it is just that I find that I now have the most difficult role and that it is the one upon which the most depends. Above all, the scene between Zeus and Demeter would have to be changed, because it was not written to come across as so profane. Perhaps also the narration of Hecate, where she announces the will of Zeus to Demeter, would have to be retouched, because things become immediately quite crude or coarse when translated into German.

Perhaps we could do individual scenes by putting together living pictures or pantomimes separated by music. In the large scenes the choirs of the nymphs, the blissful, and mystics must alternate in a beautiful manner with the spoken word.

Naturally, you are overtaxed with work; I know that. However, perhaps the genius of the drama will take hold of you, and you will succeed in putting together into a whole work what was created in individual parts....

I think back often to the peaceful Vogesental (valley in the Vosges)[†] where we found such warm and understanding hospitality. I hope to see you and Mrs. Schuré in Munich....

If you only knew how much work Dr. Steiner has to do! I don't think anyone has ever had to work this hard before.

DECEMBER 1906 TO FEBRUARY 1907
The Congress program is printed and sent out

December 8: Rudolf Steiner writes to Marie von Sivers from Stuttgart: "How is it going with your translation of the Eleusis? We must have it soon.... We must absolutely be able to send the Congress program at the beginning of January. We will, therefore, possibly have to stay in Munich."†

December 11 and 12: Rudolf Steiner holds lectures in Munich.

December 20, 1906 and January 4, 1907: Rudolf Steiner and Marie von Sivers make a personal stop in Munich on a short vacation trip to Venice.

January 13: Marie von Sivers writes to Edouard Schuré:

> I understand your thoughts of alarm about our undertaking. I share your apprehension. It is just that I have the impression that there is a necessity here. It is as if it *must* happen. For us, it is the sword of Damocles that hangs over the Congress, for we have connected it in an organic way with a mystery performance, and all the accidents and misfortunes that threaten this performance also threaten our Congress. Yet we must simply put our backs into it and take the burden upon ourselves without, however, losing sight of the stars. The composer has not given his final word, but he is enthusiastic about the idea. He is reading the play right now. His name is Mr. Stavenhagen† of Munich.

January 21: Letter from Rudolf Steiner from Erlangen, Germany, to Marie von Sivers concerning the Congress program:
I am enclosing the Congress program for you. It is now ready for the printer. Please have it printed immediately and just exactly as it is in the manuscript....

I escaped to Erlangen for a few hours today. I could not disembark anywhere along the way from Karlsruhe to Nuremberg, and if I had been in Nuremberg this morning, you would most likely still not have received this attached urgent Congress program.† For wherever I am, there are always people there.

Please give the printer a congress program from last year, so that he does not make it an impossible size. Impress upon him that he must do the text in two columns with the German and English facing each other, as it stands in the manuscript.†

Relevant excerpts from the program:

The purpose of the program of this Congress shall be to bring a unified Theosophical idea to expression. Because the Theosophical worldview represents an ideal for the future, it is obviously impossible to express such an idea completely in the present time. Yet we can perhaps still, through the arrangement and dissemination of what is to be offered, bring it about that in the Congress itself the Theosophical leading principles of concentration and clearness of ideas and the Theosophical basic mood of rest and inner composure are successfully expressed in detail.

The content shall consist of lectures from the Theosophical worldview, artistic offerings, and purely social gatherings. The artistic presentations shall be selected from the visual arts as well as the musical and poetic arts, so that each individual event joins together with what is brought forth out of the Theosophical worldview into a harmonious whole. For this reason, there will be an attempt to give a representation of a mystery in dramatic art.

Written Discourses and Lectures

According to the practice of the congresses up to this point, these will include:

1. Everything connected with brotherhood and other objectives of the society
2. Religion
   Mysticism
   Philosophy and science
   Including
   a)Knowledge of comparative religions
   b)Myth lore
   c)Folklore
   d)Science of art
   e)History
3. Administration, information
4. Occultism

The written discourses should be in the hands of the secretary of the Congress by April 10. These can be written in any language spoken in the affiliated sections.

The Visual Arts

The intention is to unite into a harmonious whole what is offered in this area with the entire form and content of the Congress. For this reason, an exhibit will not be held in a separate room but rather in the spacious and appealing festival hall of the Congress itself. There shall be incorporated into the choice of artworks to be exhibited, just as in the other decorations, a harmony that will establish a basic mood of the space for everything else that will take place. Therefore, only those works in the visual arts and handwork arts will be considered that fit within the scope characterized. Still, the underlying idea is so wide that it can include much.

Music

The musical events will integrate with the rest of the arrangements and, where possible, will be related to the Theosophical worldview, at least in mood. They will also take place in the festival hall of the Congress itself.

Poetic Art

Poetic offerings shall include recitations and a stage performance with the character of a mystery. It is hoped that the efforts of the German committee will succeed in overcoming the great difficulties of this part of the program. It is nevertheless desirable, even if only within modest limits, that for once it could be shown how the Theosophical worldview is capable of enlivening the artistic. All these events will bring to expression the fact that Theosophy must not remain merely a sum of theoretical views but can undergo the transformation into the sense perceptible and into a perceptible mood. In this way, it must fructify culture as a whole.

January 25 and 26: Rudolf Steiner stopped in Munich for two public lectures.

February 17: Death of the president and co-founder of the Theosophical Society, Henry Steel Olcott.

February 25: Steiner wrote to Marie von Sivers about Olcott's death: "Whatever may come, for the Theosophical Society everything will be fatal, but for the spiritual movement, not unfavorable. Even the falling into ruin of the Theosophical Society as such should not in any way dismay us."†

March 17-19: Steiner stayed in Munich again and held lectures.

APRIL/MAY 1907
Rehearsal time in Munich and the decorating of the hall

April 6: Steiner and Marie von Sivers arrive in Munich. In between everything else, Steiner traveled alone to Berlin briefly to arrange that which was necessary for the selection of the new president of the Theosophical Society.†

April 29: Steiner returned to Munich. During this six-week stay in Munich, Rudolf Steiner worked nonstop on the performance of the mystery drama and the room decor. He put the drama, which had been translated in prose by Marie von Sivers, into free verse, cast the players, and directed the rehearsals. The scenery and costumes were also made according to his instructions. He guided the arranging of the hall, for which he drew the sketches for the apocalyptic seals and then the planetary seals for the congress program, and he sculpted the forms of the capitals.

MAY 18-21 (WHITSUN)
The Congress as an attempt to renew the Western mysteries

Steiner, as acting president, opened the Congress of approximately six hundred participants at 10:00 A.M. on May 18. Annie Besant, as honorary president spoke after the various general secretaries. Among others who performed in the evening artistic programs, Marie von Sivers recited the Ariel scene from Goethe's *Faust*, Part II.

On Whitsunday (May 19), morning, Steiner held his first lecture of the Congress, entitled "The Rosicrucian Initiation." At 3:00 P.M. there followed the performance of *The Sacred Drama of Eleusis*, a mystery by Edouard Schuré, with music by Bernhard Stavenhagen.

Relevant excerpts from the program:

Brief Synopsis of the Content of Edouard Schuré's *Sacred Drama of Eleusis*

performed during the Congress of the Federation of the European Sections of the Theosophical Society on May 19, 1907

1. *Prologue:* Demeter warns Persephone not to be swayed by Eros to pick the bewitching Narcissus, but rather to weave the world veil where the fates of the world are woven right down to chaos, yet not into the conscious life of human beings. The nymphs work as an admonishing element. They seek to guide Persephone to the fulfillment of her vow. Eros appears as tempter. Persephone picks the Narcissus of "desire" and can thus be kidnapped by Pluto.

Act I.

Demeter appears with Hecate, complaining about her pain and asking after the whereabouts of her daughter. Upon learning that she has been kidnapped by Pluto, Demeter wants to know where she can live with a free people and give herself up totally to her pain. Hecate points the way to Eleusis. There, the king has just died. So that she might enter without being recognized, Hecate turns her into an old beggar.

Metaneira, the widow of the king of Eleusis, has her three daughters who mourn the death of their father. She herself, however, is anxious that her son, Triptolemus, should sway the people to choose him as the successor to his father. He does not want to gain the crown through persuasion but only if the people choose him freely.

Demeter enters in the form of an old beggar. She is well received by the daughters and Triptolemus but sharply rejected by Metaneira.

As Demeter speaks alone to Triptolemus, sparks become visible under her garment. She tells Triptolemus of the loss of her daughter, and he promises to descend into the underworld to get her. Demeter recognizes his great nature and says that she wants to make him "the most divine of the heroes." She touches him, which calls forth a light appearance. Metaneira hurries to him, hurling curses on Demeter, who then reveals herself and ordains Triptolemus as future sacrificing priest of Eleusis. Metaneira is banished from the sanctuary. As a result, she curses Triptolemus.

Act II.

Zeus bemoans the fate of Persephone and of Triptolemus, who also has now been caught by Pluto. He says that only Dionysus in a new form can free them. Demeter appears. Zeus tells her that a new Dionysus must arise to free the condemned and that he can only arise through a union of his (Zeus's) fire with the light of Demeter. Demeter does not want to have Dionysus, in a new form, torn apart again by the Titans. But Zeus says that this Dionysus will be stronger. Demeter sinks into sleep. Out of her dream in union with the power of Zeus, the new Dionysus is created. Before he appears, the mystery of becoming is announced solemnly by a "choir of the invisible blessed." Then Triptolemus and Persephone appear in a wagon drawn by fiery dragons. Persephone recognizes the god in Dionysus, with whom she had always been united through longing. Dionysus recognizes in Persephone the sister to whom he belongs for all eternity. Zeus sends Triptolemus as an initiated priest to Eleusis. A choir of the invisible heroes speaks of the mystery of initiation.

The Choirs are:

Nymphs:

O Persephone, O Virgin!
Chaste bride of heaven!
You weave in your veil
Light forms of the gods,
Vain illusion of Earth
Be eternally far from you!
Pure radiance of truth
Ray forth to your sight!
In the imperium Dionysus,
The husband, lives for you,
Chosen by heaven itself.
Like a chaste ray of a far Sun
His kiss touches only you.
From your breath he lives,
In his light you breathe—
No greater salvation
Is to be found in the All.
Do not consider your salvation
Withdraw yourself
From vain questioning.

Search not further!
Flee the dangers
Threatening human beings
And the gods.

O divine Virgin!
It is only a dream,
Yet it becomes being
When guilty wish
In your soul calls it forth.
In appearance must vanish
Heaven's bliss for you,
When for naught
Salvation's warning resounds for you.
Weave further the veil,
Forget what Eros would
Unchastely reveal to you.

Wretched one, stop.

Be careful, Persephone,
Evil can easily arise
From magic.

Choir of the Invisible Demons in Tartaros:

To Persephone's conqueror—
Great Pluto—
To him be honor!
Hades rejoices
In your wedding festival.
Tartaros gleams
In a thousand fires of joy.
The children of Earth
Escaped him till now
In their innocence.
They were too mild
For the kingdom of darkness.
Yet now possessing
The goddess of the heights,
In immeasurable number
We conquer her for ourselves.
For she will draw
The errors of her life
And beauty of her forms
Into our kingdom.
It must become inhabited
With vain shadows,
You Stygian, Harpies,
You monster, be glad
In the tree of lies.
Honor to Pluto.
Hades trembles
For joy,
And dark Tartaros
Will hold
Its prize.

Forget, forget,
You shall drink
From this cup
And pass it on
For us to drink.
We demand
To drink the power of life
From this cup!
The thirst of Hades
Burns in us.
It alone
Can quench it.

Choir of the Shadows:
You see in us only souls
Bowed down by misfortune's power,
Erring on this shore
We want to plead of you
Deliverance, O Queen,
Asking you
To lead us upward
In Eleusian Fields.

Drink not, Persephone,
The red blood
In the black cup.
And let us ascend
Out of Hecate's darkness
Into the Elysian kingdom.

Choir of Invisible Blessed:
When the goddess of all earthly fruitfulness disappears in spirit realm of dream
The power of becoming streams through the All,
The Ardor of gods instills the world with spirit,
And human beings quake to the depths of soul.
Creation struggles out of sense's dusk;
New gods enter into being.
Human beings shall bow in reverence
When the holy spirit powers manifest.
Countless forms stream into life,
When the eye of god looks
Into unmeasured widths of space.
Worlds spring into being out of nothing,
They sink from being to nonbeing
And so create the time of the gods,
Like light and darkness for human beings.
But you, seed of the abyss, you souls,
Who are scattered in the realm of the dead,
The rudder you lacked hitherto
Shall be given into your own hand!
The oven from which you once arose,
Was till now hidden in your soul....
It will reveal itself for you!
Dream power of the Mother God
Enliven what the Father God fashions.
Out of enlivened form shall arise
The new god, the strong light bearer.
And you shall take him up in your souls,
So his power can transform
The mortal in you into eternal being.

Choir of the Invisible Heroes:
You witnesses of deep, hidden knowledge!
What rests in deepest ground of worlds
Is naked before your prophetic eye.
The spirit shall keep what it has seen,
The memory preserves it in the realm of Earth....
May it comfort you as long as you live!
As leader, take it into the spirit land!
But closed in depths of heart this sacred relic
As secret treasure must be,
Like the rock that rests in rock.
To bear pure ray of wisdom
Into world-being is the seer's high duty,
Only those may betray its origin
Who wish to lose it.

Monday, May 20: Steiner holds his second Congress lecture entitled "Planetary Evolution and the Evolution of Humanity."

Tuesday, May 21: Steiner speaks in the morning on questions of education and in the afternoon on the arrangement of the hall. In the evening, the Congress ends with musical offerings and closing talks.

May/June 1907
Marie von Sivers reports to Edouard Schuré on the performance of his Mystery Drama

Marie von Sivers made a lively report to Edouard Schuré, who did not come to Munich, giving her impression of the performance and the challenges they had in staging it:

Munich, May 26, 1907: This is the first day that I have a few peaceful hours in my room. Soon people will come streaming in, but until then I will try to impart, if not a witticism, at least a few informational scraps. My long silence before the Congress was the most painful for me. I did not dare to persuade you to come, for if the event had failed, you would have experienced painful moments and would have taken upon yourself a long trip with hardships, only to receive unpleasant impressions. And then we did not know until the last moment whether we would be able to perform the drama or not. The obstacles were very great.

You must remember, the actors came out of various cities and could gather together only quite late. Of the two women we considered to be our stars and who promised to be wonderful in the roles of Persephone and Hecate, one had to leave to take care of a sister-in-law who had suddenly become insane, and the other developed a neurological illness herself. We had her here for a week without being able to send for her mother, from whom she had inherited the illness. Her mother had been tormented with the illness her whole life. We finally, had to take her to a mental institution. It was really a catastrophe. The chances of the performance succeeding became very slim. After much hesitation, we decided to try to substitute a poor young girl who has an exceedingly difficult life and, in moments of depression, comes across as hopeless, because she has no energy. She then sits down, lays her hands in her lap, and says, "I can't put up with this."

Happily, she "put up with" the role of Persephone. That was the question. Then we saw the sparks ignite that had lain dormant within her, and she became happier every day. Her voice, which was too weak and slid down into her chest, grew stronger with each day. Still, it was only in the last week that we could be sure that anyone would be able to understand her. This young girl is even now still transformed and still has the allure of a princess. These days will have been the most beautiful of her life. On the whole, the rehearsals were a source of delight and harmony for many. We had a great number of people in the audience who could not get enough and found the play to be so beautiful that they would have liked to hear it every day. The nymphs and phantoms were quite full of zeal, but made a lot of work for us. None of these people had ever performed. No one had any experience, except for Triptolemus, who is an actor and a member of the Theosophical Society, and myself. (I had worked in amateur theater at the same time as he.) Their enthusiasm made up for everything.

Metaneira was disappointing. The one who was supposed to play this role had to take over the role of Hecate, and the new presenter, a quite bright lady, showed no understanding of the stage at all. The role of Triptolemus was entrusted, at first, to a young man who really wanted to play him. He made a very sympathetic impression and looked like an Ephebe, but his gestures were so hopeless and his speech so incapable of any improvement that we believed we would have to give up because of him. Then the actor who was originally supposed to play the role of Pluto came and replaced him successfully. Dionysus was a charming young girl (half Italian and half Polish), who was the last to come and spoke at first with an accent that made us wince. She was indeed nice but extremely inept, and the final elevation of the character to divine status was in danger of failure because of her. We had to work intensively with her every day to improve her German pronunciation.

Through this effort, my own voice, after I had already exhausted it because of a cough and constant speaking in rehearsals, became completely hoarse in the last week. I feared that I would not be able to speak during the performance. Besides, I had no opportunity to pull back from all the other responsibilities and to take care of myself. Apart from my obligation as secretary of the German Section and of the Congress office, we had to set up studios for this performance: two painting studios for the scenery, a tailor's studio (even the costumes were all made by our members, according to indications given by Dr. Steiner), and two more studios where our painters could work on the decoration of the hall (of the subsequent temple, according to drawings by Dr. Steiner). It was as busy as an ant hill; everywhere there was great haste because we were sure, more or less, that we could perform.

May 28: Mr. Stavenhagen (who, by the way, is not Dutch) had his music ready just three days before the performance, and he didn't even get to the planned final chorus. The music was, however, very beautiful. I don't know what the foreigners thought of it, but the Germans found it to be like a harmony of the spheres. The actors also thought it was beautiful, noble, strong, and ethereal—religious through and through.

I believe it was advantageous for the poetry that it was not mingled with music. Through the wonderful prelude, a concentrated religious mood was called forth; then the word held sway, and the meaning came through all the more clearly.

The Germans were really inspired. They did not make trite compliments but were deeply moved by the drama itself and pressed us for a repeat performance, but that was not possible. The foreigners were more critical and cooler, however, as you had already surmised. Many of them had come with hostile feelings and had made the decision to resist the progressive spirit. They had decided to handle anything beyond their understanding with irony and to reject what they held to be unorthodox. Yet it was special to watch how their resistance diminished and how some were finally moved by the drama. The Blechs and Mr. Pascal† will certainly never give up their reserved stance, but Mr. Pascal is at the end of his strength, and the Blechs are extraordinarily narrow-minded. I also believe that it made a peculiar impression on them that we stress the significance of your work so strongly, while they passed right by it in their English education. For this reason, they have mixed feelings.

You were right when you recognized Dr. Steiner's hand in the translation. I didn't know why Mr. Sauerwein† told you that it was by me. By the way, I do not know Mr. Sauerwein and have never seen him. Dr. Steiner spoke of him as a theosophist whom he had met one time in Vienna, who was there at the Congress on the day of the performance and who is acquainted with you. Because he was going to Paris, Dr. Steiner asked him to give you our greetings. Perhaps Mr. Sauerwein saw on the desk the two works that I did translate and so assumed that I also had translated the *Sacred Drama*. I did the prose translation, and in the last month Dr. Steiner put into verse, but with what difficulties! He was constantly interrupted. People needed him continually. He went away, returned for five minutes to progress with his poetic work and then went away again, being called by yet another person. He worked on all the arts and on all the handwork. He directed everyone: the painters, sculptors, musicians, carpenters, wallpaperers, actors, tailors, stagehands, and electricians. If he had had the necessary material and the workers available, he would have brought about something fabulous in a short time: the temple of the future. As it was, he could only sketch ideas, but they will have a fructifying effect.

With all that, the last scenes of the drama could only be completed in a moment that appeared to me to be highly critical. I really trusted that we would accomplish it, but it would have been foolish of me to have depended on it. It would have, at one and the same time, pleased me and frightened me if you had written and said that you were coming. But I didn't dare encourage you to do so. One does not want to make demands of the guardian spirits, but rather only ask carefully for their help. What really amazes me is that my voice came back for the performance. It was so peaceful and certain, as if I had never suffered the cough or the exhaustion.

Kassel-Wilhelmshöhe, June 17, 1907: I ... regret fervently that I did not send these pages that I wrote in Munich and whose details I thought I would be able to elaborate. However, every day brought something unexpected. About two hundred people stayed after the Congress in Munich for Dr. Steiner's lecture cycle,† and they simply tore us to pieces with exhaustion. It was difficult to leave. At 9:00 P.M. on the last day we still had ten people waiting to be received. When we take the morning train, as in this case, we pack our suitcases from 2:00 to 6:00 A.M., without going to bed. Dr. Steiner went directly from the train to give a public lecture in Leipzig. Another followed on the next day.... The morning of June 15 we had to take a train to Kassel, where a two-week lecture cycle is now taking place.†

The Munich Congress as the point of departure for the separation from the Theosophical Society

The esoteric-artistic form of the Munich Congress organized by Rudolf Steiner had a strong historical effect on the Theosophical Society. From the viewpoint of life within the Theosophical Society, it constituted a large-scale attempt by Steiner to bring Occidental-Christian-Rosicrucian esotericism, out of which he had worked from the beginning, into the international circle of the Theosophical Society. This attempt, as he described it in his *Autobiography*, was rejected by the non-German Theosophists. In this resistance lay the real reason why the Anthroposophical Society could not remain part of the Theosophical Society.

Because he foresaw the fall of the Theosophical Society, Steiner had a long conversation yet during the Congress with Annie Besant, the new president, in the presence of Marie von Sivers, who served as interpreter. Marie von Sivers reported later that Steiner had tried in this conversation, "with heartfelt respect but in a deeply emphatic manner, to point out to Annie Besant some of the circumstances in connection with the coming fall of the Theosophical Society and, at the same time, to explain to her that he was compelled to base his own esoteric work completely on the ground of Western-Christian mysticism, independent from hers." She listened to him silently.† Steiner spoke of this conversation once, to the effect that "Annie

Besant, before a witness (Marie von Sivers) who is always prepared to give testimony, said in Munich in 1907 that in connection with Christianity, she is not competent. And for that reason, she cedes to me the movement, insofar as Christianity should flow into it."†

On June 7, 1907, Annie Besant wrote to the German theosophist Wilhelm Hübbe-Schleiden on the basis of the conversation, shortly after her return to London from Munich:

> Dear Dr. Hübbe-Schleiden, Dr. Steiner's esoteric practice is very different from ours. He does not know the Eastern path and, for that reason, cannot teach it. He teaches the Christian-Rosicrucian path, which is of help for some people, but is different from ours. He has his own school and carries the responsibility for it himself. I consider him to be a very good teacher in his own path and to be a man with real insights. He and I work in perfect friendship and harmony but in different directions. Always yours, Annie Besant.†

In reality, this "friendship and harmony" were in no way as "perfect" as Annie Besant expressed in this letter. This became ever more apparent in the course of the following year, until in 1912-1913 the German Section of the Theosophical Society became the independent Anthroposophical Society.

The Munich Congress of Whitsun 1907

Rudolf Steiner

Excerpt from *Autobiography*

Two poles of Anthroposophical activity developed in Berlin and Munich. Some people came to Anthroposophy to find the spiritual meaning that their souls longed for and had been unable to find in the scientific worldview or in traditional religion. In Berlin, the society branch members and audiences at public lectures consisted only of those who had rejected worldviews opposed to traditional religions. Those who adhered to worldviews based on rationalism, intellectualism, and the like considered Anthroposophy to be fantastic or superstitious. Thus, we began to see public audiences and members who took up Anthroposophy as their sole guide to a spiritual life. They were unsatisfied with what was available from other sources. This soul mood had to be taken into account in the Anthroposophical work. Thus, membership grew steadily, as did the size of audiences at public lectures. An Anthroposophical life emerged that was, in a sense, *self-contained* and that virtually ignored any other endeavor toward spiritual insight. All hopes were directed toward what Anthroposophy had to say. The expectation was that one could continually increase one's knowledge of the spiritual world.

The situation in Munich was different. From the very beginning, an artistic element was active in the Anthroposophical work there. One could assimilate a worldview such as Anthroposophy in a completely different way than one could rationalism and intellectualism. The artistic *image* is more spiritual than a rationalistic concept. It is alive and, unlike intellectualism, does not kill the spirit in the soul. Those in Munich who set the tone and built the membership and public audiences there were likewise the ones in whom this artistic feeling worked. Consequently, right from the beginning the society branch in Berlin was marked by uniformity. All who came to Anthroposophy had the same sort of interests. In Munich, on the other hand, the artistic feeling evoked individual needs in individual groups. I gave lectures to those various groups.

. . .

By describing the Anthroposophical work in Berlin and Munich as "polar opposites," I do not intend to imply that one is better than the other; it is simply a diversity of human nature—all of it valuable in its own way—that became very prominent and required consideration in the work. In any case, there is no point in making a value judgment.

Because of the way the work of Anthroposophy had proceeded in Munich, the 1907 Theosophical Congress arranged by the German Section took place there. The congresses, which were held previously in London, Amsterdam, and Paris, had included arrangements for addressing problems related to Theosophy in lectures and discussions.[†] They were based on the same pattern as the scholarly conferences. Many of the arrangements were modified for Munich. We (the organizers) provided a large concert hall to serve the Congress, along with interior decoration, whose color and form would reflect artistically the dominant mood of the subject of oral deliberations. The artistic environment would become one with the spiritual activity there. In relation to this, I placed a great value on allowing the artistic feeling to speak and to avoid abstract, inartistic symbolism.

An artistic performance was included in the program. Schuré's reconstruction of *The Sacred Drama of Eleusis* had been translated sometime earlier by Marie von Sivers, and I had adapted it for performance. We included it in the program. Thus, a connection, however slight, was established with the ancient mysteries, but the main thing was that the Congress included artistic work. It pointed to the will never to allow spiritual life into the society without an artistic element. Marie von Sivers rendered the part of Demeter in a way that indicated the nuances that dramatic art should attain in the society. Through the inner power inherent in speech, Marie von Sivers had developed the art of declamation and recitation to a decisive stage, from which further progress could be made in this art.

A great many of the older members of the Theosophical Society from England and France and particularly from Holland were completely dissatisfied with the innovations offered at the Munich Congress. It would have been good if more people had understood that the Anthroposophical attitude toward the spirit was entirely different from the one evident so far in the Theosophical Society. This inner attitude is the real reason that the Anthroposophical Society was unable to continue as a part of the Theosophical Society.

The Congress of the Federation of the European Sections of the Theosophical Society

RUDOLF STEINER

Announcement of the Congress in the magazine *Lucifer-Gnosis,* Number 33 (Spring 1907)

The Federation of European Sections of the Theosophical Society shall seek to further the goals of the society in the cooperation of members from various countries through the strengthening of all that is contained in the mission of the Theosophical Movement. It is in consideration of this goal that the program of the next Congress has been prepared. It will take place on May 18-21 in Munich, in the concert hall (Kaim-Säle) at 5 Türkenstrasse.

The program was sent some time ago to all members of the German Section and to the members of the sections of other countries. It contains information about the planned lectures and offerings in the visual arts, music, and poetry. Special care will be taken for the Theosophical arrangement of the purely social gatherings so that the Congress may be suitable to appropriately support the work together.

It is of special importance at this time to have as large a gathering at the Congress as possible. We are perhaps facing important decisions in Theosophical matters, and the Congress will, if the opportunity is not neglected, be able to contribute much to bring about advantageous turns in spiritual matters. May all members who can possibly attend do so. Whitsuntide was chosen so that as many members as possible could attend.

All mail within the German Section should be addressed to Miss von Sivers. All international communications should be sent to the secretary of the International Federation: Miss Sophie Stinde at 55 Adalbertstrasse, Stuttgart.

All other information can be found in the Congress brochure.

The Theosophical Congress in Munich

RUDOLF STEINER

Report in the magazine *Lucifer-Gnosis,* Number 34 (Summer 1907)

It was the task of the German Section of the Theosophical Society to organize this year's Congress of the Federation of the European Sections. It seems appropriate that the circle of organizers should speak less here about what was accomplished and much more about what was intended. For the organizers know how far short the accomplishments fall from the goals that could be set. Therefore we ask that you accept the following words in the sense of a description of the ideas underlying the Congress.

The place chosen for the meeting was Munich, and the time was to be Whitsuntide, May 18-21. The questions that the organizers carried during preparations were these: How can the task of the Theosophical Movement in modern spiritual life be brought to expression in such a congress? How can a picture be given through it of the ideals and goals of Theosophical work? Because the meeting was bound naturally by the limits presented by existing circumstances, it could only present to a small degree a real answer to these questions. It seems particularly important that at such occasions the comprehensive character of the Theosophical Movement should be stressed.

At the center of this movement is the nurturing of a worldview based on knowledge of the supersensible. There will be people who come together at such a congress who, with the bridging of the gap between nations and other human differences, work toward a common spiritual ideal in the sense of such a worldview. The mutual impulse, in the best sense, will be the noblest fruit of such a meeting. In addition, it is appropriate that it be shown how spiritual-scientific work should be incorporated into all of life in our time. For the spiritual foundation of this movement is capable not only of realization in ideas and theories but can work into and fructify, as soul content in our time, all areas of human doing and creating. We grasp spiritual science rightly only when we expect it to stimulate not only the imagination and inner being but also the whole human being.

If we want to interpret its mission in this way, we might remember how the Egyptians expressed the worldview of their time in buildings and artistic representations (for example, the Sphinx). The ideas of the Egyptian worldview were not merely thought by the souls alive at that time but were also made visible in the surroundings of the human being. Think, too, how everything that is known of Greek architecture and drama is the worldview of the Greek soul formed in stone and poetic works. Consider how, in the Middle Ages, Christian ideas and feelings were made visible in paintings and how, in the Gothic impulse, Christian devotion gained form and took shape. A true harmony of the soul can be experienced only where form, shape, and color mirror for the human senses in the surroundings what the soul knows to be its most precious thoughts, feelings, and impulses.

Out of such ideas the intention grew to give a picture of spiritual-scientific striving in the outer arrangements of the Congress. The space in which such a meeting is to take place can reflect Theosophical feeling and thinking to the visitor on all sides. Because of our circumstances, we could give only a sketch of the ideal that we had in mind. We decorated the meeting hall so that a fresh, stimulating red became the primary color of all the walls. This color was meant to make visible the fundamentally festive mood. Naturally, there will be some objections to the use of red for this purpose. These objections are justified only as long as we rely on exoteric judgment and experience. Such objections are well known to the esotericist, who nonetheless must use the color red in accordance with esoteric symbolism for the purpose under consideration. For it must not be a question of what that part of his or her being senses which turns toward the immediate material surroundings, but rather what the higher self experiences in hidden, spiritual working while the outer surroundings are seen physically as red. It is just the opposite from what the ordinary feeling says about the color red.

Esoteric knowledge says: "If you would attune yourself inwardly as the gods were attuned when they gave the world the green covering of plants, learn to endure the red in your surroundings as they had to."

This points to the connection of the higher human nature to red, which true esotericists have in mind when they represent the opposite essences of the creative Ground of the World in esoteric symbolism, such that toward the bottom is green, as a sign or symbol of the earthly, and above is red, as sign of the divine creator-powers of the elohim. We could say much more about the objections to the color red and much to refute them, but this brief indication should suffice to show that this color was chosen in accord with esotericism.

On the walls, to both sides and on the back wall, we placed the so-called apocalyptic seals, in a size appropriate to the room. They present in pictures certain experiences in the astral world. That is a long story. Some observers will most likely consider such pictorial representations as ordinary symbols. They are, however, much more. Those who want to explain with the intellect what is represented in the seals symbolically have not penetrated to the spirit of the matter. We should experience these seven pictures with our whole soul, with our undivided mind (*Gemüt*). We should fashion them in our souls according to form, color, and content so that we live inwardly in the imagination. For this content corresponds to certain astral experiences of the seer.

What the seer wants to express in such pictures is not in the least an arbitrary symbol or even a lifeless allegory, but rather something that we can best illustrate with a comparison. Let us consider a person who is in a room illuminated so as to cast his shadow on the wall. The shadow is somewhat similar to the person who casts the shadow. However, it is only a two-dimensional picture of a three-dimensional being. As the shadow is to the person, so is what is portrayed in the apocalyptic seals to certain experiences of the seer in the astral world. The seals are akin to silhouettes of astral occurrences. For this reason, they, too, are not arbitrary representations of an individual. Everyone who recognizes the corresponding supersensible events will find their silhouettes in the physical world. We cannot simply think up these kinds of things in their essential content but must take them from the teaching of the esotericist. Those who know of these matters will notice that certain individual seals agree with what they find about them in other works and that others do not.† The reason lies in the fact that some esoteric imaginations have already been reported in books; certainly, the most important and true may first appear only in our time. One dimension of spiritual-scientific work must be to bring into the open what was preserved strictly in secret by guardians so placed for that purpose. The development of the spiritual life of our time demands this of the bearers of spiritual science.

The evolution of humanity, whose expression in the astral world must build the most essential foundations of esoteric knowledge, is shown in these seven seals. The Christian esotericist will recognize them again, in a certain sense, in the descriptions of the Book of Revelation of John. The form they took in our congress hall corresponds to the esoteric spiritual stream that has set the tone of the West since the fourteenth century.† Such secrets of existence as described in these pictures portray ancient beings. The seers of the various epochs of humanity see them from different viewpoints. For this reason, the forms change somewhat, according to the necessary evolutionary requirements of the ages. John's Revelation sets in symbols that which is to occur "soon." Those who learn to understand the spiritual-scientific form of expression know that this is nothing other than an indication of the spiritual-scientific symbols for certain imaginations that we can experience in the astral world and which have to do with the nature of the human being inasmuch as it reveals itself over time. The Rosicrucian seals show the same thing. We shall give only a rough sketch of the infinitely rich content of the seals. In truth, everything in these pictures is important, even the smallest detail.

The first seal presents the human being's entire evolution, in the most general sense. In the Book of Revelation of John 1:12, we read:

> And when I turned, I saw seven golden candlesticks and in the midst of the seven candlesticks, one like a Son of Man, clothed with a long garment and girded with a golden girdle around his chest. His head and his hair were white like wool, like snow, and his eyes were as a flame of fire. His feet were like brass that glows in the furnace, and his voice was like the great roar of water. And he had seven stars in his right hand; and out of his mouth came a sharp two-edged sword; and his countenance shone like the full brightness of the Sun.

Such words indicate in broad strokes the comprehensive secrets of human evolution.† If we wanted to elaborate the content of every meaningful word in detail, we would have to write a thick volume. Our seals present this pictorially; we will give just a few indications. Among the bodily organs and forms of expression of the human being are some that, in their present structure, give evidence of the declining evolutionary stages of earlier forms, that is, those which have already surpassed the point of their completion. Others, however, reveal the beginning stages of evolution; they are, as it were, the predisposition of what they will become in the future.† The esotericist must know these secrets of evolution.

The speech organ is an example of an organ that will evolve into a much higher and more perfect form than it has at present. In saying this, we touch on a great secret of existence that is often called the "mystery of the creative word." This is an indication of the future condition of the human speech organ, which will become a spiritual organ of production when the human being becomes spiritualized. In myths and in various religions, this spiritual production is intimated by the appropriate picture of a sword coming out of the mouth. Thus, every detail of the seal has meaning in connection with the mystery of human evolution. These pictures are not formed out of a need to have sense-perceptible representations of supersensible occurrences; rather, living into these pictures, when they are the right ones, brings about an awakening of forces that slumber in the human soul. Through this awakening, the imaginations of the supersensible world emerge. It is not correct that, in Theosophy, supersensible worlds are described only in schematic concepts. The true way is to awaken the imagination of such pictures as are given in these seals. (If esotericists do not have such pictures on hand, they should give oral descriptions of higher worlds in appropriate images.)

The second seal portrays one of the first conditions of evolution of earthly humanity. In primeval times, this earthly humanity had not yet developed an individual soul. At that time, humanity had a group soul, which is still found among animals. Those who, through imaginative clairvoyance, can follow the old human group souls on the astral plane find the four types that are represented in the four apocalyptic animals of the second seal: the lion, the bull, the eagle, and the human being. Here, we are led to a truth about the four animals that is so often interpreted in a dry, allegorical manner.

The third seal presents the secrets of the so-called harmony of the spheres. The human being experiences this mystery during the time between death and a new birth (in spirit land or in what is called devachan in conventional Theosophical literature). The harmony of the spheres is not depicted as it is in spirit land itself but as the occurrences of this realm reflect into the astral world. We must bear firmly in mind that the seven seals are experiences of the astral world, yet the reflections of other worlds can be seen in the astral. The angels blowing trumpets, as portrayed, represent the spiritual primordial beings of world manifestations. The book with seven seals indicates that the riddles of existence "unseal" themselves in the experiences that are illustrated. The "four apocalyptic riders" represent the stages of human evolution throughout the long cycles of Earth's evolution.

The fourth seal shows, among other things, two pillars—one rising out of the sea and the other out of the realm of Earth.† These pillars represent the roles that the oxygen-rich red blood and the carbon-rich blue blood play in human development and how this blood transforms itself from primordial times into far future times, in accordance with human evolution. The letters (J, B) on these pillars point to this secret of evolution in a way known only to initiates. (All the explanations of both letters, given in public writings or in certain societies, remain superficial and exoteric.) The book in the cloud indicates a future condition of human beings, in which all their knowledge will be spiritualized. In the Book of Revelation, we find meaningful words about this: "And I took the book from the hand of the angel and ate it." The pictured Sun points to a cosmic event that will take place at the same time as the characterized future stage of humanity; Earth will enter into a relationship to the Sun totally different from the one it currently has in the universe. Everything in the seal is so depicted that all arrangements of the parts and all the details correspond to real events.

The fifth seal presents the future evolution of the human being, in a universe in which the circumstances just indicated will have set in. The human being of the future, who will have a different relationship to the

Sun than at present, is portrayed as the "woman who gives birth to the Sun." The power that the future human will have over certain forces of the world, which express themselves in the lower nature, is portrayed by the sun-woman standing above the animal with the seven heads and ten horns. The woman has the Moon under her feet. This symbol points to a later cosmic relationship of Sun, Earth, and Moon.

The sixth seal depicts the further-developed human being, with still greater power over the lower forces of the universe. The way in which the picture expresses this is suggestive of Christian esotericism: Michael holds the dragon, bound. Finally, the seventh seal is the picture of the Mystery of the Grail† as it lived in the esoteric stream that was beginning in the fourteenth century. The cube in this picture represents the world of space, out of which a serpent springs from all sides, insofar as it represents the higher forces living in the lower forces. From the mouth of the serpent comes the world spiral, the symbol of cleansed and purified world forces. Out of this spiral arises the Holy Grail, upon which the dove looks. This representation points quite appropriately to the secret of world begetting, of which the earthly begetting is a lower reflection. The deepest mysteries lie in the lines and figures of this seal.

A column was inserted between every two seals. These columns could not be sculpted but had to be painted instead. Still, they were configured as real architectural forms and correspond to the seven columns of the true Rosicrucian temple. (Naturally, the arrangement in Munich does not correspond perfectly to the Rosicrucian initiation temple. There, such columns are doubled, so that when we go from the rear wall to the front, we walk through fourteen columns, of which every two stand across from each other.† This is only a brief mention for those who know the true facts of the matter; with us, only a general imagination of the secret meaning of these columns should be awakened.)

The capitals of these columns depict the planetary evolution of our Earth system.† Our Earth is the fourth embodiment in planetary evolution and indicates a predisposition for three more embodiments in the future. (Further details about these future embodiments of the Earth can be found in essays in this magazine under the title "Aus der Akasha-Chronik" [From the Akashic Chronicle]).† The seven consecutive incarnations of the Earth we call Saturn, Sun, Moon, Earth,

Jupiter, Venus, and Vulcan. Conventional spiritual-scientific accounts leave out the Vulcan condition as one that lies too far off in the future and divides Earth evolution into a Mars and a Mercury condition. The reasons for this difference would lead us too far astray, [but also can be found in the essays, "From the Akashic Chronicle"].

These seven embodiments of the Earth—Saturn, Sun, Moon, Mars, Mercury, Jupiter, and Venus—are expressed in esotericism by seven column capitals. The forms in these capitals present the inner life of each evolutionary condition. We are not meant to delve into the forms of the capitals with the intellect but rather with our feeling, in real artistic experience and in the imagination. For every line, every curve, everything in these forms is such that we awaken slumbering forces in our souls when we immerse ourselves in them. These forces lead to imaginations concerning the great world secrets that lie at the foundation of cosmic evolution and, connected with it, the evolution of humanity on Earth.

Those who wish to find fault with the design of the columns should consider the fact that, for instance, the Corinthian and Ionian columns[†] of old arose out of the embodiment of secrets of existence and that such facts are just unknown today. From the way that the motifs of world evolution are expressed in these column capitals, we can judge how esotericism will influence art in a fructifying way. The ancient columns were born out of esotericism, and the architecture of the future will have the task of making visible what the esoteric worldview of Theosophy can give today as an indication. In Munich the attempt was made to produce in a few strokes a sketch of an inner space as held in the mood of the Theosophical worldview. Naturally, it was possible to put across only a suggestion of this space—and even that only in a very general way and, above all, not exactly in the appropriate order. However, it was meant to impart only an *idea* of the matter.

Among the furnishings in our meeting room, there were also two pillars that stood at the front of the hall. Drawing on the fourth seal, in which they are found, they point to the mystery of the blood and contain the mystery of the evolution of humanity. In their connection to the mystery of the blood, the one pillar is red, and the other is deep blue-red. Spiritual science writes upon these two pillars four deeply significant sayings. When the human soul immerses itself meditatively in these four sayings, cosmic and human mysteries spring forth from their depths. We would have to write many books if we were to exhaust their whole meaning: not only is every word meaningful, but so are the symmetry of the words, the manner in which they are distributed in the four sayings, the intensifications therein, and much more. Only a long, patient devotion to them can elucidate all that lies therein. In the German language, the four sayings of the pillar wisdom read as follows:

In reinen Gedanken findest du
Das Selbst, das sich halten kann.

Wandelst zum Bilde du den Gedanken
Erlebst du die schaffende Weisheit.

Verdichtest du das Gefühl zum Licht
Offenbarst du die formende Kraft.

Verdinglichst du den Willen zum Wesen
So schaffest du im Weltensein.

In English, they translate as follows:

In pure thinking you find
The self that can hold itself.

Transform thought into an image
And you will experience creative wisdom.

Concentrate feeling into light
And you will reveal the formative power.

Realize the will into being-ness
And you will create in world-being.

We sought to make the keynote mood vivid in the visitors' program book. Because the meaning of the color red in esotericism has already been discussed, there is no need to say more about the red color of the book's cover. In the upper-left corner of the cover, there is a black cross entwined with red roses on a blue oval field. To the right are the letters: E.D.N.—I.C.M.—P.S.S.R. These are the ten beginning letters of the words through which the principle of true Rosicrucianism is summarized: "Ex Deo nascimur. In Christo morimur. Per Spiritum sanctum reviviscimus." The cross encircled by roses expresses esoterically the meaning of Rosicrucianism.†

With respect to the relationship in which our Congress stood to Rosicrucianism, it seems necessary to mention the misunderstandings that have arisen. People have tried here and there to form an idea of Rosicrucianism based on historical traditions. Of those who have taken such note of Rosicrucianism, some look upon it with goodwill. Most, however, see it as charlatanism, rapture, or something similar—or even much worse. It can be stated without hesitation that if true Rosicrucianism were that which people know of from historical documents and traditions, it must seem that it would certainly not be worth any reasonable human beings occupying themselves with it. However, absolutely no one today knows anything about true Rosicrucianism who has not given it full consideration through the methods of spiritual science.†

Outside the sphere of spiritual science there are no true documents concerning that which bears the name of the spiritual stream referred to here and which has been setting the tone in the West since the fourteenth century. Only now can the secrets of Rosicrucianism begin to be made public. By drawing from this source in Munich, we did not want to put it forward as the only path to blessedness within the Theosophical Movement, but only as *one* path upon which spiritual knowledge can be sought. One cannot say that we gave one-sided preference to this source, while the Theosophical Movement should take all forms of religion and paths of truth into account equally. It is never incumbent upon the Theosophical Movement to study the variety of religions as an end in itself; through the study of religious forms, it must reach the point of their *unity*, their core. We did not want at all to show what Rosicrucianism looks like; rather, through Rosicrucianism, we wanted to show perspectives of a core of truth in all religions. This is the true mission of the Theosophical Movement.

In the program book there are five drawings. These are the motifs, in vignette form, of the first five of the seven column capitals referred to earlier. Something of what is called the "occult script" is given in these five drawings. For those who immerse themselves with their whole souls into the lineal forms and figures, a hint will light up within of what we describe as the conditions (Saturn, Sun, Moon, Mars, and Mercury) important for the knowledge of human evolution.

This outline was meant to give a description of the intentions of the congress organizers in preparing the framework within which the festivities were to take place. The place of the Congress was the concert hall (Kaim-Säle), which seemed especially suitable for this event.

The Rosicrucian Initiation

Rudolf Steiner

First Congress Lecture, Munich, May 19, 1907

One of the great men whose busts stand here before you,† the German philosopher Hegel, summarized his conviction concerning the nature of the evolution of humanity as follows: this evolution is a progress of humanity in the consciousness of freedom.† He wanted to indicate that evolution of humanity is not a repetition, a sequence of the same facts or events, but rather a constant and steady progress and that, from epoch to epoch, humanity climbs to ever higher and higher stages.

Whoever looks at human evolution from a spiritual viewpoint will find a deep truth in this statement from Hegel. Indeed, this is not to say that within the ascending course of the evolution of humanity there do not also occur passing epochs of decline. However, it means that we are observing the great development of humankind from a limited point of view if we do not see within these passing epochs of decline how the enduring ascent is present on a larger scale. Only those who cannot look into the depths of the course of evolution have the idea so often found today that whether we look further into the past or into the future, the human form or nature was, and will be, approximately the same as today. Even when evolution is discussed, the mentality that lives only on the physical plane can form no idea of the immense differences that exist from one epoch of the human spirit to the next, and so on, throughout the progressing of culture. To them, it often seems grotesque when one shows them the great differences in the realms of nature that have occurred in the elapsed epochs or indicates future epochs prophetically.

Only when we observe the differentiated development of humanity do we see the configuration of the higher worlds on the physical plane. Only those who know at which stage they live in humanity's evolution know their own epoch. We must look around us a bit to see where we are standing—to which plane our current human evolution corresponds. Esoteric wisdom teaches us that it is what is called *intellect* in the German language which is on a descending path of development—not the other members of the human being. It is the intellect that has descended most deeply onto the physical plane in our epoch. Since the last third of the nineteenth century, the intellectual impulse has been at the point of ascending again, and those who recognize the configuration can express it by saying that the characteristic of this epoch was the deepest entanglement of the intellect with matter and that now it is making the effort to ascend again to the spiritual. All who strive spiritually are working to come out of this entanglement.

Such an important nodal point of humanity's evolution has been in preparation for a long time. If we examine esoterically since when this decisive moment in the spiritual development of humanity of the nineteenth century has prepared itself, we arrive at the time when the human intellect descended from the knowledge born more or less on the astral plane, and we come to a special mission in the evolution of humanity that has been developing for the past four to five hundred centuries. The most important point at which human evolution made the move downward from the astral to the physical plane and spiritual knowledge passed over into the material we can pinpoint at the time when the Ptolemaic system—which was not nonsense, but rather a projection of astral knowledge onto the physical plane—was brought down to the physical plane by Copernicus.† This knowledge penetrated ever more deeply into the physical in later stages of evolution, until it was led deeper still than was intended. Whoever understands the Theosophical Movement rightly does not criticize what humanity has thus brought down. That would not be active Theosophical life. The active Theosophical life asks much more: How do we free ourselves of the fetters of the physical plane? Such a life attempts to recognize the task of this descent onto the physical plane.

We look back to the Egyptian wisdom, to the wonderful Chaldean-Babylonian wisdom, and ask ourselves: What is the difference between what the Egyptian priests, the servants of Hermes, saw when they looked up to the starry heavens or what the astronomer of the Chaldeans saw in the stars and what modern science sees? We do not attain to a correct conception, through materialistic science, of that which took place in those wise ones when they looked up to the vault of the heavens; however, we can attain to it through an analogy, when we consider a human being. We do not observe the human being in such a way that we look only at the physiognomy of his face. When we see the tears roll down, we do not study merely how gravity makes them fall—as if an angel were to come from heaven and we would calculate the rate of descent—no, we see through the teardrops the suffering and pain of the soul. And when someone smiles, we see in the smiling countenance the joy that lives in the spirit. We know that primal, elementary feelings are arising in the human being.

This looking through the material to the soul-spiritual content of the soul was what the servants of Hermes meant when they said: Everything below is as above![†] There is no earthly matter that is not the outer expression of the soul-spiritual! As ice is merely water in another form, so all matter is merely spirit in another form. If someone was to show us a piece of ice and we said that it is solidified water but he denied it, we would tell him, "You are naïve. You are mistaken. This ice is merely solidified water." In like manner, matter is merely transformed, condensed spirit. However, it is not enough just to know that; we must take all knowledge into the soul. The spiritual life demands that everything that lives in the soul becomes active. What lives in our souls as ordinary thoughts, feelings, and will impulses is not enough. If we also awaken an inner life, we can understand how the Egyptian servant of Hermes looked up to the heavens. Mars, Venus, Moon, and Mercury were only an expression of the spirits that lived in the stars. Thus, in times when life was more spiritual, these names did not signify what the modern astronomer understands of the stars. With the name Mercury, the wise of old, those who lived in the spiritual life, imagined the spirit that lives in Mercury the way the soul lives in our body. Thus the servant of Hermes taught everyone who listened to him.

Now imagine in a living way how human beings looked out into space and perceived the stars. It was not an abstract but rather an intimate spiritual life that connected them with the world. It was spirit they saw, and they floated in spiritual space and felt themselves to be members of the world, as my finger is merely a member of my hand. If their being were separated from the universal spirituality, they would die and no longer be present, just as the finger would die if one were to cut it off. Compare that with what modern astronomers see. For them, physical cosmic globes fly around the cosmos. The living feeling [for their spiritual substantiality] is lacking in them, but this living feeling is not so easy to achieve. Perhaps they are theoretical spiritualists, but it is more difficult to be a spiritualist in accordance with the whole soul than it is in accordance with a merely theoretical view. Today we live in a purely physical environment. We no longer find the living harmony between the divine and the physical. It is, however, right and of great significance that this came to be. Let us compare the accomplishments of human beings on the physical plane with those that derived from spiritual priest-wisdom. In olden times a primitive culture prevailed. When we look at the unending work and effort of that time and recognize that every single object around us is a spiritual creation of the past four centuries, we do not want to forget that we have the human spirit of these last centuries to thank. All of this could not have happened if the intellect had not descended to the physical plane. Thus, every epoch has its task. Because that was especially the case for the last epoch of world history, in the last epoch of humanity the source from which spiritual life flows had to send the spirit down to those who wanted to receive it with devotion.

If we calculate the time to the descent [of the intellect onto the physical plane] back four or five centuries and reckon two centuries for preparation, we find a stream that saw to it that the intellect could find its way back again—to give the intellect, which had to descend to the physical plane, the means to ascend once more. This is the Rosicrucian stream. Just as in olden times human beings had to be led upward to the eternal, so human beings today must seek the way to the modern Rosicrucian initiation. It is not to be maintained here that there are different truths in the course of humanity's evolution. Truth is universal, as is the Sun that illumines the whole orbit of the Earth; however, the paths to the truth are varied.

Think for a moment of the viewpoint one attains on the peak of a mountain. There we have a free view to all sides, no matter how we came to the peak. Would you not think it absurd if someone who is standing on the left mountain slope and has come up the left side of the mountain would then go around to the other side of the mountain to find another way up? So it is with the evolution of humanity. The starting points of the various cultures are like the paths on the mountain; the diverse peoples must climb by different paths. The truth—spiritual knowledge—is the same. Only those who believe that the same developmental processes are repeated in exactly the same way in the various cultures can maintain that the paths of initiation have always been identical. As different as the human body born fifteen centuries ago is from the human body born today, just so different must be the path for the student who wants to climb to the spiritual. In certain epochs, there must be a renewal of methods, an adapting to the peoples and to that which the human being has become, even though the structural circumstances escape our ordinary vision. Yet the esoteric view of physiology and anatomy knows that the structural conditions of the physical brain must evolve if the human being is to conquer the physical plane. The physical structural conditions are only the lower facts of that which lies on a higher plane. And so, today there is a Rosicrucian initiation.

Among the various kinds of initiation, we need to refer only to the three most prominent. We know what is concerned when we mention the path of yoga, the Christian-Gnostic way, and the Rosicrucian path. You all know the yoga path from the literature. The Christian-Gnostic path was taught in the early days of Christianity through Dionysius the Areopagite. Scholars speak of him as a pseudo-Dionysius who lived in the sixth century and is supposed to have written all the great books.[†] Christian tradition connects these books to the time of the apostle Paul. Scholars ask only this: When were those scrolls written? Christian esotericism knows, however, that this Dionysius the Areopagite was a pupil of the Apostle Paul and was given the task by his master to found the esoteric school of Christianity. For countless people, Christian esotericism has become truth. Today we can hardly imagine the source from which many a word of a Christian teacher is derived. The source was Christian initiation. This Christian initiation appears to be fantasy to those who think materialistically. For the people of that time, however, it was direct, immediate life. We differentiate seven stages through which every person who wanted to attain Christian initiation had to pass. Let me just name these seven stages:

1. The Washing of the Feet
2. The Scourging
3. The Crowning with Thorns
4. The Crucifixion
5. The Mystical Death
6. The Laying in the Grave and Resurrection
7. The Ascension of the Soul

These are the seven true stages that had to be endured in the centers of Christian initiation. I will characterize at least the first and fourth stations.†

When Christian pupils were far enough along that one could call them moral in ordinary life, that they were purified and had raised themselves to a higher level, and that it was clear that they would no longer stray from a high level of morality, they received Christian initiation from their master. At this point they were supposed to experience what I can describe only in the form of a dialogue, although it never took place in dialogue form.

After the pupil was taken in hand in such a way, the teacher said this: "Look at the plant world. It sprouts in the mineral kingdom. If the mineral kingdom were not present, plants could not develop, even though they are at a higher level. If plants could think, they would have to say: In the kingdom of nature you rank lower than I, but I could not exist without you. I bow in humility before you." The pupils were then led to understand this humility through all the kingdoms of nature. The animal ought to bow down in humility before the plant and the human being, in turn, before the animal and say: Without you I cannot be! Human beings, who are at a higher level, ought to bow before those that have not progressed as far, for none can stand higher without the others, which are lower. If human beings understand this ascending scale, they look down in humility to those at a lower level.

In this way, the pupils learned to grasp what it means, in the thirteenth chapter of the Gospel of John, that the highest bowed himself in humility and washed the feet of the twelve disciples, even though they were lower than he. Pupils who are thus trained [to higher morality] in the sense of esoteric Christianity understand the inner essence of the Gospel of John. The Gospel of John describes the methods of the initiation, and the Apocalypse of John [the Book of Revelation] illustrates the content of initiation. When pupils had progressed so far that this humility was self-evident to them, the thirteenth chapter of the John Gospel became truth in their souls. Then the teacher could bring them to the point where quite specific feelings could arise. The pupils felt and knew that they could climb to a yet higher stage. They felt—and it was a feeling common to all who had received Christian initiation—as if their feet were in water, as if spiritual water lapped against them. When the pupils were ready, the inner indication was that a picture from the thirteenth chapter of the Gospel of John arose before them, coming from within them through an inner force. It is not just an outer, historical picture, but rather a spiritual picture available to everyone. The pupils saw a picture of the Washing of the Feet spread out before them on the astral plane.

I will now talk about the fourth stage, the Crucifixion, as a way for us to come to an understanding. When the third stage was completed, it was made clear to the pupils that they could no longer consider their bodies as their own. They had to sense the body as an object, as something outside themselves. Ordinarily, human beings think that the body is their "I." Those who wish to attain the fourth stage of Christian initiation must come to the point where their bodies have no more worth for them than some chair or table around them. Ordinarily, people say: I go through the door. For the initiated it is self-evident to say: I carry my body through the door. Then again, two signs arise: One of these is the voluntary bringing forth of the so-called Blood Trial as the symptomatic expression of the fourth stage of initiation. Through the inner strength of their spirituality, pupils are able to induce a reddening of the skin exactly in the places of what we call the stigmata. The stigmata appear on the hands, the feet, and the right side of the thorax, accompanied by the inner symptom or feeling that pupils see themselves on the cross on the astral plane. [This is the second sign that arises.]

One does not speak of dangers in this development. It is a matter of the degree of inner development, and then one speaks no more of dangers with it. However, whoever wants to do this without the advice of a teacher is certainly in danger. Still, those who are patient and give themselves over in humility to the leadership of a master will thereby—in that they endure their martyrdom—be all the more helpful a part of human evolution. Of course, they should not take this initiation upon themselves until they feel within themselves the obligation to do so.

Christian initiation was also the source and foundation of outer Christian life. This Christian initiation had to pass over into the somewhat different form of Rosicrucian initiation about two centuries before the descent of the intellect onto the material plane. Rosicrucian initiation is not an un-Christian initiation; it is a further development of it. Those who undergo this initiation, however, do not withdraw from their physical surroundings, as is demanded by purely Christian initiation, at least for a time. Whoever wants to live as a worthy participant in the evolution of humanity today must take part in work on the physical plane. It would be sinful to pull back from the physical world. We just need to understand it and be equal to it. Had the Christian initiation kept the earlier form, human beings would have climbed high on the soul-spiritual level but would have remained weak on the physical plane. Think about the conquest of the physical plane—of the great inventions, such as the art of printing, and so on... [gap in notes]... For that, a completely different inner configuration is necessary. It is necessary to develop other strong impulses in order to lead what comes from material development along the right paths. Rosicrucian initiation gives the human the ability to use all the resources of modern culture. It teaches us to grasp the spirit in matter, in that we recognize the connection of matter itself with the spiritual, so that we can let the spiritual flow out into matter.

Rosicrucian initiation was born out of the necessity of the time. It, too, has seven stages. The first is called study in a wider sense; the second is the acquisition of imaginative knowledge; the third is the acquisition of the occult script; the fourth is the producing of the philosopher's stone—that is the technical term for it; the fifth is learning the correspondence between microcosm and macrocosm; the sixth is becoming one with the macrocosm; the seventh is attaining divine bliss or piety. You must not imagine that every pupil need go through these stages virtually one after the other; rather, the teacher must select what is suitable for a particular pupil according to his or her individuality. Every pupil must engage first in the study. Then, however, the order of the next stages must often be arranged differently, according to the pupil. Now we want to discuss the specifics of each stage.

Study in the Rosicrucian sense is not the same as what is called study in ordinary life. In the Rosicrucian sense, we would have to call it living in pure thinking. What that means is not immediately easy to understand. Indeed, Hegel tried his whole life to show the German people what it means to live in pure thinking.† By ten years after his death, what he had imparted to the German people in the deepening of thinking was forgotten. Today we are still not far enough along that Hegel would be understood, and yet his works are a good example of what it means to live in pure, sense-free thinking.

The newer philosophers, like Eduard von Hartmann,† deny altogether that we can form a thought that is not influenced by sensory nature. For this reason, one swore that nothing is found in the intellect that is not found in the senses. What does not come through the senses is not real. If this were true, there would be no mathematics. The Gnostics called the spiritual life a "*mathesis*"† not because they imagined it as mathematics, but rather because, on higher levels, it is a pure thinking and knowing, as exists in mathematics. There is, in reference to form, a sense-free type of thinking. This pure thinking does not proceed from objects but flows from thought to thought. For those who want to live into a sense-free thinking, I wrote *Intuitive Thinking as a Spiritual Path*.† It is not a personal work. It came into being like an organism. It is a thought-organism and a guide for that which is called study in the Rosicrucian sense. Certainly, many people do not go through anything like this study. For most people who cannot do this, the Theosophical teaching is enough. It is sense-free thought; no one can see it or hear it. The study of Theosophy corresponds to the first stage of Rosicrucian training. When it is done properly, Theosophy is itself Rosicrucian study. One does not need to lose oneself in the philosophical heights. The simplest, most modest soul can deepen itself therein.

Imaginative knowledge is the second stage of the Rosicrucian initiation. It is attained when the human being manages to transform a thought into an image. That is a real fact. [Goethe, who knew Rosicrucianism fully, said: "Everything transitory is but a parable."† When we have turned thought into an image, we come away from the physical plane. I would like to show with two examples how we can do so. Take, for example, the three "Logoi."† Everything that has been introduced as study up to this point is connected only with the physical plane. Imaginative knowledge lifts us higher. When we describe the three Logoi schematically—when we speak of projections—we are considering a concept taken in by the physical intellect; this is true even when we say of the second Logos that it vibrates differently from the first. This information about the second Logos remains entirely bound to the intellectual consciousness. We cannot transpose anything connected with three-dimensional space into higher realms, but only that which is not thought of as spatial.

A tone or color exists in space but is not spatial. The astral realm is a surging sea of color and light. What one perceives here on the earthly plane as qualities of color and tone confront one on the astral plane. That which is physical in color and tone we lift up to higher planes, but we must purify and cleanse it in order to raise it up. For that reason, the teacher says: "Take out the sense quality of everything you want to look at directly; imagine how a color lifts itself out. That is the method to come to imagination." Those who want to attain this stage look at the outer world so that these separated pictures present themselves differently; when we speak of the three Logoi, we no longer experience them as quantity but rather as quality. We imagine the third Logos as tone, as something that resounds throughout the world; the second, inasmuch as it appears as astral projection, we imagine as surging light; and the first we imagine as cosmic aroma, as fragrance purged to the point of perfect purity, flying through the world. Rosicrucians everywhere have experienced the Logoi in this way. They are pictures, imaginations—not descriptions, for descriptions arise from the physical plane.

A different picture that has a more ordinary appearance is contained in a myth: the myth of the Holy Grail. Rosicrucian pupils sense the inner soul life as fact. The master says to the pupil: "Look at the plant;

it lives with its roots in the Earth, sends the stem upward, and has its calyx—that which brings forth a plant again—turned to the Sun." Even the newer materialistic scholarship has drawn attention to the fact that when we compare the plant with the human being, we must find the correspondence to the root of the plant in the head of the human being.† The plant is virtually an upside-down human being. Evolution lies in the fact that this picture reverses itself: the part of itself that the plant opens chastely to the whole world is turned downward in the human being. The root of the plant—that which strives toward the center of the Earth—corresponds to the head of the human being, which is directed outward into Sun space. Between the plant and the human is the animal kingdom, in which the spine is horizontally aligned.

Now the master tells the pupil: "Imagine the plant, the animal, and the human being, and you have the cross of the world." The cross is the imaginative picture of the evolution of the beings of the world up to the human being. The plant reproduces only when it is touched by the sunbeam, which at one time was called the "holy lance of love." If the plant is struck by the sun, the plant fulfills its task. Now consider human beings with kama† (the lower astral, the seat of desire) that has taken hold of them. The lower organs must be purified and cleansed, and they must evolve to a higher stage so that, in the course of evolution, this chalice, or cup, will open from above. When we have transformed ourselves, when we have purified this cup, which the plant has at a primitive stage, then we will again be touched by the holy lance of love; we will have accomplished the purification of the human being not only in the astral or etheric but even in the physical. Thus is evolution beheld imaginatively. The astral plane reveals itself to those who live into it in this way.

The third stage of Rosicrucian initiation is the acquisition of the occult script. The occult script is not like our modern, abstract writing. We make the harmony of the qualities our own. The teacher says to the pupil: "If you climb higher and attain to knowledge of the occult script, what was called the harmony of the spheres in the Pythagorean School† will resound for you." That is a reality for the initiate and not merely an allegory. What modern science says of number systems has the same relation to the harmony of the spheres as a symphony would have to the undulating waves in the air. The pupil of esotericism learns to hear tones in the spiritual world. Goethe knew about this when he said this: "The Sun intones in ancient tourney with brother spheres, a rival air"[†] and "Intoning, the new day is born for spirit ears."[†] Occurrences on the spiritual planes, the harmonies of the spheres, are audible to spiritual ears, but not to physical ears. The symbols of the occult script are true cosmic forces, and those who know these symbols feel the stream of cosmic forces within, even down into the physical organism. As just one example, I will mention four numbers. As words, they seem abstract, but if one were to hear the music for them, one would perceive the relationship of the four lower members of the human being. These numbers are 1, 3, 7, and 12.[†] The lower four members of the human being resound harmoniously together in the spiritual world. That is the secret of the Pythagorean number system—we transform them into spiritual music.

The fourth stage of initiation is the production of the philosopher's stone. Modern scholarship has made a fairy tale out of it. In a certain respect, the scholars are right, because if it were really as science imagines it, it would be nonsense. But producing the philosopher's stone is the highest stage of development toward which the human being strives. Toward the end of the eighteenth century a certain Rosicrucian secret was divulged. We could say of it that people found a resonance with it. A peculiar passage in a German newspaper discussed the philosopher's stone in these terms: "It exists. If one comes to know it in its full worth and use, one possesses the secret of immortality. Actually, the majority of people do know it. Many have it in hand daily."[†] The man who wrote that had no idea what is involved, but he had received a report that contained a germ of truth. We need do nothing other than to examine the process that cosmically preserves the human being in the present epoch: the breathing process. We breathe in and out. We breathe in the oxygen of the air and give back to the surrounding world carbon dioxide, a poisonous gas in which we could not live. The plant takes in the carbon dioxide constantly, keeps the carbon for itself, and builds up its own body out of it. It gives the oxygen back to animals and human beings. Thus, the plant, animal, and human being form a whole, in the context of the breathing process.

The human being needs the plant today. The corpse of the plant, which takes the form of black coal dug out of the Earth or of transparent diamond, is something that we ourselves have within us, but we cannot use it. We have to hand it over as breath of life to the plants. The plant builds its own body out of carbon dioxide. It can do what human beings cannot yet do but will be able to do later. Imagine this process: the taking in of carbon dioxide by the plant; the sending out of oxygen, which is transferred into the interior of the human being ... [gap in text] ... thus the flowing together with the plant world, which is taken into human nature; then we build up for ourselves a pure, chaste body, just as the plant does today.

Humans are on the way to becoming beings able to carry out this process consciously; in this way, we will be able to develop the chalice of the Holy Grail within ourselves. The breathing process has not reached completion; it is being perfected and is poised to perform a task within the human being that today takes place outside the human being and to transform the human substance that is pervaded with kama into pure, chaste substance. That is true alchemy. We will become capable of performing the alchemy through which we will also learn to transform the cosmos. The symbol for this process is the Holy Grail. We cannot dismiss this high ideal simply because it is millions of years away; rather, it must be attained according to the maxim "Continual dripping hollows the stone." Those who make the breathing process rhythmical attain their goal gradually. The philosopher's stone is the carbon, the substance for the building of the human body in the future. This process of transformation is alchemy in the Rosicrucian sense. Naturally, the intimate instructions are given only from teacher to pupil.

In the fifth stage of initiation, the correspondence between microcosm and macrocosm, the pupil learns of the correspondence of what we have in ourselves with what we find in the outer macrocosm. Paracelsus† once said: "Look at the animals, plants, and minerals; they are all, in some way, also in our own human body." The human being is a flowing together of everything that is found in outer nature. Nature is, in effect, a disassembled human being. Nature represents the letters, but the human being is the word that is formed from these letters.

When this knowledge penetrates the consciousness, the pupil sees how the human eye was formed from light. The eye is built up from light. The human organism proceeded out of another organism that did not yet have eyes, but light called the eye forth. The condition of consciousness that knows how the human developed has not existed for a long time. The human being of today knows nothing more about this, but the seer on the astral plane sees it. On the astral plane one learns again to know that which, coming out of the interior of the cosmos, weaves into one's own nature. Then one learns through the individual parts of the human body to know the cosmos—out of the eye, the light; out of the ear, the tone; and other such things, which can be imparted only from teacher to pupil.

When we have learned the correspondence between microcosm and macrocosm, we can move on to the sixth stage: becoming one with the macrocosm. One then has a friendship with everything in nature. There exists something like a love relationship to every being in nature, similar to some extent to the love that still remains between husband and wife. The sunflower, the violet, the lion and tiger, this and that form in nature appear differently. As differentiated as the love between husband and wife, just so differentiated appears the whole cosmos. What is within us flows outward and is connected with a metamorphosis of the heart. The etheric body and astral body transform the heart so that it becomes a voluntary muscle. Here esoteric teaching, when it perfects itself still more, will have the effect of spreading light.

Today the heart poses a problem for physiologists. It is an involuntary muscle, but in that it is striated diagonally, it is a voluntary muscle. All voluntary muscles are diagonally striated, while the involuntary muscles are vertically striated. The heart is striated diagonally because it is on the path to becoming a voluntary muscle. It has the predisposition for this today. When, in the future, we can work out of the spirituality of the cosmos, we will be able to move the heart in the same way we can move our hands today. I could cite hundreds of examples where esoteric science throws light on a subject that physical science cannot explain. The teacher tells us that when we gradually attain this personal, intimate relationship to the whole world around us, when we no longer must use the physical brain, only then can we understand what the

Rosicrucian calls divine blessedness or piety, in which the independence of the human being is preserved, but the highest will be felt.

I could give only a sketch of this here, but Rosicrucian schooling has much to offer. There might be many objections to this path; the potential dangers can be brought to one's attention. If, however, we are not impetuous out of egotism concerning the ideal, but instead feel ourselves integrated; if we feel esoteric development not as a desire but as a responsibility; if we want to be a servant of evolution; if we purify what must be purified—then there is no danger. Rosicrucian schooling will also bring about moral purification. Students must immerse their souls completely in pure thinking, for pure thought is a powerful moral purification. It works as a preparation for the first six stages of initiation.

All the goals of esoteric development, however, must take place under the principle of overcoming, which Goethe expressed. Only when we have overcome ourselves can we develop ourselves higher. That must become our primary ideal, for overcoming is the most important ideal of the Rosicrucian path:

> From the might that fetters all beings
> They free themselves who overcome themselves.[†]

Planetary Evolution and the Evolution of Humanity

Rudolf Steiner

Second Congress Lecture, Munich, May 20, 1907

Yesterday I was able to speak to you about initiation in the sense of the Rosicrucian spiritual world stream, of the stages of knowledge, feeling, and will impulses, the activities in which human beings must engage if they want to move upward on the path of knowledge and approach higher stages of existence. Today let us attempt to discuss a chapter from Rosicrucian Theosophy itself. It is not as if—and this must be stressed again and again—this Rosicrucian wisdom were something other than the wisdom common to all peoples and ages; it is only adapted to our modern way of thinking, the modern temporal necessity. It is born out of the recognition that our epoch needs a particular way of speaking in order to make known the primordial, eternal truths of all ages, so that it can live into the configuration of modern humanity of Europe and America.

It is perhaps a chapter that lies quite far back in time, and yet it is one of the most essential. For nothing shows us the origin and goal of the human being as well as this chapter and at the same time points to the forces that we should develop in ourselves in order to become coworkers in the service of the evolution of humanity. We cannot contemplate the great evolution of the cosmos other than by starting with the nature of the human being. I will not say anything other than what is common Theosophical and Rosicrucian wisdom, what each one would say if they were speaking out of these sources. There is no contradiction. Many already know the things that I wish to reiterate here.

We differentiate seven members of human nature. This morning we heard[†] that one can also take another number as the basis for the human being: three-times-three. It does not matter that I today combine the three middle members and give them one name as the fourth member. The explanations coincide completely. We divide the human being in such a way that we can say that the human has first of all a physical body. The physical body is that which hands can touch and eyes can see, that which the human being has in common with all of nature and is subject to physical and chemical laws. The second part is the so-called etheric body, or life body. The etheric body calls the chemical and physical forces and matter to life and abandons the connection with physical and chemical matter at death. It is said in esotericism that the human physical body is such a combination of matter and forces that, as a physical body, it cannot exist by its own means. Only in that an etheric body is integrated with it, and only as long as it remains integrated with it, is the physical body preserved from the disintegration of physical matter and forces. At the moment that the etheric body abandons physical forces, death enters, and the physical body becomes a corpse. Thus, we may also say that the etheric body is that which keeps us from death at every moment of our lives. There is a great struggle within the etheric body against that which otherwise makes our chemical matter disintegrate.

The third member of the human being is the bearer of pleasure and suffering, joy and pain, feelings and passions. We call it the astral body. It is the part of the human being that we have in common with the animals, just as we have the etheric body in common with the plant and the animal worlds and the mineral body with the whole of the outer world. The name astral body has been used since the earliest of ages. There is no name more suitable for this member of the human being than "astral body," and there is perhaps no more beautiful explanation of the reason for calling it the astral body than the one given by Paracelsus,[†] the great Theosophist. Just as the etheric body abandons the physical body in death, so, too, the astral body leaves the etheric body shortly after death. However, the astral body leaves the physical and etheric bodies every night and is outside of us. Where is it then?

Paracelsus asks, and rightly so: "Where is the astral body, and what does it do at night?" Does it rest? Does it have a task? Absolutely, it has a task. Whoever does not have clairvoyant powers cannot see into the activity of the astral body during the night, but every person senses the consequences of this activity. You all go to bed tired in the evening. This tiredness is the expression of a disharmony in the union of our physical and etheric bodies. It must arise when the astral body does not have the power to maintain harmony between the two other bodies, the physical and etheric bodies. Considering the way in which the human being is formed today, such a disharmony must of necessity arise in our waking life. If the physical body and etheric body were under the influence of only the astral body—as these forces are supposed to be united—then there would always be harmony between the two. However, the astral body lives in the physical body and, at the stage of consciousness that humanity has reached on Earth, the whole surroundings of physical, sense-perceptible objects affects the human being. The impressions of the eyes, ears, and the other sense organs flow into us. During the waking hours of day, a disharmony must come about for every human being who has not yet reached a higher level of spiritual development. If this astral body could never dwell anywhere else than in the physical body and etheric body, it would come into disorder. Its stream of forces would not be what they should be if proper etheric and physical bodies are to be formed. During the day the inner harmony of the astral body becomes disordered, and the expression of that disorder is tiredness. In the moment when you feel tiredness, disharmony is present. Where is then the astral body during the night?

Paracelsus says correctly that when the lines of force that connect it with the physical body begin to loosen, the astral body enters into connection with the whole harmonious system of forces that flood through the starry heavens. In the moment when we go to sleep, we rest in the harmony of the spheres; from there, we bring the forces with us to restore what was used up during the day. So the astral body rests in the world of the stars at night; there it is actually at home. When it returns, it brings the forces of the stars with it, to do away with weariness. Sleep is a good doctor, because order and harmony can arise when the astral body rests a while in that world which contains the laws of the starry heavens—the laws that guide the spiritual world as a whole. If we do not sleep, it undermines our health, because the astral body has not rested for a time in the world of the stars. This is the reason the astral body was given its name. In past times, no name was given to a thing that did not correspond to its essence. Before we correct esoteric names and symbols, we must first contemplate why the names were chosen. Today, when a comet or a small planet is discovered, we open an encyclopedia of mythology and choose a name from it for a star [or comet or planet]. The principle in spiritual times was to allow the essence of the thing itself to resound in tone in its name; there resounded in the name its connection with the world.

In the fourth member of the human being, we have something through which we form the crown of the earthly creation of planetary existence. Follow closely along with me for a short time. In the whole of the German language—in other languages it is similar—there is a name that differentiates itself from all other names. All of you can say "table" for a table, "picture" for a picture, and so forth. There is one name, however, that we cannot use in the same sense. That is the name "I." None of you can call another person "I." Every other person is a "you" to you, and you are a "you" to everyone else. If this name should designate our own selves, it cannot sound from outside but must resound from out of our own selves. In all the ages those religions with an impulse of the mystery teachings sensed this truth.

In the mystery teaching, one says the name for that being. In the Hebrew mystery doctrine the unspeakable name of God, the name Yahweh, is nothing other than the name for the "I." In truth, Yahweh is the name for that in the soul which begins to hold a monologue, begins to live in the inner self. Human beings sensed this, such that in those worldviews and religions based on a spiritual foundation they said: "In the 'I,' the god begins to speak in the depths of the soul." It is just a beginning, but a beginning must be made. This "I," this single central point, is that which is the most essential characteristic that differentiates the human being from all other beings around us on this planet. Thoughtful individuals have always understood this. Jean Paul tells how he stood as a very young child in the yard of his parents' house and—he remembered this exactly—for the first time the feeling arose in him: You are an "I"-being! And he said that there was no chance of an error and that other people had added to this memory. "For at that time," says Jean Paul, "I looked into the veiled inner sanctum of my being. Then I knew that I am immortal, because I had found the connection with the god."†

Proceeding from the "I," we come to the point where we can observe the reciprocal relationships of the parts of the human being. Human development consists of the "I" working on the three bodies, within which it appears like the seed within a fruit. How does this "I" work? If we wish to understand this, we must remind ourselves of the primitive nations. Take a folk that stands at a subordinate cultural stage today. There you see that the group is dominated by its feelings and instincts, by drive and passion, quite like the animal; there is something similar to an inner devouring of one another. Compare these people with members of a more highly developed culture—with, for example, a Francis of Assisi. What differentiates these evolutionary forms?

If we want to answer this question, we must be aware that human beings, in the course of the many incarnations through which they develop, work out of the "I" first on the astral body, then on the etheric body, and then on the physical body. That is human evolution: the "I" radiates into the three bodies. The savage follows all the drives and passions that live within. Human beings of more highly developed cultures tell themselves that there are certain desires and passions that they may not pursue; they deny themselves these desires and passions. The idealists, who stand still higher, not only deny themselves in this way but also form ideals that add a new element to that which makes up the desires of the astral body belonging to the primitive cultural stage. So we see through clairvoyance that the astral body exists in two parts: that which was originally part of it and that which the "I" has made of it. Look at a highly developed idealist. This part [it is drawn on the blackboard] becomes larger through the work of the "I" than it is at first. With people like Francis of Assisi,[†] one can see how little remains of that which human beings called their own when they entered upon their first incarnation. We call this practically transformed part of the human astral body, over which we have gained control, the "spirit self," or "manas" as it is known in Theosophical literature. It is a transformed part of the astral body.

We also rework the etheric body out of the "I." What does it mean to work on the etheric body? Let us explain it with an example. You can do this in your own development. Remind yourself of what you knew as a seven-year-old child in terms of concepts and ideas and of what you know today, what you have learned and what has changed in your life of ideas. You will find that quite a lot has evolved. Now compare this learning with other things that have changed within you: temperament, memory, and certain fundamental traits of human nature. If you were violent-tempered as an eight-year-old, this temper will still occasionally show through. If you were melancholic, it will perhaps color your whole life. So we can say comparatively that what we learn progresses forward like the minute hand of a clock, but the fundamental inclinations of the human being move forward more slowly, like the hour hand. The etheric body transforms itself slowly, like the hour hand of a clock. It is denser than the astral body, and therefore work on the etheric body is substantially more difficult than that on the astral body.

When the "I" works not only on our intellectual thoughts but begins to transform our temperament as well, it is accompanied by a transformation of our etheric body. For many, this is possible only by a transition from one incarnation to the next. That is the essential part of esoteric schooling: all that you learn is only preparation for esoteric schooling. You have done more if you have made the effort to do away with some fundamental mood—for example, when you have transformed a melancholic temperament into a harmonious nature. In that moment in which we begin not only to change our feelings and impulses but also our fundamental emotions, we begin to work on the etheric body. That part of the human etheric body which is thus transformed by the "I" is, in turn, a new member of the nature of the human being. Only a very few human beings can consciously bring about this transformation of the etheric body today, only those that undertake esoteric training. For example, a law in the Pythagorean School was that the astral body had to be completely purified before work on the etheric body could begin. We must, however, differentiate between conscious and unconscious training of the etheric body. The part that is penetrated by the work of the "I" is called the "life spirit"; it is basically the same as what we call "buddhi" in Theosophical literature.

Most significant is when we begin not only to master the forces of the etheric body but also to work down into the physical body. It could seem as though the work of the "I" on the physical body is the lowest;

on the contrary, it is the highest. Work on the physical body is also more difficult than on the etheric body. When we begin consciously to make the effort to master the forces of the physical body, something new arises. The forces that work in the physical body are the same ones that work in the cosmos. If we learn to reign over the forces of the blood, over breathing, then we learn the magic of the cosmos. Then that which we can do flows from our physical body into the cosmos; this is the genuine, true work that can begin when the human being has reached a certain stage of development of the etheric body. We start with regulating a function closest to us—the breathing; thus the name for breathing is taken from "atman."† As much as we transform of our physical nature, just so much is in us of "spirit human," or "atman"; a part of spirit-matter in us is transformed.

It is not a matter of fleeing the physical world ascetically. We have the task of entering into the physical world in order to transform it spiritually. That is the great law of salvation. The physical world is a part of the spiritual that has become what it has become in order for us to attain our current stage of evolution. We now have the task to spiritualize this physical body, to redeem it. This principle is the basis of salvation. Thus we have the mutual relationships of the seven members of the nature of the human that are necessary if we are to make practical use of these members in Theosophical endeavor.

Now let us consider the evolution of the human being. Materialists, who know only the physical body, have only an abstract concept of the evolution of the human being. Whoever perceives the intricacy of the human being also sees how complicated the evolution of the human being is. Which of these four members is the oldest, the most perfect? Some people will be surprised to hear that the oldest and, in its way, most perfect member of the human is the physical; it is that part of the human being which needed the longest time to develop. The etheric body is younger, and the astral body is still younger; and the "I" is the baby.

It is incorrect to say that the physical body is an imperfect part of the human. Observe, for instance, the construction of the femur, a wonderful work of art. The beams (bones) are placed so wisely that no human engineering could bring it about. They are positioned so that the upper body is carried with a minimum expenditure of strength. Let us pass on to the construction of the human heart. Those who immerse themselves in what physiologists teach us about the heart and the other organs know that they are so wisely constructed that no human wisdom can even penetrate these physical forms. The physical body [left on its own] would always be healthy. Look now at the astral body and what it does throughout life. Through the activity of the astral body, we constantly feed toxin to the physical body, for example, to the heart. The heart, however, is put together so wisely that it withstands the attacks of the astral body. Only at a future time will the astral body be as wise as the physical body is today. The physical body is the oldest member of the human being and needed the longest time to evolve. The various members of the human being are united with the entire surrounding world. Just as the individual finger can exist only as a part of the hand, so is the human being conceivable only in connection with the whole cosmos. Lift human beings a few miles above the Earth, and it would be the same as it is with the finger if one were to amputate it. We do not admit this dependence only because we walk on the Earth .

Look back into ancient times and then look forward into the future, and you see that the forms of the members of the human being continually change. They can change, however, only when everything in our surroundings changes. It is only because human beings have an overview of such a short span of time, despite the advance of science, that they believe things were always the way they are now. But whoever sees more deeply knows that our planet must alter its form if we want to evolve. It is not merely that the Earth has changed; the human being was present before the Earth in the cosmos could be called "Earth." As the human being strides forward in the cosmos, so the planets, or the beings that dwell on them, stride forward. Our planet is the reincarnation of another planetary condition, and we can follow three preceding incarnations of our Earth and three in the future. What we call planetary evolution is nothing other than an analogy of our human evolution. The three preceding planetary conditions through which our Earth had to pass are called, in Rosicrucian terms, Saturn, Sun, and Moon. So we have to imagine that the Earth, before it became Earth, was Moon; before it became Moon, it was Sun; and before the Sun, it was Saturn. The later conditions toward which we can look are called Jupiter, Venus, and Vulcan. What does it mean that the Earth passes through these conditions?

Today, we are in the fourth incarnation of our own planet, and that is intimately connected with human evolution. On the first planetary form (Saturn), the first predisposition of the human physical body was present. During the entire Saturn evolution, the human physical body was such that there was not an independent etheric body incorporated into it. Through the Sun and Moon conditions and on to the Earth condition, the physical body perfected itself ever more and more, so that the human physical body is today at the fourth stage of its evolution; it stands at the point of Earth evolution. Only during the second incarnation of Earth was an independent etheric body incorporated into the physical body. The physical body became, as it were, more perfect through the fact that the etheric body worked in it. Then the third incarnation of the Earth (the Moon) led to the astral body's becoming part of the two other bodies. The resident of the Moon, the forefather of the current Earth-human, consisted of three bodies: the physical body, the etheric body, and the astral body. The task of Earth evolution is to incorporate the "I" into these three members; the "I" is the worker that begins to transform what had been developed in previous times. We see now that the physical body is older than the others and that the "I" is at the first stage of its evolution. We can even know from the configuration of the physical body which part of us has evolved from the Saturn condition. The sense organs stand the highest within our physical body, and the seed for these sense organs was laid on Saturn. Thus, the human being was built up member by member and became, step by step, more and more perfect as each of the other members of human nature was added.

What is called Saturn and Sun here is not the same as our current Saturn and our current Sun; they are instead phases of evolution. Still, the condition through which our Earth passed in its Saturn evolution is connected with our current Saturn. Today's Saturn is to the Earth as a boy is to an old man. The same circumstances that the Saturn of today is passing through our Earth went through earlier. Therefore, in real esotericism one does not speak of *the* Saturn or *the* Sun and so on, but rather of *a* Saturn, *a* Sun, and so forth. Our Earth is a Saturn that has grown older.

We must bear in mind the meaning of this evolution. When we look back to the Saturn evolution, where the human being still had no etheric body, astral body, or "I" as independent natures, we can determine the difference between that primordial, ancient condition and today's by referring to "consciousness." There is a state of consciousness connected with every evolutionary condition. In all, there are seven consciousness states. The modern human being is in the fourth consciousness state; no being can reach this stage that cannot say "I." Human beings first developed on the Earth the form of consciousness they now have. The task of Earth evolution is to develop day-waking consciousness. In earlier planetary conditions the human being experienced only imperfect consciousness states. On old Saturn, our human ancestors had, in its primitive form, a consciousness similar to that of minerals, or rather the human physical ancestor was that consciousness. We can hardly find words to explain this; we can only give an indication. This is a completely nebulous, deep, trancelike consciousness. It is dull and dim, but it has a certain advantage. It has a more universal, wider view. A mineral consciousness knows the whole solar system.[†]

Later, during the Sun existence of the Earth, this consciousness was narrowed down to that of the plant. It was, however, a somewhat brighter consciousness compared with that of the mineral. The third form of consciousness is the picture consciousness, also called the primary psychological or emotional consciousness. It differentiates itself from the consciousness of today in that it works in pictures, such that it conveys the emotion of another being. Think of a being—and the human ancestor on the Moon was such a being—that has no sensory consciousness and can clothe objects with color upon awakening. We have a last remnant of such a consciousness in the dream world. The dream world is not the astral consciousness. The current dream consciousness is to the Moon consciousness as a withered part is to the form it had when it still had a task in the human being—for example, certain muscles that could once move the ears but have lost their purpose in the human being of today. Of that astral or psychological consciousness of the Moon there remains as a rudiment our current dream life. It works in the way the astral imaginative consciousness does. Suppose that a man dreams that he has caught a tree frog. He sees it hopping and catches it. Then the sleeper wakes up and finds that he has a corner of the blanket in his hand. Or suppose that a farmer's wife dreams that she goes to church. She listens reverently. The minister moves his arms robustly, and suddenly he receives wings. It is not entirely strange to a pious farmer's wife that a minister who preaches about heaven occasionally receives wings. But what happened here? The minister began to crow loudly from the pulpit. At that moment the woman wakes up, and outside in the courtyard a rooster is crowing.

What took place in this whole drama? In a symbolic picture something is expressed through an object that you would have perceived in day-waking consciousness. Something takes symbolic form that actually does not exist in this manner [in the physical world]. Keep the symbol in the form and imagine that the human being uses it to perceive the real psychological or astral world; then you understand what I am speaking about. The Moon consciousness was a true symbol consciousness. Imagine people who do not have our modern object consciousness. They draw near other beings. They do not see the clearly defined form; instead, there appears before them a color shape. In the case of sympathy, they see a quite particular color, and in the case of antipathy, a particular color. This is different from color as we know it today: it is the expression of inclination or aversion for the other being. Those who have Moon consciousness act according to the Moon consciousness; they adapt their actions according to the symbols. If they perceive a certain color, for example, they know that something is happening that is antagonistic toward them, and they withdraw. Only later, under the influence of the "I," does a consciousness develop that no longer perceives the manifestation of emotion; that which arose as color then settled upon objects. The colors that you see spread out over objects today are the old colors that once arose as emotion-shapes.

If modern human beings had, in addition to today's consciousness, that of the Moon, such that they perceived the psychological or emotional world fully, just as they do the physical, the present consciousness would be expanded into imaginative consciousness. An even higher form would be added to this consciousness if today's human being had that awareness that the plant has today and that the human being had dully and faintly during the Sun incarnation. The highest form of consciousness would be the consciousness that the mineral has today, which would make it possible for human beings to merge and become one with the universal cosmos. This last form of consciousness we hold as the ideal of the human, and we call it the spiritual consciousness.

In planetary evolution, the states of consciousness follow each other. In addition, the planetary scene must become a completely different one with each stage of evolution. We have an overview of all of evolution only when we know that within each planetary condition, seven stages must be passed through. Saturn, Sun, and Moon each had to pass through seven stages, and so, too, must the Earth. These are called *rounds* in Theosophy and *kingdoms* in Christian esotericism. Each planetary stage of the Earth, in turn, has seven smaller cycles, for each state of consciousness also has degrees if it is to climb from the most imperfect to the most perfect. We also call them *conditions of life*. Each such kingdom, or life condition, must undergo seven different conditions of revelation or form states: arupa, rupa, astral, physical, plastic, intellectual, and spiritual (archetypal). Thus we have 7 x 7 x 7, or 343 conditions; they connote the 343 planetary incarnations in their entirety. The development of one consciousness state comprises forty-nine of these conditions. You thus see how we can look into an immense cosmic evolution.†

Human beings who lived on the Sun and had developed only the etheric and physical bodies were completely different beings. We cannot call them plants, but we can say, in a certain figurative sense, that they had a plant existence. With respect to their position on the Earth, they were turned around: the head, which projects freely into the ether today, was turned to the center of the Earth at that time. The conversion, or rotating, of the whole human form is connected with the evolution of consciousness. Therefore, we call the Sun-human a human being turned toward the center of the Earth; in the same sense, we call the human of the Moon a circling human being. The Earth-human is the reversed Sun-human.

Evolution progresses in this way. When we look back at the Moon evolution, we must bear in mind that what we call emotions today could develop only as an astral element on the Moon. The "I" was not developed at that time. Because the "I" first evolved on the Earth, Moon-humans did not sense pain as their own individual pain; it was Moon-pain. These physical-etheric-astral Moon-humans were not independent. Passions, emotions, and pains were not individual. For example, during certain seasons on the Moon—we can say it today, even when so few believe it—the whole world, all living beings wrapped in an astral body, began to shriek, to emit tones. That phenomenon was connected with a certain stage of evolution in animal life. A rudiment of this is still found in the sexual life of certain animals that cry out during mating season.

The law of evolution is such that, in later conditions, certain earlier conditions always repeat themselves. The Earth had to go through a repetition of the Saturn, Sun, and Moon existences. Now the Earth is in its actual Earth existence. If one were to mix all the beings that are on the Sun, Moon, and Earth today into a porridge, one would have an imagination of what was called the Sun existence; all these beings were once together as *one* on the Sun. During the Sun age, the Sun, Moon, and Earth were one body. The Sun first evolved into the Moon existence, and then the Sun and Moon separated. In the repetition on Earth, first the Sun and then the Moon separated from the Earth; the development of the human "I" is connected with the separating off of the Moon. The Moon contains the forces that prevent the other members of the human being from becoming bearers of the "I." This moment in Earth evolution, which took place in the old Lemurian time, could come about only because the Sun and Moon had separated from the Earth. Only when the Earth became independent could it bring forth the form from which the present-day human being evolved.

Thus, cosmic evolution and human evolution are intimately connected. If you look back to the predecessors of our present era, when the human being lived in Atlantis—natural science has at least discovered this in regard to the animal world[†]—there you have the human ancestor who did not yet possess the sort of consciousness that the human being has today, which can calculate and manufacture industrial products. Nonetheless, a different ability had developed to a high degree. The Atlantean human had a terrific memory, of which we cannot form a proper idea. Something more was connected with this consciousness. The physical configuration of this old Atlantis differed quite essentially from that of the present Earth. What we call air and water were not yet present as such. The air was filled with a fine watery mist, evaporated water. For this reason, the old Germanic saga preserved the name Nifelheim (Mist-home).† The name suggests that human beings at that time lived in a kind of water-impregnated air; it was only in such air that the picture consciousness of the human beings of that time could live. The myths and sagas of German mythology arose out of this consciousness. Whoever really knows that particular folk knows that they did not write in the way present-day scholarship maintains [not like authors today]. The myths and sagas were remnants of the old etheric picture consciousness, the expression of primordial, dim clairvoyance. People simply forgot the source, after they progressed to the present clear, day-waking consciousness.

You see how the evolution of humanity is bound to the cosmos. During the cycle of Earth in which the air was impregnated with water, human beings perceived the world quite differently. For the Atlanteans, the murmur of the wind was a language that they understood. There were no commandments and laws at that time. There were times when, if human beings wanted to know how they were to behave, they went out and listened to a spring and heard how it trickled. That told them something. What the Atlanteans heard was a fundamental tone and undertone that was like a musical keynote, which they understood. It was a simple syllable of several parts, and this lived in the surroundings of the Atlantean. It permeated everything, and the Atlanteans told themselves this: "In this fundamental tone, the god speaks to me." When they wanted to direct their prayers to their god, they did it in this fundamental tone. The wisdom of the old Atlanteans had to transform itself into that of our present time, so that human beings could progress. In the course of evolution we must achieve, in turn, the consciousness of the Atlanteans and add it to our present consciousness. From time to time, we must recognize that the old must lie dormant for a while.

Thus is the evolution of the human being connected with the evolution of the cosmos. Think about how far human beings have removed themselves from the source of wisdom that rests in the world itself! How far they have moved away from a direct connection with nature! Still, what we have lost, we will regain, and we will add to it that which we have achieved ourselves. Our consciousness springs out of the consciousness of individual concrete facts, which has been characterized in the Rosicrucian method as the "wisdom of the world." It pervades the whole life of the human being. If we imbue ourselves with it, we feel what the teacher connected with the name "Rosenkreutz"† wanted—he who, as a leading individuality, directs and leads the spiritual movement throughout the centuries.

When we consider the human being in connection with the whole world, it seems remote to us. However, if such a consideration penetrates our hearts, it becomes a force within us that will fill us with bliss when we want to collaborate in the transformation and reforming of the cosmos. We have the responsibility to integrate ourselves into the cosmos. As the single stone does not strive to free itself from the house, so too, human beings may not exempt themselves from the cosmos. We must recognize that we have a duty to serve within the greater cosmic evolution. Then that which is eternal in us will be integrated into world existence. There will be a reflection of this integration in the most ordinary aspects of life, so that we can express this wisdom with every movement of the hand. Then the cosmos will really have something of the human being in it, for everything is undergoing transformation. All must be transformed through the beings that are involved in the world evolution. If we collaborate in this way, we will feel livingly how true this is. The truth will be the impulse for all our behavior. In this way, the beautiful words of a highly inspired poet come true:

> Time is a blossoming meadow,
> Nature is a great aliveness,
> And all is fruit, and all is seed!†

Explanations of the Arrangement and Décor of the Congress Hall

RUDOLF STEINER

Lecture, Munich, May 21, 1907

I wish to say a few words about the color within which we have held our meetings. There is a reason that it is red. When we see red outwardly, it forms its counter-image inwardly, for the eye has the tendency to bring forth green-blue when it has red before it. That is the inner activity of the eye. With a child, much depends on how the body responds to outer impressions. I point here to what I have said in connection with red when I spoke about education.[†] The eye responds to a red surrounding with the tendency to green-blue activity, and this inner working is calming. Therefore, the color red in the surroundings has a calming effect on an excited or nervous child.

When you remember that the later stages of human evolution always lead back, on a higher level, to the stage of childhood, you will understand why we chose for this place the color that produces in the child's body a color suited to that which is sacred—even though the place itself is not a place of initiation, but yet should remind us of one through its symbols. It is not for nothing that it says in the Bible: "If you do not become as the little child, you cannot enter into the kingdom of heaven."[†] Our inner being must become as ether, pure as the blue world-ether above us. The training for this expresses itself in the red color of our surroundings. If we are surrounded outwardly by red, the counter-color[†] lives in our inner being. This explains why red is present in all ritualistic places of the esotericists, while in exoteric places, in which the mystery teachings are spoken of outwardly and in symbols, there is blue.[†] The Rosicrucian worldview expresses the esoteric in red. Were the room to be decorated completely in accordance with the Rosicrucian worldview, there would also have to be blue vaults raised above us.

What do the two pillars mean to the Rosicrucians? If we want to explain these two pillars[†] standing here before us, we must start with the Golden Legend. The legend goes as follows: When Seth, the son of Adam who took Abel's place, was mature, he was allowed to gain insight into paradise. He was allowed to pass by the angel with the flaming sword and enter into the place from which the human being had been driven. There Seth saw something quite special. He saw how the two trees, the Tree of Life and the Tree of Knowledge, intertwined with each other. From these intertwined trees Seth received three seeds,[†] which he took with him and laid in his father's mouth when he died. A mighty tree grew out of Adam's grave. This tree revealed itself to those with psychic senses as if radiating in the form of a glowing fire. For those who could see this glowing fire, there twisted together the letters "J B," the first letters of two words that I do not have the authority to express, but which mean: "I am Who was; I am Who is; I am Who will be."[†]

This tree divided itself into three parts. Seth took wood from it, and it was used in manifold ways in world evolution. A staff was made from it; the legend says this was the magic staff of Moses. The beams in Solomon's temple were made out of this same wood. There they remained as long as human beings understood the old secrets. Then the wood was thrown into a pool, in which, at certain times, the lame and blind were healed. After the wood was taken out again, it was used to build the bridge over which the Savior walked on his way to the cross. And, lastly, the legend tells that the cross itself on which the Savior hung was formed from the wood of this tree that grew out of Adam's mouth after the seeds of the intertwined Trees of Life and Knowledge were laid therein.

This legend contains deep symbolic meaning. Call to mind for a moment the process of transformation that pupils must consider when they pass through the fourth stage of Rosicrucian training: the producing of the philosopher's stone. We remind ourselves that it has to do with a certain treatment of the red blood. Let us think about the significance of this red blood, not only because Goethe's expression, "Blood is a very special fluid,"[†] gives this indication, but also because esotericism through all the ages has taught it. Red blood arises as the result of the breathing of oxygen. We can give only a brief indication of it. When such an important moment is referred to in legend and in the Bible—

the moment Seth penetrated into paradise—we must remind ourselves of the process through which the human being was brought out of paradise. The human being was brought out of paradise, the old condition of the human being in the bosom of the higher spiritual world, through a physical process that took place in parallel with the descent. Those who wish to understand the Bible must learn to take it literally. It was said: "God breathed the breath of life into the human being, and he became a living soul."† This breathing of the breath of life into the human being was a process—expressed in a picture—that stretched out over millions of years. What does it mean?

There was a time in the forming of the physical body in the evolution of humanity when the human body still had no lung and could not inhale oxygen. Human beings more or less floated in fluid elements, and they had an organ, a kind of air bladder, out of which the lung later developed. This air bladder reorganized itself into the lung, and we can follow this process. When we do so, we find that it is portrayed in the Bible with this picture: "And God breathed the living breath into the human being, and the human being became a living soul." With this breathing into the human was made possible the production of the red blood. Thus, the descent of the human being is connected with the arising of the red blood tree within the human being.

Imagine that the human being was standing before you and that you could follow the flowing of the red blood. You would have before you a living red tree. The Christian esotericist says that this is the Tree of Knowledge. The human being seized it, partook of the red blood tree. The constructing of the red blood tree, which is the Tree of Knowledge, is the original sin for which God drove the human being out of paradise, so that the human being would not eat of the Tree of Life as well. We have yet another tree in us; you can imagine it in the same way. It has red-blue blood, and this blood is death substance. The red-blue tree was planted in the human being at the same time as the red blood tree. As the human being rested in the bosom of the godhead, the godhead was able to intertwine in the human that which signified life and knowledge. In the future lies the point in time when human beings will be able, through their expanded consciousness, to transform the blue into the red. Then they will themselves become the source or cause of the blue blood tree developing into a Tree of Life. Today it is a tree of death. Thus, there lives in this picture a looking backward and a looking ahead.

You see that in the human being a red blood tree and a red-blue blood tree are intertwined. The red blood is the expression of the "I," the lower "I"-knowledge. The blue blood is the expression of death. The blue blood tree, the Tree of Death, was added to the red tree, the Tree of Knowledge, as a penalty and correction. In a far future this Tree of Death will be transformed into the Tree of Life, just as it was originally a Tree of Life. When you imagine the human being today, our whole life in the present is based on an interaction between these two trees.

The fact that Seth was allowed to enter paradise means that he was an initiate and could look back at the divine-spiritual condition in which the two trees were intertwined with each other. He laid three seeds from the intertwined trees in Adam's mouth, and a three-membered tree grew out of them. Thus the tree that grows out of the human being—manas, buddhi, and atman, which make up the higher part of the human being—is present within us as a predisposition. In the legend it is shown how, already in Adam, the threefold nature of the divine is present as a predisposition and how it grows. At first only the initiate sees it. Human beings must follow the path of initiation. The legend further expresses all that has taken place in the evolution of humanity and which leads to initiation.

Out of the knowledge that the threefold tree, the Tree of Eternity—which expresses itself in the words "I am Who was; I am Who is; I am Who will be"—rests in us, we gain the power that brings us forward and puts the magic staff of Moses in our hands. The wood of the tree that grew out of the seeds was taken to build the temple of wisdom; and the cross—that symbol of initiation that signifies the conquering of the lower members of the human being by the higher ones—was constructed out of it as well. Thus, this legend shows how the initiate looks upon a future condition in which the Tree of Life, the red blood tree, and the Tree of Knowledge, the blue-red blood tree, will intertwine in the human being. Those who want to develop themselves write in their heart what the two pillars, the red pillar indicating the red blood tree and the blue indicating the blue-blood tree, want to say to us. Today they are separate. For that reason, the red pillar stands on the left side of the hall, and the blue-red pillar stands on the right. The pillars want to urge us to overcome the present condition of humanity, in order to direct our path to the point where they will intertwine through our expanded consciousness in such a way that one calls, "J-B." We designate the red pillar with "J" and the blue-red with "B."

The sayings on the pillars will bring home to you what is connected with each individual pillar. On the red pillar stand these words:

In pure thinking you find
The self that can hold itself.

Transform thought into an image
And you will experience creative wisdom.

Those who meditate on these words imbue, through the strength of their thinking, the red blood pillar with that power which leads to the goal, to the wisdom pillar. And we imbue the life pillar with the power that it needs when we meditate on the thought that stands on the blue pillar:

Concentrate feeling into light
And you will reveal the formative power.

Realize the will into being-ness
And you will create in world being.

The one verse has to do with knowledge and the other with life. The formative power reveals itself in the first saying. It becomes magical in the second saying. The ascent from mere power of knowledge to magical working lies in the transition from the power of the verse on the first pillar to that of the verse on the second pillar. Thus, you see how that which these symbols, the two pillars, signify is connected with the ideals and goals of the Rosicrucian pupil. In many esoteric societies these pillars are erected. The esotericist will always ascribe the meaning to them that you have just been told.

The seven pictures that decorate the hall are symbolic expressions for quite specific ancient truths. They present the so-called seven seals of the ancient, and ever new, wisdom. This is spoken of in the Apocalypse of John, and this Apocalypse is a kind of interpretation of an esoteric symbol language. Whoever studies the seals will recognize the images in the visions of the writer of the Apocalypse. Every letter, every color of the seals means something. When we look at them together in the right way and sense the connection, quite specific feelings are released, which can engender inner strength. It all depends on our not having to do with dry allegories but rather with a living expression of what every [initiate] can experience as real facts on the astral plane.

The *first seal* is the man with the sword of fire in his mouth. This sword—and this feature is what matters—is connected with a secret of evolution. Speech has always been compared with the sword. It is, however, not merely a poetic picture. In esotericism everything is to be taken literally. We must only understand it correctly. There is a certain mysterious connection between that which lives in our speech—what is said in words through our larynx—and the lower human reproductive drives of today. The human form is in the process of transforming. Some can already see on the astral plane what will be present physically in the future. The seer sees in such a picture as this first of the seven seals a condition that the human being will someday attain. This is an astral picture today. It expresses the evolutionary condition of the human physical body in the future.

When we want to imagine this condition, we must think of it in such a way that we say that through their present-day lower power of reproduction, human beings reproduce instinctively and unconsciously. Through the reproductive drive, they can bring forth forms filled with matter. There is another force in human beings, which does not yet enable us to bring forth forms that linger, that remain. That is the force of our speech. In that I speak here, I produce something. If you observe what happens in this room while I speak, you can follow oscillating waves of air. These are nothing other than words converted into movement. Such words translated into movement were, in the primordial past, that which expresses itself today in the life of reproduction. What is condensed today was, when it was still spirit, word converted into movement. What human beings today can achieve out of the word, only in the form of movement, will later be a true power of reproduction.

Imagine that you could solidify my words for a moment so that the solidified waves of air would fall down: you would find a different form for every word. The word *and* would have a different form from the word *god*; a mussel form, as far as I am concerned. If I were to say "god," there would be a different form generated than if I were to say "and." Esotericism shows us that all the physical objects around us arose in this way. The spirit of the Logos rang through space, and matter formed itself; the rest is a process of solidification. What is present around us today is formed word, the condensed words of the gods. The forces in us are condensed divine forces. What was created earlier through the word is now converted into natural form.

Thus, in the course of evolution, the human larynx will become a reproductive organ. We will be able to produce not just movement; indeed, the larynx will become the true organ of reproduction. What our speech is today will be the producer of our own kind. The larynx is the future reproductive organ elevated spiritually—hence, the parallel in the development of sexuality and the development of the larynx within the human. The change of voice at sexual maturity points toward the creative power that will develop out of the voice of the human being one day. Out of speech will arise the true power of reproduction, the conscious bringing forth of the human being. As you know, in that we give those spirits that were our ancestors the name "fire spirits," because they were connected with fire as we are connected with air, so we will once more develop ourselves from air spirits to fire spirits in our ascent. From the larynx will flow not only the air force but also the fire-spirit force.

What you see in the first seal expressed as the fiery sword is that which represents the being of the human that passes through all incarnations. This eternal element in the human being is at the same time the divine creating element. It is true that the element within us that goes through all the incarnations as wisdom is of the same nature as that which created the sevenfold planetary succession. That is the reason the man pictured in the first seal holds the symbols of the seven planets in his right hand.

The *second seal* portrays the so-called apocalyptic animals: the lion, the eagle, the bull, and the human being. We get an idea of them when we remind ourselves that the animal today does not have the same sort of "I"-soul as we do. The animal does not have its I-soul on the physical plane; the individual animal has the same relationship to the "I" of a group as a member of the human being has to the whole "I." Therefore, we speak of a group soul with the animal; when you look for this group soul, you find it on the astral plane. Everyone will understand that human beings also went through evolutionary conditions in which their being on the physical plane did not yet have the "I"-soul. Human beings passed through conditions in which they had a group soul. At the same point in time—the Lemurian epoch—when the soul descended into physical embodiment, the group soul changed into the individual soul. In the far future, human beings will again raise themselves up to the group soul—but consciously, in a higher sense.

The second seal is the symbol of that higher group soul. The unity in the far future is portrayed through the outer forms of those group souls that humanity had earlier. These group souls, out of which proceeded the human individual soul and to which we will again return, are divided into four archetypal groups. They are four astral groups. The first is characterized in the group soul that is embodied today as the rudiments of the bull-soul, another as the lion-soul, and the third as the bird-soul. The fourth soul, which lifted the human being, bringing it into individuality, is designated as the human being. Out of these four group souls the human being arose and into them the human being will again return. We see in the symbol in the middle of the seal—surrounded by the four soul groups—the group soul that is the most advanced and which is individualized as the human soul on the astral plane. It is the Christ-soul, symbolized by the lamb. The Christ-soul completes the four other group souls.

In the rainbow that surrounds the whole in seven colors, the creative cosmic principle is pictured. It is the sevenfold creative principle that lies at the foundation of the inner course of human evolution, at the stage of evolution represented by this seal. In connection with the numerals I to XII, which are to be read like the numbers of a clock imposed on the colors of the rainbow, we must remember that once the

Earth, Moon, and Sun were one body. This unity is connected with the conditions portrayed here. This form of the cosmic order was necessary so that the human being could have a group soul. Our present division of time is connected with the position of the cosmic bodies. In the primordial past, when there was not yet an Earth circling the Sun, all time relationships were different. At that time there was no day and hour. The Sun itself went its way, and there was a great cosmic dial. This dial represented the places that the Sun passed. The hour hand on our clocks circles the dial two times each day; thus, in that ancient cosmic calendar, the Sun passed through the zodiac not once, but twice—through a time of light and a time of darkness. This twofold passing, the twofold traveling through these stations, is called "passing by the Elder Brothers of the cosmic order." They are the twenty-four Elders of the Apocalypse.† Hence we have here a kind of cosmic clock.

Looking to a far future, you see expressed in the *sixth seal*† future cosmic conditions in which human beings will ascend higher in their outer form. We see that Earth and Sun will be united and the Moon will be eliminated. Remember that Goethe calls the highest ideal to which the human being can strive, the "eternal feminine."† That which overcomes the unusable material in human nature is designated as feminine. When the Earth will have united with the Sun, the human being will have brought about this union. The unusable material is portrayed as the Moon, which will be trod underfoot. What must be eliminated when the Earth becomes Sun again is represented by the dragon. It will be overcome when the Earth will again be Sun.

The *third seal* shows an open book with a semicircle of chalices and angels blowing trumpets above it, all encircled by flooding light and colors. The trumpet-blowing angels express the harmony of the spheres. When we rise from the astral plane to the devachan plane, we have the experience that the harmony of the spheres pervades the flooding light and color worlds of the astral plane. That which one can see within the astral plane as flowing light and color begins to sound, and it proves to be the expression of the essence of the mental plane. The Pythagorean School called this harmony the "music of the spheres." Goethe also speaks of it when he says, "The Sun intones in ancient tourney" and "Intoning, the new day is born for spirit ears!"†

The chalices signify the cups of wrath, suggesting that the human being will have attained the spirit that has overcome and transformed what we call anger. All anger must be eliminated; hence, the cups of wrath are being poured out. The book indicates that the human being, in the course of evolution—if we are able to rightly solve its mysteries—is an image of eternal world evolution. If we recognize this, that the human being is a picture of world evolution, then we can read our own being; we ourselves have become a book. Then comes the moment, which is spoken of in the Apocalypse, when John must eat the book. The next seal carries this idea further.

The two pillars of the *fourth seal* portray the red and blue blood trees. The cloud is the present-day air, which only the larynx controls. Out of it will arise the future human ability to produce in matter. Over the two blood pillars will form the initiated human being, who ate the book. Human beings will develop within themselves the power that will transform the Earth into the Sun. This power is characterized in the face born out of the Sun. When human beings reach this stage, their seeing is a seeing into the astral world. That is intimated in the rainbow above the Sun face. This rainbow points to that power which human beings will have acquired when they become cosmic, creating beings.

In the *fifth seal* we have a being that conquers the dragon—the future human being, who will have overcome the so-called lower nature completely. That is connected with the cosmic conditions that set in at the point when the kama[†] is trod underfoot. The condition that will arise is symbolized in the Holy Grail of the *last seal (the seventh seal)*. At the bottom is pictured a cube of transparent diamond, which consists of pure carbon. When human beings are far enough along in evolution that they use carbon itself to build up the body—without the involvement of the plant world—they will then produce the cube. This cube of crystallized, pure carbon is the best indication of that future condition of the human being.

Human beings will then be able to know not only the ordinary space in three dimensions but also the approaching counter-space; we see the counter-space come to meet ordinary space in mirror image.[†] The counter-space indicates what human beings will attain someday, when they have overcome the physical in the spirit. The serpents signify this evolving upward to a higher level, which is indicated in the violet-blue winding, curved lines of the seal. This image of the serpent denotes the devotional nature of knowledge. Only this selfless, devotional attitude can grasp the cosmic spiral in the Mercury staff, which then becomes fiery and winds out of pure knowledge. It then transforms itself into the downward-turned pure chalice or cup. The plant "cup" is chaste today and is turned openly upward. With the human being it is reversed. In the future the human cup will become chaste and will turn itself downward; hence is the Grail shown here as a chalice turned downward. The pure human being, the human being who has become guiltless, is portrayed in the dove. The rainbow points to the sevenfold creative human being.

Thus, the entire evolution of humanity is indicated in the seven seals. Through contemplation of such seals, which represent effective elements in evolution, we will develop the devotional attitude that we must achieve.

The *program book* is circumscribed with the symbols of the Rosicrucian school:

E. D. N. I. C. M. P. S. S. R.:
Ex Deo nascimur;
In Christo morimur;
Per Spiritum sanctum reviviscimus.

In English:

Out of God we are born;
In Christ we die;
Through the Spirit we are reborn.

The secrets of initiation are expressed in the seven seals; they are given planetary expression in the seven columns. These columns bear the heavens, that is, all of evolution. The capital motifs have in their individual features quite specific significance. If you can sense sculpturally how that which is above tends toward that which is below, feelings are set free in you that tell of the streams in the corresponding conditions of these cosmic bodies. The motifs of the first column have simple slopes and curves. Through the contemplation of them, a feeling is called forth of the streams that moved through the Earth as it was embodied in its first evolutionary condition, called the Saturn condition. This is the Saturn column.

When you sense the progression of the organization of the motifs through examining the second column—the lower part is structured like the ovary of a plant, and, from above downward, it is arranged so that it can become a cup—feelings are released in you that correspond to the streams that passed through the Earth when it was in the Sun condition. Therefore, we speak of this as the Sun column. We can continue in this vein in examining the third, fourth, and other columns. When we pass from one to the next, different feeling-streams develop.

The first half of Earth evolution has its particular characteristic from the influence of Mars. The second half now stands under the influence of the power that the esotericist sees proceeding from Mercury. For this reason, Earth evolution is divided into Mars and Mercury halves. If we leave out the Vulcan condition as an octave of the Saturn condition, the following sequence of conditions of Earth evolution results: Saturn, Sun, Moon, Mars, Mercury, Jupiter, and Venus. With the Mercury column, the Saturn motif is woven into the Mercury motif. The serpent staff comes organically out of what went before it and develops further. We sense, through deep study of the capital motifs, the Earth streams that will arise in future development. In the last capital, we have the cup form again.

The secret of the seven planetary conditions of our Earth were laid into the naming of the seven days of the week.[†] They have these names:

Saturn day: Saturday, Samstag, Samedi
Sun day: Sunday, Sonntag, Dimanche
Moon day: Monday, Montag, Lundi
Mars day: Tuesday, Dienstag, Mardi or Ziu
Mercury day: Wednesday, Mittwoch (literally Mid-week in German), Mercredi; note that the German "Mittwoch" is a profane name,[†] and the English "Wednesday" is from the god Wodin, or Odin
Jupiter day: Thursday, Donnerstag, Thor, Donar, Jeudi
Venus day: Friday, Freitag, Freya, Vendredi

The names of the days of the week are deeply symbolic. In their sequential order, the initiates wanted to tell us to think about the fact that we were placed into the living evolution of time. Thus, the highest teaches us to understand the nearest, that which is immediately around us. The idea of the evolution of humanity should be indicated in the columns. It is expressed in the way it has always been expressed in the esoteric symbol-script. The centers of esotericism were arranged and decorated symbolically. In the form, in the picture, in the color we are to see what lives in the soul. What lives in the soul should shine toward us from outside; then we have worked in the sense of world evolution. Above all, our task is to think selflessly about this great evolution. It will be fulfilled when we allow the inner life to flow entirely into the outer.

Report of the Congress in the Berlin Branch

RUDOLF STEINER

Given before the lecture in Berlin, June 12, 1907

The Munich Congress, which is the fourth,† after those in Amsterdam, London, and Paris, should be considered as a certain stage in the development of our Theosophical Movement. It will establish a kind of connection among various nations, also with regard to our Theosophical affairs within Europe. I do not want to give an actual report on the Congress but rather to make a few comments to those who were not able to participate.

I have stressed again and again with regard to our Theosophical concerns that Theosophy should not be the object of personal brooding and living into oneself. Theosophy should engage in practical life; it should be a matter of culture, a participation in all aspects of everyday existence. Only someone who has a deeper understanding and a more profound conception of the true impulses of the Theosophical knows the possibilities that Theosophy will offer in the future. It will be the unity between what we behold and what we feel inwardly. For those who can see more deeply, a main reason for the absentmindedness of human beings is the discord between that which is and that which Theosophy intends. It is not just Theosophists who have sensed this but also other significant personages, for instance, Richard Wagner.†

In earlier times every door lock, every house, every structure was a construction of the soul. Soul material flowed into it. In ancient times artwork belonged to human feeling and thinking. The forms of the Gothic churches corresponded in olden days to the mood of those who made pilgrimages to them. These churches were the expression of their own soul mood. Those making pilgrimages to the churches sensed the forms like a folding of the hands [as in prayer], just as the old Germanic peoples sensed a folding of the hands in the coming together of the treetops [forming an arch]. In those times everything was more intimate. You still see this attitude expressed wonderfully by Michelangelo† and Leonardo da Vinci.†

That the entire village was arranged around the church was nothing other than the expression of its whole soul life. All the etheric streams collected together at the place where the church stood. The materialistic age has split this unity apart. Those who cannot reflect on life do not know this. The seer, however, knows that today, when we travel through a city, there is almost nothing to see but things that have to do with the stomach or fashion. Those who know how to follow the hidden threads of life also understand that materialistic culture has brought about this division.

A healthy outer world can come about through the expression of our inner soul moods. One cannot immediately reach the most perfect expression, but an example of it was given in Munich. The Theosophical worldview was brought to expression in the congress space. One saw nothing but the Theosophical. The entire hall was red. Often mistakes are made with regard to the color red, but the deeper significance of red is not to be misjudged.

The evolution of humanity comprises an ascent and a descent. Look at aboriginal peoples. They have green in nature. And what do they love the most? Red. The esotericist knows that red has a specific effect on a healthy soul. It releases in the healthy soul the active forces, the forces that spur one on to deeds; they are the forces that will shift the soul out of comfort into the discomfort of doing. A room with a festive mood must be wallpapered in red. Those who wallpaper a living room in red show that they do not understand a festive mood; they profane the red color. Goethe expressed this most beautifully: "The effect of this color is as unique as its nature. It gives the impression of both earnestness and dignity, and of grace and beauty. It accomplishes one thing in its dark, condensed condition and another in its bright, thinned condition. And so, the dignity of age and the charm of youth can both be clothed in one color."† Those are the moods that are produced through red; one can attest to these moods with esoteric methods. Look at the countryside through a red glass, and you have the impression that it must look like this on the Day of Judgment. Red is an enemy of retarding moods, against moods of sin.

Then there were the seven motifs of the columns, looking toward the time when, out of Theosophy, we will be able to build buildings as well. Column motifs come from teachings of the initiates of ancient times. Theosophy will be able to offer truly new column motifs to architecture. The motifs from ancient times have not said anything to the human being for a long time. The new ones have to do with Saturn, Sun, Moon, Mars, Mercury, Jupiter, and Venus. An inherent lawfulness expressed itself in the capitals. We placed the seven apocalyptic seals between the columns, in the manner of Rosicrucianism. Here the Grail seal appeared for the first time before the public.[†]

We can also build Theosophy; we can develop it in architecture, in education, and in the social question. The principle of Rosicrucianism is to introduce the spirit into the world and to accomplish fruitful soul work. Theosophy will also raise art to a mystery art—an art for which Richard Wagner had such an intense yearning. Such an attempt was made in Edouard Schuré's mystery drama, which reworks the Greek mystery plays. The program has the festive red color and bears a black cross encircled with roses on a blue field. Rosicrucianism takes what Christianity has imparted to us and leads it into the future. The initials given on the program represent the fundamental thoughts of Rosicrucianism.[†] What underlay the whole Congress was the intention to crystallize Theosophy into the building-up of the world.

The Apocalyptic Seals†

RUDOLF STEINER

Lecture, Stuttgart, September 16, 1907

By far the most important symbol we have—which has been recognized as such by esotericists in all ages—is the human being. The human being was always and will always be called a microcosm, a little world. Whoever comes to know the human being exactly and intimately will understand more and more that everything arrayed in outer nature is contained in the human in miniature. That is perhaps difficult to understand at first, but when you think about it, you will grasp what is meant. In the human being there is to be found, as a kind of extract, an excerpt of the rest of nature, in all its substances and forces. If one were to study the essence of a plant and search deeply enough, one would find that in the human organism something of this same essence is contained, even if only to a small extent. If one were to look at an animal, one would always find something of it that was taken into the human organism.

Certainly, it is necessary to contemplate the evolution of the world from the esoteric viewpoint in order to understand it rightly. For instance, the esotericist knows that human beings would have a heart of a completely different nature from the one they have today if there were no lion in nature. Let us shift to an earlier time in which there were no lions. There were human beings, because the human is the oldest being, but their heart was formed entirely differently then. Everywhere in nature there are connections that are certainly not always obvious. As, in remote ages, the heart of human beings developed to its present-day form, the lion came into being; the same force formed both. It is as though you were to extract the being of the lion and, with divine skill, form the heart out of it. Perhaps you think the human heart has nothing of the nature of the lion, but that is the case for the esotericist. We cannot forget that when a thing is placed into a certain connection within an organism, it works totally differently from when it is free. We can also say it the other way around. If you could take out the essence of the heart and form a being that corresponded to this heart, when it was not being determined by the forces of the organism, then you would have the lion. All the characteristics of courage and boldness or, as the esoteric says, the "regal" characteristics of the human being stem from this association with the lion. Plato, who was an initiate, transferred the regal soul into the heart.†

Paracelsus† used a very beautiful comparison for this connection of the human being with nature. He said: It is as if individual beings in nature were the letters and the human being were the word made out of these letters. Outside is the great world, the macrocosm; within us is the small world, the microcosm. Outside everything exists separately; within the human being everything is determined through the harmony in which it is placed with the other organs. It is precisely for this reason that we can look at the evolution of our entire universe in the human being, insofar as it belongs to us. In the seals that hung in the festival hall during the Congress, you have a picture of the evolution of human beings in connection with the world to which they belong. Let us see what they portray.

The first seal shows a man clothed in white, with feet like metal, like flowing bronze. From his mouth protrudes a fiery sword, and his right hand is surrounded by the signs of our planets: Saturn, Sun, Moon, Mars, Mercury, Jupiter, and Venus. Whoever knows the Apocalypse of John will remember that it contains a description of this picture that is in fair agreement, for John was an initiate. One could say that this seal portrays the idea of the whole of humanity. We will grasp this when we recall a few imaginations with which the older among you are already acquainted.

When we look back on human evolution, we come to a time in which the human being was still at a very incomplete stage. For instance, human beings did not yet have that which you carry on your shoulders: the head. If we were to describe the human being of that time, it would sound quite grotesque. The head has evolved gradually over time and will continue to develop. There are organs in the human being today that are, so to speak, at their end; they will later no longer be present in the human body. Other organs will transform: the larynx has a powerful future, particularly in connection with the heart. Today the larynx of the human being is just at the beginning stage of its development. It will one day be the reproductive organ transmuted into the spiritual.

You will gain an idea of this mystery when you realize what we do with the larynx today. In that I speak, you hear my words. Because this hall is filled with air and in this air certain waves are produced, my words are transmitted to your ears, to your soul. When I speak a word, for example "world," waves of air vibrate. Those are the embodiments of my words. That which we produce in this way, we call production in the mineral kingdom. The movements of the air are mineral movements. Through the larynx we work in a mineral way on our surroundings; we do mineral work. However, the human being will rise higher and one day will work in such a way as to do plant work. We will produce not only mineral vibrations but also plant vibrations. We will speak plants. The next stage will be when we speak sentient being, and on the highest level of evolution we will, with the larynx, speak our own kind into being. The way we now can speak only the content of our soul through the word, so at a future time, we will speak our own self. The way human beings will speak in the future, so the predecessors of humanity, the gods, were endowed with an organ through which they spoke into being everything that is in existence today. They spoke all the human beings, all the animals, everything into being. You are all, literally, the spoken word of gods.

"In the beginning was the Word, and the Word was with God, and the Word was a God!"† That is not a philosophical saying in a speculative sense. John put down a primordial fact that is to be taken quite literally. In the end will be the Word; creation is a realization of the Word. What the human being will produce in the future will be a realization of that which the Word is today. Then, however, human beings will no longer have the same physical form as they do today. We will have progressed to that form which existed on Saturn, to fire matter. Thus the creative force in the beginning of world evolution connects with our own creative force at the end of world evolution. That being, who spoke everything in the world into being, is the great example, the model, for the human being. This being spoke into the world Saturn,

Sun, Moon, Earth—with both of its halves of Mars and Mercury—Jupiter, and Venus. The seven stars point to this truth; they are the symbols for the heights to which the human being can evolve. The planet will come to an end in fire matter, and the human being will be able to create through speaking in this fire matter. This is the fiery sword that protrudes from the mouth. Everything will be fiery; hence, the feet of flowing bronze.

When you compare the human being with the animal, the difference presents itself in such a way that one must say that the individual human being has something that the individual animal does not have. The human being has an individual soul, and the animal has a group soul. Each human being is a whole animal species unto himself or herself. All lions, for example, have only one soul together. These group "I" beings are just like the human "I," but they are not descended into the physical world; they are to be found in the astral world. Here on the Earth, you see human beings, each of whom bears his or her own "I." In the astral world, you meet in astral matter beings that are like you; they are not in physical sheaths but rather in astral sheaths. You can talk with them as with your own kind; those are the animal group souls.

The human being, too, had a group soul in earlier times. Only gradually did we evolve to our present-day independence. These group souls were originally in the astral world and then descended to live in the flesh. When we examine the original group souls of the human being in the astral world, we find four kinds from which the human being came. If we wanted to compare these four types to the group souls of today's animal species, we must say that one compares to the lion, another to the eagle, a third to the cow, and the fourth to the human of olden times, before the "I" descended. Thus, in the second seal, the apocalyptic animals—the lion, eagle, cow, and human—portray an earlier evolutionary condition of the human being. Then there is, and will continue to be, as long as the Earth will be, a group soul for the higher revelation of the human being. This is represented by the lamb, the mystical lamb, which is the symbol of the Savior. The second seal portrays the five group souls—the four of the human being around the great group soul that belongs to all human beings in common.

If we follow human evolution far, far back many millions of years, we are confronted by something quite different. The human being is a physical being on the Earth, but there was a time when the being that wandered on the Earth could not yet have taken up a human soul. This soul was on the astral plane. Still further back, we come to a time when it was on the spiritual plane, the devachan plane. In the future it will again climb up to this high level, when it has purified itself on the Earth. From the spirit through the astral to the physical and upward again to the spirit: this is the long evolution of the human being. And yet it seems like a short period when we compare it with the time involved in the evolution of the human being on Saturn and on the other planets. There the human being went through not only a physical transformation but spiritual and astral tranformations also.

If one wishes to follow these transformations, one must go up into the spiritual worlds. There one perceives the music of the spheres, tones that flow through space in this spiritual world. When human beings live into this spiritual world again, the harmony of the spheres will sound toward them. In esotericism it is called the trumpet tones of the angels; hence, the trumpets in the third seal. Revelations coming out of the spiritual world are revealed only when the human being progresses ever further. At that point the book with seven seals will be revealed to us. These seals are precisely those we are examining here. They will give up their secrets. For this reason, the book is placed in the middle of the seal, and below it are the four phases of humanity. The four horses are nothing other than the evolutionary stages of humanity through the ages.

There is a still higher development. Human beings come from even higher worlds, and they will again ascend to these higher worlds. The form that human beings have today will by then have disappeared from the world. We will take up again that which is in the outer world, the individual letters from which we are assembled; our form will have identified itself with the world form. In a certain trivial presentation of Theosophy, it is taught and talked about that we should seek the god within ourselves. However, anyone wanting to find the god within must seek in the works that are spread out in the universe. Nothing in the world is mere matter; it just seems that way. In reality, all matter is the expression of spirituality, tidings of the effectiveness of the god. Human beings will, as it were, expand their being in the course of the coming ages. More and more, human beings will identify themselves with the world, so that we will be able to portray them with the form of the cosmos, instead of the human form. This you see in the fourth seal, with the rock, the sea, and the pillars.

That which moves through the world today as cloud will give up its substance in order to form the body of the human being. The forces that are with the spirits of the Sun today will deliver to human beings in the future the power that builds their spiritual forces in an infinitely elevated manner. It is to this Sun power that the human being strives. In contrast to the plant, which sinks its head—the root—toward the center of the Earth, human beings turn their head to the Sun; one day we will unite our head with the Sun and receive higher forces. This we see portrayed in the Sun-face that rests on the cloud-body on the rock and the pillars. Human beings will have become self-creative then; as the symbol of this completed creation, a colorful rainbow surrounds the human being in the fourth seal. You can find a similar seal in the Apocalypse of John. In the middle of the clouds, there is a book. The Apocalypse says that the initiate must eat this book. Here is indicated the time when human beings not only will receive wisdom from without, but will also permeate themselves with it as they do with food today—when they will themselves be an embodiment of wisdom.

Then the times approach in which great changes will occur in the cosmos. When the human being will have drawn the Sun power near, the Sun will again be united with the Earth. The human being will become a Sun-being and, through the power of the Sun, will give birth to a Sun; hence we see [in the fifth seal] the woman who bears the Sun. At that point, humanity will be so moral, so ethical, that all the ruinous powers that lie in the lower human nature will be overcome. This is portrayed by the beast with seven heads and ten horns. At the feet of the Sun-woman is the Moon, which contains all the bad substances that the Earth could not use and which it has cast out. All the magic powers that the Moon still exerts upon the Earth today will be overcome. When human beings are united with the Sun, they will have overcome the Moon.

[The sixth seal] presents to us the way in which the human being, who has risen to a high level of spiritualization, is like the form of Michael. He holds the evil in the world fettered, in the symbol of the dragon.

We have seen that at the beginning of the evolution of humanity, and again at the end, the same conditions of transformation are to be found. We find these conditions depicted in the man with the molten feet and the sword protruding from his mouth. In a deeply meaningful symbol, the Holy Grail, the whole being of the world is revealed. I want to place this seventh seal before your souls in a few words. Any esotericist, who comes to know our world, understands that space is something quite different for the physical world than a mere vacuum. Space is the source out of which all beings have crystallized, as it were. Imagine a glass cube-shaped vessel that is totally transparent and filled with water. Now imagine that certain cooling streams are passed through this water so that ice forms in manifold ways. You get an idea of world creation: the divine Word of creation is spoken into space and all things and beings crystallize out of it.

The esotericist portrays this space into which the divine Creation-Word is spoken through a water-bright cube. Various beings develop within this space. Those closest to us we can best characterize in the following way: The cube has three directions perpendicular to each other, three axes—length, height, and width. These represent the three dimensions of space. Now, in your imagination add to these three dimensions, as they are in the physical world, the counter-dimensions [of counter-space]. You can imagine these counter-dimensions more or less in this way: a person goes in one direction, and another comes toward him, and they bump into each other. In a similar way, there is a counter-dimension for every space dimension, so that we have six rays in all. These counter-rays [from counter-space] represent, at the same time, the primordial germ of the highest members of the human nature. The physical body, crystallized out of space, is the lowest member. The opposite is the spiritual, the highest; it is represented by the counter-dimensions. These counter-dimensions form at first a being that we can best portray by letting it flow together with the world of the passions, desires, and instincts. That is what it is at first.

Later it becomes something different. It purifies itself ever more and more—we have seen to what heights—but it came out of the lower drives, symbolized by the serpent. This process is represented in the converging of the counter-dimensions in two serpents that face each other.

By purifying itself, humanity rises up to what one calls the world spiral. The purified body of the serpent, this world spiral, has a deep significance. You can form a conception of it through the following example. Modern astronomy is based on two statements made by Copernicus.[†] A third has been ignored. He said that the Sun also moves. The Sun moves forward in a spiral, so that the Earth travels in a complicated curve with the Sun. The same holds true for the Moon that moves around the Earth. These movements are much more complicated than one assumes from elementary astronomy. You see here how the spiral has significance for the cosmic bodies; these cosmic bodies represent a form with which human beings will one day identify themselves. At that time, the human reproductive force will be cleansed, purified; the larynx will be the organ of reproduction. That which the human being will have developed as purified serpent body will no longer work from below upward, but rather from above downward. The transformed larynx will become the cup that one calls the Holy Grail. Everything connected with the reproductive organ will be purified, and it will be an essence of the world power, the great world essence. We depict this essence of the world power in the dove that looks upon the Holy Grail. Here it is the symbol of the spiritualized fertilization that will work from out of the cosmos when, one day, human beings will have identified themselves with the cosmos. This whole creative process is represented through the rainbow: that is the all-encompassing seal of the Holy Grail [seventh seal].

The whole seventh seal imparts wonderfully the sense of the connection between the world and the human being, like a summary of the meaning of the other seals. For that reason, the world mystery stands as an inscription on the outer rim of the seal. This world mystery presents how the human being was born out of the primordial forces of the world. All of us, when we look back, have undergone that process that we go through spiritually today when we are born anew out of consciousness forces. Rosicrucianism expresses this with the letters E. D. N.: Out of God I am born.

We have seen that in the revelation a second element comes in addition to life: death. In order to find life again in death, human beings must overcome the death of the senses in the primordial source of all life. This primordial source is the middle point of cosmic evolution. We must find death in order to achieve consciousness, but we will overcome death when we find its meaning in the mystery of the Savior. Just as we are born out of God, so we die, in the sense of esoteric wisdom, in Christ: I. C. M.

Because wherever something reveals itself as a duality a third must be joined, we human beings will identify with the world-permeating spirit (the dove) when we have overcome death. We will be resurrected and live again in the spirit: P. S. S. R.

That is the Theosophical Rose Cross. It shines into those times when religion and science will become reconciled. You see how in such seals the whole world presents itself; a powerful force lives in these seals, because the world is laid into them by magi and initiates. You can turn to these seals ever anew; you will again and again discover that you can find infinite wisdom revealed through meditation. They have a powerful influence on the soul of the human being, because they are created out of world secrets. Hang them in a room where such things are discussed the way we are speaking here, in which we lift ourselves up to the sacred mysteries of the world, and they will have an enlivening, illuminating effect in the highest degree, sometimes without the human being even knowing it. At the same time, because they have this significance, they are not meant to be profaned. As peculiar as it may seem, when you hang them in a room where nothing spiritual is talked about, where trivial words are spoken, they work there, too—but in such a way that they make the physical organism ill. As trivial as it may sound, they ruin the digestion. What is born out of the spiritual belongs to the spiritual and may not be profaned. That shows itself through its effect. Symbols of spiritual things belong where spiritual things take place and achieve effectiveness.

Symbols and Signs as Effects of Chaos†

Rudolf Steiner

Lecture, Berlin, October, 1907

Today let us begin with an examination of a subject that is quite remote but which, as you will see, can interest us in terms of our daily life. We will try today to connect not only the sky, but also what is behind the sky, with the Earth and our daily life. The leading motif of our examination will be what is called by a name borrowed from olden times: *chaos.*† As you see, it is a somewhat remote theme but one that really still lies behind our understanding of the sky, which we should connect with our daily experiences.

You know that the wonderful Greek myths and sagas take up the theme of chaos, in that they say that the oldest gods—thus the oldest spiritual beings—are born out of the chaos. You also know that the myths and sagas of other peoples know this chaos by various names. What exactly is the gaping abyss of the Norse-Germanic saga "Ginnungagap"† other than the chaos out of which arose, on the one hand, the cold Mist-land (Niflheim or Nebelheim) and, on the other, the hot Fire-land (Muspelheim)? What is it that the beginning of our Bible itself points to? In Genesis, you find the words "In the beginning God created the heaven and the earth. And the world was without form, and void; and darkness was upon the face of the deep. And the spirit of God moved upon the face of the waters. And God said, Let there be light: and there was light. And God saw the light, that it was good: and God divided the light from the darkness."† "The world was without form, and void" is just another expression for the chaos out of which the highest spiritual beings came forth.

What is chaos? Such old words for such lofty concepts have suffered a peculiar fate in the evolution of humanity. Quite some time ago human beings lost all feeling for gaining a correct conception of what is meant by such words. The materialistic age, into which all people of the present have been born, hardly has words yet to characterize what is behind the world of chaos. Over time our words have taken on a completely different meaning than they had earlier—even a short while ago. Earlier, words corresponded to the spiritual significance and meaning of an object, the concept. Today our words are attached to the materialistic meaning of outer, material objects and are no longer used for their spiritual meaning. When one hears a word today, one focuses on what it means in the sense-perceptible world but thinks no more to bring it into relationship with the spiritual world.

Among the many reasons for inaugurating the present Theosophical stream, there is one that is connected with this transmutation of the word into materialism. That the Theosophical Movement has come, and had to come, into the world at precisely this time is connected with various facts, both sense-perceptible and supersensible. However, one of the reasons is that if this Theosophical Movement, this spiritual world stream, had not arisen at the end of the nineteenth and beginning of the twentieth centuries, such a spiritual movement would probably not have been possible for another hundred years. It is indeed a seizing of the opportune circumstances of the moment. More and more, words are being used only for the material. If we had waited yet another hundred years, our words would no longer have been able to express what spiritual science has to say. Human beings would no longer have a feeling for it, because they would hear only that which is used for the world of matter. There would be no more words with which we could make ourselves understood, and so nothing that the spiritual scientist has to say would be suitable anymore. Theosophy must therefore press new words upon everything. It must give a new character to all words. Theosophy must virtually renew language. People must regain a feeling for the fact that a meaning lies in certain words that is not meant merely as something that can be touched or seen but that points into the higher worlds.

Now we will seem to leave the theme completely and try to seek the feelings of those human beings who were much more strongly directed and drawn to the spiritual world than human beings with the feelings and imaginations of modern humanity. It is always very interesting for anyone who becomes absorbed in the mysterious, and yet clear, course of the human spirit to take up any book and immerse oneself in it, not simply in the way many scholars do when they gather "their own meaning" from it, but as one feels one's way into the spirit of the author, puts oneself in the author's place. One could examine any book in this way. We want, however, to take the "Physics" of Comenius, which came out in 1633. This is a physics about which the modern human being can no longer think properly, because in this work physical things are spoken of in a manner in which it is clear that the author is pointing, in each case, to the spiritual background. He sees in all matter and in every force an instrument, a product of the spiritual beings and spiritual forces standing behind it. In this book much is described that was known in those days. Still, Comenius, the great pedagogue and thinker of the seventeenth century (born in 1592),† did not just summarize the knowledge of his time, but had great original thoughts about human beings and events and found deep spiritual connections. Comenius is a curious personality; there has been a string of such personalities since the fourteenth and fifteenth centuries.

You know from other discussions that the so-called Rosicrucian Order—that Order which works with and preserves the ancient secrets in a modern form—was founded in the fourteenth century.† The Order, which had only seven members at its founding, has, until now, worked completely in secret. No one knew who was a Rosicrucian other than another Rosicrucian. No one could ever find out anything about the secrets of the Rosicrucians. For this reason, everything in the outer world that was written by followers or enemies about Rosicrucianism is charlatanism, or a misunderstanding, or has come out through betrayal. Today the time has come when some Rosicrucian secrets may be communicated openly to the world. However, there are, and were, other methods and ways by which such secrets, which flourish in esoteric schools, flow into general spiritual and cultural life.

For example, it was nothing other than a hidden Rosicrucian stream that flowed through Gotthold Lessing,† even though he had no inkling of it, when at the end of his *The Education of the Human Race* he says, like a shot out of a pistol, that the human being comes again and again to Earth, that we reincarnate. This important treatise—which closes with the question "Is not the whole eternity mine?"—is, for any one who understands it, nothing other than a sign that the Rosicrucian worldview was put before humanity through Lessing's mouth in what was, for him, an unconscious manner.

Much has come to us this way through Rosicrucianism. There are many methods through which the spiritual world works, without the people whom it affects always entirely realizing it. It does not matter whether that which is done in the world is connected with a name. The movement as such is connected with a name. Still, Rosicrucians have never taken legal action because of plagiarism. They would never have pursued any so-called borrowing of their ideas. They have been indifferent to it. To a person for whom the effect is what matters, what could be less important than the personal source from which such ideas derive? The main thing has been that they came into the world. In our time, in which people take legal action because of the stealing of ideas and other such matters, the people who do the taking, as a rule, cannot be understood.

Thanks to a higher spiritual development, Comenius was among those who had higher knowledge and, through a strong, energetic will, rose into the higher worlds as a result of Rosicrucian influences. It is useful for people of today to immerse themselves in the ideas of Comenius. And it would be just as useful to immerse oneself in the thoughts of Johann Baptist van Helmont,† his contemporary, who also was a Rosicrucian. They interest us today from a completely different perspective. I want to note expressly that what I now say should serve only for clarification of what we mean by the word *chaos*, for seeking a path to its understanding.

There is a word that all or many of you probably believe is quite old. The word is "gas," which most of you know only as coal gas. You have learned from physics that there are many gases and that basically most substances can be changed into gas. If one does not think any more about it, one could easily be misled into believing that this word is as old as all the others. That is not the case. Before the time of Comenius and Helmont, "gas" and "gaseous" were not yet understood as concepts. Helmont was the first to coin this word and use it.† Only since that time is it to be found in language. The work in which this word first appears was written in 1615. Just think how short a time ago that is. You have to realize, of course, that a person must have a reason to use such a new word. Helmont was simply the first who had the imagination, the conception, of gas and communicated it, as it is usually used, to humanity.

Let us be clear about the modern concept of gas, as learned in school. You know that when you bring water to a boil, at first steam arises. Steam is not gas—according to the modern school concept. Roughly expressed, steam, which one can still see, is the same material that was in the water but is just split up into finer particles. Thus, we can say that water passes over into steam through heating. You can transform all, or at least most, substances into steam through a lower or higher or an extremely high temperature. You can take the heating still further, however. If you do so, the substances in question will no longer be visible, as it were; they will pass over into a really different form—a form we call the gas-form today. While the steam-form is a kind of intermediate between the water form and the gas-form, this gas-form is basically just the steam form at a higher level of development, that arose through subjecting it to a higher temperature. Before Helmont, the steam-form and the gas-form were not clear ideas. Comenius, too, worked with the steam-form.

Helmont came to understand the nature of gas with carbon dioxide, which he studied closely. Indeed, he connected ideas with carbon dioxide and other gases that the modern physicist and people in general no longer quite understand. Through his study it came to light that under various conditions, substances arrive at a state that he termed *gas*. A fundamental statement in Helmont's *Ortus Medicinae* is made in the sentence "Hunc spiritum, incognitum hactenus, novo nomine gas voco,"[†] which means: "Such spirit, which was not known until now, I will call gas." That is the first time that this word appeared in this type of study or treatise.

This sentence teaches us quite a lot. Above all, Helmont calls gas "spirit," so that it is clear that what he sees as gas was for him the instrument of a spiritual being. He had the feeling that he must address this transparent substance as spirit, and he gave this spirit the new name of *gas*. Let us grasp exactly what imagination he had in mind. He knew that when he cooled gas down, it took on peculiar appearances: dark, cloudlike elements formed. Gas becomes steam again and then watery, or fluid. For him, the gas was a basis—a clear, transparent foundation out of which something thick and concentrated came into being. He thought of gas as a parable in the same sense as Goethe, when he said: "Everything transitory is but a parable."† Helmont saw in this simple process how gas cools and condenses. For him, little worlds came forth out of the gas. A human being who felt this could still say: "Hunc spiritum incognitum gas voco."

The answer to the question of how all matter in the world originally came into being was clear to him. He knew that something filled the world that was perhaps very much finer than what he had discovered as gas. It was a substance through which light could pass and which people could not see at all; it was a transparent, radiant spirituality that contained no darkness. Just as steam separates itself out from this gas and looks like masses of fog, so, too, all things that now are minerals and plants and animals—all that we see in matter—have formed out of the transparent, clear infinity. All spiritual substance has become thickened, has condensed into the structures of today.

As early as ancient times and in primitive cultures, we find parables that are useful in calling forth a similar imagination. Primordial and also primitive peoples sometimes still look spiritually at what occurs outwardly in the material world. Such human beings know that breath comes out of their mouths and becomes steam in the cold air. They see that something is created within the soul that thickens out of the transparent clarity of human breath. And they feel in the breath of the soul, in the exhaling and condensing, a parable for the great macrocosmic process, the coming into being [the genesis] of the world. Hence, there is the view among many that the world is the result of a breathing out of the godhead. That is really an ancient imagination.

We must be clear about what this ancient imagination involves. This ancient imagination contains a conception of space completely different from the dry, abstract concept of space that we have today. What do modern people think about space? They imagine an unending expanse of emptiness, a great void that is nothingness. This is a concept you can find wherever space is discussed. What did those who based their thinking in spiritual science imagine about space? For them, space was outpoured, extended spirit, which has its comparison in the clear element out of which steam arises, the source from which all the seeds of things were created through the Word of the original spirit of God. Space is not an endless void, but rather original spirit. We ourselves are condensed space, born out of space. If all things were dissolved again, we would seem to have an unending emptiness or void around us. This apparent void contains all the things that were there before they dissolved. In truth, this endless void would be just as little a nothingness as is the gas into which substances have evaporated. Those who think esoterically understand this about space.

Helmont shows quite clearly that he had such an imagination behind his thinking, that he had the following thought:

> Such a gas as I have discovered is quite thin and permeable; light goes through it. No one has any idea at all of its presence, if he or she does not sense its effect there where the gas spreads itself out. Yet in relation to the primordial foundation, this gas is a condensation, a darkening. There is something else, more spiritual, at its foundation. We can discern the deeper element if we take the gas as a comparison—when we imagine the whole world proceeding out of the seed-rich space, like steaming and evaporating, and that the gas is a mist of the spirit itself, just as the steam is the mist of the gas.

Because he had this imagination in his soul, Helmont made a particularly beautiful statement: "Halitum illum gas vocavi, non longe a chao veterum secretum,"[†] meaning, "That breath which I have called 'gas' is not far different from the 'chaos' of the ancient ones." You see, he connects the concept gas with the word *chaos.* Yes, he fashioned the word *gas* entirely according to the word *chaos. Gas* is transformed *chaos.* Helmont formed this word to imbue it with his esoteric scientific concepts. That is an extraordinarily interesting scientific connection.[†]

Thus we are led by someone who knows about these matters to a concept of space that is not a sterile, empty, abstract one, such as physics knows, but rather one that is infinitely rich in seeds, for it contains, invisibly, the seeds of all things. The things that are made of matter today were all a mist and were condensed out of space. Space springs to life, becomes the seed of that which is spread out in the world. So we put in the place of empty, abstract space the living spirit out of which all things proceed. We transform in this way all kinds of abstractions into living concepts. It is good that we are moving away from such abstract concepts, which have a killing effect on all human thinking.

When we imagine the condition of space when it was still spiritual and follow with our souls how beings condensed out of this infinite space, according to its innate laws, we sense clearly the beautiful words of the Bible: "In the beginning God created heaven and Earth. The Earth was without form and void, and the spirit out of the godhead hovered, brooding over the deep." Think for a moment of what the pure, spiritually transparent space was like in the beginning. What took place in this pure, clear space? Let us imagine this very vividly: Here, in this space, air is spread out. My words are being spoken into the space where there is air. There arise vibrations, and the words press into your souls. Every word that is spoken forms itself in this space, which is filled with air. Imagine the air to be still; nothing is spoken. The air comes into regular movement through my speaking, and every word builds itself into forms in the air, still and invisible. Now imagine the space that stretches into infinity and is not an abstraction and, into this, the Word of God resounding and forming the space according to the Words that the godhead speaks. That was in the beginning. The Word resounded in space, and there arose first the spiritual world, the chaos, this mist structure that developed out of the space and which showed for the first time, in dimness, what would be formed later.

Now listen to the words of the Bible: "The chaos—this developing mist structure of the Earth—was still empty and without form, and the spirit of God worked and hovered, brooding over the depths." There we have the moment of the coming into being: that is the chaos. Very deep indeed are the imaginations at the foundation of such a religious document. Human beings must once more develop the feeling for understanding such a thing.

The chaos worked not only in the beginning of world evolution, but it continues to work. It is still present today. That which leads us behind the sky and into our daily life is the knowledge that this chaos is present, that just as the harmonious heavens, the beautifully formed worlds, are around us, so is the chaos. Everything is permeated with it. It was the first primordial forming. Then it darkened, it built seeds, and it formed the worlds into their present-day perfection. Just as when we have a gas mass and a part of this mass cools, such that between the individual parts there is still gas that works on, so also a part of the primordial spirit stayed back. In this way chaos works and lives on in our world. Everything is still permeated with chaos—every stone, every being. You yourself are permeated with this chaos. It is not only the beings in the outer sense world that are permeated with chaos but also your own soul and spirit. The soul and spirit of human beings who are in the world still participate in what has remained of the original chaos. Only a part separated itself out from the chaos. The chaos is still there all around us. It works in all beings and, at the same time, is the foundation of the continual, further-working fertility, or fruitfulness.

Let us build an imagination of how chaos works by way of a simple example. You see that the effect of chaos appears where there are waste products of, for instance, the animal organism. These waste products are apparent results of destruction, but this animal excrement, which is spread on the field as fertilizer by the farmer, forms the basis of renewed fertility. The new seedling comes forth because fertilizer was laid into the ground. What happened there? What was the fertilizer at first? It was all kinds of beautifully formed plants and other beings in the world, that which had formed out of the chaos. It took its course and served the animal as feed. The unusable matter was excreted through the laws that work in the body. The fertilizer mixed with the soil; the being returned to the chaos. The chaos works on in the fertilizer, in all that is thrown out. And unless you mix the chaos into the cosmos at some time, further development is never possible.

Through this process—an example of which we have examined at its lowest level—we can work our way up to grasping the fact that it is necessary for all evolution to free itself from the ancient causes and to somehow take in the chaos again. No one can continue to exist if only the cosmos works upon him. For what is the cosmos? The cosmos is nothing other than that which was formed out of preceding causes and forces. Not only all physical things but also all moral and intellectual teachings arise out of causes that were previously established. I want to make this clear with a radical example.

It is only cosmos working when, for instance, in Germany, Goethe, Schiller, Lessing, Herder, and Schelling have written their works† and then a schoolmaster comes along and recites the magnificent works and ideas of Goethe, Schiller, and the others. The schoolmaster would not be able to recite anything that was not already there beforehand. Or let us consider people in another field. They base their work completely on what has developed over time. This is not the case with genius. Genius works out of the chaos. It is unique, in that a new spark comes into the human soul. Fresh concepts arise and take effect. In genius we find the marriage of the cosmos with chaos.

No progress could come about if there were only outer causes, if these causes did not merge again into the chaos. By all earlier laws of effect being thrown back into the chaos, genius arises. And through the effect of genius, something comes out of other worlds—something that was not taken from the past but is brand new. In every moment the world must again become chaos. The marriage of the past with the present is a union of the cosmos with the chaos. From that union come the deep, significant feelings that the ancient human being had and that the esoteric researcher still has when the word *chaos* is spoken. For those who cannot sense it, chaos is muddled and unclear, just as the thoughts of a genius are without form and confused in the eyes of most people. But the feeling of formlessness and confusion—the way in which the thoughts of genius are typically sensed—is to be found only in human beings who consider simply the effects that derive from the past. New elements can come into being only out of the chaos, which must really unite with us, if we want to make a contribution to the progress of humanity.

The Theosophical Movement should be a movement that is able to fructify humanity with new spiritual seeds. Those who understand the Theosophical stream must realize that they cannot continue working only with what comes to us from old Father Cosmos. Instead, new sprouts of the spirit, streaming in from out of the chaos, must enter humanity. In this way, humanity will be fructified in the right sense.

The imaginations that humanity gains today through true Theosophy have not been taken from the past. Whoever, like a geologist, investigates the layers of the Earth and can speak only about what has come about in the sense world in the past, can never investigate what is important in terms of Theosophy: the knowledge of the future form of humanity, which enters the sense-perceptible cosmos from out of the chaos. For that reason, it is of the utmost importance that the human being, through the Theosophical worldview, takes on ideas, feelings, and will impulses that do not derive from our sense-perceptible cosmos but which come directly out of the form that the spirit had before it took outward shape. These come from the chaos. Such imaginations that are received from chaos are the symbols and signs brought in from higher worlds by the esoteric schools, and they form the foundation for all esoteric science and imaginative knowledge. These imaginations work on the human soul from out of the chaos. If they have a living effect, then the chaos weds itself with the human soul.

You remember the decoration of the congress hall in Munich. What was portrayed in the seven seals is not yet present in the cosmos; no one can find this portrayal in the cosmos of natural law. It will become form in the future, in what is to come. These imaginations still work from out of the chaos upon the human soul in such a way that we have an entire picture of the world in the manner I described in my introduction.† When they are properly taken in, they work in a living way and guide the human being into higher worlds. Then chaos works in the human soul and leads it into worlds that lie beyond the sense-perceptible universe. The human being must thus come to a new connection with the spiritual worlds; that is the reason that human beings reach for such pictures. When we come to such pictures, we sense the effect of the great power that works on through the eternity of the ages. We sense the overwhelming effect of that chaos which contains the seeds of all things. When we allow these seals to work upon us, they plumb the deepest sources of the soul.

In the seven seals, we see pictures of the astral world. In the seven columns, we find the concepts that come into our universe, into our world, when we examine the world of devachan. When you contemplate these column capitals, you will find that they work in you. When you live into them in a feeling way, you will discover that which orders your feeling in a way in which it could never be ordered within the sense world and which can provide a concept for you of that spiritual music or harmony of the spheres that is devachan. These capitals are a direct stimulus to lift our feelings out of the old connections and to bring them into entirely new ones. Through this alone something new can arise; that our feelings be torn away from the old connections and build new connections. We may not tear them away senselessly, though. If we do, we rip ourselves apart. We unite with the new connections when we take that which we allow to work upon our feelings, from the spiritual world, from the chaos. Thus, such imaginations belong to the means through which the spiritual-scientific stream in the world accomplishes its mission. All that appears in this world stream must be looked upon as a unity, for a single thought permeates the entire stream. Only when a single thought permeates this stream can we promise the [Theosophical] Movement its proper fruitfulness.

You can see for yourselves that these seals have a [positive] effect, yet they can also work in a very detrimental way. These seals are meant to lead the human being into the most beautiful spiritual harmony. Those, who contemplate them in a true Theosophical attitude and in a place where Theosophical life flows, will find that they have a soul-freeing and enlivening effect. If you were to hang them, for instance, in the dining room and examine them with everyday thinking, you would ruin your physical organism as far down as your digestion. These things cannot be enjoyed with an unholy soul, but rather, only in the proper mood. You see that a strong light can also have a strong shadow. A weak light has only a weak shadow. Theosophy may not be held at fault when it becomes darkness for those who enjoy it in an improper manner. We cannot work by talking abstractly, but rather by passing on what esoteric schools have to impart and giving the human being the means through which to engage with the larger scope of these things. Theosophy is not a playing with imaginations, but a real force that must flow into the spiritual life of humanity. Hence, we may not fool around with such matters, but must realize that these are effective forces. Taking our present example, it can be shown how encompassing the concept of chaos is for those who understand it correctly. All have known what stands behind the physical, out of which the physical is made and is born: the chaos. Whether the Greeks called it chaos, whether Genesis depicts it the way we have seen, or whether the Indian philosopher speaks of the *achaos*, the *akasha*, the esoteric schools will remind us that it is always the same as what was in the beginning and works on through all ages.

Only in that the human being unites with his or her true source, or beginning, can progress take place. For those who are bound to the sense world, chaos appears to be without form and confused. For those who know and understand, this is not the case. Those who penetrate it in the spiritual sense perceive how it is permeated with the resounding of the harmony of the spheres, of which the Pythagoreans spoke and whose translation into words is communicated to the public in the Theosophical Movement today, at just the right time. Because it is still possible for a few human beings, who stand out from the great majority, to receive words out of the spiritual world, the time has come to speak of these things.

All art has come out of these feelings. Just as earlier the ordering of the Corinthian and Ionian columns proceeded out of ancient Egyptian esoteric teaching, so these columns will become the expression for spiritual-scientific truths. New column arrangements will proceed out of them, for all art is but crystallized esoteric teaching. At one time, human beings sensed the working and weaving of the gods in the sacred groves. Who could not sense what was felt in a Gothic work of art, such as the cathedral in Milan! The same mood prevailed there as in the sacred groves of the Druids and Drottens. Thus, all future art will be crystallized esoteric teaching. The Gothic is nothing other than the crystallized esoteric teaching of the pre-Middle Ages. In the same way, that which we now clothe in words will be poured artistically into color and form in the future. The Theosophical stream will flow in a living way, not only when it streams in thoughts and words, but also when it imprints itself on the things around us, when it permeates all things.

Excerpts from the Discussion [Fragments]

The forces that the "hollow"-"I" calls forth [are an] intensification of the forces which are already present in the developing threefold nature below. When this trinity develops further, then the "hollow"-"I" arises. At a particular stage, these bodies are complete. When they are mature enough, they hollow themselves out as the self approaches and enters. Everything hollows itself out when it reaches its completion in evolution.

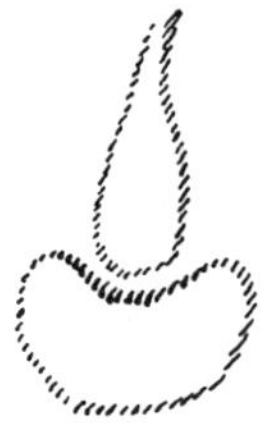

The "substantial"-"I"

The "hollow"-"I"

Let us think about the chaos, which—still perfectly transparent, spiritual—contains the seeds of things. Only through condensing can they ... [gap in notes]. This comes about because the spiritual presses out material in such a way that hollow spaces arise. When the spirit works, there arises a hollow space in matter. These spaces arise in all matter when the spirit works on it, when the spirit broods over it. The Logos bores holes into the space, in a manner of speaking; here is the principle of the words from the "Verses of Dzyan" in the *Secret Doctrine* [by Blavatsky].

Report on the Congress at the Sixth General Meeting of the German Section of the Theosophical Society†

RUDOLF STEINER

Berlin, October 20, 1907

From *Mitteilungen für die Mitglieder der Deutschen Sektion der Theosophischen Gesellschaft*, No. 6 [News for members of the German section of the Theosophical Society](February 1908)

. . .

What was further incumbent upon us, in the international connection, was the holding of the Munich Congress. You have seen what our intentions were through the arrangement of the congress space, the pictures of the seals and the columns with which the hall was decorated, and the nature of the program. They were to be a beginning towards not letting Theosophy be a mere sum of abstract dogmas but an influence on the life around us. No one can harbor the illusion that the harmony in connection with the whole arrangement of the Congress succeeded in being more than a weak beginning, compared with what lives as Theosophical thought. Yet, everything must have its beginning. If the German Section showed thereby only what intentions could hold sway with such a congress—if it showed how the life of the soul can make itself evident in form, in art, and in coming together with each other—then the German Section made such a contribution on this occasion. Out of such a stimulus, the force can develop that will make it possible gradually for the Theosophical Society not only to be a center for the spreading of this or that dogma, but to reach deeply into the whole life of the human being.

What is still to be noted is the circumstance that we went over the 4,500 Marks budgeted for the Congress, which we thought would suffice. The Congress was just that much more beautiful because of it. We must say with profound gratitude that a deep understanding of this situation was shown, especially in the German Section. We needed a lot of money. It became apparent, however, that when

Theosophical life matters, there is also understanding and an inclination to make a contribution. Therefore, there is no deficit to record.

We should stress no less strongly the very satisfying fact that those who could help worked in an immensely devoted manner. Everything that had to be done was done by our Munich friends, not only devotedly but also with comprehensive understanding, so that in this work there lived most beautifully what we call Theosophical unity and harmony. There was no one who was not prepared to do the highest spiritual work along with the smaller tasks that are necessary with such a congress. People who were never accustomed to such work in their lives lugged large things meant for this or that purpose. Some hammered, and others painted the columns and pillars. In short, it was all devoted work. Gifts from 1,000 Marks to ten pfennige were collected.

The management that Munich had undertaken was circumspect, even down to the labor that showed how the real accomplishment of a true working together brings about harmony among human beings. We brought it to the point that the deeply satisfying performance of *The Sacred Drama of Eleusis* could take place. Consider all that had to be done to make it possible—from the translation from the French to the sandals for the feet of the players, who were all members of the Theosophical Society and had to rehearse for weeks. If you knew how all of that went, how beautifully and harmoniously it took place and how the work was carried by the common thought and dedication of feeling, then you would realize the practical worth that results when a joint bond of work enfolds everyone. Just as the plant strives harmoniously toward the Sun, so also human beings become harmonious when they are governed by the same feelings.

We have the good spirit of the corps of co-workers on the Munich Congress to thank for the fact that it all came to fruition. In these preparations there truly lived the spirit of unity in the Munich work community, which could be, to a certain extent, a model for the way in which we in the Theosophical Society can act and work together. It is hoped that this somewhat different manner of working, which the German Section has undertaken in the past five years,[†] will be recognized in the international Theosophical Society and that it would also have a somewhat fructifying effect there. Only in this way can the international Theosophical Society flourish, if every section contributes what it can upon the altar of communal Theosophical international effectiveness.

It hardly needs to be said that the German Section of the Theosophical Society sends deeply felt thanks to Edouard Schuré, the author of the mystery drama. We should stress expressly that we owe a great debt of gratitude to Bernhard Stavenhagen, the famous pianist and sensitive composer, who in the midst of a rich and pressing workload undertook, at my request, to give us the gift of the musical part of the dramatic performance. All the participants will always remember the deep impression that this composer had on them. We all felt the beautiful unity of the musical creation with the mystery.

Pictures of the Apocalyptic Seals and Columns: An Introduction to the Portfolio of the Fourteen Plates

RUDOLF STEINER

October 1907

The fourteen plates here are reproductions of the seals and symbols that served as decoration of the interior spaces in which the Congress of the Federation of the European Sections of the Theosophical Society took place on May 18-21, 1907, in Munich. They are not just any symbols, which we can interpret intellectually; they are spiritual-scientific "script-symbols," which must be taken in a way that corresponds to true spiritual science. Spiritual science does not invent such symbols out of the intellect or the arbitrary imagination but merely describes what is present to spiritual perception in the supersensible worlds. No speculation or intellectual explanation—even if it is ever so clever—is appropriate for such symbols, because they are not just thought up. They give an actual description of what the seer perceives in invisible worlds. These reproductions have to do with the descriptions of experiences of the astral and the spiritual (devachan) worlds.

The seals of the first seven plates portray real facts of the astral world, and the seven columns depict the same of the spiritual world. While the seals convey directly the experiences of spiritual seeing, this is not precisely the case with the columns. For the perceptions of the spiritual world cannot be compared with a "seeing," but more with a spiritual "hearing." Here we must note that we should not think it similar to hearing in the physical world, for although it can be compared with physical hearing, it is quite different. The experiences of this spiritual hearing can be expressed in a picture only when we translate hearing out of the tones into form. That is what happened with these columns, whose essence is understandable only when we imagine the forms in a plastic, molding way (rather than as in painting).

In the sense of spiritual science, the causes of the things of the physical world are located in the supersensible, invisible worlds. Those things that reveal themselves physically have their archetypes in the astral world and their spiritual primordial forces (primordial tones) in the spiritual world. The seven seals give the astral archetypes of the evolution of humanity on the Earth in the sense of spiritual science. When the seer follows this evolution on the astral plane into the distant past ages or the far future, it presents itself in these seven seals. The seer does not have to invent anything but must simply understand the spiritually perceived facts.

SEAL I portrays comprehensively the entire Earth evolution of the human being. This seal, along with the others of the series, we can find described in a certain sense in the Revelation of John.† Whoever is able to understand this document in the spiritual-scientific sense, sees in it nothing other than a description given in words of that which the seer perceives on the astral plane as the archetypes of the evolution of humanity. Such a person also understands the first words of this document: "The revelation of Jesus Christ, which the god offered him in order to show his servant how the necessary events will take place shortly; this is sent in symbols by the angel to his servant John. This one has brought to expression the 'Word' of God and its revelation through Jesus Christ, in the way he has seen it."†

The symbols that he saw are portrayed by the recorder of the esoteric revelation. We find that the following seals are also similar to what is described in the Apocalypse, and yet not completely. For our pictures are based on a spiritual-scientific method, which is indeed in accord with all traditions and yet developed in its own form, corresponding to the modern spiritual needs that arose in the fourteenth century in those circles that had the task at that time to care for and nurture these things. Nevertheless, when it matters, the description will be given with reference to the Revelation of John (Apocalypse). It should be expressly noted that some pictures from the seven seals have already been made public in this or that modern work,† yet those who are initiated in such things will be able to find that these other reproductions stray in many points from the form given here, which presents the true spiritual-scientific foundation.

We can compare the first seal with the description in the Apocalypse:

> And I turned around to perceive the sound which came through to me; and there I saw seven golden candlesticks, and in the middle of the lights the image of the Son of Man, with a long robe and a golden girdle around the loins; and his head and hair shining white as white wool or snow, and his eyes sparkling with fire. And his feet were flowing fire, as if glowing in a fiery oven, and his voice was like the harmony of the rushing of many waters. And in his right hand were seven stars, and out of his mouth came a two-edged sharp sword, and the radiance of his countenance was like the shining Sun.†

The most encompassing secrets of the evolution of humanity are given there in general pictures. If we wanted to present a more detailed version of what the seer can see in these pictures, we would have to write a thick book. Only a few indications are given here. Every symbol, every form in the seals is full of meaning, and what is said here can impart only some of that richness. Among the organs and methods of expression of the human being† are some that, in their present form, represent the declining stages of evolution of earlier forms that have already gone beyond their point of perfection. Others represent the beginning stages of an ascending evolution. Such parts of the human being are as yet incomplete and will have entirely different tasks to fulfill in the future. One organ that will take a much higher form and be much more perfect in the future than it is now is the speech organ and everything connected with it.

We touch here on a great secret of existence, which is also the "mystery of the creative word." This is an intimation of the future condition of this organ—that it will one day become an organ of production (procreation) when the human being is spiritualized. In myths and religious narratives, this future spiritualized form is indicated through the appropriate picture of the fiery "sword" coming out of the mouth. The first stages of the Earth evolution of the human being took place when the Earth was still "fiery," and the first human embodiments developed out of the element of fire. At the end of the human's Earth evolution, human beings themselves will ray outward their inner being creatively through the force of the fire element. This development from Earth's beginning to Earth's end discloses itself to the seer when he or she perceives, on the astral plane, the archetype of the developing human being in the way it is reproduced in the first seal. The beginning of Earth evolution is presented in the fiery feet, and the end lies in the fiery countenance; the last perfect force to be achieved, that of the "creative Word," is represented in the fiery sword that comes out of the mouth. While this evolution runs its course, the development of human beings, along with the forces that unfold with it, is under the influence of forces expressed in the seven stars on the right. Thus, every line, every point in the seal, portrays a connection with the comprehensive mystery of the evolution of the human being.

SEAL II portrays one of the first conditions of the evolution of Earth humanity, with all that belongs to it. The Earth human in ancient times did not yet have what we call an individual soul. At that time, all that was present was what belongs to the animals, as beings that have remained behind at an earlier stage of the evolution of humanity: the group soul. When, through clairvoyant sight, we look into ancient times and we follow human group souls on the astral plane, it comes to light that their various forms can be traced back to four basic types. These are pictured again in the four apocalyptic animals of the second seal: the lion, the bull, the eagle, and that form which, as a group soul, is close to the individual soul of the present-day human being and is called the "human being." We touch here on the truth of what is often so dryly and allegorically construed with respect to the four animals.

SEAL III portrays the secrets of the so-called harmony of the spheres. The human being experiences these mysteries in the time between death and a new birth (in spirit land, or what is called devachan in conventional Theosophical literature). It must be remembered with all these seals that they represent only the experiences of the astral world. Still, worlds other than the astral world itself can be observed in this seal. We can examine our physical world according to its archetypes on the astral plane. The after-images of the spiritual world are to be seen on this plane. Thus, the third seal portrays the astral after-images of spirit land. The trumpet-blowing angels represent the primordial spiritual beings of world phenomena. The trumpet tones themselves are the forces that stream from out of these primordial beings into the world, and through which the beings and things of this world are built up and maintained in their development and working. The apocalyptic riders represent the main points of evolution through which the human individuality evolves in the course of many incarnations.† These are portrayed on the astral plane as the riders on the horses: a white gleaming horse, expressing a quite early stage of soul evolution; a fire-colored horse, pointing to the warrior stage of soul evolution; a black horse, corresponding to that soul stage in which only the outer physical perception of the soul is developed; and a green shimmering horse, the picture of the mature soul, which has dominion over the body (hence the green color, which brings to expression the life force working from within outward).

SEAL IV depicts, among other things, two pillars, the one coming out of the sea and the other out of the realm of the Earth.† In these pillars is indicated the mystery of the roles that the red (oxygen-rich) blood and the blue-red (carbon dioxide–rich) blood play in human evolution. The human "I" evolves in the Earth cycle by bringing its life to expression physically in the interaction between the red blood, without which there would be no *life*, and the blue blood, without which there would be no *knowledge*. Blue blood is the physical expression of the knowledge-giving forces that, in the human form, are connected with death, and red blood is the expression of the life that, in the human form, can give no knowledge. In their working together, the two portray the Tree of Knowledge and the Tree of Life, respectively—or both of the pillars, on which the life *and* the knowledge of the "I" develop to that point of perfection at which the human being will become one with the universal Earth forces. This last condition of the future is depicted in the upper body made of clouds and through the face that has taken on the spiritual forces of the Sun. The human being will then no longer take in from outside the "knowing," indicated in the middle of the seal, but will have devoured it from within. Through such a "devouring" on a higher plane of existence, the seven seals of the book open, as indicated on the third seal. Concerning this, in the Revelation of John, we find these meaningful words: "And I took the book out of the angel's hand and ate it."

SEAL V presents a higher stage of the evolution of the human being, as will come about when the Earth will have united again with the Sun and the human being will no longer work merely with Earth forces but with the Sun forces as well. The "woman" who bears the Sun is connected with this future human being. Human beings will have set outside themselves certain forces of a lower nature, which live *in* human beings now and hinder them from fully developing their higher spirituality. These forces are portrayed in the seals by the beast with "seven heads and ten horns" and by the Moon at the feet of the Sun-human. The Moon is for spiritual science the middle point of development of certain lower forces that still work today within the being of the human and which human beings of the future will force "under themselves," as it were.

SEAL VI portrays the cleansed human being, who not only is spiritualized but who has become strong in spirituality; this human being has not only overcome the lower forces but has transformed them in such a way that they stand reformed, at the human being's service. The tamed "animal" communicates this. In the Revelation of John we find its expression: "And I saw how out of heaven the angel descended, who held the key to the abyss and had in the hand a great chain. And he brought the dragon, the serpent of old which is the devil and Satan, under his control and bound him for a thousand years."

SEAL VII is the rendering of the mystery of the Holy Grail.[†] It is that astral experience which describes the universal meaning of human evolution. The cube represents the "world of space," which is not yet filled with physical beings or physical events. For spiritual science, space is not "empty," but rather is the invisible bearer of the seeds of all that is physical. Out of it the whole physical world condenses, as salt precipitates out of a still transparent solution. That which forms in the human being out of the world of space goes through development from a lower to a higher level. Firstly, to grow out of the three dimensions of space, expressed in the cube, are the lower human forces. These lower forces are illustrated by the two serpents [thus formed out of the six], bearing the purified higher spiritual nature portrayed in the world spiral. Through upward growth, the human being can become a receiver (a cup) for the taking in of the pure spiritual world-being, expressed by the dove. In this way, the human being becomes the master of spiritual world powers whose image is the rainbow. That is a quite sketchy description of this seal that bears within it immeasurable depths that can reveal themselves to devoted meditation. Written around this seal is the maxim of modern spiritual science: "Ex Deo nascimur; in Christo morimur; per Spiritum Sanctum reviviscimus": "Out of God I am born; in Christ I die; through the Holy Spirit I am reborn." The meaning of human evolution is indicated fully in this saying.

These seals were hung in the hall of the Munich Congress in such a way that between every two seals there stood one of the seven columns shown in Plates 20-26 at the back of the book. In the capitals of these columns is portrayed what the seer experiences in the spiritual world. The term "seer" is actually no longer appropriate in this realm, as the experience is the perception of the primordial forces that exist in spiritual tones. The sculpted forms of the capitals are translations of what the "seer" hears. These forms are in no way arbitrary, but come about in a completely natural way when the "seeing" human being allows the spiritual music (harmony of the spheres) that streams through his or her whole being, to work on the creating hand. The sculpted forms here are really a kind of "frozen music" that expresses world secrets.

That these forms should appear as column capitals is self-evident for those who understand the matter. The foundation of the physical evolution of Earth beings lies in the spiritual world. It is supported from there. All evolution is based on advancement through seven stages. (The number seven should not be interpreted as the result of a superstition, but as the expression of a spiritual lawfulness, just as the seven rainbow colors are an expression of a physical lawfulness.) The Earth itself strides in its evolution through seven conditions, which are characterized by seven planetary names: Saturn, Sun, Moon, Mars, Mercury, Jupiter, and Venus conditions.† It is not only the heavenly body that progresses in such a way through evolution; indeed, *every* evolution runs through seven stages that we distinguish with the expressions for the seven planetary conditions in the sense of modern spiritual science. The spiritual supporting forces of these conditions are reproduced through the forms of these column capitals.

We will not come to a true understanding of this matter if, in looking at the forms, we base it only on an intellectual explanation. We must look into the forms with artistic sensing and allow the capitals, as form, to work upon us. Those who do not do so will believe to have only allegories before them or, at best, symbols. They would then have misunderstood everything. The same motif goes through all seven capitals: one force works from above and one from below, and they strive toward each other and, when they meet, work together. These forces are to be sensed in their fullness and in their inner life; then it is experienced by the soul itself how the forces, in lively forming activity, expand, contract, intertwine, open, and so on. One will be able to feel this complexity in the way one can feel the plant developing itself out of its living forces. One will be able to sense how the line of force grows vertically in the column and unfolds in the plastic form of the capitals, which open to the approaching forces from above so that a meaningful bearing capital comes about.

First the force from below develops in the simplest manner, and the force from above strives just as simply toward it (Saturn column); then the forms fill up from above and form into peaks from below, and the lower forms move off to the sides. At the same time, these lower forms open themselves up into living structures (Sun column). Then the upper part becomes more diverse; a peak that was pushed out turns into a fructifying principle, while the lower part transforms into a fruit bearer. The force motif between these two becomes a bearing support, because the relationship of the intermediate parts was not felt to be strong enough as a bearing force (Moon column). Furthermore, there entered in a separation between the lower and the upper parts. The strong bearers of the Moon capital have themselves become column-like, and the upper and lower that lie between have grown together into one form; from above, a new motif is indicated (Mars column). The formation out of the combination of the upper and the lower took on life and now appears as a staff that is wound about by serpents. We can have a sense of how this motif grows organically out of the one before. The middle forms of the Mars capital have disappeared; its force is absorbed by the supporting inner part of the capital. The intimations of form from before in the Mars capital that are coming from above have become fuller (Mercury column). Now the form has simplified once more but includes the fruit of the diversification that has taken place. The upper element opens up, cuplike, and the lower simplifies life into a chaste form (Jupiter column). The last condition shows this inner fullness with outer simplification most deeply. The growth forms from underneath have enticed a fruit-bearing cuplike form from above (Venus column).

Whoever can sense all of what is expressed in these columns of world events, experiences the comprehensive laws of existence that solve the riddles of life in a totally different way from the abstract laws of nature. These images are intended to provide a sample of how spiritual vision can become artistic form, life. Take note that the images reproduce living forces of existence of the higher world, and these higher spiritual forces work deeply upon the observer of the seals. They work directly on corresponding forces that slumber in every human being. However, the effect of these seals is only correct when one observes them with the appropriate inner soul state. Whoever views them with Theosophical ideas in their minds and with Theosophical feelings in their hearts will take in something most sacred from them. Those who want to hang the seals anywhere or place them where they survey them with ordinary thoughts and feelings will be negatively affected, and this effect can go so far as to become a bad influence on bodily life. One must comply with this admonition and enter only into such a relationship with the seals that is in harmony with devotion to the spiritual world. These seals should serve to decorate a space serving the higher life. Never again should we find or study them in a place where the thoughts of the human being are not in harmony with them.[†]

The History of Our Society: Four-Times-Seven Years Ago

MARIE STEINER

Essay from *Was in der Anthroposophischen Gesellschaft vorgeht. Nachrichten für deren Mitglieder* (1935) [What's happening in the Anthroposophical Society: news for its members]

The Munich Congress of the Federation of the European Sections of the Theosophical Society took place at Whitsun in 1907. Dr. Steiner attempted, through the decor of the space and in the choice of artistic offerings, to bring that to outward expression, which spiritual goals placed in the stream of time and world events. The Theosophical Movement is to be credited with having pointed to the ancient wisdom that runs as a uniting band through all religions. But Theosophy, with its Oriental tendency, did not agree with the point of view that the general cultural level of humanity has ascended gradually and that human self-consciousness, through which an individual "I" understands itself within the divine Self, has evolved and developed. Theosophy did not have this understanding of historical evolution and the meaning of Christianity. In that Rudolf Steiner pointed to the Western (Occidental) mystic, to the connection of Christianity with the old mystery knowledge,[†] and to modern Christian esotericism, which takes the present into account and is also the source of inspiration for Goethe, he was known as the bringer of a new element. In this regard and despite his initial resistance, he was called into the Theosophical Society as teacher and leader of still unknown areas of knowledge. His books were respected and translated abroad.

On the occasion of this Congress of the European sections, the new element, which was accepted at first with gratitude, was to come to expression in the outer forms of the pictures and through the choice of literary work. The attempt was to be made to fructify more intensively the artistic life of the society, in order to awaken an understanding of the significance of art in the spiritual life of humanity; it is an understanding that had been missing to a very great extent. The impression was enormous. The festive red with which the walls were covered had an enlivening effect on some participants like the power of the resurrection; on others, it worked almost like divine wrath, for they could not master their fury. In addition, the organizing committee, to which Dr. Steiner did not belong, insisted upon choosing Dr. Steiner as president of the Congress, instead of Mrs. Besant, who expected to be the obvious choice.† There was nothing else he could do but offer her the position of honorary chairperson. The German Section acted demonstratively and necessarily against the work with mediumistic declarations which had begun during the long illness and passing of Colonel Alcott in Adyar.† The choice of Rudolf Steiner for president rather than Mrs. Besant was necessary also for the special character of the Munich events to be maintained.

The seals indicated secrets that were not yet unlocked to most participants and which either ignited a new desire for knowledge or offended the loved opinion that one had oneself already come so magnificently far in knowledge. Greek history spoke its eternal, living word from the stage in Schuré's reconstruction of the Eleusinian drama. The column motifs told the primordial story of the evolution of humanity in picture form. They encouraged the desire for picture forming; they let the new building idea become deed. Realities stood behind these symbols, and they had an effect. The essence of so many riddles of existence was combined in the basic principles of the pillar wisdom that proclaims the secret of the blood, which held the attention of the onlookers in the front of the hall. In the red of the program there shimmered for the first time the initials of the threefold statement of objectives [EDN ICM PSSR] so familiar to us and containing in the symbols the source of being, of life, and of becoming.

The reality of these working forces was so strong that they could become the impulses which, on the one hand, made the Mystery Dramas possible, like a joyful gift of the spiritual. On the other hand, they led to the courageous decision to erect a building specially to frame the mystery plays and for Rudolf Steiner's spoken word. In the form of the Congress of 1907, in the Kaim-Säle in Munich, lay the germ for the establishment of the recurring festival plays in the course of the year and for the Dornach building (the first Goetheanum), which was at first meant to be in Munich. Here lies the starting-point for what led to separation from the Theosophical Society. Effect and counter-effect were equally strong here. The Theosophists refused to accept the element of Western and Christian esotericism in their old and new forms; we, however, had to strongly reject the reaching back to atavistic forces and to the mediumistic tendency that was coming out of Adyar. When the name of Christ was usurped for the nonsense that went on with the "Order of the Star of the East"† and, at the same time, pressure was exerted through impure methods on the leadership of the Anthroposophically-oriented movement, it came to a separation and, later, to the founding of the Anthroposophical Society. The inner soul separation first came to expression in those days of the Munich Congress.

Thus, many stimuli were present then that have become components of our Anthroposophical life. Faust's regaining strength after the mental breakdown in the Ariel scene†—which has belonged to our annual Whitsun program since the art of eurythmy came into being—could be spoken as a monologue at that time. Dr. Steiner later described these stages for us in detail: this extinguishing of consciousness after a difficult agony, a diving down into the elemental world, a bathing in the dew of the ether after going through the flaming, scorching fire-sea—the recapturing of Earth consciousness. "In the colorful reflection, we have life." Here we have Faust's re-enlivening! Here lies the starting point for what we have retained as the wonderful commentaries on Goethe's *Faust.*†

The Congress in Munich

Mathilde Scholl†

From *Mitteilungen für die Mitglieder der Deutschen Sektion der Theosophischen Gesellschaft*, No. 5 [News for the members of the German section of the Theosophical Society] (August 1907)†

This year's Congress of the Theosophical Society, which occurred at the time of Whitsun in accordance with the decision of the Paris Congress last year, and which was prepared by the German Section, took a quite significant course.

At this, the first congress held in their region, the German Section had the great joy of greeting Mrs. Besant, who was here after a two-year absence from Europe and, on the occasion of her visit in Munich, lectured again for the first time. A large number of national and foreign members of the society also came; including the Munich members, about six hundred participants attended the Congress. After the meeting of the international committee took place, according to the statutes, on Friday evening in the rooms of the Munich Lodge, the four-day Congress was opened at 10:00 A.M. on Saturday, May 18, by the General Secretary of the German Section, Dr. Rudolf Steiner.†

After a musical introduction, of Johann Sebastian Bach's Toccata in F-major, performed by Mr. Emanuel Nowotny, Dr. Steiner greeted the section representatives and the participants of the Congress. Above all, he spoke heartfelt, eloquent words to Mrs. Besant, thanking her for coming and for honoring the Congress with her presence. At the same time, he asked her to take on the honorary presidency.... At this point he remembered president-founder Colonel Olcott,† who had passed away. The assembly stood as he spoke. Among other things, he said that Colonel Olcott had possessed an extraordinary organizational genius, which was needed to give the Theosophical Society the necessary direction on the physical plane. Olcott's work was of great worth, because he respected the being of every individual in his or her striving to develop. After this address of the General Secretary of the German Section, the representatives of the various countries' sections brought greetings to the Congress from their members. The representatives and secretaries from England, France, Holland, Belgium, Scandinavia, Italy, Hungary, Bohemia, Russia, Bulgaria and the United States of America all gave, in their own language, an almost perfect, vivid picture of the widening circles of the Theosophical Society. Then, Mrs. Besant greeted the Congress....

The participants of the assembly made use of the opportunity to look more closely at the impressive décor of the large concert hall as well as the small unified, fascinating picture collection in the entrance hall. The first sight of the large hall covered with red material made a special impression on the guests; the longer one looked, the more the intensive, but not harsh, color of the room called forth a calming, if not uplifting, mood. This mood was supported by a number of sculptural works of art, seven mighty painted columns, seven round paintings [seals] with symbolic representations that hung on the walls, along with the busts of Schelling, Hegel, and Fichte† at the front of the stage on which the representatives of the sections sat, and two powerful round pillars with spherical ends on which the following inscriptions could be read:

J

In pure thinking you find
The self that can hold itself.

Transform thought into an image
And you will experience creative wisdom.

B

Concentrate feeling into light
And you will reveal the formative power.

Realize the will into being-ness
And you will create in world being.

Saturday afternoon was dedicated to lectures and performances....

At approximately 8:00 P.M. the same day, the congress participants came together in the concert hall for a declamatory and musical performance, which was suitable for bringing members closer together socially, because long intermissions were interspersed between the various numbers. A richly set buffet in the green-decorated room was supposed to serve this purpose as well. After the Prelude and Fugue in B-flat by Johann Sebastian Bach were played by Mr. Emanuel Nowotny, who gave masterly performances of all the organ offerings during the Congress, Miss Marie von Sivers recited excerpts from the second part of Goethe's *Faust*, which specifically highlighted the spiritual depths of this work. Then Alice von Sonklar and Toni Völker played Robert Schumann's atmospheric "Pictures out of the East" on the piano, while Gertrud Garmatter sang Franz Schubert's "To the Music" and "You Are the Peace." Last, Toni Völker played a pastoral and a capriccio by Scarlatti on the grand piano. After these very pleasant offerings, the participants remained together several hours in enthusiastic conversation.

The Congress opened on Sunday, May 19, at 10:00 A.M., with Johanna Fritsch, Marika von Gumppenberg, and Hermann Tuckerman playing the first movement of the Trio in E-flat for piano, violin and horn by Johannes Brahms; it is a work full of feeling. Then Mrs. Besant gave her noteworthy lecture, "The Place of Phenomena in the Theosophical Society."...

The second lecture of the afternoon was "The Rosicrucian Initiation," in which Rudolf Steiner examined the methods for attaining knowledge of spiritual worlds in accordance with the leading esoteric path in the West since the fourteenth century. He likewise discussed humanity's need for these methods in the present evolutionary period.

At 5:00 P.M. on Sunday, *The Sacred Drama of Eleusis*, a mystery play by Edouard Schuré (translated from the French), with music by Bernhard Stavenhagen, was performed. This took place on the stage of the hall, which was framed with painted pillars... The poetically beautiful work created a festive mood, for which Dr. Steiner was to be thanked for his careful preparations, down to the minutest details. The gestures of the cast, which were executed according to his direction, came to expression like those of antiquity. His direction strove not to limit the personal characteristic of the performer; it was meant much more to intensify a mood of enthusiasm for the beautiful work, out of which the united ensemble acting of the entire cast arose on its own. The play was arranged according to Dr. Steiner's indications, and the costumes, decorations, and all the details of the scenery were made according to his intentions. Those who had the opportunity to attend the evenings of script readings and rehearsals know what a vast amount of work he had to accomplish. Bernhard Stavenhagen's music introduced the ensuing scenes in a mood of solemn preparation. By means of the music's rich instrumental arrangement, into which the organ was integrated, and in dramatic note sequences, it seemed to point to a mysterious world occurrence, which the audience then was meant to see and experience on the stage. The engaging effect of its majestic tones asserted itself overall. The performance ran until 7:30 P.M., after which the participants spent the evening together socially, enjoying a buffet in one of the side rooms.

The third day of the Congress began on Monday, May 20, at 10:00 A.M. with the reading of Goethe's "Prometheus" and "Song of the Spirits over the Waters" by a Cologne member, Mr. Richard Jürgas, who recited with beautiful speech of impressive power. Then the participants had the great joy of hearing a second lecture from Mrs. Besant....

After these lectures, our member, Mrs. Hempel, pleased the participants with her excellent singing. Then Dr. Carl Unger of Stuttgart spoke on "The Paths of the Theosophical Worldview." It was his intention to describe the work of the Stuttgart Lodge. Connecting with Dr. Steiner's book *Theosophy*, he tried to clarify the relationship of the member of the lodge to communications out of the supersensible world from the leadership of the lodge. He connected closely with those philosophical teachings that can throw a light on our spiritual existence. His precise explanations met with great approval from the assembly. After Dr. Unger had spoken, Mrs. Elise Wolfram expounded on "The Esoteric Basis of the Siegfried Saga."...

In the afternoon meeting, beginning at about 3:30 P.M., Baroness Gumppenberg read a work by Arvis Knös in English: "Absolute and Relative Truths." Then Dr. Rudolf Steiner held a lecture "Planetary

Evolution and the Evolution of Humanity." In lengthy, detailed explanations, he showed how the evolution of the macrocosm is connected with the evolution of the microcosm. He explained that we can observe seven stages of our planet—three before and three after the present one. These are the Saturn, Sun, Moon, which preceded our present Earth condition (Mars and Mercury conditions) and those that are still to follow—the Jupiter, Venus, and Vulcan conditions.

The third day ended at 8:00 P.M., when the participants of the Congress assembled in the concert hall for musical performances, which were accompanied by an invitation to tea during the intermissions....

The meetings on the last day of the Congress, Tuesday, May 21, began with an adagio out of Violin Concerto op. 16 by Max Bruch, performed by Johanna Fritsch and Paulina Friess, and Mr. Richard Jürgas's recitations of the thoughtful, deeply moving poetry of our member Mia Holm. There followed an open discussion of Theosophical matters, specifically about the necessity of nurturing esotericism within the society. Those who took part in the discussion were Mr. Jules Agoston of Budapest, Bernhard Hubo, Ludwig Deinhard, Dr. Carl Unger, Michael Bauer, D. Nagy, Mr. Wedgewood, Miss Sivers, and Mrs. Elise Wolfram. The discussion was initiated by Jules Agoston, who stressed the necessity of nurturing the spiritistic experiment.† Bernhard Hubo then developed an opposing point of view based on his long years of experience. Ludwig Deinhard discussed the necessity for the Theosophical circle to become acquainted with the scientific attempts to penetrate into the deeper foundations of soul life. It is not possible to report here on the rich, many-sided speeches of the speakers I have named. It is just as impossible to report on the stimulating perspectives that Mr. Nerei of Budapest offered on "Education Questions" in the afternoon discussion. At the end of these discussions, Dr. Rudolf Steiner also said several things about education.

Then Dr. Steiner gave an explanation of the arrangement of the concert hall, which, like the design of the admission ticket and program brochure, was fashioned in accordance with Rosicrucianism. He stated that there was a good reason for the choice of the red color for the hall. When we see the red color in our surroundings, the complementary color forms within us. One can remind oneself of the role that red plays in the soul life of the child. The Bible says: "Unless you become as a child, you cannot enter the kingdom of heaven." Dr. Steiner went on to say that exoteric centers, in which secret teachings are discussed outwardly and in symbols, carry the blue color. The Rosicrucian worldview expressed the esoteric in the color red. If this Rosicrucian worldview had come completely to expression in the decoration of the hall, there would have to have been a blue ceiling spread out above the red walls.

With respect to the two round pillars, with the inscriptions already cited, Dr. Steiner commented that they played an important role in Rosicrucianism, because they have a connection to the Golden Legend. The legend is as follows: When Seth was mature, he was allowed to wander to paradise and gain insight into it. The angel with the fiery sword allowed him to pass by and enter the place from which the human race had been driven as it climbed out of the bosom of the godhead in order to clothe itself in earthly sheaths. There Seth, the substitute son of Adam, saw something special. (He gained an insight into an etheric-physical occurrence.) He saw two trees, the Tree of Life and the Tree of Knowledge (or of death), intertwined with each other. From them he took three seeds[†] and laid them in the mouth of his dead father, Adam. Out of Adam's grave there grew a mighty tree, which revealed itself to many in jets of flame, and its glow formed into the letters that mean: "I am Who was, Who is, and Who will be." This tree divided into three parts. Seth took wood from it, and the wood was used in manifold ways. The staff of Moses, with which he performed wonders, was made from it. Likewise were the beams of Solomon's temple erected with it. Then, when the time came that the human being no longer understood the old mysteries, the wood was thrown away. But it was also used to build the bridge over which the Savior went on his way to the cross. The cross itself was also fashioned out of the tree that had grown from Adam's mouth.

Dr. Steiner went on to say that this legend has a deep symbolic meaning. One should think of the Rosicrucian initiation, specifically the fourth stage, which portrays the creating of the philosopher's stone. It is a matter of the production of red blood. Red blood is the result of the breathing in of oxygen. When the Golden Legend and the Bible point to such an important moment, to Seth's entering again into paradise, it raises the question: How did this come about? We must ask which physical process took place parallel to the climbing out of the bosom of the godhead. It is said: "God blew the living breath into the human being, and he became a living soul." The development of the breathing of oxygen is portrayed there pictorially.

There was a time when there were no lungs in the organization of the physical human being, when human beings more or less floated in the fluid element, in which they had a kind of air bladder that only later developed into the lungs. This air bladder that the human once used has transformed into lungs, and this process of reorganization can be traced. It shows itself as that event which the Bible expresses with this picture: "And God breathed the breath of life into Adam." With this breathing of the breath into Adam, the production of the red blood is instilled. In this way, the human's descent is connected with the generation of the red blood tree within the human being.

Of this living tree, the esotericist says that it is the Tree of Knowledge. That is the sin, the erecting of the red blood tree, which is the true Tree of Knowledge. God drove the human being out of paradise so that the human would not partake of the Tree of Life. That is the tree of the red-blue blood. This red-blue blood is a poison, a death substance. The red-blue tree was planted in the human being at the same time as the red tree. When the human being still rested in the bosom of the godhead, the godhead was able to intertwine life and knowledge in the human being. We can foresee a time when human beings, through their expanded consciousness, will have within themselves a tool with which they can bring about the transformation of the blue blood into the red. Thus, one looks to a time in which human beings will have the plant nature in themselves, a point when human beings will have within themselves the tool with which they can bring about this transformation.

Thus, there is in the human being a tree of red blood, or the outer instrument of "I"-knowledge, and a tree of blue blood, or the expression of death. In the future, the tree of death will be transformed into the Tree of Life. The whole life of the human being rests on these two trees, on their alternating effects. That Seth was permitted to enter paradise and see how the two trees join together, indicates that he was allowed to become an initiate. He took three seeds and laid them in Adam's mouth. From that grows the threefold higher human being. Human beings have, as an inclination within themselves, manas, buddhi, and atman (spirit self, life spirit, and spirit human). In the human predisposition—and thus in Adam's—the threefold element is present. Seth, the initiate, sees them. The legend expresses the evolution of humanity that leads to initiation. Out of spiritual power and the knowledge that the threefold tree, the tree of the eternal, rests in the present human being, we progress forward and receive the magic staff: the staff of Moses, the wood of Solomon's temple, the wood of the cross, the symbol of initiation. Thus the legend shows us how the initiate looks to a future condition.

The initials "J B" on the two round pillars are the first letters of veiled words; the sayings on them should ever and again be thoughtfully considered. Those who meditate on the words under the "J" of the red pillar imbue their red-blood soul with knowledge that leads to the goal. Those who meditate on the verse that stands under the "B" of the blue pillar, fill the life soul with power. This power works magically when the soul is stimulated by the second saying. An intensification of the power of knowledge to magical effect lies in the transition from the first to the second saying.

The seven round pictures on the walls form the symbolic expression of specific ancient wisdom; they portray the seven seals of ancient wisdom. The seven seals of the Apocalypse of John are, in their way, an interpretation of this wisdom. The seals were painted by Miss Clara Rettich of Stuttgart, according to the esoteric indications given. Every detail of these seals has meaning; when one devotes oneself to such a picture properly, specific feelings arise, through which spiritual forces that slumber in the soul are stimulated. The first seal shows a man with a flaming sword in the mouth, an image pointing toward a later evolutionary state of the human being. That which realizes itself instinctively in the reproductive drive, the creating of material-filled forms, will later be formed consciously through the force that flows in speech today. Every word produces an air form. If these forms were to harden, we would see a solid body. The spirit of the Logos resounded in space, and the rest is a solidifying process. Everything that exists is the condensed Word of God and condensed divine force. There are connections between the present-day human being's lower drives and human speech. The larynx will become the future reproductive organ raised to spirituality. The speech of the human being will transform into a higher force of reproduction.

The spirits that were our ancestors were called fire-spirits, because they were connected with the fire as we are with the air. Human beings will one day evolve again from air-spirit to fire-spirit. Out of their bodies will then flow the force that pours out from the fire-spirits. That is contained in the flaming sword as an astral imprint. The eternal being of the human is, at the same time, the divine, the divine creator. That in us which goes through all incarnations is of the same nature as that which created the entire seven-stage planetary sequence. As an indication of this, the man with the flaming sword in the mouth, which portrays this being, holds seven stars in his right hand.

The second seal presents the four apocalyptic animals: lion, eagle, bull (cow), and human. The four animals brought together in a circle have significance. It is known that animals today have no "I"-soul, but rather a group soul on the astral plane. The circle that the animals build represents the astral plane. The human being also passed through a group soul state; in the Lemurian epoch the human group soul transformed to an individual soul. The symbol for this condition lies in the forms of the earlier group souls. The group soul that makes the transition to individuality is characterized as human. Out of the four typical group souls of lion, eagle, bull, and human, the human being went forth with the individual soul, and the human being will, in the future, return to this group soul. The most highly developed human soul, which is individualized on the astral plane, is portrayed as the lamb in the middle of the seal, as it was in Christianity.

In a circle around the symbolic animal forms are the seven colors of the rainbow, which indicate the sevenfold creative principle. It must be noted with respect to the numbers I-XII, which can be read in the rainbow like the numbers of a clock, that the circumstances which the seal portrays are connected with the fact that the Earth, Sun, and Moon were once one body. This organization was necessary so that the human being could have a group soul. Our present division of time is connected with the place and movement of the cosmic bodies. In that ancient time the Earth did not orbit the Sun. Relationships were different then; there were no days or hours. The Sun moved on its path through space, and there was a great cosmic dial that showed the places the Sun passed; that is portrayed by the twelve numerals on this seal clock. Its hour hand passed two times around the dial—for in olden times, the Sun passed not once but twice through the zodiac: once each through a time of light and a time of darkness. This twofold circling was called esoterically the "passing by the Elder Brothers of the cosmic order." They are the twenty-four Elders.

The third seal shows an open book surrounded by bowls and trumpet-blowing angels, which are encircled, in turn, by flowing light and color. When we ascend from the astral plane to the devachan plane, we have the experience that the world of streaming light and color is pervaded by the harmony of the spheres. The Pythagoreans spoke of this, and so did Goethe: "Intoning, the new day is born for spirit ears; it trumpeted, horns blew,"† and so on. The words of the Apocalypse also refer to this plane in this way; one recognizes the allusion to the world of tone. After the astral pictures from the Apocalypse have been unsealed, the trumpets of the angels sound, and there opens up the world of devachan. The bowls signify the bowls of wrath. If love is to be developed, wrath must be done away with; hence are the bowls of wrath poured out. Lastly, the book represents the human being as the image of eternal world evolution. When human beings know this, they can read their own selves. If we ourselves are become a book, then we have arrived at the moment of initiation in which we eat the book. The next seal presents that picture.

The fourth seal portrays two pillars with a book, over which floats a cloud. We are meant to recognize the present-day air in the cloud. Out of this air will develop the force of production, the power to shape matter. The form in the cloud over the pillars is the initiated human being who has eaten the book, and this human being generates the force of production; this is characterized in the face. The human being's vision is then a seeing into the astral world, which proceeds out of the surrounding rainbow colors.

The fifth seal shows the so-called Sun-woman, a feminine form that stands on the Moon and stamps down the dragon. Before her body, a sun gleams. This picture shows that Earth and Sun were once united and that the unusable element was eliminated as Moon. In all mystical writings the conquering element is characterized as feminine. When the Earth reunites with the Sun, the human being will become the Sun-woman; that which must be eliminated is portrayed as the Moon being trod underfoot, and the unusable portion is depicted as the dragon.

The sixth seal shows a being that overcomes the dragon. This is the human being who will have overcome and bound the lower nature. When this is achieved inwardly—when the kama[†] is overcome and trod underfoot—such conditions, as are portrayed here, assert themselves. The initiate ensures that it occurs; the seventh seal shows that. We see in it the outer image of the Grail above a transparent cube, which represents pure, transparent carbon. There the human being recognizes, in addition to ordinary space with three dimensions, counter-space with three dimensions. Thus, in mirror image, ordinary space is confronted by counter-space, indicated in the seal by the violet-blue winding arrow-like formations. This demonstrates the devotional nature of knowledge, which the human being must develop in order to rise to this state. At that point we grasp the world spiral, which will then be fiery, like the glowing red color of the spiral shape in the representation of the seal. Then arises the pure, downward-turned chalice, or cup, that floats above the spiral. The human cup will again become chaste and pure and will turn downward. The purified human being is portrayed in the form of the dove, as the human being who has become guiltless.

The same process of development is expressed in the columns of the hall. They represent the planets. The motifs of the capitals are such that they bring about feelings that grasp something of the streams that are present in these cosmic bodies. The first half of Earth incarnation had a particular characteristic that stood under the influence of the force of Mars. Now the Earth is under the influence of the Mercury forces. For this reason, esotericism speaks not of the Earth but of the first half and second half, of Mars and of Mercury. Rudolf Steiner leaves the last condition out as the octave to the prime. Thus, the seven planets—Saturn,

Sun, Moon, Mars, Mercury, Jupiter, and Venus—come about, whose names are also contained in the days of the week.

For the end of the Congress, the participants came together again in the concert hall for musical offerings. As given in the program, the following performances were heard:

"Adagio in D-major" by Adolf Arenson—Adolf Arenson, piano; Johanna Fritsch, violin; Dr. Carl Unger, violoncello

"Tröstung Nr. 1: Werde Heiter, Mein Gemüter" ("Comfort") by Felix Mendelsohn-Bartoldy—Hilde Stockmeyer, soprano

"Ave verum" by Wolfgang Amadeus Mozart—Gertrud Garmatter, alto; Emanuel Nowotny, organ accompaniment

Recitation—Mrs. Rieper

Solos for Violin by Johann Sebastian Bach: Air; Gavotte—Johanna Fritsch and Pauline Friess

Variation of the Choral "Sei gegrüßt, Jesu gütig" ("Greetings, Dear Jesus") by J. S. Bach—Emanuel Nowotny, organ

The composition by Adolf Arenson proved to be a distinguished work of chamber music, which can be praised for its noble instrumentation and soul-deepening, emotional content.

The Congress came to an end with brief closing addresses from the representatives of individual sections; Mr. Wallace spoke for the British; Miss Aimée Blech as substitute for Dr. Pascal, who had to leave early for health reasons; Mr. Fricke for Holland; and Professor Penzig for Italy.

Then Mrs. Besant directed deeply touching words to the participants. Lastly, Dr. Rudolf Steiner spoke a few words of farewell to all who had come to the Congress and thanked them for their thoughtful participation. He communicated that the next congress would take place in two years in Budapest, where, it was hoped, all could assemble in the same spirit as in Munich.

The sculptural works, which were all from Dr. Ernst Wagner of 29 Hohenzollernstraße, Munich, and were exhibited in the main hall, are not to be taken as formed in the sense of Rosicrucianism but as work created out of the spirit of Theosophy. There were four busts and also pictorial works [literal translation]: "The Praying," "Relief for a Crypt Chapel," "Grave Relief," "King's Child," "Resolution," "Sibyls," "Relief for a Burial Niche," "Pain," "Christ Mask," "Mask," "Death," and a bronze statuette. Among the busts was an accomplished bust of Dr. Rudolf Steiner on a black-and-white marble pedestal. A relief of Colonel Olcott was sent by M. Cailland of Paris, and a sketch, "H. P. Blavatsky," by Julia Wesw-Hoffmann. "The Great Babylon" came from Mr. Haß of Munich, and a small tapestry from Miss Lehmann of Munich. The sources for the exhibit of paintings, reproductions, and other items in the anteroom, were as follows:

Etchings by Hans Volkert;† reproductions of two pictures by Gustave Moreau;† reproductions of two pictures by Schmiecher; a statuette, "The Master," by Heymann; a painting, "Out of Deep Need," by Stockmeyer; reproductions of various paintings by G.F. Watts;† three reproductions of works by Leonardo; paintings by Kalckreuth the Elder;† landscapes by Sophie Stinde;† five pine studies by Haß;† "After the Storm," "Fairy Tale," "The King's Daughter," and "The Storm Cloud," a reproduction by the painter Knopf.

Through the décor of the hall, in which the signs of the zodiac were present in the columns and seals, as well as through the mystery play—and indeed, through the organization of the whole Congress—the attempt was to be made, as Dr. Steiner noted, to show art in closer connection to real-life occurrences. If we want to see a cultural factor of significance in art again, as it had in antiquity, then it must seek a connection to the processes of life lying behind the manifestations. Artists must gain the power to intimate the processes of life themselves in pictorial and sculptural form.

About the Munich Congress

LUDWIG KLEEBERG†

From *Wege und Worte: Erinnerungen an Rudolf Steiner aus Tagebüchern und Briefen* [Ways and Words: reminiscences of Rudolf Steiner from diaries and letters]

The year 1907 brought the Theosophical Congress to Munich. Sophie Stinde was named as secretary of the Congress and Pauline von Kalckreuth as treasurer. There the work was placed in true and energetic hands. In July 1906, both friends were at the Landin estate in the Mark, along with Marie von Sivers and Dr. Steiner. Dr. Steiner wanted to work quietly there on his *Lucifer*. Here they could discuss matters concerning the Congress. Sophie Stinde wrote me: "There will be a winter full of strenuous work. Whitsun is quite early next year; the Congress will most likely be in the first half of June, however. In any case, you must come to it. I will take care of your travel expense and accommodations.... We are assuming, for now, that Annie Besant will come, but it is not at all certain. In any case, our General Secretary, Dr. Steiner, will be the president. We hope, however, that Annie Besant will come as our honored guest."

It was suggested before the general meeting, in October 1906, to postpone the Congress until later, as Whitsun would fall too early. Steiner had recommended Whitsun, however. As he said, there are—thank God—still people among us who have a profession.† Thus the Congress took place at Whitsun. It began on the morning of May 18, in the Kaim-Säle, which was decorated with pictures and other representations. There were the seven seals of the ancient wisdom, the seven columns of the Earth conditions or weekdays, and the red and the violet pillars portraying both the Tree of Knowledge and the Tree of Life. At the front of the stage stood the busts of Fichte, Hegel, and Schelling. The Congress was quite well attended; people even came from other countries. Most of the participants were women. Steiner opened the Congress, whereupon the General Secretaries of the various nations spoke words of greeting. It was an important and edifying moment, to hear the representatives of the nations speak in their own languages with unity of thinking, feeling, and willing. Mrs. Besant was present. She looked exactly like the picture of her that Sophie Stinde brought me from London: an impressive older woman with silver hair and wearing a white silk garment. Her speech was quite curious: very musical and rhythmical. It was a memorable sight to see Rudolf Steiner and Annie Besant standing beside each other. They represented two opposite poles. In five years the opposition broke out openly, a prelude to the world struggle of Germany and England [in World War I]. The proceedings and events went according to a program that was artistically produced and given to every participant. The poppy-red admission ticket was decorated with the Rose Cross on a blue oval. The evening of the first day was dedicated to a social gathering with musical offerings and recitations....

On May 18, Rudolf Steiner held his lecture on "The Rosicrucian Initiation." It was characteristic that he began by making reference to statements from Hegel about knowledge and closed with an aphorism from Goethe. On Sunday, May 19, the Greek mystery play by Edouard Schuré was performed. Steiner's friend Bernhard Stavenhagen wrote the music. The whole made for an excellent presentation of the Eleusinian mystery art. The original Eleusinian mysteries may well have been thus. On Monday there was a social gathering....

The last day of the Congress was May 21. Steiner explained the symbols in the hall. In the evening a photograph was taken, and the individual representatives, as well as Mrs. Besant and Dr. Steiner, gave their closing talks. Dr. Steiner thanked Annie Besant for coming and also thanked all who had helped with the Congress. Much praise was to be given. Indeed, we saw only the finished product and not all of the never-ending effort and work that was necessary to make the Congress run as it did. At approximately 11:30 P.M., the Congress ended.

II

THE EFFECTS OF THE MUNICH CONGRESS

MALSCH

FOREWORD

HELLA WIESBERGER

In 1887, on the edge of the village of Malsch not far from Karlsruhe, the painter Karl Stockmeyer† built the Waldhaus, a house in the woods of that name. His wife, Johanna ran it as a boarding house starting in 1908-1909, mainly for friends of the movement who were seeking relaxation and recuperation. After the death of Karl Stockmeyer [in 1930], the Waldhaus became a home for the mentally handicapped.

The older of the Stockmeyers' daughters, Hilde, who was the first in her family to find her way to Rudolf Steiner, founded and ran the Francis of Assisi Branch of the Theosophical (later Anthroposophical) Society in the Waldhaus, until her early death in 1910. The younger daughter, Waltraut Stockmeyer-Schopflin-Döbelin, made significant contributions to biodynamic farming in Norway. A son, E. A. Karl, was a pioneer not only in the Waldorf School movement but also in working with Rudolf Steiner's architectural impulses. As a twenty-one-year-old student, he took part in the Munich Congress with his parents and siblings. Deeply impressed by the new forms of the column capitals, he asked Rudolf Steiner questions in 1908 about the bases and the architecture of the columns. Based on the instructions given to him by Rudolf Steiner, he developed the idea for a model building by the Waldhaus, which he erected with the help of his father in 1908-1909.

Rudolf Steiner went to Malsch three times in connection with this building project. He went first in the summer of 1908 and again at Easter 1909, for the laying of the foundation stone of the model building and for the dedication of the Francis of Assisi Branch. The laying of the foundation stone took place at the rising of the first full moon of spring on the night of April 5 through the morning of April 6. Besides Rudolf Steiner, Marie von Sivers, and the Stockmeyer family, a number of other friends of the movement were present. Hilde Stockmeyer later wrote down from memory the account of Rudolf Steiner's address, which appears on the following pages. Steiner dedicated an impressive obituary to her when she died a year later.† The actor Max Gümbel-Seiling gave a brief description of the event and Steiner's address at the laying of the foundation stone in his recollections *With Rudolf Steiner in Munich*.† This description comes before Hilde Stockmeyer's account of the address. The third time Steiner traveled to Malsch was in October 1911, immediately before his trip to Stuttgart for the dedication of the Stuttgart House. The Stockmeyers, father and son, were both also involved with the basement cupola room in the Stuttgart House that was built according to the Malsch model.

At that time, E. A. Karl Stockmeyer could only build and plaster the model building in Malsch in the rough. It was not until he moved back to Malsch in 1956-1957, old and ill, that he took up the project for the model building again, together with other interested friends, above all the architect Albert von Baravalle of Dornach and Klara Boerner of Malsch. In 1959 the Malsch Building Association was founded and assigned the renovation, completion, and further maintenance of the small building. The renovation work and the artistic decoration were carried out by Albert von Baravalle and were completed in 1965.

The Laying of the Foundation Stone of the Model Building in Malsch

MAX GÜMBEL-SEILING

Descriptions of the event on April 5-6, 1909

We were in the living room of the Waldhaus belonging to the Stockmeyer family. There were approximately twenty-four people present.† Rudolf Steiner stepped in front of the table behind which we stood, with the document he had written. First he explained the sign of the macrocosm that he had drawn on it with simple lines. Around the six-pointed star, formed by two intersecting triangles, were two dragons that bit each other in the tail. Above was a white, winged dragon and below a dried, dark one. On the right, written from above downward, were the words "All above as below."† On the left, written from below upward, were the words "All below as above."

We all signed the document, which Steiner rolled up and put in a bottle to lay under the foundation stone. It was late in the evening, but Steiner still wanted to wait for the Moon before we followed him outside to a ravine in the forest where the little building stood. The building was open to the sky. "Dear Sisters and Brothers," he began. We stood pressed close together before him in the small room. First he spoke about the laying of foundation stones in olden times, in which priests allowed themselves to be walled up in the ground, then about the slaves that the Romans forced into being walled up, and, finally, about the present meaning of the foundation stone. Then he laid the foundation stone himself.

Address by Rudolf Steiner at the Foundation Stone Laying for the Rosicrucian Temple of the "Francis of Assisi" Lodge of Malsch

Hilde Stockmeyer

An approximate rendering from memory

Digging under the ruins of many ancient houses, one can find human skeletons. There is a reason for them to be there. In earlier times, one knew that a new building must develop an inner life. This meant, originally, that spiritual life must flow through every building if it is to bring blessing. A decadent time understood this outwardly and established the practice of embedding a living slave under the building. What should really be buried with the foundation stone are the feelings and thinking and wishes of blessing of those who built the building and of those who wish to use it.

Thus, we want to lower the foundation stone of this temple into the womb of our Mother Earth, in the face of the rays of the full moon shining upon us in the middle of the plant world that sprouts around the building. And as the Moon reflects the bright sunlight, so we want to reflect the light of the spiritual-divine being. We want to turn trustingly to our great Mother Earth, which bears and protects us lovingly, and we want to entrust to her the document of the building.... [Here followed the description of the document.]

At the same time, all of us assembled here want to bury our wishes and blessings with the document and remind ourselves again and again of this moment and of that which has flamed through our souls and hearts. Then will our attitude and way of thinking work on, supporting and protecting this temple building, the existence of the Malsch Lodge. We want to call down upon this stone and the Malsch Lodge the blessing of the masters of wisdom and harmony of feelings and the blessing of all high and highest beings, the spiritual hierarchies, who are connected with Earth evolution. We implore that they let their power stream into this foundation stone and allow it to work on within it so that all that is thought, felt, willed, and done over this stone may be in harmony with them and be ensouled by their spirit.

Let the light of the Spirits of the East
Shine upon this building;
May the Spirits of the West let it ray back;
May the Spirits of the North strengthen it
And the Spirits of the South warm it through,
So that the Spirits of East, West, North, and South
Stream through this building.

Our Mother Earth suffered pain as she solidified. It is our mission to spiritualize Earth again, to redeem it by reworking it through the power of our hands into a spirit-filled work of art. May this stone be a first foundation stone for the redemption and transformation of our Earth planet, and may the power of this stone multiply a thousandfold.

As we still rested in the bosom of God, cared for lovingly by divine forces, there wove in us the all-pervading and enveloping Father Spirit. But we were still not conscious or independent. Therefore, we descended into matter, to learn to develop consciousness of self here. There came the evil; there came the death. Yet, Christ also worked in matter and helped us to overcome death. When we die thus in Christ, we live. We will overcome death and spiritualize matter and make it divine through our strong power. Thus will awaken within us the power of the Hallowing One, the Holy Spirit.

Thus resounds at this place as truth-wrought Word:

Ex Deo nascimur,
In Christo morimur,
Per Spiritum sanctum reviviscimus.

Out of God we are born,
In Christ we die,
Through the Spirit we are reborn.

Concerning Forerunners of the Goetheanum

E.A. Karl Stockmeyer

Written for *Mitteilungen aus der Anthroposophischen Arbeit in Deutschland*, Christmas 1949 [News out of the Anthroposophical work in Germany]

At Whitsuntide 1907, I was able to participate, as a quite young member, in the Munich Congress of the Federation of the European Sections of the Theosophical Society. Dr. Steiner led it as the General Secretary of the German Section. He formed it completely in the sense of what he had built up since the turn of the century in Germany, even into the outer arrangement of the space. He often said later of the forms of the Goetheanum structure that this building, in its visible aspects, should correspond to living spiritual science in the same way as the nutshell to the nut. That spirit lived in the impulse of the outer "dressing" of the first actual Anthroposophical congress—which was still, in 1907, presented as part of the Theosophical Society. The so-called Kaim Hall, later called the Concert Hall, on the corner of Prinz Ludwigstraße and Türkenstraße, was covered in deep red material, as were the ceiling and the large galleries. Thus, a fairly wide, square room without windows was formed, a true inner space.

The red walls of material were totally smooth. In one end of the room was set a little rectangular stage space, its floor easily a meter higher than the floor of the hall. On the stage stood a long table (for the leaders of the Congress), covered in red and decorated with the signs of the zodiac. To the side, and somewhat to the front, was the speaker's podium. Above the stage opening hung a picture by the Munich painter Haß, *The Great Babylon*. Below the stage the busts of the great German idealists Fichte, Schelling, and Hegel stood on pedestals, and to the right and left of them stood two pillars, one red pillar decorated with a "J" and one blue pillar with a "B" on it. Each had its respective verse:

J

In pure thinking you find
The self that can hold itself.

Transform thought into an image
And you will experience creative wisdom.

B

Concentrate feeling into light
And you will reveal the formative power.

Realize the will into being-ness
And you will create in world being.

The side walls and back walls were decorated with seven columns approximately two and a half meters high, which were simply painted on wide boards. The motifs that were to be used later in the columns of the first Goetheanum were depicted here in capitals on top of smooth round shafts without bases. The planetary signs were mounted on the shafts, and in the spaces between the columns the seven apocalyptic seals were hung. Both the columns and the seals were painted according to Rudolf Steiner's sketches. The columns were painted by Karl Stahl of Munich, and the seals were painted by Clara Rettich of Stuttgart. Otherwise, as far as I remember, there was no other decoration in the space. Despite their artistically undemanding nature, one sensed the columns and seals to be mighty intimations of a comprehensive supersensible life of being. The painted columns standing free of beams and ceiling, with the apocalyptic seals hanging on the red walls between them, became a challenge to the viewer to construct a room in one's imagination in which the columns were the bearing element and in which the seals, as pictures, directed the sight into a nonspatial, spiritual life.

The red of the walls became the color of the space itself, illuminating all objects and enveloping them with a delicate nebulousness, giving the space so created a profound festive quality. It received the souls of those present and spoke to them in the same spirit out of which the words of spiritual science sounded. It was a living indication of the imminent, not yet known, architecture of the Goetheanum. It was an addressing of the innermost part of the human being; the spiritual world itself invoked the human being, even if only in introductory tones.

I can no longer remember the content of the lectures; the questions and answers so blended together with the enormous amount that Rudolf Steiner let us experience that I can no longer sort it out. However, the effect of the space stands firmly there in memory in its appealing and stimulating solemn festiveness.

The thought would not let go of me that here only a hint of a true architecture was given. It seemed inconceivable that Steiner could arrange new columns with these unique capitals without placing them in an appropriate space with a ceiling for them to carry. I then occupied myself intensively with the seals and columns and tried working with them through painting and sculpting. In Munich I was able to see the original models of the column capitals sculpted by Dr. Steiner. In the meantime, they have unfortunately been lost. In the spring of 1908, I showed Steiner my first attempts and asked about the bases of the columns. He explained that, for each, the lower motif of the capital should be used as the base, as then did happen in the first Goetheanum. In the summer of the same year, I asked about the architecture of the columns. He addressed this question immediately and drew for me in a few strokes how the seven columns running in two rows from west to east enclose an elliptical room and should bear a cupola in the form of an ellipsoid with three axes, whose large axis runs from west to east. The entrance should be in the west, and there both rows of columns should begin with the Saturn column. Behind the columns should be an ambulatory, which likewise should be covered over "mussel-like" with ellipsoids with three axes. An elliptical wall should form the boundary of the whole to the outside, with no windows. The seals are to be mounted on the wall so that the first is between the Saturn column and the Sun column, the second between the Sun column and the Moon column and so forth, up to the seventh, which should be mounted twice on the other side of the Venus column, to the right and left of the center.

The space receives light only through a single opening in the main ceiling vault. It is to be constructed in such a way that at the spring equinox, at about 9:00 A.M., the sunlight falls on a certain point inside. The wall is to be painted red and the cupolas blue. The zodiac should be painted on the main vault, beginning with Pisces in the west over the Saturn column.[†] Actually, the room should be carved in stone; the best would be granite. The columns should, if possible, be made out of Siberian syenite.[†] All of these instructions were answers to my questions that went ever more into the details.

That was in the summer of 1908. In thinking these instructions through, it became clear to me quite soon that realizing them would bring significant difficulties. It was a question of fitting together fifteen ellipsoids of three axes each. Even though the problem of the five ellipsoids incorporated in each of the four quadrants could be minimized through the east-west and north-south symmetries, this problem, too, was quite complicated. One had to strive to make certain, for the sake of structural stability, that on the elliptically formed intersecting arches between the main vault and side vaults the contact surfaces of the main ellipsoid take in the main axis of the side ellipsoid, such that the shearing force of the main vault would be absorbed most beneficially by the side vaults. For this reason, these had to be placed diagonally in a particular way. Further, one must succeed in making the side ellipsoids meet, with perpendicular tangents, the columns and two points on the wall that were determined beforehand.

Therefore, a particular question arose. It was presumed that the dimension of the main vault and the distribution of the columns connected with it could be determined freely within the framework of Rudolf Steiner's instructions, along with the width of the entrance and the form of the arches leading from each column to the wall. They had to be shaped the same, so that the floor plan and the boundary of the individual ceiling areas would, in any case, be symmetrical. Otherwise, the fitting of the ellipsoids would be still more difficult, if not impossible.

Within this established framework, the conditions already cited were to be accomplished more through engineering and aesthetics. It was a mathematical task. It soon became apparent that this problem could not be solved directly, either through construction or through calculation.

That is not really surprising. It was actually a matter of an artistic question that was translated into the realm of mathematics only because the ellipsoid has its own particular mathematical lawfulness that must be taken into account when forming it into an architectural structure. For this reason, mathematics must behave here as an artistic technique. It had to help solve the artistic problem that goes beyond mathematical determination. That meant, practically, that one could use mathematical methods, construction, and calculation only as a way to come gradually closer to the sought-for form and placement of the ellipsoids through arbitrary and repeatedly modified assumptions.

I did this complicated work in the fall and winter of 1908.† At first, it was a purely theoretical matter. In order to have a concrete starting point, I established only the height of the columns, which I modeled. They were 87 centimeters (about 34 1/4 inches) high. When one also made the cupola 87 centimeters high from the tops of the columns to the highest point, this resulted in 174 centimeters (about 68 1/2 inches). The horizontal dimensions were about 3 1/2 and 2 1/2 meters (about 11 1/2 and 8 1/4 feet), which gave a nearly usable model structure. My father, who is always highly enthusiastic about his children's ideas, took this up. He believed that this model structure should become reality. We sank the floor to table height; in other words, we set the columns on table-high supports and formed a room into which one could really enter, a model building that has its ideal floor at table height and into which we could enter in such a way that our legs were still, so to speak, under the floor. Sitting, it looked as if we were in a huge space with high columns.

This model building was actually begun. It was built in a thicket in the forest by Waldhaus, and Rudolf Steiner dedicated the Francis of Assisi Lodge of the Theosophical Society there during Passiontide 1909. He laid the foundation stone in the night of April 5-6, 1909. Of Steiner's address, only the record made of it from memory by my sister, who died in 1910, is available. In this, the following words are recorded: "May there shine upon this building the light of the Spirits of the East. May the Spirits of the West let it ray back. May the Spirits of the North make it firm and the Spirits of the South warm it through, so that the Spirits of East, West, North and South stream through the building." Whoever has become acquainted with the symbolic-ritualistic activities of the time before World War I,† mentioned by Rudolf Steiner in his *Autobiography*† will find again, in the quoted words, that which lived there and shines over the Mystery Dramas right down to the laying of the foundation stone at the Christmas Conference and also throws a light on Goethe's *Fairy Tale of the Green Snake and the Beautiful Lily.* At that time the little model building was still open; the bare framework for the side vaults had just been erected. Just as the laying of the foundation stone was carried out, the Easter full moon rose and shone from the east upon the small assembly.

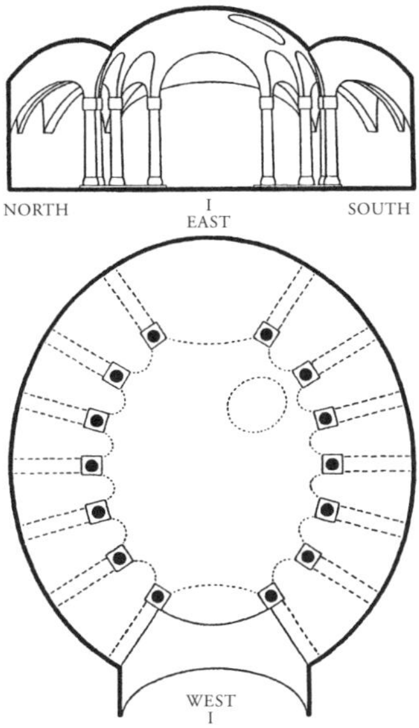

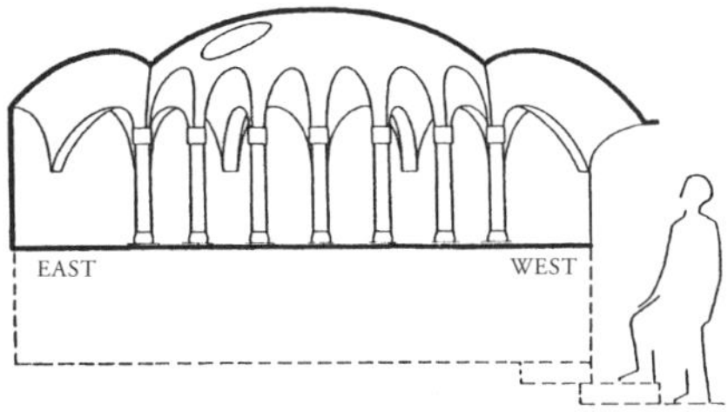

The Malsch Model Building (Drawings by Erich Zimmer)

Left: The floor plan

Above left: Cross-section towards east.

Above right: Lengthwise cross-section towards south. The dashed line shows the height of the floor necessary in order to enter the model building. The human figure gives a scale for the relative size of the building, but the exact proportions necessary to carry it to completion are not known.

We were able to erect the structure of the building and use it for the Francis of Assisi Lodge, but it could not be finished and is today still not finished. However, it could become the beginning point for another structure. A question arose ever again in my soul: What should this building be? The Greek temple is the home of the god; the Christian church is the house of the community that assembles to find the spiritual through ritual. What task does this new building have? I could find no other answer than that this building should be the center for the work of the human being—that work through which the human being strives to draw near to the spirit. There came to me, by dealing with the harmony of the forms that presented themselves in such overwhelming unity, self-containment, and perfection, the single thought: such a temple will have an effect on human beings, such that those who cannot travel the path of thinking can also come to self-knowledge, if they give themselves over to the forms.

When I said this [about such a temple and self-knowledge] to Rudolf Steiner, he answered: "Yes, it is true, but to *higher* self-knowledge." I took him to mean the knowledge of the human being as such. At that time no Mystery Drama had been written, and the idea of establishing a central Anthroposophical building had not yet arisen. So at that time, I could experience only in this imagined underground temple what is regarded as Steiner's entire artistic creation—from the architecture of the Goetheanum, to the creative speech work, to the spiritual discernment of the *Mystery Dramas*,† the *Truth-Wrought Words*,† the *Anthroposophical Leading Thoughts*, and the "Letters to the Members."†

As the Stuttgart Branch decided to build its own house, the architect Schmid-Curtius,† who knew the Malsch model building, had the idea of building a space of this type for the symbolic-ritualistic events I have already mentioned. In the basement under the large hall there was a designated space that he wanted to arrange accordingly. I was engaged, with Schmid-Curtius's agreement, to work on the project.

The task was still more difficult than working out the Malsch model building, because the available room in the basement was not only very narrow but also unfavorably oriented. In order to remain in accord with the four points of the compass, one had to place the column room almost diagonally into the space available. So as to lose as little of the rectangular room as possible, we made the circle-like wall ellipse so large that it overlapped somewhat with the straight walls of the cellar. The low height of the room forced a quite flat cupola-form and led to our laying the floor under the main cupola about three steps lower than in the ambulatory. The columns were hewn out of sandstone from Main by my father, together with the young architect Gerbote. The shafts were round. It was impossible to let sunlight fall in through the vault. For this reason, the opening for light was installed in the southeast, as in Malsch, but it had to be lit artificially. Imme von Eckhardstein† painted the cupola. On a very cold day in the winter of 1910-1911, Rudolf Steiner laid the foundation stone of the house, on the place where, later, the east niche of the column hall was to be built. In the course of 1911 the house was finished, and the column hall was then to be installed in the fall. I used the summer for calculations.

This hall served its original purpose until World War I broke out. Then it remained unused and finally was used as a multipurpose storeroom. This remained so until at the beginning of the 1930s, Mr. C. S. Picht,† editor of the magazines *Anthroposophie* and *Die Drei,* moved his office into the house. He "discovered" the column room and cleared it out. It is thanks to his understanding effort that the hall was set in order again. It was to become a Rudolf Steiner memorial room and was arranged as such. Mr. Picht had photographs taken, and two of them are in the special joint issue of the magazines published for the tenth anniversary of the death of Rudolf Steiner.

When the Anthroposophical Society was banned [by the National Socialists, the Nazis] in the fall of 1935, the house at 70 Landhausstraße had to be sold. The Regional Educational Film Center of Wurttenberg took it over. The column room was torn out; only the columns themselves remained. Dr. Friedrich Husemann† bought them during the demolition and moved them to Wiesneck. There they are arranged as bearers of a beautiful arbor around a small pond and remind us painfully of the lost temple room in Stuttgart. The column hall in Stuttgart was finished in about 1911-1912.

At that time, plans were already developed for the Johannes building in Munich, which then became the Goetheanum in Dornach. In place of the elliptical vault was the unique double cupola, and a building arose that was intended for the performance of the Mystery Dramas. Its stage, with twelve thrones and the image of the Representative of Humanity,† portrayed the most exalted ritual center.

In the lectures on *Architecture as a Synthesis of the Arts,* Rudolf Steiner says:

> What should our building become? It shows, in its floor plan and its cupola form, the characteristic of what it should become! It has two parts, both equal in their architectural forms. There is

> no differentiation, such as exists between the altar space and the congregation of a Christian church. The distinction here signifies only that, in the large cupola, the physical is predominant and, in the small cupola, the spiritual is meant to be paramount. There is already an elevation to the spirit expressed in this form. It must be expressed, in all its details, the way in which the elevation to the spirit corresponds to the fact that in the building an organ is created, that the gods can speak to us here. When I say that whoever understands the building fully will discard the habit of lying and wrongdoing, that the building can be a lawgiver, one can see it in the individual forms.[†]

One could experience this idea as germ in the prototype of the Malsch model building and in the Stuttgart building. Both forms—the elliptical as well as the double cupola—should be considered sheaths for the work of human beings, not profane work but work through which humans allow themselves to hear the speech of the gods and take it into earthly tasks.

The first Goetheanum combined two functions, ritual center and mystery stage. The second Goetheanum took over only the second function. It also became a commemoration building for the first Goetheanum. Rudolf Steiner called attention to it in the words he spoke at the Stuttgart Delegates' Meeting in the spring of 1923,[†] after the burning of the first Goetheanum, when he called that which the Anthroposophical Society is to accomplish the "reverse ritual." This is a ritual through which the human being, together with others, seeks the way to the spirit and, in this seeking, builds *community-out-of-freedom* into the future. The religious ritual, on the other hand, wants to lead human beings to a symbolic re-living, a re-experiencing of that which we went through together in past spiritual fervor. As a reminder of what must still be a task of the Anthroposophical Society, to create this reverse ritual and to place it in an appropriate space, stands the fact that the old Goetheanum is only a memory and that the stages leading to it could not as yet progress to lasting reality.

The primary fact is, however, that we are worlds away from the realization of the reverse ritual in our society. The first stage towards fulfilling this task can only be that we succeed to build a society that unites, in a truly brotherly manner, all who seek the spirit of Anthroposophy in the most varied ways. People can disagree about the word of Anthroposophy, if they do it in such a way that they do not refuse love to others. We will find each other ever again when we strive to reach the spirit of Anthroposophy. This may lead us once more to the point where we can think about erecting spaces out of the spirit of the old Goetheanum, as sheaths for the true spirit of Anthroposophy, as realized in our work.

The Architectural Problem of the Munich Congress Hall of 1907 and the Design for the Malsch Model Building of 1908

E.A. Karl Stockmeyer

(Unfinished essay from the last year of his life)

It is obvious from the start that taking the direction for an ellipsoid with three axes as a cupola-form does not provide a building plan for a hall. The ellipsoid is a very abstract concept that must be more clearly determined in every building plan, if it is to become a concrete building element. The work of the architect begins with this question, if he or she wants to erect an elliptical construction. It is simplest when we can set the dimensions and proportions ourselves, where perhaps only money or the overall size sets a limit. That was the case with the construction of the Malsch model building, where the low height of the columns (87 centimeters) made it such that a real hall could not be created, but rather only a model structure that could hold just twenty-four people. Everything had to be oriented to these 87 centimeters. Within this framework one could, however, move freely; for instance, one could set the axes of the ellipsoid according to the Golden Mean or in some other way.

It was different with the Stuttgart Hall of 1911, which had to be forced into a quite unfavorable size and, above all, in an unfavorably oriented room, through choosing a floor plan that was a bulbous ellipse. In this way, the cupola became very flat and, in outline, almost a circle in form. The cupola rested on 2 x 7 newly-shaped columns that form the boundaries of the nave of the main room. They were not evenly spaced in the main ellipse; that would have corresponded to a circular floor plan. The attempt was made here to maintain an appropriate distribution of the columns that would make the distances between them, measured from the center, appear to be equal. If one had made the apparent distance similar to an eighth of the elongated angle, then one would have 2 x 7 column places, and in the east and in the west, there would be a gap double as wide as the spaces between the columns. Thus, a column order appropriate for the ellipse was produced.

The arrangement of the columns gives the starting point for the construction of the side nave-like ambulatory, and for that problem Rudolf Steiner gave only the simplest direction—that the individual areas, like the main room, should be covered by ellipsoids. With this, we depart fundamentally from the Gothic construction of the vault through girders and triangular fields and form each individual vault as an aesthetic and dynamic whole. It is the same for the main vault as for the individual vaults, which one could also call ellipsoid vaults.

These ellipsoid vaults should absorb the shearing force of the main vault and transfer it to the uniform outer wall in such a way that the "weight-bearing" [load] and the "holding-up" [support] will be sensed by those who look at them. The wall is especially weight-bearing when it is carved in stone. Every encircling wall is only a substitute for the bearing stone wall. The cornice of the ellipsoid vaults rests, pressing upon the wall or outer wall, yet these ellipsoid vaults bear the main vault themselves, and the movement concludes in the keystone that rests hovering in the highest point of the main vault. The cornice of the columns takes on a part of the weight of the main vault and transfers it through the elliptic arches onto the wall. The arches and the ellipsoid vaults together build a uniform cornice in which the ellipsoid vaults form the load element and the arches form the support element. Thus, the whole vault, with all its support and load elements, is an indissoluble unity with a fixed middle point and an unmovable circumference. In the floor plan the area of a cornice-ellipsoid appears as a rectangle with somewhat curved sides. Each of these rectangles is determined by four points. Two of them mark the axes of the two neighboring columns; the other two indicate where the ellipsoid surface passes over into the wall surface. The four points have to be chosen such that an ellipsoid that has a perpendicular tangent on each of the four points would be determined by them. This condition is met, however, by an infinite number of ellipsoids.

One must therefore seek a different, more specific condition that cannot be satisfied by so many different ellipsoids, and one finds it in the relationship of the cornice-ellipsoid to the main ellipsoid. These two surfaces should also be perpendicular to each other where they intersect. For then the load and support will be most clearly experienced. This perpendicular placement is achieved when one of the three axes of the cornice-ellipsoid touches the main ellipsoid. With these conditions of perpendicular tangents on the four points mentioned, there is the right angularity of the main ellipsoid and cornice-ellipsoid....

The Roof Vault Resting on Two-Times-Seven Columns

E.A. Karl Stockmeyer

(From Notes Out of the Estate of E. A. Karl Stockmeyer)

The vault, in the form of an ellipsoid with three axes resting on two-times-seven columns of a new form, is the primary architectural motif that Rudolf Steiner gave me in answer to my question in the summer of 1908. This form-motif stands between the Greek temple, with its straight lines, and the cupola building, with its restless circle tendency, which is then subdued only through a cross-form in the floor plan. The temple from antiquity knew only two spatial dimensions; one does not move forward inwardly when walking from the door to the picture but repeats the same two-dimensionality. The cupola construction makes the ancient temple into a Christian structure. Rudolf Steiner's temple building, with its elliptical floor plan, merges the straight-line tendency of the older temple buildings with the turning tendency of the cupola buildings through the uniform ellipse form.

BERLIN

FOREWORD

Hella Wiesberger

The Berlin Branch was the starting point of Rudolf Steiner's teaching activity. Originally it was called the German Theosophical Society Berlin and was founded as such in 1894 as a branch of the European Section of the Theosophical Society, with its headquarters in London. Steiner was invited in the fall of 1900 to hold lectures for this group. Soon thereafter he met Marie von Sivers (later Marie Steiner). Together with her, in 1902, he took over the leadership of the German Theosophical Society, as well as the German Section, which was in the process of being founded. From 1905 until 1912, the German Theosophical Society, or Berlin Branch, was called the Besant Branch, and from 1913 on, it was called the Berlin Branch of the Anthroposophical Society. Rudolf Steiner and Marie Steiner remained the leaders of this first branch of the Anthroposophical Movement until, with the new founding of the society at Christmas 1923, as the General Anthroposophical Society (with headquarters at the Goetheanum in Dornach, near Basel), Steiner became the first chairman and moved permanently from Berlin to Dornach.

From fall 1903 until May 1909, the home of the Berlin Branch was in Berlin (later West Berlin), at 17 Motzstraße, Hinterhaus. This was a large building that housed the business of the German Section, the publishing company for Rudolf Steiner's writings, and his and other coworkers' dwellings. On May 5, 1909, Steiner dedicated the long-needed larger branch meeting place at 2 Geisbergstraße. The decoration of the space, which strove, above all, for a uniform surface effect through being colored completely in blue, was done according to Rudolf Steiner's instructions.† Besides Steiner's own description of the room in his address at the dedication of the space, there is also a short description by Assyia Turgenieff:

> The branch meeting place in Geisbergstraße was like a ship or island in the roaring sea of modern city life. Dr. Steiner here made his first attempt at decorating a space. The walls were painted in a dense blue and the doors, floor, windows, and chairs were painted in a still darker blue. The speaker's podium, set to the side, was dark blue as well, with a bouquet of radiant red roses on it. The curtains at the windows were light blue, and the ceiling was covered with light blue material that was firmly stretched and so hung down, billowing in peculiar waves, that were not intended. Much care was taken to build drop-like forms as a transition to the darker walls. The busts of Hegel, Schelling, Fichte, and Novalis, as well as two etchings from Raphael's *Stanze*, took up the spaces between the windows.[†]

Steiner established the uniform blue coloring (which was also used for the branch space at 17 Motzstraße) at the dedication of the Stuttgart House. On October 23, 1911, in Berlin, he said how necessary it is to have our own space:

> We have seen that something can be achieved when we can fashion the space ourselves, not only in small beginning steps, but even now in the first Middle European Theosophical building, the Stuttgart Branch. Those who were present at the dedication will have convinced themselves sufficiently of the significance of an inner room dedicated in the Theosophical sense and will know how totally different it is to enter such a space than some other hall—apart from the individual refinements that I discussed when I spoke in Stuttgart about the significance of color, space demarcations, and so on, for the cultivating of esoteric knowledge in such a space.[†]

In 1919 it was necessary to arrange a larger space in Berlin, and new rooms, with a stage, were set up at 98 Potsdamstraße. The meeting place was dedicated by Steiner with a lecture on September 12, 1919,[†] although at that time he could only rarely be in Berlin. It served the work in Berlin until the banning of the Anthroposophical Society in

Germany by the National Socialists in 1935. After World War II, many Anthroposophical activities developed in Berlin, and they created their own spaces.

The Dedication of the New Berlin Branch Space

RUDOLF STEINER

Berlin, May 5, 1909

Today, we have assembled together for the first time in the space that is intended for the cultivating of the ideas and life that we have until now cared for in smaller, more limited rooms. Today we have come together, less in order to receive something new, but much more, to be together for the first time in the consciousness of the meaning and significance of the Theosophical ideal in Theosophical life.

With the opportunity to exchange our smaller spaces for a larger one, we also tried to arrange the space in an appropriate way. Still, there underlay the awareness that this is only a beginning of what is to develop more and more, if Theosophy is not to become merely empty dogma but rather life in the most eminent sense—life that will pervade and take hold of our entire culture, of everything we do. In this first intimation, we should attempt to create a certain harmony between what will work onward here as word and that which confronts us in the outer space of the branch. One could do this more perfectly. These things will be done quite differently at a future time, perhaps best when we are all no longer here in the physical body. However, in order for anything to become more perfect one day, a beginning must be made. The beginning, in its imperfection, is in many ways more important than the more perfect vision that will develop in the course of ages.

The feeling must gain ever more ground in Theosophical minds and souls that what answers us, so to speak, from the walls of the space in which we come together for the cultivating of Theosophical feelings and Theosophical ideas is not without consequence. It lies in the nature of things that those who become interested in the ideas of a worldview that is in its initial stage behave disdainfully toward what is in the outer sense world. However, that view should give way to a totally different fundamental feeling in our lives. Theosophy can achieve its highest ideal, which naturally goes beyond the outer sense world, by also working on that which many people sense as merely outer reality, perhaps also as only the ordinary.

Whoever is able to recognize and judge the associations of spiritual facts knows quite well that customs, habits, soul inclinations, and certain relations of good and evil of an age depend on the qualities of the things that we pass by from morning until evening, and among which we are active from morning to evening. What is around the human being from morning to evening is, for the most part—forgive the harsh expression—often hair-raising. Human beings today frequently bother about nothing other than that which is in their surroundings during the day! Did one's judgment, eye, or taste influence the way one fashioned a particular table or chair? The most ridiculous results in this area are possible today. Our factories send out some catalog that shows that chairs are formed in this style and that style, and tables are formed thus and so. In most cases, when we do not like abstract, impractical items that are sent out a thousand-fold into the world, we are told: "Yes, well, one cannot have anything different!" People do not notice that in that moment in which they would only want or will something different, they would have something different. The individual, naturally, can do little about it. However, those societies that cultivate ideals in common should aim to have in that which surrounds them an expression of what lives in their hearts, in their judgment.

Everything you see here in this room was worked on mostly by those who are sitting here, impractical Theosophists, so to speak. There is only one impractical element in this room at the moment: the lamps. And they must be changed in the next few weeks. They are the only things in this room that were made by a cooperative that has nothing to do with Theosophy but which is known as an eminently practical firm. I can assure you that the appropriate instructions were given more than six weeks ago for how these shades, through which the light was to fall into the room, should be made. They should be *blue*. Yet a world-famous firm was not able to manufacture something that differs from what they normally make. The practical ones have proven themselves to be the only impractical ones. Here it becomes apparent, in other words, that this practice, when looked at rightly, is the most impractical that one can imagine. There is nothing else behind it but the brutal insistence that we are dependent upon them, because we cannot manufacture electric lamps for ourselves. This is said only to point out how senseless it is when, proudly and with a shrug of the shoulders from on high, our Theosophical direction is looked down upon as estranged from and at enmity with the world. Indeed, something impractical has gradually crept in among Theosophists, and that is the practice of arriving late. One should understand that one basically cannot arrive late to Theosophical lectures. For a Theosophical lecture is comprehensive, and if one has missed hearing the first sentences, then one has actually heard nothing at all.

This space should thus really be an expression of Theosophical life-practice in the small area where it is possible today. That which lives spiritually can perfectly well imprint itself on the forms and colors of our surroundings and can confront us again in what we perceive around us. What is around us can, in a certain connection, be an echo of what we feel in our hearts and souls. In this connection, Theosophy should more and more penetrate our whole cultural life and even become absolutely the life blood of our spiritual development. One can say, in relation to this, that our highest ideal is connected to what we have around us wherever we go. After we have entertained the meaning of why we built this space precisely in this way, then we can use this opportunity to bring our great Theosophical life ideal a little closer before our souls.

Housed here are two of the world's most important pictures—pictures that show the way in which Theosophists can make their life-ideal the content of their souls. They are two pictures by Raphael,[†] in which he, in the great time of artistic evolution, brought to expression everything that went through his soul in sensing and feeling the nature of humanity's evolution over many centuries. The one picture is called *The School of Athens* (in the travel book by Baedeker, and it would be better if this name were to disappear). The other is the so-called *Disputa*. What do these pictures portray when we let the content appear before our souls in such a way that the great ideas underlying them come to life in us in the same way as the artistic element in them does?

It was possible for me to see these pictures often. They are in Rome in the Vatican as part of the famous Raphael *Stanze*. One sees there how the people stand before them and read in their travel guide books: that is Socrates, that is Plato, that is Diogenes, and so on. These people are immensely happy when they can decipher, according to the Baedeker travel guidebook, who this or that figure is, whether this or that one is a bishop or a church father, whether this is Paul or Peter, or if that is Moses, and so on. How meaningless that all is artistically! I want to use a quite grotesque comparison to point out how one can approach such pictures; in this, the artistic approach will coincide fully with the Theosophical approach.

We know that there are also inhabitants of Mars, even though these Mars inhabitants look completely different from Earth inhabitants. For us, they are quite real beings. The confounded ideas of many modern visionaries will not interest us—for example, whether it would not be possible to design the Pythagorean Theorem of electrical power lines on a great plain of Siberia, such that a correspondence with the inhabitants of Mars could be initiated. We will leave such reverie to the materialistic visionaries of the present day. Whoever stands on the ground of reality knows that we have to do with Mars inhabitants who are of a completely different nature from Earth inhabitants.

Let us suppose that such a Mars inhabitant were to come down onto our Earth and could see what happens here. We would not immediately have the peculiar expectation that they would already know our Earth history. It is possible that such Mars inhabitants could come to Rome. We could well expect that they would go to the Vatican collection and look at these pictures by Raphael. We could not imagine, however, that they would immediately study the entire history of Greek philosophy and the whole evolution of the Middle Ages, so that we could talk with them in our manner. It would seem quite strange to them if we explained that this person is Augustine or that is Ambrosius, and so on. They would probably reply, if they could speak an earthly language, that they do not know the gentlemen! We know them generally because we have formed certain conceptions of them. It does not matter if they are right or wrong. The artistic impression of these pictures is not changed by the fact that Mars inhabitants know absolutely nothing about Mr. Aristotle, Mr. Plato, and Mr. Socrates or that we might know the entire history of Earth evolution. The artistic impression depends solely on what confronts us in the picture. We gain a feeling for the picture's artistic impression best when we pay attention to absolutely nothing but what the picture itself says. Thus, the Mars inhabitants would be the best observers in a purely artistic sense.

Let us put ourselves into the place of the Mars inhabitants to whom we have not given a handbook on Greek or Middle Age philosophy and who have just come down to Earth. They would say to themselves: "I see certain figures, human figures in these pictures; among present-day human beings there are, for the moment, no such figures." For I do not believe they would recognize those standing around them as being of the same significance as the figures in these pictures. They would sense something that must have evolved out of the life of the Earth itself. They would see in the pictures themselves that Earth inhabitants wanted to say something that is not connected with the moment but with much that lives in Earth-life. They could direct their attention to the one picture and say: "Here I see quite peculiar forms and figures; two figures there in the center and other figures to the right and left. I see a certain expression: the one has the hand raised, the other points to the ground with the hand." All of this they could say without knowing anything about Plato or Aristotle. One sees there, too, persons doing this or that in the most varied positions. One sees nothing other than simple architectural forms around these human beings, but one sees that in the heads and souls of the human beings something lives. One sees this.

Let us assume that such Mars inhabitants turn their attention from the one picture to the other. It looks entirely different. They see a world below that looks similar to the outer world today. Above they see a part that can be reproduced only by combining elements that do not belong together in physical life today: cloud structures and human shapes, yet definitely still reminiscent of the real, of reality. Still further above, over this weaving into each other of clouds and human shapes, one sees, on a golden background, forms that are not reminiscent of that which is human anymore. What would those beings have to say who look at these pictures and know nothing further about spiritual life on the Earth but who judge only from the picture itself?

They would have to say to themselves that these humans have the Earth around them, but they had the need to express in certain signs what they do not see of the world with physical eyes: a world removed from the physical senses and which they can portray only through clouds combined with human figures and through figures on a gold background that are in no way similar to the human. There must thus be something to which these human beings have been able to elevate themselves through certain inner forces that can see more than what confronts them in the sense world. They have built up another world outside this sense world. This other world must have thus entered into a relationship with them.

Then they would ask themselves how the human being came to a relationship with this world. They would see there the curious group that we call the "Father God," the "Son God," and the "Dove" as the expression of the Spirit. Under that, they would see an altar and upon it the Eucharist as symbol of Communion. Since the Mars evolution is not as far along as Earth evolution, there is nothing for the inhabitants of Mars to draw on that we call the two-thousand-year tradition of Christianity. Therefore, the Mars inhabitants would not know what is portrayed in this picture. Yet from the way the groups on the right and left behave toward the middle group, the Mars inhabitants would say to themselves that through the power of the symbol, human souls are given that through which the higher worlds arise for them.

Now the Mars inhabitants would look more closely. They would notice that in the other picture there are various figures, among them, two women—one standing to the right and the other to the left. Curious! When one looks at them, they are quite different in their expressions, even different in their clothing. But now study these two female figures. When we face *The School of Athens*, the figure on the left seems to be pointing to the earthly sense realm below. There are male figures standing around her. What lives in their thinking from the sense world is divined and intimated. What confronts us in this female figure? Her expression, her gesture, and even her clothing indicate what lives in the heads and souls of the men. The pure white dress shows us that nothing of the force that comes from a mere clinging to things of the sense world has worked upon the woman yet. We understand every expression of the men when we understand what this female figure expresses.

Now we will turn our attention to the other feminine figure, on the right in the same picture. There we see how she is different and how she immediately draws attention to what the men are doing. While the left figure only pointed to the surrounding sense world, the figure on the right follows what the men have done. Our attention follows that which the human spirit has produced. We see quite precisely, even if we know nothing of Greek philosophy, that there is progress, a moving forward, from the left to the right side of the picture. On the right side we see what the men have already made out of the surroundings. That will develop still further, and this is also expressed in the color.

Both of these women also appear in the other picture, which bears the name *Disputa*. We see one female figure on the left side. There are human beings standing and looking in rapture upon the symbol in the middle. There we see portrayed the time when the Christian religion was still completely feeling and sensing, when even wisdom itself still lived in feeling. Working in the countenances and hearts of these figures, we see a kind of Christianity that was immersed in feeling and enthusiasm. This is also expressed in the female figure. Then, when our gaze travels to the other side of the picture, we see a progression. There we have those Christian philosophers who have worked on Christian wisdom. We see how Augustine dictates and the female figure records his words. One can construct a great deal of human history from the way Raphael executes the motif: to allow what lives in the souls of men to be expressed in these female figures whose appearance is repeated twice in the pictures.

These are only quite sketchy strokes in a consideration of such pictures. The two pictures can be grasped only when taken together and only the one after the other. The pictures express artistically that which occurred from pre-Christian times to deep into the Middle Ages. Imagine how great and powerful must have been what went on in really sensitive souls who had the one picture on the one side of the room and the other on the other side and said to themselves: "You are interwoven in this course of humanity's evolution; you belong to what happens there in the sense of what both pictures portray!" For this is what the human beings felt who grasped the true meaning of evolution at that time. They saw back into pre-Christian time, when the simple sense-world surrounded the human being like the simple architecture of the first picture. And, in the second painting, they looked at their own time, which revealed the spiritual for the human being, through the entrance of Christ Jesus into humanity's evolution. They sensed that they belonged to this evolution; they felt that their existence entered into the existence of millennia. What lived in the soul streamed into the imagination and also into the hand of the painter who painted these pictures, such that what lives in the inner world of the soul could confront the human being in the outer world.

For Theosophists, these pictures can become the summons to inscribe this great ideal on their souls. Let us look spiritually at the *Disputa.* There we see the Father God in the middle and then the Son God, or Christ, and below him the Dove of the Spirit. Think of the many other pictures that we can find in manifold galleries. Everywhere, when you have the occasion to look at those galleries, you can find these pictures, which are created out of great traditions. You will frequently find the picture of Christ proceeding out of the form of a bird, as if being born of a winged being. For humans once sensed the mystery of Christ, the whole descent out of the higher worlds, as a wresting out of a nature, which is also portrayed spatially as the higher world—hence the wresting out of a bird form. Let us place this picture of Christ born out of a bird before our souls, and, with this picture in mind, let us study the *Disputa.*

There, too, we find a bird being, the Dove of the Spirit. This Dove of the Spirit, which stands among all of the Christian symbols as a great riddle, implies a great deal. The painter of the future will have to paint what will be born out of this Dove of the Spirit. It is a passing symbol; it will be replaced by another in the Trinity. One day the symbol will arise, as the freed human soul is born out of the Dove, through the Theosophical Movement and Theosophical wisdom. Each human soul that wants to take into itself the impulse of Theosophy will be born again on a higher level in a new form. This Dove of the Spirit will change its form, and what proceeds out of it will be the human soul that has as its lifeblood the worldview that meets us today, in its initial form, as Theosophy. There will be other, new forms around this symbol—the freed figures of those around the Dove who show in their expressions what lives in their souls. They understand how, through the events of the spiritual worlds that reveal themselves to the sight of human beings who raise themselves above the sense world, the soul will be freed and, as a free soul, can then face every other individual soul in true brotherhood and love.

For this reason, it seems right that these two pictures should be shown, because they are a prophetic indication of a third picture. The first picture expresses a pre-Christian worldview, and what came to be through Christ is expressed in the second picture. What will come into being through the Spirit, which is sent through Christ and which will dispose of its sheaths, will be expressed in the picture that can stand as a great ideal before the soul of every Theosophist. It cannot be painted today, as there are as yet no models for it.[†] However, within our souls these two pictures are meant to complete themselves as a trilogy.

Thus may the present moment sink beneficially into your souls, so that you hold it and carry it away as an objective and concrete ideal and take with you the feeling of the spiritual flight that the Theosophist should take. We are not together today for learning; rather we are gathered so that we say to ourselves: may such a great ideal of encompassing human freedom and love penetrate our thoughts, ensoul our feelings, and lend wings to our will impulses. Then the small Theosophical group will be a seed around which future humanity can place itself. It will be a seed of human beings who cultivate, in a true sense, that which is so badly needed in our culture: inner truth and veracity. Such human beings feel something—for they will only gradually achieve full insight into what it means—of the Dove of the Spirit revealing itself. They feel how the human soul will live in complete openness in the world. They may vow to carry into our time of manifold untruthfulness and dishonesty in the entire spiritual life a germ of the fundamental honesty and truthfulness to which Theosophists should train themselves. It is precisely the Theosophist who should be an example of the mouth that speaks everywhere what the soul feels and of the hand that executes what the will wills.

Each of us today may make this vow, for the time is right. It is the moment when we can experience a certain satisfaction with how the nearest arena of our activity has widened. May we not look back today to the times during which we were very few people in the rooms left to us by our unforgettable Countess Brockdorff?† We had no worry at that time that the rooms would become too small. Now we have been able to enlarge the space considerably, and one of our friends has just noted that it is already completely full again. That is the main thing—that the Theosophical ideal should penetrate into more and more souls. When it truthfully penetrates, it will assert itself in its true significance.

Precisely on such an occasion, where we are feeling the immediate process of growth may we vow anew to hold our ideal. This growth is quite certainly not something that is mentioned only because it has just occurred or for trivial reasons, but is symptomatic of the entire Theosophical Movement at present. We also see the spreading of the Theosophical Movement in the fact that we now can assemble here in a larger space. In a few days, I will be allowed to lecture on the same topic in Christiana.† A few weeks ago I could make this teaching known in Rome.† At the lecture held there, there were Theosophical friends present from Palermo, a very southern point in Europe. In Düsseldorf† there was a friend from Hammerfest, the northernmost point in Europe. This, of course, is put before you in all modesty, yet as something that may satisfy us in the interest of Theosophy. However, something else appears to be much more significant, and it is perhaps not unimportant to mention it here as symptomatic.

We spoke of Raphael's pictures. They are in the Vatican chambers. They are the expression, captured by a great genius of humanity, of human evolution from antiquity to far into the Christian Middle Ages. Near these pictures there still lives today that person who is for many people the personal representative of Christianity. Not far at all from these pictures, I was able to hold a course on Theosophy in the last weeks for people who had been thoroughly accustomed to hearing messages about the themes of spiritual life only from their own official representatives. These lectures took place in rooms in which, up to now, only cardinals had entered† to speak about the meaning of Christianity. Thus, the words of Theosophy could be spoken to people who were accustomed to hear about the meaning of Christianity and the mission of Christ on Earth only from their cardinals, and this could be done in rooms where previously the meaning of Christianity was spoken of only by cardinals. That means nothing less than that the need has arisen in this place to be enlightened about the meaning of Christ Jesus!

This speaks volumes. It says that human beings there are no longer satisfied with what can be said by the official custodians about that which they have made the content and orientation of their hearts. Christ Jesus is greater than every proclamation that endorses him. Those who are in the immediate proximity of the most official representatives of the proclamation of Christianity want to hear today from the Theosophical perspective who Christ Jesus was and what significance he had for the world. There was really nothing uttered there that was different from what has often been said to you. Does that not make it clear that Theosophy will be called in the future to explain and enliven the most important impulses in humanity's evolution? When people come to us to hear who Christ was, is it not proof that the answers given from other directions are unsatisfactory? We should feel such things out of the spirit, for it is the spirit alone out of which Theosophy wants to work, disregarding all personal interests, all small human interests. It is a mighty power.

Only parenthetically will I mention something else as well. I must mention it, because in Theosophical circles things have a quite peculiar tendency to be transformed. I said things about this symptomatic significance, using almost the same words as here, to a smaller circle at the dedication of the Malsch Lodge. After a few days—only the days spent in Cologne and Düsseldorf—the news that I was in Rome to speak on Theosophy had changed so much that I was already being told that I was in Rome to bring the Pope to Theosophy! We are not that far along to be sure! However, I may well point out that we must take proper care that things do not go through such metamorphoses. Otherwise, we will experience that the one tells that I had wanted to convert the Pope and the other, that the Pope had wanted to convert me! When this tendency to change things is once let loose, it no longer has any boundaries.

However, the matter remains undoubtedly symptomatic. For it appears to me absolutely true that when Theosophy is desired in such places, it means that Christianity is venturing out, or at least that it longs to venture out, into future forms, which it can receive only through the Theosophical world stream. Such a thing must paint the third picture yet more concretely and more visibly before the soul. Theosophy must become the life content of the most important branches of spiritual life in the future. Let it be our special satisfaction that we can work immediately in these initial stages. May that be what we vow to ourselves in the present hour, as we stand before this enlarged space around us. If we keep the promise in the true sense, perhaps the space will have to be made larger more often.

We can then make another connection with our local event—even though the commemoration day is a few days early. I speak of a day that is characterized as a death day in physical life but as a birthday by Theosophists. May 8 is called "White Lotus Day" in the Theosophical Movement, because it is in the physical-material sense the death day of the founder of the Theosophical Movement, Helena Petrovna Blavatsky.[†] On this day we commemorate, in general, those personalities who founded our Theosophical Movement. For this reason, we want to be united for a short while with the images of those who established the Theosophical Movement, as we do on a White Lotus Day.

Of both founders of the Theosophical Society, the last to leave the physical plane was Henry Steel Olcott, who served as president of the Theosophical Society from its founding in 1875 until his death two years ago. If one wanted to speak about Olcott, there would be much to say that would move this unique personality into the light to which it belongs. It should always be stressed and never forgotten that, above all, Olcott was a personality that was entirely and perfectly suited to be president of such a society through the most manifold characteristics. When the German Section was founded nearly seven years ago, there were a number of voices outside the German Section in Germany that said this Theosophical Society allows all of its orders to be dictated from Adyar. They also said to the people in Germany: "That is tyranny! We want to be free of this tyranny from Adyar!" Some people founded other societies alongside the society to which our section belongs, with the objection that this society was nothing other than a kind of marionette whose long strings are pulled from Adyar.

The best refutation of such a statement was Colonel Olcott's character—it lay so completely in his nature to fully understand the freedom of personality of each worker wherever he or she was. No one understood how to respect and value the free individuality of every personality and, above all, not to hinder it as Olcott did. One felt nothing of the tyranny that was supposed to be coming from Adyar. Those, who knew nothing of this freedom that flowed powerfully from Olcott's character and who talked of there being no need for a central power, understood nothing about what it means to found a society around the world that has virtually the same idea content in common. That which is free must be cemented together, in order to make a whole out of the free societies. Olcott understood this in a unique way, and he understood it not merely through what he did, but through what he was.

What Olcott was greeted us everywhere. When I met Olcott for the first time,[†] I had the impression that within the Theosophical Society, one must judge Olcott artistically. The artistic standard, of which I spoke a moment ago, could be used for both Olcott and the Theosophical Society. One could assume for a moment that Mars inhabitants had come down to Earth and had looked at Olcott and the Theosophical Society. Even if they had known nothing of the society's elections or of any statutes, it would have been clear to them, through the whole nature of Olcott, that he obviously was the president of the society. One saw that in the nature of the society and in Olcott himself when he was in the midst of the society. Thus, the Theosophical Society has really had the great fortune of having an exemplary founder in Colonel Olcott. It would be very bad for the Theosophical Society if the day were ever to come in which the spirit that streamed through Olcott would no longer flow into it. It must become outwardly evident that the Theosophists in the world belong together. Without this spirit, the breath that blows through the whole Theosophical Society everywhere would no longer be present and the society would not hold together. It is a beautiful, wonderful framework that Olcott brought into being in this way.

When we pass from outer organization to content, we find not only a personality like Olcott—whose character, wise leadership, great tact, and much more, we can admire—but also a personality like Helena

Petrovna Blatvatsky, who could actually be called a wonder for world evolution. She could only be called a wonder if what she said (cited below) were not true. What is so unique about this person? In her we are confronted with someone who, through her own abilities, would quite certainly never be able to bring about a worldview of even minor significance. A person meets us here who would not have been able to present great ideas to the world on her own. Blavatsky had no great logic or great intelligence. It would be easy for someone who places importance on logic to establish proof of logical blunders on every side in what Blavatsky wrote; likewise, one could easily prove a lack of intelligence in her. Everything that makes a human being great was missing in this woman, and yet she gave the world works that belong to the most powerful that have been imparted to humanity in the course of millennia.

Human beings should not *believe* in Blavatsky; they may think about her what they want. However, you may take *Isis Unveiled* and the *Secret Doctrine*† and examine what is in them with your healthy power of judgment, no matter from where these works have come. The ordinary scholar will have no ability to make such an examination, but that is not what matters. Those, who have the ability to judge, may examine it. Scholars are naturally not able to judge. That seems somewhat strange, but the ability to judge is something different from scholarship. One can be a great scholar and even have a brilliant world reputation, and yet, be more ignorant than a child when it comes to the ability to judge. That is completely consistent. The ability to judge is needed for understanding Blavatsky's works and, strangely, much more ability to judge and much more logic than Blavatsky herself possessed. She knew that and therefore said: "These truths do not come from me! These works come from those high individualities who stand behind the movement that should flow into the culture today!"

Let us assume that she spoke the truth. Let us assume that there really were great Masters of Wisdom and Harmony of Feelings who inspired her.† If we accept that, then everything can be explained without a miracle. For powerful individualities stood behind her, and she was the suitable instrument to impart their secrets to the world. At most, someone could ask: "Why precisely Blavatsky?" Yet, whoever asks that, does not understand the time. If someone else had been suitable as a conduit for the words of the masters of wisdom and harmony, they would have chosen him or her. At that time, Mommsen,[†] Taine,[†] and Du Bois-Reymond,[†] and probably even Haeckel,[†] were not suitable, and so another personage had to be used.[†] For scholarship was not necessary—the masters already had that themselves—nor was intelligence or intellect. It was necessary, rather, to have a largeness of soul and a devoted, selfless heart to take in that which should flow into humanity. This Blavatsky had. If we presuppose this to be true, then everything is understandable. Then admiration for this woman grows with every thought we turn toward her.

If one is without insight, one says that there are no masters of wisdom and that Blavatsky must have invented everything she wrote. This is a thought that could go around like a mill wheel in the head if one wanted to unravel it logically. Let us assume that what Blavatsky said about the masters of wisdom standing behind her is not true. Then what she thus said on this basis is also not true. Blavatsky would have had to have made up everything, and what is in her books would be contestable. However, one should examine her works again. In that they contain things that belong to what is greatest in humanity, which one cannot find even in the great scholars, she cannot have made them up. The world will have to understand this more and more every day. Words really do not suffice to characterize the situation when one does not want to admit that Blavatsky spoke the truth when she said that the ideas did not come from her. It would be a miracle if someone without intelligence were to cleverly disseminate all kinds of teachings, for which the brightest heads of the time are not sufficient to bring into being. What Blavatsky said about the origin of the Theosophical Society speaks for itself.

All of this, appropriately, increases our high regard for the founder of the Theosophical Society with every thought that we turn toward her. When do we best value Blavatsky? Will we best value what she was through swearing by every sentence of the *Isis Unveiled* and the *Secret Doctrine*? If we form new dogmas out of Theosophical teachings, we will be very poor followers of Blavatsky, for she swore by no dogmas. She had only a large heart for what flowed into her from the spiritual world. The springs that were opened then have not oozed away, but flow yet today. They sin against the spirit of Blavatsky who swear by her sentences and make what she has written into dogma. Those honor her, however, who have an open mind and an open heart for that which flows into us from the spiritual worlds. Let us do as she did. Let us not close ourselves off to all that she has left us by making it into dogmas. It is emulation of the deed that she described for us so thoroughly. If she could talk to us today, she would say, "Those who are a joy to me are those who do not swear by my statements, but who do as I have done: listening to the masters of wisdom and harmony of feelings! Those deny me, however, who swear by my words literally. I brought the wheel to a roll; now you drive the vehicle that I have given you!"

I know quite precisely that the words I have just spoken to you—which I express here in this festive hour—are not merely hypothetical, that Blavatsky, if we could hear her, really says this literally! We celebrate White Lotus Day in an attitude worthy of Blavatsky when we remind ourselves that we want to keep the Theosophical Movement growing and progressing, that we do not want to let it ossify, and that we want to consider the Theosophical Society as a framework for spiritual and esoteric life. Let that be the fundamental tone of our admiration for the great individuality who stands at the starting point of our movement. That is the viewpoint that alone can lead us beyond everything that is narrow and personal.

It is more difficult than one thinks to get beyond the narrow, personal element. There are people who stress at every opportunity: I want nothing for myself, I want everything to be in service of humanity, and so forth. There are people who, when one listens to them for five minutes, mention the word "I" fifty times; when one reads a letter from them, the word "I" appears three to four times on every page. To stress that one wants nothing for oneself but only for humanity has something alarming about it. It is entirely negative. It is positive when one stands confidently on that which flows into us out of the spiritual world and then willingly accepts it. Blavatsky was such a noble example, such a beautiful, great model, that she never made the claim that what she gave was from herself. Yet indeed, she invoked her own personal nature in that she committed all her keenness and strength to that which was entrusted to her.

You can rest assured that we act according to her wishes when we expand widely the boundaries that she herself had to draw for the Theosophical Movement. She had an openness of feeling for a number of things that concern certain great early cultures in the spiritual life of humanity. We want to recall just one example: how she again and again pointed out that the Orientals understand nothing of what oriental wisdom means. The Orientals could not derive meaning from the legend that Buddha was thought to have perished from eating too much pork.† There are indeed Orientals who cannot go beyond taking this legend literally. Some believe that Buddha was a vegetarian throughout his life but that he let himself get carried away and ate meat once, and it disagreed with him. Blavatsky was quite right to point out that a significant esoteric truth lies behind this tradition; one can sense this if one takes the words of the Bible as a help: "You shall not cast your pearls before swine!" In a certain sense, Buddha had ventured too far, had given too much to his time; this had given rise to karma. One expresses this thought when one says that he perished through that which worked in opposition after he had cast his pearls.

Blavatsky laid that out in a wonderful way, and she said that every Eastern esotericist knows it. We Western esotericists will admit it without hesitation. We need not deny what she has affirmed. At the same time, however, she speaks of the Apocalypse and its author and says that it was written later by a fanatic. She asks, since the Apocalypse supposedly came into being on Patmos amid thunder and lightning: "Has then anyone ever heard of someone writing a book in the midst of thunder and lightning and declaring that the thunder and lightning were especially inspiring?"† Here we must say, charitably, that she certainly could not yet know, although every Western esoteric knows, what is meant when it is said that John received the Apocalypse amid thunder and lightning on Patmos.

What would Blavatsky say today to those who still want to maintain what she herself said some time ago: that no one could believe that a book was written amid thunder and lightning when one took it literally? She would say: "You have not grasped anything of my spirit at all!"

For she said of everything about her that was imperfect: "Do it better!" We act in her sense when we work on in her spirit. We do not celebrate something in the true sense of the word by looking back to the past, to what was accomplished, and embalming it. Those who are esotericists are not friends of jubilees, because they do not look merely to what has happened; rather, they like life-festivals in which one looks forward. Blavatsky's spirit asks us to look forward at all times to new creating and to consider the past as stimulus for new creating and new working. Then we will celebrate her White Lotus Day with proper feeling.

When we live in her spirit, she lives in us. Not when we embalm what she was or what she accomplished do we celebrate this personality, but rather when we give her the opportunity, now that her spirit is in other spheres, to be with us in the feelings that live and weave through our branches. She can come in only when we develop living feelings and not feelings of memory or of embalming. When our souls, full of the power of life, look into the future and rise up to higher realms of concrete pictures—of which one is of the spirit freeing itself and looking toward us out of the Spirit-dove—the moment has come when our feelings will vibrate through space in such a way that our dear Blavatsky can be with us in her present form of existence. Then she will be among us gladly; then we will have her in the way in which she wants to live among us. For at no time did she want to found Theosophy as some kind of dead, artificial product but rather as a living organism.

That is the second thing that we want to promise ourselves today, on our White Lotus Day: not to cultivate in Theosophy anything that is dead or dogmatic or that is to be embalmed. We want to cultivate something living, which we know will take us a bit further every day. Yes, truly, the more evenings we can spend in this space that take us ever further in our soul experiences and closer to our great ideal, the better it is for us in this space that we have entered now for the first time. In this spirit, we want to be united in this place of new working, creating, feeling, and life.

STUTTGART

FOREWORD

HELLA WIESBERGER

The house built in 1911 at 70 Landhausstraße, Stuttgart, was the first building owned by the society in the history of the Anthroposophical Movement. Until then society events took place in various rented spaces; the larger events and public events were arranged jointly by the three branches existing at that time, which joined together as the Association of Stuttgart Branches in the public museum across from Hegel's birth house. The initiative for a house of our own was set in motion in 1910 through a gift by a Stuttgart member. The Building Association of the Stuttgart Branches was formed. The laying of the foundation stone was carried out on January 3, 1911, and the dedication on October 15, 1911.

The fashioning of the house, principally the inside arrangement, was executed by the architect and Stuttgart member, Carl Schmid-Curtius, according to the instructions of Rudolf Steiner. (See illustrations 4-10.) The polarity of the coloring with blue and red that had been evident in Munich and Malsch metamorphosed in the Stuttgart house. The main events room was deep blue (dark blue-tinted wood), broken up only by the gold ornaments of Rudolf Steiner's planetary seals. To the five seal drawings from Munich were added the sixth and seventh seals. On the other hand, the anteroom, serving as reception area and meeting room, was colored completely red and called the Red Room. In 1921-1922, the large hall was expanded to include a stage and side rooms. The columns with the capital forms that can be recognized in the photograph were added during this renovation. The stage was officially dedicated on February 24 and 25, 1922, with two eurythmy performances of various scenes out of Rudolf Steiner's Mystery Dramas.

At the same time as the building of the house in 1911, the architect designed a cupola room in the basement, according to the model in Malsch, for the symbolic ritualistic functions of Rudolf Steiner's

Esoteric School. This Stuttgart cupola room was the second such architecturally-realized room—after the Malsch model building (which remained unfinished at that time)—with the new column forms, the red-blue polarity of the walls and cupola, and the apocalyptic seals, with each set of seven repeated on the right and the left between the columns and new zodiacal pictures in the cupola. This cupola room was dedicated in connection with its purpose, presumably on November 27, 1911. In any case, this is the first known date of such an event after the opening of the house on October 15, 1911.† According to a statement by the participant and painter of the cupola, Imme von Eckhardstein, the first festive communication of the founding of a "society for Theosophical proceedings and art" was made on this date—November 27, 1911.

The Stuttgart column hall was the only space in which Rudolf Steiner could truly accomplish the uniting of knowledge, art, and ritual. In the first Goetheanum, the center of the Anthroposophical Movement, this step could never be carried out, because it was destroyed before its completion. According to E. A. Karl Stockmeyer, the blue and red pillars from the Munich Congress belonged to the ritualistic layout of the Stuttgart column hall. The room could serve its original purpose only for a short time, as Rudolf Steiner stopped the symbolic-ritual events with the outbreak of World War I in 1914. It was not until Christmas 1934 that the room was again made accessible, when it was transformed into a Rudolf Steiner commemorative room through the initiative of C. S. Picht. Just one year later, however, the house had to be given up, following the banning of the Anthroposophical Society in Germany by the National Socialists. The inside furnishings were removed. The sandstone columns of the column hall underneath (height of 1.98 meters) were removed and erected as an arbor in the park of the clinic Wiesneck in Buchenwald near Freiburg im Breisgau. They stand there today. In Stuttgart a new building was built in 1957, the Rudolf Steiner House.

Report of Rudolf Steiner's Address at the Laying of the Foundation Stone of the Stuttgart House

Stuttgart, January 3, 1911†

Concerning the laying of the foundation stone on January 3, 1911, it is said in the protocol of the Building Association of the Stuttgart Branches: "Today the laying of the foundation stone for our own house took place. Dr. Steiner held a longer address for those assembled at the lecture hall of the public museum. Afterward, the document for the laying of the foundation stone was read and then signed by the architect Schmid and also by Heim, Arenson, Unger, Völker, Kieser, del Monte, Molt, Schrack, Benkendörfer, von Sivers, and Dr. Steiner. Then Dr. Steiner and Miss von Sivers went to the new building with Mr. Heim, Mr. Schmid, the boards of directors of the three Stuttgart branches, the members of the board of the Building Association, and Mr. Stockmeyer, Jr., as a guest. There Dr. Steiner carried out the laying of the foundation stone.

Of the above-mentioned "longer address" by Rudolf Steiner, only the following passage remains:

> We should be clear that as long as we are forced to come together in such halls whose forms belong to a declining culture, our work must, more or less, meet the destiny of that which is ordained with respect to the decline. The spiritual stream will be able to bring up the new culture that it is called to form, only when it is allowed to work right into the physical form, even into the walls that surround us. Spiritual life will work differently when it flows out of spaces whose proportions are determined by spiritual science, whose forms grow out of spiritual science. You can be assured that spiritual science would disappear in the sand if it did not live in the hearts of human beings who are prepared to make the sacrifice that a building like the one intended in Munich demands.

The Dedication of the Stuttgart House

Stuttgart, October 15, 1911 (Afternoon)

Address by Architect Carl Schmid- Curtius[†]

As the builder of this house, it is granted me to speak the first words of greeting and welcome to you at today's dedication. The fullness of the feelings that move me with the handing over of this building, of our new Theosophical home, will find expression in heartfelt thanks to all of those who furthered the work—yes, actually made this building possible through their advice and deeds. If I have thus discharged the noble task of fulfilling a work with the help of others, I may summarize my many wishes for this house, in which countless generations will be taught Theosophy, by saying: In these spaces the esoteric motifs are ordered according to an underlying idea, under leadership and approbation of the spiritual world. We know that everything that surrounds us here is the expression of the spiritual. May all of these forms serve to foster Theosophical work and may this building always be dedicated to the spirit in which it was built! To the Building Association of the Stuttgart Branches I hand over the key of the house with heartfelt thanks for their devoted assistance and with best wishes for beneficial work in these beautiful spaces.

Address by José del Monte[†]
Chairman of the Building Association of the Stuttgart Branches

In the name of the Building Association, I accept the key of this house. Although you, my dear Mr. Schmid, have directed words of thanks to all those who have helped do this work, we are quite conscious of the fact that this thanks must be directed specially to that person out of whose deep knowledge the ideas embodied in these rooms could arise, and all of us share your feelings wholeheartedly. Insofar as this thanks is directed toward us, let me tell you that we have seen it as a special fortune to be allowed to help with the work. We want to leave it up to our dear guests to decide if our work has succeeded. Let me just add that working harmoniously together with you gave us great satisfaction, and we appreciate how much devoted effort this work has demanded of the builder. We thank you warmly and are very happy to be able to say so in this place. Moreover, our thanks go out to all those who have given generously to this undertaking, and we especially thank that member who, through a large foundational gift, made our long-held wish possible.

And, lastly, in the name of the Building Association, let me express our joy that we can celebrate the dedication of the house together with so many out-of-town friends. We thank you for your participation and welcome you warmly. We were allowed to build, through working devotedly together, a stronghold for Theosophical life. The house is now finished; the Building Association has completed its main task.

Address by Adolf Arenson†
Chairman of the Association of the Stuttgart Branches

In the name of the Association of the Stuttgart Branches, I accept the key to this house. It was designed and executed in correspondence with spiritual rhythms and spiritual laws that were communicated to us by our honored teacher. The shapes and forms that meet us, the signs and pictures that give the space its imprint, are created out of those spheres that lie behind our earthly sphere. We want to bear this in mind, and the work that we have to do in this house will strive to attain harmony with what surrounds us. The symbols that look down upon us will become inner life through our striving.

The space is sacred in its arrangement; it will be ensouled in its sacredness through our own work. It will become a home for the highest that has taken shape through high spirit powers. We want to protect the possession entrusted to us with all our strength. This we vow solemnly. Pervaded by such a fundamental attitude, we ask our honored leader to consecrate the place for our future working.

Dedication Address by Rudolf Steiner

All of us assembled here today sense the significance of this moment. Perhaps many a heart here will ask, at this time, wherein lies the greater significance and glory of this house. Are they in the accomplished work that we have before us, and whose importance for the Theosophical life in our circles we cannot appreciate enough, or are they in the symbolic meaning and importance of what we are allowed to begin here today? The most beautiful and most solemn words spoken at this moment are, without a doubt, those that sound softly in the hearts of those assembled here, and it is incumbent upon me to do little else than to give expression to these unspoken words that now fill our hearts.

We feel the significance that lies in the fact that for the first time and from now on, in the spirit that we have kept in our Middle European Theosophical Movement for years, we can work in a space that surrounds us with the signs and features that are so intimately connected with all of that for which we strive as impulse for the knowledge that will lead us into the supersensible worlds. Basically, the entire weight of this hour is summarized in these few words: we are encircled for the first time by a home, by a space that is ours. Such words might suggest a concept that can easily become associated with something that must be far from our minds: the concept of egotism. We cannot and may not understand these words in this sense, but solely in the sense that we have a room around us that belongs profoundly and intimately to that toward which we strive in the spiritual world. When we let the weight of these words work upon our souls, the encompassing feeling of thanks already spoken will grow toward all who have made it possible for us to be gathered in this place today.

We must certainly look back many years if we want to find the source of this initiative. We have to look back at the devoted Theosophical work that has been done here for years. We must keep in mind how beautifully the most manifold Theosophical impulses work here at present and how a mystical inner striving, as well as Theosophical intellectual striving, has been cooperating lovingly over the years. We must see how peaceably people of different temperaments, ways of working, and characters were able to harmonize their ways of working, temperaments, and character, because there lived in them the deepest impulse, which we can express as Theosophical love, as a Theosophical feeling of freedom and striving for peace. We would have to reach far out on the horizon of our Theosophical life, if we wanted to characterize what finally concentrated into an impulse and was realized here. Thus, we can say that out of industrious, energetic Theosophical work was born understanding for the need of Theosophical life.

This moved the heart of our dear friend† who was in a position to translate an idea into a reality that certainly must always live in all of our hearts. We must direct our gratitude toward the man who has given his noble, Theosophically intended foundational donation, which should be long remembered in connection with the development of Theosophy. Thus was created, in the relatively early years of our Theosophical striving, a home for Theosophy, which shows in all its details a reflection of our thinking and meditation. In the impulse given by our dear friend lies the stimulus to work worthily in the home that was given to us. We feel from the very beginning that what we see, what works on our senses, is ours Theosophically, and we also feel that the space, in a certain sense, is morally ours. Likewise, we feel this space to be pervaded by Theosophical love and Theosophical willingness to make sacrifices—by the love of those who have worked for years with devotion and willingness to make sacrifices, in order to provide the impulse of Theosophical understanding, and by the love of the one who first made the space possible. We may say further that we feel in many ways the exemplary nature of the present moment. It has often been stressed how Theosophy must find its way into all branches and ways of acting of the human spirit, soul life, and outer life.

Thus, as all comes from the spirit, so should all human working be penetrated and ensouled by spirit. We must recognize it as a Theosophical result that we found in our own midst a man who could penetrate the artistic knowledge of today with our Theosophical spirit. You all doubtlessly know that our dear Mr. Schmid, who undertook the work on this building, united his best Theosophical feeling, sensing, and thinking with the artistic ability that was bestowed on him by the outer world. We are as fortunate as he is in this respect. What do we feel when we turn our attention to all that surrounds us? We feel, above all, that not only the ability of a master builder worked here but also the heart of a Theosophical master builder. As true as it is that we stand with full acknowledgement before our friend Schmid's interpretation of Theosophy into art, just so true must it be that we reciprocate the love that he was able to put into this building. I think, my dear Mr. Schmid, that it was also a task that filled your heart with joy, a joy that belongs to the realm of spiritual feeling arising where human beings are allowed to let their ability, their drive, and their talent flow into the forces of spiritual life. We consider it the beneficial karma of our Theosophical Movement that we found precisely this master builder, who—as I, probably better than anyone else outside of Stuttgart, can assure you—showed a wonderful devotion and understanding for what architecture should offer to spiritual life in this instance. We may be happy if, in the future, a similar relationship can be achieved.

Now let us, who have assembled here from many different regions to celebrate this hour with our friends, bring to mind—besides the general self-sacrifice and devoted work that was done—the work closer at hand that had to be accomplished in just the last years. Recall the moment nine-and-a-half months ago when we were able to lay the foundation stone for this building, and call to mind what had to be done beforehand in self-sacrificial work. Think further of all that had to be accomplished by our Stuttgart friends, by the association that took over possession of the key to this building today, so that we could be united within this new Theosophical building. It would be impossible to describe this arduous and dedicated work. However, let one thing about this work be stressed. Let me call to your attention a fundamental challenge for such Theosophical work! You are all doubtlessly filled with joy and inner satisfaction about how our Theosophical Society has grown. Still, it should never be forgotten that, even when it is the greatest fortune that it has grown so much, with this growth the difficulties in management also multiply.

When challenges arise, such as have now come solemnly and significantly to our attention, they must be met by people who can bring their whole heart to the work. This makes it necessary to speak of the fundamental challenge. The more our society grows, the more it appears as if such work should be laid in the hands of all Theosophists. That cannot happen at all! It is impossible! Something else is possible—that the genuine work on such a deed can, in an ideal way, have a pedagogical effect on all who declare support for us. What will be the best social relationship if our movement is to translate into numerous fruits that which we have as a seed? It will not be elections and majority decisions, but rather that we can trust, personally and individually, the other—that trust that consists of our allowing a little circle to work on a particular task without hindrance. Such small circles can work in the way in which the work here was done. Let us not disturb those who offer their hearts to that which will further our great goal, and let us give them the full freedom for their work. Let us not surround them with hindrances of knowing better, which should absolutely not be present! If a small circle has worked quietly for years and claimed that trust, then we may say this: If we may infer the seed from the fruit, then that which is working in the Theosophical sense has proved itself brilliantly. The deed before which we stand today is, in the fullest sense, the magnificent justification of the trust that we came to have for the loyal work of the small Building Association that carried it out. With understanding and trust, we express our gratitude for the exemplary work of this Building Association.

Take with you today or tomorrow, when you leave this space, the feeling of how different it is to devote oneself to Theosophical thoughts in such surroundings than in the surroundings in which we otherwise work. Let us feel in this moment how the feeling that this space is ours can expand. What does it mean in still another sense? In a different way may be repeated what was said with the laying of the foundation stone: "We have built a temple for the spirit that we serve." How could we feel otherwise than united with the spirit within such a building! We understand then the longing for images of the beautiful, marvelous example that was given to us here. Perhaps more than anything that could be said in words, this space itself can speak to those who are in the position to create such images. In a clear, perceptible way it speaks of the necessity to be surrounded by our spirit temple. And if we spoke in Munich about a similar building,[†] only to be built with larger proportions, so consider what this space is able to speak to you as an intensification of those words. When we enter it with understanding, remain in it, or leave it and come back to enter it ever anew, does this space not clearly stress the necessity of such buildings in other places?

If we let our feelings run free, we must say that human karma works mysteriously. It could rightly fill us with emotion that our building was placed precisely in this region. Think about how much has arisen in terms of the spiritual life of Middle Europe out of this area of the country. Think about how, in a quiet, earnest, intimate way, a great mind of the eighteenth century made a friend take note of the fervent veneration for the spirit that works and weaves through worlds with just three words: "One in all." This phrase, which was written out of deep feeling, has often been repeated. The unhappy Hölderlin, sensing the spirit in the universe, made the philosophical friend in this region take note of the words "One in all."† A man was thus made aware whose philosophical spirit filled all of Germany and, indeed, the whole educated world.

Think further how, in the eighteenth and nineteenth centuries, spiritual life took its starting point in this area—that Theosophy, which was possible at that time, had its origin here. Within Swabia there were Theosophical centers of the eighteenth century from which many colonies proceeded, some of which still operate today. Let us think about the fact that there was a son of this area who went to Thüringen to a seer in the eighteenth century; this was Oetinger,† who represented the Theosophy that was possible at that time. Because of his own temperament he found that seer in central Germany whose name is of local significance here.† Let us be mindful of the fact that Völker of Thüringen gave a great deal out of his clairvoyance to the Theosophy of this region. Recall that the great philosophers were sent to us out of the spiritual substance of this region,† and that profoundly interwoven with that spiritual substance is the one who became so popular in spiritual life and spoke the beautiful words, "an immeasurable realm is the thought, and a winged instrument is the word."†

When we call to mind that we want to be servants of the spirit through the word in this building, which should be an expression in symbols and forms of the spirit that we serve, then there may sound in our souls in a somewhat changed form—translated into our Theosophical thought—

the words that long ago took hold of and edified countless hearts of those who collected all that they could spare to build such a temple. He who was allowed to set his whole self at the service of the building of this temple spoke the following words, translated into our language:

> You, Spirit of the Cosmos, who makes yourself known to our true self-knowledge, you have graciously kept the word that you gave us, because you saw how the work was accomplished over the years by your servants; it becomes manifest today in this hour. Indeed, the furthest spirit realms are not able to grasp you, Great Spirit of the Cosmos, who penetrates all our works with your spirit, who wants to live in the words that may sound from our lips. How much less can these temple walls, which we have built for you, grasp you! Spirit of the Cosmos, who announces yourself in our true self-knowledge, look upon the will of your servants to understand, upon the longing for knowledge! Spirit of the Cosmos, who pervades each "I," look down upon us and let your eyes watch over this building, where you have decided to live! Accept our feelings, which urge us, through our work, to be worthy of your spirit, flowing into the space that we have dedicated to you.[†]

I had to reach for the words of the Old Testament, to Solomon's words, to express what we ourselves have to direct, out of the spirit of advanced human development, like a prayer to the Spirit of the Cosmos, who lives in every heart that strives after true self-knowledge. If we can develop within us the feeling of devotion, through which in all times the spirit of a community has been called upon in relation to a building, so let this feeling arise in our hearts! By our further working in this space, we will see how differently our work can be accomplished than in some other space that is indifferent to it.

What will, above all, be possible here? It will be something that we need and that we can put into a single expression: composure of our spirit, seclusion of our souls, while we devote ourselves to Theosophical ideas. We can feel what the voice of the cosmos itself can say to us when we put ourselves into the mood of spring. Even when it is autumn outside, we have spring in this space. Then we can understand, out of the language of the cosmic spirit in nature, how justified it is to seek self-communion and composure. If those should come who ask why we isolate ourselves with our work, why we do not carry it out as work of love, we will not answer but will let the great Spirit of the Cosmos answer, who speaks out of nature itself.

How much depends on what happens in the spring! What is necessary for the well-being of the plant world that sprouts out of the Earth in the spring? It is that the seeds are removed from full outer sunlight; in order for them to be able to thrive, they must come into the darkness and seclusion that they enter in the autumn. So must the spirit-seed of life be carried into the inner stillness and containment, the knowledge, the love, and peace, to work here quietly like a seed in the womb of the Earth. Only then can it be effectively carried back out into the full sunshine of life. Such places are necessary for the collaboration of the evolution of humanity. Inasmuch as we ourselves want to be bearers of the best seeds of our culture, it is necessary that what can be obtained from the outer world be carried into seclusion, which only here can be cultivated and can thrive.

Thus, it is a wonderful fulfilling of karma that our first Theosophical house was placed precisely on this ground, like a tribute from the new spiritual life to the old. If the spirit that we serve has received this sheath, we feel ourselves incorporated into the organism of the entire human spiritual life and know, in the highest and most sacred sense, that we have a timely work before us—timely because this work is connected with the spiritual stream that at the present time flows out of the source of spiritual life toward the karma of all of humanity.

For this reason, we can admit today that with regard to those whom we consider to be the source of our work, and also of our possibility to work, we feel that we can serve them with this work. With our outer work, we have been allowed to serve the masters of wisdom and harmony of feelings, with whom the sources of our knowledge lie. Because we feel this, we also sense that they help us with our work. May their spirit hold sway in this space that arose out of Theosophical devotion, a devotion that makes the space worthy of the Masters of Wisdom and Harmony of Feelings[†] and allows the forces of the supersensible worlds to flow in; those forces necessary to strengthen and invigorate our soul capacities! It stands before my soul how the Masters of Wisdom and Harmony of Feelings look down with satisfaction upon this hour today and especially upon the feelings living in our hearts, which are the finest when we vow to fulfill, in this space that we have built for them, the work of the masters. These spirits, which have been connected with Theosophy in its best form throughout its existence, will send their help into this space. Thus speaks the wish that they may do so; thus also speaks a quiet prayer that may be directed to them. When the Masters of Wisdom and Harmony of Feelings, upon whom we call, work within the place where we strive for knowledge, for harmony, and for support of our life, then our work will flourish.

May these good spirits of thc Theosophical Movement bestow their blessing on what I wish to draw out of all of your hearts in this hour, not with physical but with spiritual words! This can be considered an accompanying verse or leading thought over the entrance of this house, words that should be written in our hearts so that we do not need physical eyes to read them upon entering and which we will keep in our hearts, both when we are in this house and when we leave it and take with us the longing to come together again and again for the cultivation of Theosophy. May there be written over the portal:

Who enters, bring love to this home.
Who tarries within, seek knowledge at this place.
Who departs, take peace along from this house!

The Esoteric Aspects of the Stuttgart Building

RUDOLF STEINER

Stuttgart, October 15, 1911 (Evening)

It seems appropriate to remain today with that which is so close to us: our home for Theosophical work in Stuttgart. Perhaps for all of you, who have entered this space today and who are trying to look, with a kind of inner vision, at the feelings that came over you, a word comes to mind that can describe what one would like to indicate as the uniqueness of our experience: it is doubtlessly *mood and atmosphere* that flows through our souls while we are in this space.

When we follow this further esoterically, we can see clearly into the foundations of our life from this viewpoint. We are surrounded in this space mainly by a certain shade of color. That the choice of color matters to us in many respects, you will also have learned from the way we endeavored to outfit the mystery performances† and also from the coloring of other rooms that we have dedicated to Theosophical study and contemplation. It is in no way immaterial which color of a defined space surrounds human beings in one state of soul or another. Moreover, it is not immaterial which color, in the main, works upon a human being of this or that temperament, intellectuality, or character. And it is not unimportant for the whole human organization whether a color works over a long time, in frequent and recurring repetition, or if it works only in passing. You will recall that we covered the hall that we used for the 1907 Congress with a certain red color. One may not draw the conclusion that we swear by red as the right color for decorating a space. This space in Stuttgart we have decorated with blue. The reason is that the hall in Munich served a specific festive occasion for a few days, an event that swept by quickly and was supposed to call forth a mood appropriate to this circumstance. Here we have a space for working; it is meant for our Stuttgart friends to carry out their Theosophical studies and work again and again, from week to week. Essentially, it is a matter of a space for recurring study meetings.

We will best bring the significance of color before our souls when we describe how it works upon esotericists. It is necessary that human beings detach themselves fully from everything and give themselves over to the hue of the color, that they merge with it. If those, who devote or surrender themselves to this color that covers the physically opaque walls, were esoterically advanced human beings, it would happen that after a time of such complete surrender, the walls would disappear to clairvoyant sight. The walls cease to be boundaries for the consciousness in relation to the outer world. What at first takes place is not that they see the neighboring houses—that the walls become like glass—but that there arises at the periphery a manifest world of a spiritual nature; a series of spiritual facts and beings become visible. We need only to think about the fact that behind everything physical in our surroundings, spiritual beings and facts are present.

What thus lies behind the physical outer world becomes visible in a certain way. However, the same will not become visible in every kind of spatial enclosure. All kinds of worlds surround us spiritually. There are the most manifold elemental beings around us. These elemental beings are not boxed in; they do not live in different dwellings. The law of impenetrability holds good only for the physical world; for the higher worlds, penetrability asserts itself. These beings, however, are not visible to ordinary sight. In the same space, depending on clairvoyant ability, visible and invisible beings can be present together. Which spiritual beings become visible in an individual instance depend on the color that we give ourselves over to. With a red boundary, different beings become visible than with blue, when one gets through to them through the effect of colors.

We can now ask ourselves: how is it for those not trained in clairvoyant sight? What the clairvoyant does consciously, the human etheric body does unconsciously, when not schooled clairvoyantly. The nonclairvoyant enters into a certain relationship with the same beings. There follows nothing less than that we, depending upon the spatial surroundings, come into a relationship with one or another kind of spiritual being. It is also a matter of our making a favorable or unfavorable connection with the beings that surround us. Let us assume we produce a color surrounding that brings us into connection with beings which disturb us in what we are trying to carry out in the space; in that case, the coloring is unfavorable. On the contrary, through the appropriate color, our etheric bodies can be supported by spiritual beings. Naturally, that is favorable.

Now we have seen that this space is dedicated to recurring study, through which we want to progress in our knowledge. We need to be in a position to give ourselves fully, with our whole human organization, to that which approaches our souls in such a space as this. We do not want to be disturbed by anything, in order to be able take in these things in the best way possible. One person will always take it in better or worse than another, but the ideal environment should be produced, such that each person can give himself or herself wholeheartedly to the studies, according to his or her inner organization. The color surrounding us puts us in connection with the beings of our spiritual surroundings that come to our aid, in our etheric body, with the spiritual work we need to inwardly assimilate spiritual truths. We will be disturbed least by this surrounding. Nothing is asked of the etheric body with respect to the battle of harmful influences of elemental beings; the forces of our etheric bodies are, in fact, called to lighter work. Thus we see that, for a way of working that always repeats itself and behind which a certain quietness of soul lies, precisely this surrounding had to be chosen.

Let us assume we are taking up earnest work for a short period of time. In this case, when we take into account esoteric law, it is of great advantage to surround ourselves with a red spatial enclosure, in order that we not enter into a festive mood only, but that we come to inner strength. When we must make strong will decisions, we must overcome the spiritual beings coming in. This means that we must become strong at festive occasions, so that that which is approaching becomes a lasting impulse. Unsympathetic feelings at such an occasion would indicate only that one refuses to become lord over the weakness of the heart and mind (Gemüt) and does not consent to making firm resolutions, which, briefly stimulated, should become permanent.

The effects of color are of the greatest conceivable significance. You know that under certain circumstances of general existence in our world surroundings, we see a primary color spread out above us: the blue of the sky. The blue of the sky has great significance for the human being of our epoch: human beings, when they let the blue of the widths of space work upon their souls, receive ever again the exhortation to come into contact with beings in the cosmos that call our etheric bodies to contemplation of the spiritual. With regard to the blue of the sky, it was not always this way with human beings. People today believe that human beings were always the same as they are now. The whole constitution of the human being has changed in the course of time. In those olden times, when an original clairvoyance was present, there was no blue sky as there is for present-day human beings; instead, the human being's gaze could reach out into the widths of space, and they were not closed off by the blue of the sky but saw into the spiritual worlds that spread out in the widths of space. When the ancient people said that heaven, in which the spiritual beings are to be sought, begins there above, they spoke the literal truth.

It is different with colors that appear transparent than with a color that is on an opaque wall. When we examine what surrounds us as radiant color, we must say that just as we enter into a relationship with certain beings through the color on an opaque wall, so we enter into a relationship with different beings through transparent, radiant color. The beings with whom we form a relationship through the color on an opaque wall spread out for the time being in the space of the room but have nothing to do with the three kingdoms of nature: the mineral, plant, and animal kingdoms. Through the radiant colors we enter into a relationship with beings that are directly occupied with bringing into being the things of the three kingdoms of nature. When we look, in particular, through radiant red, we enter into connection with beings within our kingdoms of nature of a quite special type. When the radiant red forms a kind of window through which to look clairvoyantly into the kingdoms of nature, we meet beings whose work builds the best forces for the future of our Earth existence. They must be there in the kingdoms of nature so that inner forces can grow for human beings which make them ever more chaste in their blood, that is, in their life of passions. When we look into the kingdoms of nature in this way, we gaze upon those who admonish us, who rouse us the most to make progress in the purification of our passions.

Besides being surrounded here by certain colors, we see all kinds of signs and symbolic figures in this space.† They are in no way without significance. I do not mean the kind of significance that the brooding intellect can find. Intelligent people can discover all sorts of intellectually stimulating things, but such explanations are nothing to esotericists. The main thing is that they are present. Let us assume that we direct the physical eye to any one of these figures. It is not merely the physical eye that is stimulated but also the entire organization. Above all, it is also the streaming of the etheric body—which comes into quite specific movement—that is stimulated through the course of the lines and the forms of the figures, so that the etheric body has different movements according to whether one looks at one or another of these figures. Within the world of etheric substance that surrounds us, with all the beings embodied in it at the moment, the forms that we draw here really are present. There are beings that truly have these forms in the etheric world.

While we look at one of these figures, our etheric body adapts itself in such a way that it fashions its own forms of movement according to the lines of the figures themselves; it brings forth a thought form that proceeds from it. According to the thought-form, the etheric body will be able to put itself into a true connection with one or another kind of being. These figures are the mediators through which we are led to shape within ourselves thought-forms, in other words, the movement-forms in our etheric body. These figures are so chosen that they result in a whole that has a rhythmical sequence, that corresponds to a certain evolutionary stream in the etheric outer world. Indeed, this stream of evolution is favorable for the etheric body through a quite specific fact. The etheric body has within it the tendency to change; it becomes different when it becomes more perfect. The sequence of the forming that corresponds to the perfecting of the etheric body takes place in the sequence of these figures. When we use symbolic figures that correspond to the esoteric facts and look more deeply at them, it is a help for us. When we bring forth the corresponding thought-forms in the correct sequence, we come to the aid of that which opens our inner understanding for the rhythm that is present when we speak of the seven members of the human being. We did not hang these figures up merely as decoration, but because they are intimately connected with what we want to do here.

Just as we are brought into connection with the etheric environment through the thought-forms that we are supposed to build, as was just described, we can, through music, be brought into a relationship to the astral of our environment, on a path that more directly influences the astral body's own movements. The musical element works directly upon the astral body and the astral body works from within on the etheric body so that we are stimulated by all that is incorporated in the astral world—not in the sense that one speaks of the astral world as containing kamaloca† but the universal element of the astral world into which the devachanic also rays down. Revelation through the musical is more direct than when the higher worlds clothe themselves in forms that are spread out in space. But that which spreads out in space, when it is properly suited to the esoteric results, allows us more independence. The musical element has a compulsory effect on the human being. We meet this kind of effect, which stimulates the etheric body more in that the astral body is stimulated first, through the spatial element as well, and we can study an example of this kind of effect in this space.

You see above two pictures, which have been contributed to our festival by our friend Stockmeyer.† These pictures will be painted again one day in a different way and will then be able to give completely what it is that they are to give. In the effect of these pictures taken together, not from each one singly, we have approximately the following: whether we want it or not, when first the one and then the other works upon us, they will, sounding together, stimulate thought-forms through specific formations of the astral body. That process remains in the subconscious. Because the thought-forms are laid into the ideas of the picture, they have to be described in abstract concepts. Our feeling can make somewhat perceptible those thought-forms which our astral body will one day draw out of these pictures more completely, when we succeed in painting them in the right way.

In the picture to the spectators' right, a certain astral form—a kind of dragon—is conquered by a high being of the upper hierarchies, Raphael, through a merely magnetizing look. When, through the development of their will, human beings come to the point of taking the power of this being into their own will, then they have within their power that which Greek culture considered to be the forces of Aesculapius, with which he healed. All that lies in the spiritually magnetic look, which can have healing effects if it is appropriately trained, can be called up in thoughts if we then immediately connect with what is portrayed in the other picture. The activity of the eye must be carried to the form-shape (phantom) of the human being, so that with the aid of these form-shape forces of the physical body,† the dragon's effect will be intensified; the dragon's effect is then conquered by the power of Michael. When we acquire the ability to sense this thought out of the forces of the cosmos and to think how it can be borne by the physical body, in that it strengthens the will forces, as a sequence of feelings and formations of the astral body, then, mostly from out of our subconscious, we will give rise to something that can have a morally strengthening effect. Then we would no longer need to say with respect to such forces that "the spirit is willing, but the flesh is weak." Thus, we can draw moral strength directly out of the succession of the two pictures and still more out of three pictures.

Let me stress that this holds good only for the working together of such motifs—and never for a single motif. If it were a matter of *one* picture, then it would have to be differently composed: two motifs would have to work directly together, as, for example, in Raphael's *Sistine Madonna*. There we have the intersecting of two motifs, which can be deeply morally strengthening. Above we see the clouds, out of which the heads of angels form. When we look at the Jesus child in his mother's arms, we sense that he came into being out of the condensing of the same forces that allow the angels to form out of cloud existence. That is the first motif, in which we sense the coming into being of the pure light being, the human being, out of the cloud-light of the cosmos.

This motif intersects with what is expressed in the mother; she is complete innocence and love. We see proceeding out of what appears as body—as the glance, the countenance, the lines of the mother—the warmest love. The light from above that condenses to the pure light-body of the Jesus child and the warming love from below meet each other and touch in the position of the arm: two motifs running into each other that give our astral body at the subconscious level—whether we want it to or not, and only if we are patient enough to devote ourselves to it—the following feeling: you have the obligation to bring your love to what reveals itself to you out of divine heights in such a way that you take it into your own arms and turn it into a reality in the world. You get your impulses in life from out of the spiritual world. The Sistine Madonna is an altarpiece in which this thought-form works together with a community. Here we have to do with two motifs that should stimulate in us the mood that we may become able to hold on, in our thinking, to the laws and effectiveness of beings of the spiritual world.

That is what matters in our Theosophical work. Spiritual things are flowing, and for untrained clairvoyants they are like dreams. As difficult as it is to hold on to these flowing characteristics of being in our thinking, the reverse path is just as difficult. It is not easy to give the thought itself such an inner consistency in our thinking that we have the feeling that we think a reality of the real spiritual world. We can gain this feeling if we allow the pictures to work upon us. We need nothing more than not to remain dull in relation to these matters but instead to look at them deeply and often. Then the forces of the astral body will sense the effect that formulates itself in the following way: We are coming more and more to the point of understanding the real content of Theosophical ideas. We are not overpowered in a compulsory way; our acceptance is fully free. The working together of two motifs releases these freeing forces in the human being. Thus you see that, in putting together what surrounds us here, all the laws are fulfilled that so-called white magic establishes: the laws that tell us not to work upon modern human beings through overwhelming forces but, to consider that part of other human beings as an untouchable, sacred shrine that should allow the forces of the spiritual world to rise out of itself.

If you bring before the soul what has been imparted here with a few indications, you will realize the significance of what having its own home has for Theosophical work, for you will feel that such a home must be built and inwardly arranged according to the laws of esotericism and, indeed, according to laws of esotericism that do not come to mind at first. You will also grasp what it means when we are forced to set up Theosophical studies in the surroundings commonly available to us, in places where we have no such home as we do here. The people of our age have very little talent for the area that has been touched upon today, and no area has been so greatly sinned against as that of design and coloring.

If we may speak of a trivial matter, how people dress today and the way they choose colors are enough to make one scream. If we wander through a large city and look with esoterically sharpened vision in the display windows, the question arises as to whether what we see came from a healthy mind or something else. As with the colors, so it is to an even worse degree with forms. This poor talent is also at work in the decorating of spaces. When it is done with full consciousness, it is terrible to set up Theosophical studies in the crass, philistine spaces we are forced to use. When we put this fact side by side with what has happened in this space—what proceeded out of our intentions themselves and thus surrounds us, not out of obstinacy, but because it must so surround us if we want to work beneficially—then we will appreciate the significance of what has happened here. The words that I have spoken to you today should serve to make us appreciate that.

In What Sense Are We Theosophists, And in What Sense Are We Rosicrucians?

RUDOLF STEINER

Stuttgart, October 16, 1911

What can harm a spiritual movement the most is one-sidedness. When we apply ourselves to such a consideration as that of the esoteric viewpoints of the Stuttgart building, we must be clear that, with the stressing of a single truth, a strong light falls upon this truth. One can easily fail to appreciate the other side of the matter, which is also to be taken into account. In order to come to a comprehensive view, we must always keep this before us. We must, for instance, add one thing to all that was said yesterday. Certainly, a still greater perfection is attained if we can erect such a temple around us in pure thinking, if we can imagine ourselves to be enclosed in such a home in thought. For this, our thoughts would have to be so strong that they work in a way similar to a physical home. This strength can be attained through a strong power of concentration, when we follow in privacy such rules as are given in *How to Know Higher Worlds*.† However, so that we do not form a false imagination of the necessity of such a building, we must tell ourselves that when we devote ourselves to our studies in the branch work, we need not only what we, as individuals, establish as the conditions for our concentration, but we also need to be disturbed as little as possible by our surroundings.

Because the human being consists not only of a physical organism but also of supersensible members, and because these parts of the human being are active and form connections with our surroundings, it is necessary, when we exert our physical thinking, that we support our will exertion for the sake of the etheric and astral bodies. We can do that if we establish for our subconscious—that is, for the etheric body and astral body—ideal conditions similar to those we have in an esoteric surrounding. Such a building is a great relief and becomes a necessity for us. We must keep this in mind—that the great truths are difficulties in a certain sense. They are something that we must learn to bear, something that can be shocking at first and that can throw us, because they are so different from what we experience in our daily life. To approach higher truths in the most beneficial way, it is necessary to create a spatial enclosure so that the spiritual knowledge that waits for us may indeed come into us. The Masters of Wisdom and Harmony of Feelings can hand down much to us in our age. Since the end of the nineteenth century many doors to the spiritual world have been opened, and many streams of spiritual life can now be passed on to us.

It may be said that in the near future, which humanity is now approaching, conditions will become even more favorable for the flowing in of spiritual knowledge, which can bring the human being forward in every respect. But to do away with the hindrances that develop through the fact that human beings, after having just slipped out of materialism, are not yet mature enough to receive the great truths, we must produce in ourselves a mood that creates less danger of disturbances. That can happen through a worthy surrounding. All that the esoteric standpoint calls for is being carried out, there where, in our sense, care should be given to assure that everything is in agreement.

It is natural for the individual who enters Theosophy to go quite far to one side or the other with his or her needs and wishes. This is difficult, because the one side does not have the necessary insight to deny things that the other considers as justified. Often insight is not there at all that allows one to see that the denial is for the best, and thus it can be very difficult to wait to receive an answer to one or the other question. Because all information is exoteric, one is accustomed to expect that almost anything that a person might ask can always be answered. Answers have at least two prerequisites. First, the one wanting the answer must be in a position to understand it. This means that he or she has come so far through his or her Theosophical development as to understand the answer. One has, for abstract reasons, the need to ask questions much earlier than one has the capacity to understand the answer, which is given out of esoteric worlds. Second, the one asked must know the answer. In connection with spiritual knowledge, we are at such an early stage that very easily for our whole age—not just for the individual human being—questions can be very premature, even when the right form of the answer will doubtlessly be given in the course of time. It is for that reason that I said in the Karlsruhe lecture cycle† that, what is called for in esotericism, is to be able to wait! Especially those who perhaps have passed through a certain development, but most of all those who have attained a certain height of esoteric development, must be able to wait. When one does one's utmost to answer a question at a certain point in time, the intellect, which always wants to reply, can conjure forth an answer, even out of the mind of the trained esotericist. This answer is not simply false or insufficient; it eliminates, for a longer time, the possibility to come to the right answer at all. Therefore, the ability to wait until one is blessed to receive an answer out of the spiritual world is a necessity.

This refers not only to the deepest questions but also to elementary questions. It is a temptation for trained esotericists to draw the answer from within themselves; they can err easily in this way. The two pictures are an example. Our friend Stockmeyer said a long while ago that he wanted to finish them. The spiritual world promised to give him the answer to his question about how to finish the paintings as soon as an answer was possible. That took a long time. The pictures were finished very late, to the despair of the architect. In what lay the fault? It lay in the fact that the answer that was necessary, as a kind of esoteric instruction for forming these pictures, could be imparted only quite late. One had to wait until the intuition arose. One could think up these ideas very easily, but then they would be worth nothing.

That is what is so necessary: one not only must follow an upright path but also must have the resignation not to think up things with the intellect. We should apply the intellect to esoteric truths only once they are before us, not in order to find them; for that, the intellect must be completely turned off. When esoteric truths are before us, then they must be dealt with and substantiated by the intellect; the intellect must give them logical character. One must cultivate that as a discipline and practice, if one wants to make progress; one must do this precisely when one needs details that are otherwise elementary, in order to incorporate them into a whole connection.

How will it be if we want to build a large building in Munich and we do not have the conception that should be imparted to it at the right time? Yes, we are Theosophists and know that karma works not only for individual human beings but in all of life. If we have this belief, then we also know that, if something is necessary, it can let us wait, but it does eventually come and, indeed, at the right time. We just cannot judge when the right time is. For that we need to trust in the future. If it does not come, then it is not to be. That is not fatalism, for such a belief does not keep us from making every effort; it guides our efforts in the right paths. We are making no false efforts with our intellect but want to prepare ourselves for the moment when we will be blessed. It is better, instead of torturing oneself before a piece of paper, to immerse oneself in prayerful meditation and to ask karma that this moment of intuition come.

Connected with this is also what one could call the right conception of the Rosicrucian principle. If a pedantic exoteric authority on the Rosicrucian temple were to come into this building and were to remember the rules that were taught to him or her out of old traditions, this authority would say: "You have done everything wrong; it is not Rosicrucian." We would have to answer that what such a person wants we do not want and cannot want. Rosicrucianism does not mean that we carry certain truths through all the centuries but rather that we develop the sense for that which a particular time can provide the human being out of the spiritual world. What might perhaps be wrong in the fourteenth century is right in our time, for the relationships of the spiritual powers around us call for just this form. Thus, this building is not made according to an old template but instead, according to the demands of our time. What is this demand from the side of the spiritual powers?

I hardly hold any lecture without using the word *Theosophical* to the extent that it is linguistically possible, even if it is not grammatically correct. Many would perhaps find our form of address—"My dear Theosophical friends"—reprehensible. This word is purposely used, because the fundamental nerve of our task can be characterized through this word. Theosophy has lived at all times in humanity and is nurtured in all epochs in a manner in which human beings had to nurture it according to their requirements—at times in larger circles and at other times in the smallest circles, completely out of the nature of the individual epoch. After all the developments that have gone before, Theosophy can be brought in a form today that, within certain limits, comes into every human "I"-being, every mind, and every manner of intellectual maturity. There need not be any human beings who, with goodwill, could not receive Theosophy. Hence, Theosophy is both eternal and a special task for our time. From this viewpoint, we must consider ourselves the bearers of that world stream that is characterized as the Theosophical.

It should be self-evident that within this stream many different shades of Theosophy can occur, depending on the insight of an individual; this is characteristic of our movement at all times. When Theosophy becomes the fundamental attitude of soul, it creates the foundation on which the most varied findings can flourish; however, they must be gained on the paths of truth. It is always true among those who understand the fundamental nerve of esotericism that they absolutely cannot disturb one another. It is impossible for human beings who have taken up an esoteric practice to be disturbed because they proceed from different starting points and come to different formulations. That is a strict law. An esotericist may not fight with another when he or she sees that the other has begun at the right starting point and has striven correctly—even if he or she finds the other's formulations to be awkward. It can happen that different esotericists formulate what they have to say in various ways, when they begin from different starting points and from different considerations of what it is necessary to derive from the higher worlds.

It is quite different when it is clear that other streams are not on the same level and work with more elementary conditions and then these streams maintain that theirs is the only truth. Not to recognize a higher standpoint is false. If someone were to say that a particular being, which for years in our spiritual stream has been identified as the Christ Being, can incarnate on Earth in a physical body more than once, from what would that stem? Out of what you have heard and will yet hear, you will gain a clear understanding that there is a being that works in such a way that it could dwell in a physical body only once, for three years, and cannot return ever again in physical form. That is a truth that has certainly always been stressed in Rosicrucianism, as was also illustrated in the Mystery Drama. Whoever does not know this truth, because of a lack of deeper knowledge in this area, can come to a wrong formulation, because it is not correct to use the name "Christ."

On the other hand, one can also ask why others say something different. They speak differently because they do not have in their thoughts what we here have called the Christ. They characterize something else as Christ. It is perhaps true what they say concerning this being, but it is not the same being spoken of in our spiritual stream. The Christ being is spoken of in our stream because it is an absolute necessity of our time; it is a demand of the Masters of Wisdom and Harmony of Feelings that this high being be spoken of. This being, whom we call by the Christ-name and recognize when we read the Gospels and identify with, has been so characterized for two millennia. That is an historical prerogative but, naturally, is not absolute!

Even though this knowledge was very incomplete for two millennia, Christ has been characterized thusly, and we do the same for historical reasons. This name should not be used for other beings.† This has been stressed and can be easily understood by every human being today. It is interesting to follow how difficult it is to come to clarity about these matters. Those who do not have a special sympathy to delve into subtler discussions will feel uncomfortable that we do not simplify matters with respect to the Christ. One could see that again in the Karlsruhe lectures. What could be presented there could only be presented because of all the other that had preceded it. It is still not easy today to come to the Christ principle, but it is a necessity laid upon us by the leaders of the spiritual movement.

It is very peculiar that a certain difficulty has existed in allowing the special research of Rosicrucianism to flow into the Theosophical stream. Even the relationship with this movement here is quite misunderstood, especially insofar as this movement lives up to the name of Rosicrucian. I will, however, never say: My dear Rosicrucian friends! You can infer from this that it was never a matter of considering the Rosicrucian as something exclusive. If a person, who stands outside our movement, wanted to say that we are Rosicrucians, it would not only be a misunderstanding but also a somewhat slanderous characterization. It is as if a person goes to market and maintains that someone is phlegmatic, to which a woman replies: "So that's what he's supposed to be, and yet I know he is a butcher!" It is similar when someone calls us Rosicrucians as a way to make a distinction. That makes no sense. Rosicrucianism has flowed into our stream; it will be assimilated and practiced to a certain degree.

You can see how difficult it is to let this stream flow in when you look at the curious destiny of that personality whom we members of the movement look up to with great admiration: H.P. Blavatsky.† If you follow her development from *Isis Unveiled* to the *Secret Doctrine*, you will see that a great deal of Rosicrucian knowledge flowed into *Isis Unveiled*. Blavatsky then made a switch (for a reason that cannot be discussed now†) in the *Secret Doctrine*, which took a sidetrack from what it could have developed. Yet we can see in the third volume of the *Secret Doctrine* how strongly these Rosicrucian principles worked. There one finds the highest truths beside the really impossible. Whoever has the power of discernment can connect with this book that which was revealed today.

Blavatsky keenly stressed that it can never be thought that the Christ who is to come again will return in a physical body.† The coming of Christ, she said, may be understood only as an event that the human being experiences through a connection with the spiritual world. We work in her spirit when we make this statement clearer than was possible for her. When she turns with such keenness against the idea that Christ could incarnate again in the flesh, it weighs heavily upon our hearts that our movement is accused of breaking with her most important findings, which are sometimes not well formulated. What we are doing has continuity, and we do not need to break with the original starting point simply because we have come into conflict concerning the coming of Christ. We articulate at all times the correct in place of the false, but in many respects we can go back to the original statements of Blavatsky. And we can know that she, in the form in which she now lives, wants absolutely for this continuity to be further developed; we should not hold on rigidly to formulations, but rather we must work in the spirit that was then present in Blavatsky's time. It was not a spirit that advocated standing still and, least of all, going backward. We work the best when we bring forward that which was still unknown to Blavatsky. Namely, the spiritual portals have opened quite differently since 1899.†

We are trying, without consideration of preceding formulations, to penetrate the meaning and importance of the Christ principle. That leads us to connect with those esoteric streams of research that have been cultivated with special care in Rosicrucianism since the thirteenth century. Whoever has listened to the various lecture cycles will know, however, that it is not a matter of teaching Rosicrucianism as it was understood in the thirteenth century. We are Rosicrucians of the twentieth century! For us, it is only a matter of connecting with the principles that Rosicrucianism has held and of making them useful for Theosophical progress. However, we must—it cannot be otherwise—recognize that which has been found in all areas as something higher than what is otherwise expounded in the world with regard to the Christ principle. At the same time, we must admit that because of the energy put into working out this principle, the teaching of karma and reincarnation had to take a back seat. What is of importance does not concern the spirit of a historical epoch and not even of Rosicrucianism; it concerns the spirit of truth.

It does not matter to us where these various confessions arise. What matters is the spirit of truth; for this reason, all placing in categories and fixing in patterns must always call forth misunderstandings. We want to serve only the truth. We do not want to represent what this or that time said but the truth that flows from the spiritual world. What can be recognized through human reason matters to us; we lead our movement further accordingly. In the face of all other confessions, we may call ourselves Theosophists in accordance with the first principle of our movement: "No religion is higher than the truth." In this way, we stand on the highest Theosophical basis. For this reason, we do not surround ourselves with spatial surroundings created according to some Rosicrucian pattern but with that which is given to us for an individual purpose. For this purpose, for instance, an outer condition is the size of the room. Perhaps one would not be able to bring particular things at all if a room were larger or smaller. No scheme can apply; but only to wait on that which comes to us as grace out of the spiritual worlds. This means that all of our striving goes toward understanding that which sounds so simple: to open the heart to the spiritual world, which is always around us, and toward understanding such a word as the Christ Jesus spoke: "I am with you always, even to the end of the world."†

With respect to what was represented in past years, no one can say that we embody a form of Christianity like that of the first centuries. We want to acquire a way of thinking that allows us to draw near to the Christ as he lives today. Only when we have recognized that this Christ is a living being, do we want to illuminate what happened in earlier times. Equally, we consider the Buddha as a living being who follows the same principle: the Buddha cannot come back in the flesh anymore. If people were to maintain that the Buddha could return in the flesh, we would have to reply that they understand nothing of Buddhism, for whoever rises from Bodhisattva to Buddha does not return. Buddha lives and works precisely in our movement, and in his work today he illumines what he accomplished 2,500 years ago. As only those who know the Buddha may speak about him, so also only those who know the Christ can speak about him.

We can say that a being of great significance might indeed be represented in a body of flesh, but it has nothing to do with the Christ. The fact is that those who deepen themselves in the being of Christ, come to understand that those who think otherwise err. It can never be the other way around. This brings difficulties, however. Those who have the opportunity to practice Theosophical principles in the true sense, in perfect tolerance with respect to error, must take this into account. Still, practicing tolerance does not mean confessing to an error but instead treating it with love; otherwise, it would be a sin against the Holy Spirit. We must practice tolerance precisely because we, with respect to the Christ, represent the Rosicrucian principle. We can wait until someone voices opposition to us about the Christ. If you understand the principle of genuine seeking after the truth and also of real tolerance, you can answer the question yourself: In which sense are we Theosophists, and in which sense are we Rosicrucians?

Report on the Dedication of the Stuttgart House

[Author unknown]

From *Mitteilungen für die Mitglieder der Deutschen Sektion der Theosophischen Gesellschaft*, No. 12, November 1911 [News for the members of the German section of the Theosophical Society]

One can certainly say that Sunday, October 15, 1911, brought our whole Theosophical life an event of historical significance! It brought, first of all, the fulfillment of a long-held yearning, a desire that slumbers more or less in the heart of every sensitive Theosophist and which Dr. Steiner noted when he said that we are "surrounded by a home, by a space that is ours."

In Swabia, on a ground that seems to be predestined through its esoteric traditions, the immense work matured in stillness, with the help of indefatigably active, devoted forces, to build our own Theosophical house on an appropriate place! Nine and a half months after the festive laying of the foundation stone by Rudolf Steiner, that which lived at first only in the creative spirit of the builder, grew up to a wonderful harmonious reality on the physical plane, a reality that could not be characterized more beautifully than with the words "Theosophy translated into artistic ability." All of our members who, as guests of the Stuttgart Lodge, came from near and far—mostly on the special train out of Karlsruhe—and, in the early afternoon of October 15, saw the sunny, stately building greeting them, were fully conscious that they had been deemed worthy to experience something quite specially significant! Like a tremor of devotion, the realization must pass through the soul of everyone present that here, in truth, a Theosophical deed has been done, that, to speak again with Dr. Steiner's words, "a temple was built for the spirit that we serve."

The entire inside of this solemn temple space, designed with so much understanding love, worked beautifully and harmoniously, beyond all expectations, upon the spectators. There is a certain measure of effectiveness for that which forms into a reality out of artistic feeling. Such effectiveness is measured in the involuntary, non-arbitrary sensing that it cannot be otherwise than it is! Nothing of what we see here looks like a calculated straining for effect; nothing looks like forced deliberateness. On the contrary, all is suitable to produce the right mood and the true soul reflection that should be connected with such a building meant to serve Theosophical work. Precisely so must the mystical, muted shades of color of the lamps shine from the walls and the clear daylight stream down upon the assembled humanity out of the triangularly framed oval windows! One could see that the symbolic triangle form was repeated in the outer shapes, even in the chairs, and was incorporated into the lofty style of the whole. The only decorations on the walls were the two deeply esoteric pictures by Stockmeyer, which expressed the triumph of the spirit over matter. Whoever then looked up to the ceiling saw what looked like a radiant tent cover spread out over the space and pouring over the edge all the way around in a well-known esoteric drop-motif.

The same rights for all—this principle seemed to make itself known in the wise use of the large, long room: from all the places in the hall, as also from the gallery, everyone could see, freely and without obstruction, the raised speaker's podium at the farthest end. The blossoming red roses of the cross attached to the front of that podium had, in the light of the electric flames, an infinitely atmospheric effect. Behind the speaker's podium, concealed behind a quite artistically designed altar-like construction, was a magnificent harmonium, which sounds like an organ and whose festive tones filled the space at the beginning of this dedication like a mystical harmony of high feeling experience: "One in all!"

Everyone must have felt deep gratitude at the fact that, in this new Theosophical home something related to spring grew and blossomed, and that a blessed artistic hand was allowed to serve the masters of wisdom here devoutly and in truth. Dr. Steiner's dedication address permitted the assembled audience to experience all of this once again, consciously in the depths of the soul. To the great joy of all the Theosophical members, we are now in the position to print in the *Mitteilungen*[†] the transcript of this talk, made available so kindly by Dr. Unger, along with a report of the rest of the dedication ceremony. Both of the other lectures by Dr. Steiner—"The Esoteric Viewpoints of the Stuttgart Building," held on October 15, in the evening, and "In What

Sense Are We Theosophists, and in What Sense Are We Rosicrucians?", given on October 16, at midday—should also appear in print shortly. They will be of great interest to everyone.

Much remains to be said about the beautiful Stuttgart Theosophical home and its various rooms so well adapted to their purposes—for example, the council room, clad completely in red, and the library, which is exceedingly comfortable and invites one to tarry. Many of the guests were kindly allowed to have a look at the beautiful and ideally-situated apartment of Mr. and Mrs. Kinkel, which is on the upper floor. Mrs. Kinkel, who fought tirelessly for years for the realization of the Stuttgart building, may now experience the satisfaction of being allowed to move into a home here herself, with the hope of being allowed to welcome Dr. Steiner in the special spaces.

At the end of this report, in addition to the festive celebration—which was shared by all Theosophists so magnificently and without any feelings of jealousy—we must mention a talk given by Marie von Sivers before the beginning of the third lecture, which was as impressive as it was convincing. Marie von Sivers stressed in this address that we should greet with joyful satisfaction the founding of a Theosophical home, such as Stuttgart now has, which proceeded out of the most beautiful impulses and was made possible with the aid of generous gifts. We must never lose sight, because of the special interests of individual lodges, of the exemplary goal of creating a building for the quite exceptional center in Munich for the cultivation of spiritual science. We must understand that such an institute of Theosophical spiritual striving[†] has become a necessity of life. This school will not ray out to just a small surrounding; as a result of Munich's favorable location, it will extend its effectiveness to the furthest periphery.

It must be felt as a lofty and unfailing goal of Theosophical striving to prepare a worthy center for the cultivation of the wonderful well-spring of spiritual-scientific revelations that has flowed into our souls over the years, bringing us ever more powerful findings concerning the being and destiny of the human being and, at the same time, crystallizing in the forms of a new spiritual art! Thus, it cannot only be a matter of founding Theosophical centers in individual places for the time being. Instead, we must take the vantage point of looking far outward. This can give our spiritual perspective the right focal point to ignite a guiding light for all of those near and far who, following a deep and abiding longing, desire to satisfy their spiritual hunger at this particular source.

This Munich building will set an example, in its design, for future Theosophical centers, just as the Munich Mystery Dramas have already carried an excellent example into the realm of art. May we all, therefore, feel it to be our next and most important task to support this deep cultural-historic work, so that its fulfillment is not postponed too long and thereby seriously endangered. May, in the depths of our willing, that feeling lead us that Goethe once felt arise in his soul at the fulfillment of a dearest wish and which he clothed in the following words:

What lofty thanks be given to the one,†
Who brought us anew to work,
Who has made a sudden end
Of all weeping, and complaining.

APPENDIX

Concerning the Unity of Temple and Ritual in Connection with the Goetheanum Building-Idea[†]

Excerpt from *Um die Goetheanum-Bauidee*, [About the Goetheanum building-idea] Private Printing, Basel, 1957

E.A. KARL STOCKMEYER

Evidently, Rudolf Steiner picked up a thread from Goethe's *Fairy Tale of the Green Snake and the Beautiful Lily* with his building-idea, by allowing Goethe's subterranean temple with the three kings to come to life in the Mystery Dramas in the subterranean temple and in the Sun temple with the three altars. One could think that Steiner found a fruitful motif in Goethe's work. In reality, however, it was quite different. He describes what Goethe also saw but had portrayed in a more or less incomplete way. Thus, Steiner connected with much more—for instance, Plato's dialogue "Timaeus"—in that he dealt with the "Atlantean ancestors" and the "planetary evolution" in his essays in the magazine *Lucifer-Gnosis*.[†] In this way, he lifts the work of art out of the sphere of human isolation and characterizes it as an individual portrayal of something that is objectively, that is, intuitively, experienced. Just as in the free deeds of human beings there is to be found the synthesis of the necessity in the world with the arbitrariness of the "I," so it is especially with art. The genuine motif is objective knowledge, yet its forming belongs to artists working in freedom. The motif of the temple, with Goethe as with Rudolf Steiner, is to be a vessel for the supersensible ritual, which Goethe allows the three kings to fulfill, and which Steiner lets speak at the three altars.

This ritual was performed by Steiner, before World War I, with a group of members.[†] Entirely independently of this ritual which was supposed to connect the participants with the ritual in the spiritual world at the beginning of the nineteenth century, the development of the building-idea took place. It proceeded out of the Munich Congress—where only "abstract" construction elements were described—to the model building in Malsch, then to the lower hall in Stuttgart, and finally to the Johannes Building designed for Munich and the first Goetheanum in Dornach. However, the uniting of both the ritual and the building-idea was fulfilled: in the Mystery Dramas the ritual appeared in the Sun temple with the planetary columns; and in Stuttgart the lower hall, with the ellipsoid vaults, became a physical sheath for the ritual of the three altars and the two pillars. The first Goetheanum, with its two interpenetrating cupolas, was of such a nature that the ritual was to be conducted under the smaller cupola and was to be experienced by a larger circle of people under the large cupola. It is significant that Marie Steiner transferred this ritual one time to the stage of the so-called Schreinerei (carpentry studio) after Rudolf Steiner's death.[†]

As focal point, the statue of the Representative of Humanity was meant to stand under the small cupola and, beneath it, the east altar. The second Goetheanum was to incorporate all the previous construction elements, including the Representative of Humanity—we know this through the notes that Mr. Aisenpreis[†] left behind. It was also supposed to incorporate the ritual, the pictorial-artistic as well as the extended ritual, meaning the Anthroposophy, which Rudolf Steiner called the reverse ritual in 1923.[†]

We have to do with the unity of ritual and temple, with temple and ritual. The one is out of the question without the other. Rudolf Steiner brought both out little by little and gradually merged the two. This fusion is found in the Goetheanum, with the Anthroposophical life within it. Hence, it would be a grievous error to believe that for the second Goetheanum, Rudolf Steiner gave up this building-idea of the merging of the ritual with the construction elements specified a long time ago and that we do not need to take it into account anymore.

What one can read from the history of Anthroposophy concerning the union of architecture and ritual in the widest sense will become especially clear in the following exposition by Rudolf Steiner, given within the framework of the Dornach karma lectures of 1924, on April 27th:[†]

> Humanity was not always so obtuse and insensitive with regard to the problem of destiny. We need not go very far back in time to

find that blows of destiny were felt to strike in from other worlds—even the destiny human beings have brought upon themselves.

What is the explanation of this? The explanation is that in earlier times human beings were not only endowed with instinctive clairvoyance but even when this faded, its fruits were still preserved in traditions; moreover, external conditions and customs did not conduce to such a superficial, commonplace view of the world as prevails today in the age of materialism. There is much talk today of the harmfulness of purely materialistic, naturalistic thinking which has become so universal and has even crept into the various circles ... and one talks in theory of the need to fight this trend. However, that is not the most important thing. The point of salient importance is that by reason of the conception of the world which led human beings to freedom,... a certain means of healing that was available in earlier epochs for outer sense-observation has been lost.

In earlier centuries of Greek civilization—in fact, it was so for a considerable time—human beings saw in nature around them the outer, phenomenal world. The Greek, as well as the modern human, looked out at nature.... However, the Greek had a remedy for the damages that the human being incurs through looking out into nature only.... And, actually, it holds good for all of perception, for hearing, for feeling, and so on.... There are some things not satisfied by merely looking out into nature.

...It is more or less the same as if we wished to live our whole life in physical existence without taking in adequate food. We would deteriorate physically. But when we merely gaze into nature, the perceptive faculty in our life of soul deteriorates. We get a kind of emaciation of the soul in our sense world. This was known in the old mystery wisdom.

But it was known how this emaciation in the life of soul can be counteracted. It was known that in the temple architecture, when human beings beheld the equilibrium between the weight-bearing and the support, or, as in the East, they beheld forms that were really sculpted representations of moral forces, or experienced the musical element in the forms, that in this was the remedy against the emaciation that befalls the senses when they merely gaze out into nature. And when the Greeks were led into their temple where they beheld the columns, above them the architrave, the inner composition and dynamic of it all, then their gaze was given a boundary, a limit. When we look at nature, our gaze is really no more than a stare, going on into infinity, never reaching an end. In natural science too, every problem leads on and on in this way, without coming to finality. But the gaze is given a boundary, comes to an end, when we face a work of great architecture created with the aim of intercepting the vision, rescuing it from the pull of nature. There you have one feature of life in olden times: this capturing of the outward gaze.

And again, when human beings turn their gaze inward today, it does not penetrate to the innermost core of their being. If they practice self-knowledge, what they perceive is a surging medley of all kinds of emotions and outer impressions, without clarity or definition. People cannot lay hold of themselves inwardly; they lack the strength to grasp this inner reality in imaginations, in pictures—as they must do before they can make any real approach to the innermost kernel of their being.

It is here that ritual that fervently engages the human being has an effect. Everything of the nature of ritual, not the external rites only but comprehension of the world expressed in images and pictures, leads the human being towards his or her innermost being. As long as people strive for self-knowledge with abstract ideas and concepts, nothing is achieved. But when they penetrate into their innermost being with pictures that give concrete definition to experiences of the soul, then they achieve their aim. The inmost kernel of their being comes within their grasp.

How often have I not said that human beings must meditate in pictures, in images so that they really come into their inner being....

And so, looking at human beings in the past, we find, on the one side, that their gaze and perception, when directed outward, are captured, intercepted, by architectural forms; on the other side, their inward-turned gaze is captured and held firm by picturing their soul life; and this can also be presented to them through the imagery of ritual.

On the one hand, therefore, there is the descent into the inmost being; on the other, the outward gaze lights upon the forms displayed in the temple and church architecture. A certain union is thereby achieved. Between what lives within and that which throws the gaze back (architecture is meant), there is an intermediate domain, imperceptible to human beings in their everyday consciousness because their outward gaze is not captured by forms of architecture born of deep, inner knowledge, nor is their inward gaze given definition by pictures and imaginations.... if you let that work in your life, if you go about with inner self-knowledge deepened through imagination, and with sense perceptions made whole and complete through forms created and inspired by a real understanding of the human being ... then your feeling in regard to strokes of destiny will be the same as it was in olden times. By cultivating the domain that lies between the experience of true architectural form and the experience of true, symbolic imagery along the path inwards, one becomes sensitive to the strokes of destiny. One feels that what befalls one comes from earlier lives on earth....

But what is of salient importance is that within the Anthroposophical Movement there shall be right thinking. The architecture that would fulfill the needs of modern humanity, that would be able to capture the gaze in the right way, and that would lead naturalistic perception, which veils and obscures the vision of karma, gradually into real vision—this architecture did exist at one time, in a certain form. And the fact that Anthroposophical thoughts were uttered in the setting of those forms, kindled the inner vision. Among its other aspects, the Goetheanum building, together with the way in which Anthroposophy would have been cultivated in it, was in itself an education for the beholding of karma. And that is what must be introduced into modern civilization: education for the beholding of karma.

But needless to say, it was in the interests of those who are opposed to what ought now to enter civilization, that, that which educates the human being and is necessary for civilization [the building], should fall prey to the flames... (And one might add

> that there was a wish that it not arise again in the unmistakable form given to it by Rudolf Steiner.) There, too, it is possible to look into deeper connections. But let us hope that, before very long, forms that awaken a beholding of karma will again stand before us at the same place.

Steiner stresses yet again *forms that awaken understanding and beholding of karma*. Can anyone misunderstand who has seen the first Goetheanum? Those who have ears, let them hear! An understanding of architecture, with inner knowledge deepened through imagination, matters for gaining the right stance to the strokes of destiny.

The architecture of the Goetheanum, with forms appropriate for modern human beings, and Anthroposophy, with all the ritualistic and esoteric elements that belong to it, combine to become the path that can bring the beholding of karma into modern civilization. Properly understood, art (architecture), knowledge of the spiritual world, and religious life (ritual) work closely together in the Anthroposophical Movement. In one of the esoteric circles in Stuttgart, Rudolf Steiner explained in a lecture held on March 7, 1914 (only a few months before the outbreak of the World War I) how this all appears in the history of architecture. He gave this lecture elsewhere also around that time. There follows here an incomplete report of this lecture produced from memory. Writing notes was not allowed at these events:

> As the year 1000 A.D. approached, European humanity lived in great fear of the expected end of the world. People imagined this, in the physical sense, as a dissolving in smoke and mist. The Ahrimanic spirits gave this idea to human beings that something terrible would take place on the physical plane, while, in reality, a number of things took place in the spiritual world. In every millennium the Luciferic and Ahrimanic spirits gain special power. Humanity does not need to be particularly proud of the decimal system that is predominant today. Every numerical system is brought into the world by specific spirits, and each has the tendency to reveal certain facts and connections more clearly and to obscure others, to let them recede.

The Ahrimanic impulses work very strongly in the decimal system. It is evident that with every millennium—thus in the years 1000, 2000, and so on—an especially strong attack by Lucifer and Ahriman, working together, takes place. In the other centuries they keep themselves more in balance. In the centuries that include the number 9, and thus in our own century, when we approach the new millennium, they unite themselves, and together, they influence human beings. This fact lives in the popular belief that Lucifer and Ahriman are bound by chains for a thousand years and then are set free for a short time.

In the millennia before Christ—1000, 2000, and 3000 B.C.E.—there was an especially strong influence of the beneficent, progressive powers, which kept this united Luciferic-Ahrimanic effect in check and let rise out of it a special good. Thus, we see how in 3000 B.C.E. the pyramids were built. The year 2000 B.C.E. was the age of Abraham and everything that came into being out of that; at the same time it was a high point in Babylonian culture. The year 1000 B.C.E. was the age of David. The building of Solomon's temple was prepared at that time. In the year zero, Christ appeared. We have often explained how, according to the Gospels and especially the Fifth Gospel, Christ had to take up the battle with Lucifer and Ahriman. In the times after Christ, the good, progressive spirits could not intervene in such a way anymore, and so humanity was left open to the attacks of Lucifer and Ahriman. They managed, in any case, to confuse the thinking of human beings, so that an entry for error was found, the error of the approaching physical end of the world. They are interested in having things be imagined much too spatially and temporally.

At this time, there arose for the first time a proof of the existence of God, which the Bishop of Canterbury brought forward, as well as the counterviews of his opponent Roscellin. It was also at this time that the popes trod Christian humility under foot and raised themselves to power, so that Kaiser Heinrich had to bow before the pope in Canossa, as the whole exoteric church came to practices that awakened derisive laughter of the Ahrimanic spirits.

It is these same Ahrimanic spirits that will assert their influence when we near the year 2000 C.E. Evolution proceeds like the swing of a pendulum: in the year 1000 C.E., one expected the end of the world; in the year 2000 C.E., one will expect exactly the opposite; and in the year 3000 C.E., one will again expect the end of the world, but the world will have become such that whole groups of people will long for this end. One can say without sentimentality: European humanity is heading toward terrible times.

Let us take architecture and the influences upon it. In 3000 B.C.E. the pyramids were built, in 2000 B.C.E. came the hut constructions (Abraham's age). In 1000 B.C.E., Solomon's temple was prepared. In 1000 C.E., the new element that was meant to arise could not struggle to enter into the world, as a result of the working of the opposing forces of Lucifer and Ahriman. We see the Normans, who spread out from Scandinavia over western and central Europe, and how they tried to express something in their wooden buildings that could not fully develop. Certain lines are suggested there but not worked out further, because the Ahrimanic spirits hindered it. Instead, the culture of the Moors appeared on the scene and, with it, the architecture of Cordova and Granada—the horseshoe-shaped pointed arches, which drive out the truly Christian round arch of Romanesque architecture. In the culture of the Moors one can see the anti-Christian element directly in the pointed arches, which should have been round.

That is Ahriman's sign. Thus Ahriman worked as the Antichrist in architecture, in that he replaced the round Romanesque arch with the horseshoe-shaped or pointed arch. In this way he worked through the Moors and the Turkish people and did not allow the art of the Normans to develop, so that the wooden buildings that they had erected throughout Europe could not impart that which they should have. For that reason, we do not find a flowering of architectural works in 1000 C.E., as with the turning of earlier millennia. Now the architecture for the next millennium should be created anew. We must express the round lines that Ahriman suppressed in the Norman buildings. If we leave out certain lines that we find in these buildings, we have our Dornach building as a true continuation of the wood buildings of the Normans.

Terrible times stand before humanity in Europe. We know that when the first third of the century has passed, Christ will be seen in his etheric form and that this will give a powerful impulse over against all the tendencies of decline of this century. In older times, as for instance in 1000 C.E., human beings had to believe what Lucifer and Ahriman made them believe, because they did not yet have within themselves the conscious Christ impulse. We do not have to believe them anymore; we should freely take in this new Christ impulse so that we can achieve resistance to Lucifer and Ahriman. In the twentieth century, Lucifer and Ahriman will seize hold of the name of Christ. Human beings will call themselves Christians who have no trace of true Christianity in themselves. And they will rage against those who follow the living Christ, who continues to work, and those who hold to what Christ said at one time, according to the tradition of the Gospels: "I am with you always, even unto the end of the ages of Earth."

Confusion and devastation will reign when the year 2000 C.E. approaches. At that point, there will be not one piece of wood of our Dornach building resting on the other. All will be destroyed and devastated. We will look down upon this from the spiritual world. However, when the year 2086 C.E. arrives, one will see all over Europe buildings arise that are dedicated to spiritual goals and which will be reflections of our Dornach building with its two cupolas. That will be the golden age for such buildings in which the spiritual life will flourish.

A quite concrete goal is set before us. Human beings, who have taken into themselves the Anthroposophical impulse, are called to work in a very brief span of time in such a way that buildings will arise that are reflections of our Dornach building. Without our effort, without our commitment and our tenacity, they will not come into being. And if the stance that now wants to disregard the essential elements of the Goetheanum-idea persists, even though there is no doubt that Rudolf Steiner wanted to hold to them, then these buildings will not come into being, because the essential counterpart to Anthroposophy, as the extension of the ritual of the present time, will be missing. Anthroposophy would lose its spiritual power if one were to eradicate that which Steiner characterized as the integrating element of its effectiveness. Anthroposophy would then have to become an intellectual and dogmatic teaching.

Deep, persistent study of Rudolf Steiner's building-idea, which has been concretely available since 1907, in harmony with the inner being of Anthroposophy as extended esotericism, allows us gradually to be able to better understand the meaning of this building-impulse.

Steiner left the idea for the rebuilding of the Goetheanum in the form of concrete construction elements. He developed the meaning of this building out of the interaction of the outer form of the building with the human being's pictorial inner vision, leading to the beholding of karma. In this way, Steiner developed the entire task of the Anthroposophical Movement for civilization, which should proceed out of the temple vision that is directed outward and heals sense perception and out of the inner vision deepened through imagination; and through the balance of these two, blossoms the beholding of karma. The building-idea has lived among us in various forms: in the Munich Congress, in the Mystery Dramas in harmony with the ritual, in Malsch as a first model, in Stuttgart as sanctuary, and, finally, in Dornach in its unforgettable glory. It stands there today as a skeleton. [Rudolf Steiner could create only the model of the outer shell of the second Goetheanum.]

Letter Exchange between Hermann Ranzenberger† and E. A. Karl Stockmeyer

Concerning the Model Building in Malsch

(Dornach, January 24, 1956)

Dear Mr. Stockmeyer,

It is an inner necessity for me to thank you warmly for your kind permission to visit your Malsch temple property. I was delighted and inspired by it and still am, naturally, and always will be. One wants to immediately take the restoration of it in hand. Then the many little wonders of form, for which one has your intensive mathematical-geometric working to thank, would be shown in their true worth. It has been worked through thoroughly. Despite the rough condition, one senses everywhere the disciplined, powerful spirit-framework of this sacred, ritual space. An etherically pure spirituality is, visibly and invisibly, intrinsically present. The objectively clear spirituality in the form reveals itself, for instance, in the arches ascending from the columns to the circumference wall. These are the best asymmetrical arches I have ever seen and experienced. How wonderful is the growing—at first slowly and then ever more intensively—inner tension of these arches, in correspondence to the measure of the load. It achieves its maximum in the vertex and then sinks down, in the manner of a fulfilled accomplishment, with a smaller, almost vertical line upon the pillars. How peacefully, lightly, elegantly the asymmetrical arches grow out of the wall. Another example of the lively, moving, and disciplined play of forms is the view when looking up from the entrance to the bases of the vaults, the cross-arches, and the lightly bowed vault surfaces arising between them. There everything is enlivened mathematically. Precisely this part, plastered subtly, had to afford a purely spiritual pleasure for the sculptural sense and for the eye. Especially impressive for me was, for example, the sculptural negative working force between the asymmetrical arches. These "vault copings" hit home; their hollow form has a strong power as hollow space.

Of my general impressions, I will purposely say nothing. Many members of the Anthroposophical Society must have concurred concerning these impressions and must be, for that reason, well known to you, Mr. Stockmeyer. When one compares the many inner impressions of historical religious buildings, "little Malsch" ranks as the most significant beside them, for it is completely new and is filled with actual, genuine spiritual substance.

With heartfelt greetings and all best wishes for a speedy recovery.

Yours,
Hermann Ranzenberger

(Malsch, January 27, 1956)

Dear Mr. Ranzenberger,

You have given me a great gift with your letter. Many have already seen the small model building. Many have gotten impressions from it and found joy in it, and have sought the connection to the Goetheanum, above all to the old one. However, no one has spoken about this attempted realization of an idea as you have. The fact that this comes from one who participated as architect in the entire work on the old and on the new Goetheanum and whose eye for the architectural was schooled by Rudolf Steiner himself, was especially important to me.

You discovered immediately that here the individual construction elements are not just put together randomly, but instead, derived of necessity from the uniform building-idea as they then arose. The asymmetrical arches between the wall and the columns, which you especially emphasized, could not be built differently. They are the only element of all the varied forms that, in complete uniformity, repeats fourteen times. Their form, which you find so beautiful, came from the requirement to build all the side vaults as ellipsoids [with three axes]. This requirement of Steiner's could be realized only if the spaces that were meant to be covered by the ellipsoid cupolas had a symmetrical trapezoid form (in the floor plan). Then I could also ensure that the small ellipsoids would pass over with perpendicular tangents into the column architraves and on into the outer wall. With that, there was yet another demand to be met: namely, that the main axes of the ellipsoids [the largest axis] should be tangents of the main vault, because they—besides the column wall arches—were supposed to take up the shearing force of the main vault. This shearing force is taken up, therefore, by the little ellipsoids in what was felt to be the most favorable place. The girder arches also help, in that they, with their (geometric) main vertex—which is not above but to the side—press against the main vault. Indeed, one senses these small ellipsoids, as you put it, as having a hollow form with strong power.

There are many interpenetrations of ellipsoids here. If one estimates only modestly, there are forty-two. For that, the large interpenetrating of the small cupola with the large cupola of the old Goetheanum is missing. Among these forty-two are two, however, that can be compared with that on the old Goetheanum, which is between the main vault and the two especially large side ellipsoids in the east and the west. The one in the west is easily overlooked, because there part of the wall is taken out so that a connecting opening to the anteroom could be made.

My question concerning the entire forming of the model building was always this: What *must* be done in order to meet the requirement of Rudolf Steiner? For this reason, nothing was developed out of arbitrariness, out of free imagination.

Many warm regards.
Yours,
Stockmeyer

Biographical Sketches of Helena Petrovna Blavatsky and Annie Besant

DANIEL HINDES

Helena Petrovna Blavatsky

By far the most significant of the three founders of the Theosophical Society was Helena Petrovna Blavatsky. HPB, as she was often called, was born on August 12, 1831, to a distinguished family of Russian nobility. She could trace her lineage back to Rurik, Viking founder of the Kievan Rus in the 9th century, the first government of the region. Her family also included German and French Huguenot nobility, and her grandmother, Princess Helena Pavlovna Fadeyev, was an important scientist and self-taught polymath, fluent in five languages, and an important influence on HPB. Her mother, Helena Andreyevna von Hahn was an important novelist, considered the George Sand of Russia, whose books examined the status of women in society and social justice in general, still managing to be critically and commercially successful. On her father's side, HPB's grand-aunt Countess Ida Hahn-Hahn was an important novelist in German, writing about the same topics as HBP's mother. And her first Cousin, Count Witte, was a major reformer, first as Minister of Finance from 1894-1902, and later as the first Prime Minister of Russia in the reforms of 1905.

As a child HPB moved frequently. Her father was a military officer and was frequently transferred. She experienced all of Russia from the capital city St. Petersburg, the Central-European small towns of the Ukraine, to the exotic Caucuses on the Eastern frontier. This allowed her to experience the range of cultures from Central Europe to the East and become familiar with non-European cultures and traditions while still a child. Her mother placed great importance on education; the young Helena learned five languages (including English from a native speaker) and became an accomplished musician. She was a voracious reader and diligent student but was also quite mischievous. She seemed indifferent to her status as a member of the nobility, preferring to play with the common children, to the horror of her relatives.

Life brought her into contact with spiritual streams in many ways. An old nurse who was a master teller of fairy tales found a most earnest listener in HPB. As a teenager she sought out a local holy man who lived in a ravine of a nearby forest. He was versed in the secrets of nature, and she visited him frequently to learn all he could teach her about plants, herbs, and their properties. Her grandfather's library contained a large collection of books on alchemy and esotericism. By age fifteen she was thoroughly versed in the writings of Paracelsus, Heinrich Kunrath, Heinrich Cornelius Agrippa von Nettesheim, and a host of others. What distinguished her were a keen intellect and a desire to understand systematically the hidden side of things.

When HPB was eleven, her mother died. She and her sister Vera then moved back with their maternal grandparents in the Ukraine. When she was fifteen, her grandfather was made State Treasurer of the newly-conquered Caucusus region, and a year later the family moved to Tbilisi. There she met another person who was significant to her development, Prince Alexander Golitsyn, son of a family friend. Described as a famous Freemason and mystic, he was a frequent visitor at the Fadeyev household for the three months that he was in Tbilisi, and he and HPB had many long conversations. By this time she had grown into a fiercely independent and willful young woman. Therefore, the family began to look around for a suitable husband. HPB proved a challenge, for she was clearly not going to be the model of domesticity. Destiny struck through impetuousness.

One day HPB mocked an old man, a regional governor, calling him a "plumeless raven." Her governess, in dismay, declared that no man would ever be her husband, and that even the old man would decline her as a wife. Her dander up, HPB made the man, Nikifor Blavatsky, propose within three days. Thus, at seventeen she was engaged. Startled at what she had done, she tried to back out, but the prevailing code of honor demanded that, if he would not release her, she had to go through with it. He would not release her. So she married and already on the day of the wedding made plans to escape. These plans were discovered, and she was placed under guard. They journeyed to his estate, and for three months she struggled, denying him conjugal rights, until one day the opportunity presented itself and she rode away on a horse, alone, all the way back to Tbilisi. This was a very dangerous undertaking in those days of banditry (the trip up to her new home had required a mounted guard of 200). From there she boarded a ship, ostensibly to travel back to her father in the Ukraine. But she gave her escort the slip, and sailed instead to Istanbul.

From Istanbul she moved around the near East, visiting Athens, Egypt and what is today Iraq. Everywhere she sought spiritual teachers, and everywhere she was disappointed. No one had much to teach her. "In Athens, in Egypt, on the Euphrates, everywhere I went I sought my [philosopher's stone], ... I have lived with the whirling Dervishes, with the Druses of Mt. Lebanon, with the Bedouin Arabs, and the Marabouts of Damascus. I found it nowhere! I learned necromancy and astrology, crystal gazing and spiritualism—of 'red Virgin' [an alchemical symbol for higher knowledge] no trace whatsoever!" [From her letter to Prince Dondoukov, printed in *HPB Speaks*, volume 2, quoted in Sylvia Cranston's *The Extraordinary Life and Influence of Helena Blavatsky Founder of the Modern Theosophical Movement*, Santa Barbara: Path Publishing, 1993.] She sometimes traveled in disguise, dressed as a young male scholar. In the end she would wander for over 20 years, sometimes spending time in Europe, visiting the United States several times, crossing the North American continent in the days before railroads, journeying to South (and probably also Central) America, India, Ceylon, and Kashmir. Her life reads like an improbable Victorian adventure novel and so unlikely for a woman traveling alone that it has been the source of contention from the outset. But enough of it has been documented that even if every last event is not proven and the exact dates of some are uncertain, she can easily be said to have been among the most widely traveled people of her generation. She was always searching for spiritual knowledge. She tells of learning voodoo in Louisiana, seeking out shamans in Eastern Canada, visiting Inca ruins in Peru, and, of course, of her attempts to find her spirit guide and Master in Tibet.

Returning to visit her family in Russia in 1859 at the age of 29, she manifested remarkable spiritualistic powers. Indeed, accounts of her abilities appear quite amazing, even impossible to skeptics and detractors. After five years in Russia, she again toured through the Middle

East and at one point found herself in Italy in 1867, where she volunteered to assist Garibaldi in the cause of Italian independence. She was severely wounded in battle, but recovered and went east through the Balkans to India and again into Tibet, where she stayed for several years. Her stay proved to be the culmination of her quest. Through study at a Tibetan monastery she became thoroughly familiar with esoteric Buddhism. She would later write up what she had learned, along with commentary, in her book, *The Voice of the Silence*, published in 1889. It was the first work to popularize Mahayana Buddhism in the West, and its authenticity and accuracy has been attested by many experts. It was even printed in Tibet and endorsed by the ninth Panchen Lama in 1927, who said she knew his predecessor well.

After her time in Tibet, she returned through the Middle East and sailed from Athens to Cairo. She became shipwrecked along the way when the boat she was in exploded (it was transporting gunpowder). Of 400 aboard, she was one of 20 to survive. In Cairo she attempted to set up a spiritualistic society, but it was a disaster, as most of the "mediums" she recruited turned out to be frauds. She returned to Russia, then went west to Paris. While in Paris she received notice from her Masters in Tibet to proceed to New York, and left the same night. She had a first class ticket, but on the way up to the ship met a woman with two small children crying. She stopped to ask what the matter was. The woman lamented that she had spent her last penny on steerage tickets to join her husband in New York, and they turned out to be counterfeit. Now she was stranded in a strange town with no money. HBP traded her first class ticket for four steerage tickets, and crossed the Atlantic in the cramped quarters of the lower class rather than above in luxury. It was a difficult crossing, but she arrived in New York in 1874.

HBP arrived in New York with a mission. Her teachers in Tibet wanted her to help save humanity from materialism. Her first job was to help convince people of the reality of other planes of existence, and towards this goal she sought out Olcott. She dazzled him and everyone else she met with her erudition and abilities. In articles and lectures they promoted spiritualistic phenomena. After about a year she started speaking out against the spiritualism, claiming the phenomena were insignificant, poorly controlled manifestations of a much larger and more important realm. She took on a few pupils and started imparting deeper esoteric secrets. Olcott was one, W.Q. Judge another. Then she was told to found a society. A group of interested people were already meeting regularly to hear lectures. At one such meeting, Judge proposed to Olcott that they found a society, and Olcott agreed. At the next meeting they came up with the name: they would call it the Theosophical Society. A few more meetings were required to work out the rest of the details. On September 7, 1875, Olcott gave the inaugural address as president, and the Theosophical Society was officially founded.

The Theosophical Society grew slowly. HPB's attention was focused on writing a book, the 1800-page *Isis Unveiled*, which was published to much critical acclaim in 1877. *Isis Unveiled* was the most significant book on esotericism yet published. It demonstrated a thorough knowledge of numerous esoteric traditions and exceeded in detail what was available from all other sources put together. Scholars of esotericism, including numerous university professors, were amazed. Practitioners confirmed various claims. Interestingly, HPB did not claim direct authorship, but instead said she was presenting the message of her Masters.

Then in 1878 she suddenly moved to India, taking Olcott with her and leaving Judge in charge in New York. They initially set up headquarters for their Theosophical Society in Bombay, and it started growing. They traveled much over the next years, lecturing, holding private audiences, and writing numerous articles and pamphlets. Their work was popular, and they attracted many new members. Yet their work was not without opposition. While many yearned for spiritual knowledge, the general attitude of the educated classes at the time was empirical and scientific, with a strong materialistic bent. Such mainstream thinkers declared Blavatsky's work "hogwash"; she was clearly making everything up. A substantial exposé was published, and public opinion turned against her. She left India and traveled to London, leaving Olcott to manage the Society in India.

She returned to London well-known for her writings and immediately attracted a circle there. After a few years, this too ended with allegations of fraud, and HPB left for seclusion to Germany where she wrote her next book. This was *The Secret Doctrine*, a substantial two-volume work published in 1888. This would be her *magnum opus*, and the foundation of Theosophical work for the next century. Among many other effects, it garnered a positive review from a young social activist named Annie Besant, who would come to dominate the next phase in the development of the Theosophical Society.

Annie Besant

Annie Besant was born Annie Wood on October 1, 1847, in London. Her family was middle-class, with an Irish background, making them somewhat outsiders in the society of the time. Her father was a doctor, but he died in 1852 when Annie was only five. From then on her mother, Emily, struggled to provide for the family and keep them from abject poverty. In Victorian England, there was no social safety net, and the drop from the middle class to utter penury could come abruptly. Emily Wood took a job providing for boarders at the Harrow School. However, her position did not allow her to care for Annie or her brother. Annie was placed in the care of Ellen Marryat, a family friend, who ran a small school for girls out of her home. Ms. Marryat, a spinster, ran an Evangelical Christian household in a strict manner. Sundays were for Bible study, theater was evil, and the purpose of life was to serve God. The young Annie absorbed these teachings willingly and enthusiastically. Visiting Paris at age fifteen, Annie witnessed a Catholic Mass and was struck by the beauty and ritual of the ceremony. Having been brought up reading the works of prominent Protestant theologians, she now turned her attention to the early Church Fathers, the theological basis of both the Catholic and Anglican churches. Her whole heart and mind were devoted to religion; she was absorbed in the subject and all her passion went into understanding the life of Christ. She experimented with fasting and even self-flagellation, trying to test her dedication and endurance. She yearned for a great challenge, an opportunity to be a martyr for her faith. In trying to relive in imagination the events of the last week of Jesus' life, she made a chart to synchronize the events as related in each of the four Gospels. And here she discovered on her own what many a theologian had already noticed: there are contradictory descriptions in the different parts of the New Testament. This was her first crisis of faith, and her reason struggled mightily with her passion. She settled the matter by deciding that God had placed the discrepancies there to test the faith of those like herself who thought so much about these things.

The young and still very idealistic Annie was still determined to live a life dedicated to the service of Christ. Frank Besant, a 26-year-old Evangelical Anglican clergyman appeared to be a kindred spirit. Due to the social customs of Victorian England, they were not very well acquainted when their marriage was arranged, but it seemed to everyone, including Annie and Frank, that it was an ideal match. And so the 19-year-old Annie was married at Hastings in Sussex in 1866. Frank became vicar at Sibsey in Lincolnshire, and by 23 Annie Besant was a vicar's wife with two children, a boy and a girl. It could have been an ideal life. Instead it was already cracking at the edges. She and Frank were poorly suited; temperamentally and philosophically opposed on almost every level. Frank was a typical Victorian male: chauvinistic, traditionalist, narrow-minded, and possibly a little insecure with a wife whose intellectual talents far surpassed his own. Annie was progressive, independent, and very intelligent; in every way ill suited to being a Victorian middle-class housewife. Their problems started early. Annie wrote short stories, children's books, and newspaper and magazine articles. Frank took the money she earned. In Victorian England, women were not legally allowed to own property. Philosophical differences showed in other ways. The parishioners of Frank's parish were mostly farm laborers, who lived a miserable and bleak existence—just the kind of people Annie had hoped to dedicate her life to helping. The biggest political issue for the area was the attempts by the farm laborers to unionize, probably the only way they had to introduce real improvements to their living conditions. Frank Besant was a staunch Tory, an anti-unionist who sided with the landowners and capitalists. This was the source of more than one argument in the household.

Three years into their marriage, Annie reached a complete crisis. She was a loving, doting mother, and her youngest child became violently ill. All her strength and attention went into caring for her sick child. But her heart was filled with despair. In every way her life was miserable. She could not comprehend how a merciful God could allow such suffering in the world: her own, that of her parishioners, and that of her child. With her child nearly recovered, she collapsed; a physical and emotional breakdown. In the depths of despair she contemplated suicide. Frank was no help, and his attitudes remained unchanged. One day when he hit her, she left him and returned to London with her two children. And she began to seriously question her faith. She took her questions to leading theologians, such as Dr. Pusey, leader of the Catholic wing of the Church of England. In the patronizing manner of a British Victorian, he told her she had simply read too many books. Others were more helpful, suggesting the books of F. D. Maurice and J. S. Mill, liberal theologians who argued that the Bible was to be interpreted symbolically. She soon resolved never again to say "I believe" unless she had proven to herself the truth of what she was saying. She also decided to return to her husband and try to repair her marriage. She managed the first, but the second proved futile. Her spiritual striving led her to question the utility of Communion, and when her refusal to take it embarrassed her husband in front of his parishoners, she was banished from her home. She moved again to London, but Frank kept their son Digby. Divorce was impossible for Frank, both because of social convention and his religious beliefs. Society would not accept a woman divorcing a good man for no valid reason; therefore Annie remained Mrs. Besant for the rest of her life. Forced to choose between convention and her own intellectual integrity, she chose independence. The choice would cost her dearly.

With her voracious intellect, she was now exposed to new currents of thought. She read the latest works of critical theology, such as Renan's *Historical Life of Jesus* which takes as its premise the fact that the Bible is an unreliable guide to history. The rising scientific picture of evolution also caught her attention, and she studied the latest advances in various fields. She later described how Darwin "had done much towards freeing me from my old bonds." In her quest for truth, she came, after much study, to reject the entire Bible and all that was based upon it. The devout protestant girl who dreamed of martyrdom had, through experiencing the worst of her age and at great personal cost, won through to spiritual independence. She had become an atheist. Within two years she joined the Secular Society, a group notorious for its efforts to separate civil society from the influence of the Church of England.

As a single mother in London, Besant turned to writing to support herself. Socially an outsider, she fell in with other dissidents against Victorian social constraints. In the Secular Society she met Charles Bradlaugh, editor of the *National Reformer.* He gave her a weekly column, and her sharp pen fought for moral and spiritual truth and justice. She abhorred state-sponsored religion, as well as the ways religions of all forms interfered in people's lives. Of personal interest was the status of women in society, and she wrote many an article on marriage and the rights of women. She and Bradlaugh advocated for freedom of conscience and free speech, things that many take for granted today. Besant was allowed to speak publicly for the Secular Society, and soon became an accomplished orator. Attending public lectures was a major form of entertainment in Victorian Europe—a world before radio and television—and Besant was soon in demand. She traversed the nation by railroad, reiterating the themes of her columns.

In 1877 Besant and Bradlaugh decided to take on reproductive rights by publishing the American reformer Charles Knowlton's book *The Fruits of Philosophy* in England. Tame by today's standards, it consisted of a philosophical argument for birth control—that working-class families would never be happy unless they could choose how many children to have—and suggested medical methods to accomplish this. The result was a prompt trial for obscenity, where they stood accused of publishing material "likely to deprave or corrupt those whose minds are open to immoral influences." In court Besant and Bradlaugh argued that "we think it more moral to prevent conception of children than, after they are born, to murder them by want of food, air and clothing." They were found guilty of "obscene libel" and sentenced to six months prison. The conviction was overturned on appeal. The trial was the topic of conversation for months. Opinions raged back and forth in the columns and letter pages of newspapers and magazines throughout the land. Besant and Bradlaugh became household names. Besant then wrote her own book advocating contraception, titled *The Laws of Population.* Newspapers like *The Times of London* accused her of writing "an indecent, lewd, filthy, bawdy and obscene book." And Annie lost custody of her daughter Mabel; such a woman was not fit to be a mother.

Bradlaugh was a strict individualist, and Besant understood and agreed with his individualism whenever it was threatened by social or religious convention. But at heart she maintained a deep moral commitment to the improvement of humanity. And as she observed the depth and extent of suffering around her, it became clear to her that workers would improve their lot best through collective action to address the injustices forced upon them through social inequality. She and Bradlaugh parted ways, philosophically and literally, over the issue. It was George Bernard Shaw, the young Irish playwright, who introduced philosophical socialism to Besant. They became close, and she joined the Fabian Society. She was now in her 30's.

Through the 1880's Besant worked for socialist causes. She joined the Social Democratic Federation, and started her own newspaper called *The Link*. She used all her powers as a public orator to advance socialism, and was notably successful in several instances, including unionizing a match factory, opposing the most powerful industrial lobby in England at the time. In 1889 she was elected to the London School Board, where she ushered in a host of far-reaching reforms, including the first program of free lunches for undernourished children. By 1890 she was a prominent public figure in Great Britain, a progressive advocate for a host of liberal causes, and a household name. The next major turn in her destiny would puzzle many.

As early as the mid-1880's Besant, who was a widely read intellectual, became interested in phenomena which could not be explained by ordinary science. She was hardly alone in this. Many late Victorian intellectuals explored the limits of science and were interested in the paranormal. Spiritualism was a fairly widespread movement by that time, and the reality of the phenomena of manifestations and séances were widely accepted. Besant began to hold séances in her home. The reality of the events impressed her, but she felt dissatisfied with the explanations given for such events. A friend with an interest in esotericism gave her Blavatsky's *Secret Doctrine* to review for her newspaper. She studied it diligently and gave it a positive review. Upon reflection, she was even more intrigued and wanted to meet the author. She found Blavatsky in Paris and soon joined the Theosophical Society.

To some her path from fervent Christianity to atheism, socialism and Marxism, and then on to Theosophy was a riddle of contradictions. But her evolution is better seen as an organic development along the path of striving for truth. She was unafraid to go where the truth took her, no matter the cost.

With her usual energy she threw herself into promoting Theosophy. Upon Blavatsky's death in 1891 she was the best known member of the Theosophical Society, and organizationally the most capable. Her conversion was not without personal cost—old friends abandoned her, a phenomenon that Steiner would experience as well. George Bernard Shaw wrote disparagingly that, "She was born an actress. She was successively a Puseyite Evangelical, an Atheist Bible-smasher, a Darwinian secularist, a Fabian socialist, a Strike Leader, and finally a Theosophist… She saw herself as a priestess above all. That was how Theosophy held her to the end." [Quoted from *Star in the East* by Roland Vernon.] These are not exactly kind words from a former close friend. Within two years she moved to India, the home base of the Theosophical Society, arriving in 1893.

In India Besant continued her program of social reform in a new context. Already in her pre-Theosophical period in England she had campaigned for home rule (independence) for Ireland and India. She received a hero's welcome on account of her status as a campaigner for social justice and Indian home rule. In India she spoke for the advancement of Theosophy, but her way of doing so gave special emphasis to the Hindu aspects. She saw it as her job to revive Indian culture and make the country proud of its heritage, while reforming certain aspects to which she objected, such as child brides and widow burning. She established a college in Benares and planned an entire network of universities. She then went around the world raising money for her educational initiatives. Membership in the Theosophical Society surged, especially in India. Older European and American members, however, became concerned with what they called the orientalization of the Society and complained about its emphasis on all things Hindu. The American branch under W. Q. Judge broke with the leadership in Adyar, and to this day the American Theosophical Society remains independent. In India, Besant's closest colleague came to be Charles Webster Leadbeater.

A Special Note on the Golden Legend and the Two Pillars

Hella Wiesberger

The Golden Legend

In the lecture in Munich, on May 21, 1907, about the arrangement of the congress hall, Rudolf Steiner said that if we want to explain the red and blue pillars, we must start with the Golden Legend.

Rudolf Steiner had already told this legend elsewhere in various versions and interpreted them out of spiritual science. He usually called it the "Golden Legend" and meant thereby the legend of the wood of the cross of the Middle Ages, as is found in Jacobus de Voragine's legend collection from the 13th century entitled *Legenda aurea.* In this collection the legend is called "The Finding of the Holy Cross." The corresponding part reads as follows:

> "When Adam became ill, his son Seth went to the portal of the earthly paradise and sought the oil from the Tree of Compassion in order to anoint his father and heal him. There appeared to him the archangel Michael and spoke: 'Seek not to receive the oil of the Tree of Compassion and do not weep over it, for this cannot be until 5,500 years have passed.' However, it is believed that from Adam's time to the passion of Christ not more than 5,199 years would have passed. One also reads that the angel gave Seth a small branch and commanded him to plant it on Mount Lebanon. In a Greek story, which is apocryphal, one finds that the angel gave Seth some of the wood, through which Adam had sinned, and spoke: 'When this branch bears fruit, so shall your father be healed.' When Seth came home, his father was already dead. He planted the branch on Adam's grave, and the branch grew into a great tree and existed until Solomon's time. Whether this is true or not, we leave to thc judgment of the reader, as it is not written in any preserved history or chronicle. When Solomon saw how beautiful the tree was, he had it cut down and gave it for

the construction of the forest house. However, the wood would not allow itself to be used anywhere in the house, as Johannes Beleth writes, for it was always too long or too short. If one shortened it according to the correct measure of a place, it would turn out too short, so that it would never fit. That angered the construction workers, and they threw the wood away. They laid it over a lake so that it would serve as a footbridge for those wanting to cross over the water. When, however, the Queen of Sheba heard of Solomon's wisdom and wanted to travel to him over the lake, she saw in the spirit that the World Savior would one day hang on this wood. For this reason, she did not want to pass over this wood, but knelt and worshipped it. Yet, in the *Historia Scolastica* [Scholastic history], it says that the Queen of Sheba saw the wood in the forest house and when she returned home to her country again, she sent a message to Solomon that one would hang on that wood, whose death would bring the destruction of the kingdom of the Jews. Because of this, Solomon had the wood buried in the bowels of the Earth. After a long time, a sheep pond was built over the same place; it was a pond in which the Nathanites washed the sacrificial animals. Therefore, the movement of the water and the healing of the lame took place there, not only because of the arrival of the angel, but also through the power of the wood. When the time of the passion of Christ approached, the wood floated to the surface. When the Jews saw this, they took the wood and prepared the cross of the Lord out of it."

The three seeds, as they were spoken of by Rudolf Steiner, are not found in the literary tradition of the *Legenda aurea*. According to the religious-historical examinations of Otto Zöckler in his work, "Die Kreuzholzlegenden des Mittelalters," in *Das Kreuz Christi* [Legends of the wood of the cross from the Middle Ages in the cross of Christ], the sagas of the three seeds built a separate grouping of sagas, appearing from the 12th century on. The earliest literary-historical basis is considered to be the tradition put forward by the Church Father Origen of Alexandria† in the 2nd century, that Adam was buried on Golgotha; to this was connected, in the 3rd century through the Gospel of

Nicodemus,† the tradition of the sending of Seth to paradise, originally with the version that Seth gets the oil of mercy from the Tree of Life. Only in later centuries did the connection of the wood of the paradise tree with the wood of the cross of Christ then appear in various versions.

Rudolf Steiner, who used various elements in his renditions, but especially that of Seth getting the three seeds that become the two paradise trees intertwined into one, traces the origin of the legend back yet much further to the pre-Christian mysteries. When he was asked, after the first presentation of the legend in the lecture on May 29, 1905, in Berlin,† whether this legend was already quite old, he answered: "It indeed appears literary-historically in the Middle Ages, but was developed already in the mysteries and was simply not written down. It connects with the Antioch Adonis Mysteries in which the crucifixion, the laying in the grave, and the resurrection were already celebrated as outer images of the inner initiation. Also the wailing women are already to be found, which appear in Christianity in Mary and Mary Magdalene. Similar things happen with the Apis, Mithras, and Osiris Mysteries. What was at that time still apocalyptic, fulfills itself in Christianity. Thus, as John portrays the future in his Apocalypse, so similarly the old Apocalypses transformed into new legends. The Queen of Sheba was the one who could see more deeply, who recognized the actual wisdom.

Also in the lecture of June 29, 1907, in Kassel,† the "Golden Legend" was characterized as the doctrine of esotericism since ancient times, and of Seth it says that "his mission" was always so conceived that he sees what is "at the end of times: the harmonizing of both principles in the human beings themselves." Both principles refer to the red and the red-blue blood-trees, symbolized by the two pillars.

As explained by spiritual science, the pictures of this legend are the expression of the fourth stage of the Rosicrucian initiation, which one characterizes as the producing of the philosopher's stone, which is also called the "golden" stone. This is the esoteric reason that Rudolf Steiner usually calls it the "Golden Legend."

The Two Pillars

When it says in the lecture about the arrangement of the hall that we designate the red pillar with "J" and the blue pillar with "B" and that these letters are the beginning letters for words that Rudolf Steiner is not authorized to express, he certainly did not mean the names Jakin and Boaz, known from the Bible (1 Kings 7:21) and which were taken over by the Freemasons. This proceeds out of the report on the Munich Congress for the magazine *Lucifer-Gnosis.* According to this report, these letters indicate, in a manner known only to initiates, the mystery of evolution connected with them, which Rudolf Steiner then presented in a modern spiritual-scientific way. All of the public writings and the indications given in certain societies remained only a superficial, exoteric interpretation.

In spite of it, there shall be a particular interpretation selected that throws a light on the pillars in cultural history. In the *Vergleichenden Handbuch der Symbolik der Freimaurerei mit besonderer Rüchsicht auf die Mythologien und Mysterien des Altertums* [Comparative handbook of the symbolic in Freemasonry with the special consideration of the ancient mythologies and mysteries] by Joseph Schauberg, it says that in the Masonic lodges, it is not without significance that the rising Sun and the setting Moon stand across from the two pillars. Their meaning as the eternal alternation between day and night, light and darkness, becoming and passing away, life and death, good and evil, pure and impure, true and false, belonged to the most ancient cultures of the Egyptians and Semites, and presumably, the two towers of the cathedrals and churches of the Christian Germans of the Middle Ages proceeded out of that.... Often two high obelisks were set up in front of the entrance of a temple in Egypt, and these obelisks represented, for the Egyptians, the sunbeams.... With the Semitic peoples, especially the Syrian tribes and the Phoenicians, two pillars of wood, bronze or stone appeared in the sacred shrines of the gods as divine symbols. Thus, at Tyre, in the old Temple of Makarth, shining of gold as the symbol of the glory of the sunlight, that is, in the temple of the City King, stood two famous pillars: the one pillar was of pure gold erected by King Hiram, who was a contemporary and friend of King Solomon, and the other pillar was of emerald that shone brilliantly at night. Also in the Temple of Melkarth in Gades, stood two iron pillars eight cubits high on which the costs of the temple construction were recorded. However, the god himself was supposed to have erected the largest pillars of the world at the end of the Earth: the stone boulders, Calpe and Abylyx at the Strait of Gibraltar. According to the images on old coins that have been found, there were also two trees standing at the entrance of some temples in Syria, especially two cypress trees as symbols of the Sun and Moon. In front of the east side of Solomon's temple stood the two pillars, Jakin and Boaz, whose names were carried over to the two pillars of the Masonic lodges. Movers explained that, out of the Phoenician tradition, Jakin was the one standing firmly, the upright one, and Boaz was the moving, progressing one....

Bunsen said in relation to the Sun-God, the pillars are also called Set's or Seth's pillars, because Set is the oldest documented name for the Sun-God.... In Hebrew, as well as in Egyptian, Set also means the pillar itself, actually the upright, the raised up, the high....

Bunsen also mentioned the following passage in the Free Mason Constitution document by York from the year 926: "Cain's son, Enoch, was an especially great master builder and astronomer. He foresaw in the stars that the world would perish once in water and once in fire and, therefore, set two pillars, one of stone and the other of clay, onto which he wrote the fundamental teachings of the arts so that the sciences of Adam and his descendants would not be lost."

Bunson went on to say: "These are thus the Seth's Pillars or Enoch's Pillars, just as the two pillars are also called Jakin and Boaz outside of Free Masonry. Present-day Free Masonry, however, has made greater use of this Jewish-Masonic myth...."

Rudolf Steiner gave an explanation of the pillars as suggestive of "world pillars," as Pillars of Birth and of Death and gave the names Jakin and Boaz in the lecture in Berlin on June 20, 1916: "The human being enters into earthly life through Jakin, assured through Jakin that that which is outside in the macrocosm, now lives in you. You are now a microcosm, for that is what the word 'Jakin' means: the divine, which is poured out over the world, now within you. Boaz, the other pillar, is the entrance into the spiritual world through death. That which is summarized in the word 'Boaz' means approximately: that which I have sought in myself up until now, the strength, I will find poured out over the whole world; in it I will live."† From this characterization follows the essential comment that each pillar individually portrays life only one-sidedly, for life is to be found only in a condition of balance between the two: "Neither is Jakin life, for it is the transition from the spiritual to the body, nor is Boaz life, for it is the transition from body to spirit. The balance between the two is what matters."

The presentation of the two pillars in the painting of the large cupola of the first Goetheanum building pointed to this aspect of birth and death in the threefold motif "I – A – O" over the stage arch. Based on a personal direction from Rudolf Steiner for the premiere of his third Mystery Drama, "The Guardian of the Threshold," the two pillars—red and blue pillars as at the Munich Congress—belong to the stage picture of the last scene (the Temple Scene) in the performances at the Goetheanum.

In the lecture in Dornach, on December 29, 1918,† Rudolf Steiner notes that the pillars in the present-day secret societies are no longer set up in the correct way, because the correct placement shows itself only in the real, inwardly experienced initiation. Besides, one could not set them up in physical space in the way in which they disclose themselves in reality if the human being were out of his or her body.

In the lecture in Berlin on June 20, 1916,† it says further that today spiritual science relates more about these things than the secret societies, which indicate them only symbolically, so that humanity does not lose them completely and so that later human beings can come who understand what is preserved in the word.

Notes about Other Editions of the Seals and Columns

HELLA WIESBERGER

1907 : For the General Meeting of the German Section in October 1907, Rudolf Steiner published black-and-white reproductions of the seals and columns of the Munich Congress as a folder edition, "Pictures of the Occult Seals and Columns—Fourteen Plates with an Introduction."

1924 : Black-and-white renditions of the colored seals and the columns were made by Arild von Rosenkrantz and were exhibited in London.

1945 : The seven seals from the 1907 folio were published as an appendix to Rudolf Steiner's lecture cycle, *The Apocalypse of John* (CW 104); the 1954 German edition has, in addition to the seven seals, the seven columns as well. The fourteen pictures were published simultaneously as a special edition. The 1962 and later German editions of the Apocalypse cycle contain only the seven seal pictures.

1947 : On the occasion of the fortieth anniversary of the Munich Congress, at the suggestion of Marie Steiner, Assya Turgenieff did a rendering of the seals and columns, using her new light- dark stroke technique. This was an attempt to take the seals beyond a basic naturalistic representation. These drawings were published as a folio edition by Marie Steiner.

1957 : On the occasion of the fiftieth anniversary of the Munich Congress, the seals and columns of 1907 were published as a festival edition, expanded with the original sketches by Rudolf Steiner for the Apocalyptic seals, the seven planetary seals, and black-and-white reproductions of two sketches by Rudolf Steiner with indications for the column and architrave forms. It became apparent only later that these were not actually photographs of the original drawings, but of a copy or tracing of them.

Notes on the Text and the Plates

HELLA WIESBERGER

Notes on the Text

The transcripts of the Munich Congress lectures come from Georg Klenk of Munich. For this new edition they were compared with the notes by Ludwig Kleeberg of Kassel and by Franz Seiler of Berlin. Changes from the 1957 edition are due to this comparison of the texts. Additions in brackets are from the editors. The notes about the address at the laying of the foundation stone in Malsch were written by Hilde Stockmeyer of Malsch from memory. The transcripts of the Berlin lectures are from Franz Seiler of Berlin, those of the Stuttgart lectures from Carl Unger of Stuttgart. The name of the notetaker for the Stuttgart lecture of September 16, 1907 is not known.

Prior individual German publications:
The lectures of Stuttgart, October 15 and 16, 1911, with the title: "Die okkulten Gesichtspunkte des Stuttgarter Baues. In welchem Sinne sind wir Theosophen und in welchem Sinne sind wir Rosenkreuzer?" ["The Esoteric Viewpoints of the Stuttgart Building. In What Sense Are We Theosophists, and in What Sense Are We Rosicrucians?], Berlin 1912.

The following lectures were printed in periodicals:
Munich, May 19 and 20, 1907; Stuttgart, September 16, 1907, and Penmaenmawr, August 24, 1923 in: *What Is Happening in the Anthroposophical Society—News for Its Members*, 25th year (1948) or 13th year (1936).

Berlin, October 20, 1907 and Stuttgart, October 15, 1911 (inauguration talk) in "News for the Members of the German Section of the Theosophical Society", No. VI, February 1908 or No. XII, November 1911.

An additional note on the text for this edition from the translator: The works by Rudolf Steiner are referred to by their Complete Works

(CW) numbers. These correspond exactly to the German GA numbers. For more details about each volume, see the list of the Complete Works (literal translation) at the end of this volume.

Notes on the Plates

Plates 1–5 : Only the sketches for the second, third, fourth, and seventh seals remain.

Plates 6–19 : The colored plates made in 1907 for the Congress hall were not preserved. Already in 1907 Rudolf Steiner made small black-and-white reproductions available as a folio, for which he then gave an introduction. Clara Rettich, presumably at the request of friends, prepared several series of the seals out of this folio and colored them by hand, in accordance with large exemplars from the Congress hall. Two of these series are in the archive of the Rudolf Steiner Estate. One of these series is reproduced here.

In 1911 Rudolf Steiner had Clara Rettich paint the seals again; this time for the column room of the Stuttgart house, where they were hung between the two-times-seven columns. These paintings, in oil and with a diameter of 79 centimeters, are now to be found in the archive of the Rudolf Steiner Estate.

Plates 20–26 : The Painter Karl Stahl painted these columns, from sculpted models by Rudolf Steiner, on large boards for the Munich Congress. Neither the models nor the pictures from 1907 remain. The reproductions included here come from the folio that Rudolf Steiner published in 1907.

Plates 27–33 : The original drawings for the planetary seals were not preserved. It is also not known if they were made available graphically. Rudolf Steiner drew the sixth and seventh seals only four years later for the Stuttgart house. These last two seals were drawn by architect Erik Zimmer for the anniversary folio in 1957. One of Rudolf Steiner's sketches for the seventh seal, which varies from the final version, was preserved and is to be found earlier among the facsimiles and notes in this volume.

Plates 34–35 : The sketches for the columns and architraves of the small cupola and large cupola rooms of the first Goetheanum were done in 1911. The details given on them for the kind of wood to be used was presumably added in 1913 for the Dornach building, as there had been no intention to use wood in the interior rooms of the central building planned for Munich.

Plates 36–38 : These drawings to scale by Friedrich Bergmann, reflect a decade of working with the forms of the first Goetheanum from Rudolf Steiner's model, architectural plans, and photographs. Friedrich Bergmann (born in 1900) was a student of Oswald Dubach and Carl Kemper, both of whom worked extensively on the building of the first Goetheanum.

EDITORIAL AND REFERENCE NOTES

Page 1, "Baron Rosenkrantz"
Baron Arild von Rosenkrantz (1870-1964) was a Danish painter who spent most of his life outside of Denmark, primarily in England. He joined the Anthroposophical Society in 1912, and worked on the first Goetheanum building during World War I. From 1914/15 to 1916 he painted the middle motif in the small cupola of the First Goetheanum. In 1917/18, at the wish of the other painters, and with his agreement, it was painted over by Rudolf Steiner himself. Von Rosenkrantz was active in the Anthroposophical Society in England in the 1920s, organizing two one-week summer conferences at which Steiner was the featured speaker, one in 1921, and this one in 1923. In 1925 he moved from Dornach to London, where he remained active in the Anthroposophical Movement as a painter and decorator. He returned to Denmark in 1940 and was unable to leave because of the National Socialist (Nazi) invasion. He remained in Denmark up to his death in 1964, painting numerous canvases exploring themes from Steiner's work, and using techniques and indications given by Steiner.

Page 1, "Goetheanum...in the future"
The first Goetheanum, a center for spiritual research and massive lecture hall, theater, and conference center made of painted and carved wood as a complete piece of art, was destroyed by arson six months prior. Steiner was working out the design for a second Goetheanum (which was completed in 1928) to be made of poured concrete.

Page 1, "my lectures here"
Rudolf Steiner held a series of lectures in Penmaenmawr from August 19-31, 1923. These are published in CW 227.

Page 9, "Julius Stinde"
Julius Stinde (1841-1905), satirist, trained as a chemist, earning his Ph.D. in 1863. He started writing on the side in the late 1860's, publishing plays and stories under various pseudonyms. He became moderately famous in the late 1870s and 1880s with several novels. Half-brother to Sophie Stinde.

Page 11, "Whitsun would come very early that next year"
From "About the Munich Congress" by Ludwig Kleeberg in *Wege und Worte: Erinnerungen an Rudolf Steiner aus Tagebüchern und Briefen* [Ways and Words: Reminiscences of Rudolf Steiner from Diaries and Letters].

Page 11, "Marie von Sivers to Edouard Schuré...July 18, 1906"
Marie von Sivers corresponded with Eduard Schuré in French. The English version here has been translated from the German translation.

Page 11, "who is...very musical"
Referenced here is Adolf Arenson, who did not end up composing any music for Schuré's *Eleusis* Drama, but did compose music for all four of Steiner's Mystery Dramas between 1910 and 1913.

Page 12, "Schuré was joyfully surprised"
From Marie Steiner's Foreword to Das Heilige Drama von Eleusis [The sacred drama of Eleusis], Dornach, 1939.

Page 12, "[Theosophy in Light of the John Gospel]"
CW 94.

Page 13, "Vogesental...Vosges"
A mountain range in the east of France near the border with Germany and Switzerland.

Page 14, "stay in Munich"
CW 262.

Page 14, "Mr. Stavenhagen"
Bernhard Stavenhagen (1862-1914). From 1885 to 1897/98 he worked in Weimar, and up to 1907 in Munich. Thereafter he lived in Geneva until his death in 1914. Stavenhagen was one of Liszt's favorite students, having been one of the most brilliant virtuosos of his school. He went on many successful concert tours throughout Europe and America. Rudolf Steiner and Bernhard Stavenhagen became friends during their time together in Weimar, where Stavenhagen was the Court Pianist for the Grand Duke of Sachsen starting in 1890 and Court Conductor from 1895. In 1895 he took over Richard Strauss' position of Director of the Court Opera in Munich. Between 1901 and 1904 he was also Director of the Academy of Musical Art and the leader of a master class for piano. Between 1904 and 1907 he was more intensively active as Soloist and Concert Director (most frequently with the Kaim Orchestra). In Geneva he was the Director of the Subscription Concerts and leader of a master class at the Conservatory.

Page 14, "Erlangen...congress program"
Erlangen is about 10 miles north of Nuremberg. Steiner arrived in Nuremberg, but then took another train out of the city for the day before anyone could see him. The program for the Congress must have been sent a little bit later. For the actual Congress Rudolf Steiner created a different "Program Book, that could be handed out to attendees."

Page 14, "as it stands in the manuscript"
CW 262.

Page 16, "in any way dismay us"
CW 262.

Page 16, "new president of the Theosophical Society"
Just before the start of the Munich Congress Annie Besant was chosen as the successor to H. S. Olcott.

Page 22, "The Blechs and Mr. Pascal"
Prominent French Theosophists.

Page 22, "Mr. Sauerwein"
Jules Sauerwein (1880-1967) translated *Outline of Esoteric Science, How to Know Higher Worlds*, and most of Rudolf Steiner's lectures to the public in France into French. He was the most famous journalist in France between WWI and WWII. The focus of his life's work was to mediate between what Rudolf Steiner brought and world politics; and between German and French culture, politics, and speech. Sauerwein met Rudolf Steiner in Vienna. Although not yet a member of the Theosophical Society, he was given permission by Rudolf Steiner personally to attend a lecture. The lecture impressed him deeply, and he began his study of Theosophy. He sought to have conversations with Steiner about the world situation. Sauerwein published an interview with Rudolf Steiner in *Matlin*, titled "Ein Licht auf die Ursachen des Krieges. Die unveröffentlichten und in Deutschland verbotenen Memoiren des Generalstabschefs von Moltke betreffend." [A light on the causes of the war. Regarding the unpublished and, in Germany, banned memoirs of the Chief of General Staff von Moltke.]

Page 23, "Dr. Steiner's lecture cycle"
The lecture cycle of May 22-June 6, 1907 was announced in the Congress program as "A course about Theosophy from the Rosicrucian Methodology." It is published as CW 99.

Page 23, "lecture cycle is now taking place"
The course was titled "Theosophy and Rosicrucianism" and is published in CW 100.

Page 23, "listened to him silently"
Source: Marie Steiner, in an introduction to a privately printed book titled "Studienmaterial aus den Sitzungen des Dreißigerkreises Stuttgart 1922/23." (Dornach, 1947, not translated).

Page 24, "in so far as Christianity should flow into it"
Said in an address in Berlin on December 14, 1911, planned for CW 251.

Page 24, "Always yours, Annie Besant"
A copy of the original English letter was printed in Emil Bock's book *Rudolf Steiner, Studien zu seinem Lebensgang und Lebenswerk* (Stuttgart, 1961).

Page 26, "congresses...held previously...discussions"
On July 4, 1903, on the occasion of the General Meeting of the British Section of the Theosophical Society, the first meeting took place of the Federation of the European Sections of the Theosophical Society, consisting of the British, Dutch, French, Italian and German Sections. Then the decision was made to organize annual congresses in other countries. The first of these congresses took place in Amsterdam, the second in 1905 in London, the third in 1906 in Paris, and the fourth in 1907 in Munich under the leadership of Rudolf Steiner. After that they followed every two years. The fifth took place thus in 1909 in Budapest, and the sixth was supposed to be in 1911 in Genoa. However, it did not take place for the reasons described by Marie Steiner's essay on pages 121-123 of this volume.

Page 31, "certain individual seals agree...others do not"
For comparison we bring a rendering of this kind out of Eliphas Levi's *Dogme et Rituel de la haute Magie*, 1862, Volume 2. Rudolf Steiner was the first to offer an image for Levi's pictureless seventh seal.

Page 32, "spiritual stream...since the fourteenth century"
See CW 130.

Page 33, "comprehensive secrets of human evolution"
See, among others, CW 104 and 104a for a detailed exegesis on the symbols in the Book of Revelations.

Page 33, "Among bodily organs and forms of expression...what they will become in the future"
Every evolution proceeds in cycles, at first in a descending direction out of the spiritual into the materiality, in order then to return in an ascending direction out of the material to the spiritual. In the lecture in Berlin of January 27, 1908, (in CW 102) it says: "...Yes, there are two forces there that move in and out of the human being, forces that descend and forces that ascend. For every such force there is a moment in which it transforms from a descending into an ascending force. All forces that become ascending forces were first descending forces. They climb, so to speak, down to the human being. In the human being they achieve the power of the ascending."

Page 34, "two pillars...sea...realm of Earth"
See "A Special Note on the Golden Legend and the Two Pillars" in the Appendix.

Page 35, "picture of the Mystery of the Grail"
In his "An Outline of Esoteric Science," which appeared three years after the Munich Congress, in *Cosmic and Human Evolution Now and in the Future*, Rudolf Steiner gives the following description of the Grail symbol:

Symbolically, this hidden knowledge, which is taking hold of humanity from the other side and will do so increasingly in the future, can be called "the knowledge of the Grail." If we learn to understand the deeper meaning of this symbol as it is presented in stories and legends, we will discover a significant image of what has been described above as the new initiation knowledge with the Christ mystery at its center.

The path to supersensible worlds whose first stages have been described in this book leads to "the science of the Grail"... To the extent that human evolution will absorb Grail knowledge, the impulse supplied by the Christ event can become ever more significant. Increasingly, an inner aspect will be added to the external aspect of Christian evolution. What we can recognize through imagination, inspiration and intuition about the higher worlds in conjunction with the Christ mystery will increasingly permeate our life of ideas, feeling and will. "Hidden" Grail knowledge will become evident; as an inner force, it will increasingly permeate the manifestations of human life.

Page 35, "columns...across from each other"
In Steiner's Malsch model building, in the Stuttgart column hall, and in the first Goetheanum it was designed as Steiner describes here.

Page 35, "The capitals...evolution of our Earth System"
In the program of the Congress it says: "The seven column sketches in the circumference of the main hall portray the evolution of the macrocosm. They are painted by Karl Stahl according to esoteric specifications."

Page 35, "[From the Akashic Chronicle]"
These essays appeared the first time in the magazine *Lucifer-Gnosis*. They were collected into a book in 1934 and now comprise CW 11.

Page 36, "the Corinthian and Ionian columns"
See CW 286.

Page 38, "The cross encircled by roses...meaning of Rosicrucianism"
See Plate I. To the fact that here eight roses are around the cross, Rudolf Steiner explains as follows with a letter on November 15, 1908, to Wilhelm Hübbe-Schleiden: "Seal Rose Cross: blue background – black cross – 7 stars (in Munich exoteric eight should stand for esoteric seven)."

Page 38, "no one knows...Rosicrucianism...methods of spiritual science"
See also CW 130.

Page 40, "busts...here before you"
They are the busts of the three great German idealist philosophers, Johann Gottlieb Fichte (1762-1814), Georg Wilhelm Friedrich Hegel (1770-1831),

Friedrich Wilhelm Joseph Schelling (1775-1854), which Rudolf Steiner also set up in the Berlin Branch space. Rudolf Steiner also wrote extensively about them in CW 20.

Johann Gottlieb Fichte (1762-1814) studied at Meissen, Pforta, Jena, and Leipzig, intending to become a clergyman. After teaching in Switzerland and en route to teach in Poland, he met Kant, who influenced him to write *Study for a Critique of All Revelation.* The printer neglected to place his name on the title page, and people thought the work was by Kant. When the true identity of the author became known, Fichte was hailed as an extraordinary philosopher. He lectured in Jena, Berlin, and Erlangen. In 1807 he was made Rector of the University of Berlin. He died at the height of his fame. Rudolf Steiner turned to the first draft of Fichte's *Science of Knowledge* as a starting point for his own work on knowledge for his doctoral thesis *Truth and Science.* Perhaps Steiner's most memorable study of Fichte's life and thought was presented in the public lecture in Berlin, on December 16, 1915 (CW 65).

Georg Wilhelm Friedrich Hegel (1770-1831) was one of the most influential of the German idealist philosophers. He studied at the University of Tübingen, taking his doctorate there in 1790. Hegel worked as a private tutor in Berne and Frankfurt a.M., before being called to lecture at the University of Jena in 1801. He wrote his *Phenomenologie des Geistes* [Phenomenology of the spirit] in 1807. In 1808 he became Rector in Munich, where he remained until 1816, when he was made professor in Heidelberg. In 1818 he accepted the invitation to become professor of philosophy at the University of Berlin. The years 1823-27 were his most prolific and influential time. In 1830 he became the Rector at the University of Berlin. He remained in this position until his death. In his written work and lectures Hegel sought to establish, from logical starting points, how history has systematically progressed.

Friedrich Wilhelm Joseph Schelling (1775-1854) was one of the main representatives of German idealism. With special permission, he began his studies at the Tübingener Evangelische Stift [Tübingen evangelical seminary] already at the age of 15 years. Among his fellow students were Friedrich Hölderlin and Georg Wilhelm Friedrich Hegel. Schelling studied Kant and Fichte. The closeness of his own ideas with those of Fichte came to expression in his dissertation in 1795. He later distanced himself from Fichte's ideas. Spinoza's philosophy, however, always had a strong influence on Schelling. He deepened his views through studying mathematics, natural science, and medicine at the University of Leipzig. He laid the foundation for his *Naturphilosophie* [Philosophie of nature] there. He also became acquainted himself with Leibniz's ideas. In 1798 he was called by Goethe to take a professorial position in Jena. He taught from 1803 at the University of Würzburg; from 1806 in Munich; from 1820-26 in Erlangen; from 1827-41 again in Munich; and from 1841 in Berlin.

Page 40, "progress of humanity in the consciousness of freedom"

In the introduction of Hegel's *Philosophy of History* it says literally: "History is the progress in the consciousness of freedom, a progress the necessity of which we have to recognize." *Hegel's Works*, Verlag Duncker and Hublot, Volume 9, 3rd edition, Berlin 1848. According to Ludwig Kleeberg, Rudolf Steiner used the Reclam edition at the time.

Page 41, "Ptolemaic system...by Copernicus"
Claudius Ptolemy (A.D. 87-165), astronomer and geographer, put the earth in the center of the universe. Nicholas Copernicus (1473-1543) caused a revolution in science when he put the sun at the center instead.

Page 42, "Everything below is as above"
Steiner is referring to the first sentence of the *Tabula Smaragdina* (the Emerald Tablet) the origin of which is ascribed to Hermes Trismegistus. According to legend, Alexander the Great, upon conquering Egypt, is supposed to have stolen an Emerald Tablet with this inscription from the hands of Hermes Trismegistus' mummy in the burial chamber of the Great Pyramid at Giza. A Latin translation of the text became known in the West in the 12th century through Albertus Magnus. In 1923 another copy of the text was found as two papyri in Arabic from the 9th century in a grave in Thebes, Egypt. These are the earliest known copies. See Julius Ruska, *Tabula Smaragdina* (Heidelberg, 1926).

Page 44, "pseudo-Dionysius...all the great books"
Rudolf Steiner stated several times that the content of the writings of Dionysius Areopogite from 533 A.D. on does indeed originate with the Dionysius mentioned in the Bible (Acts 17:34), whom the Apostle Paul made the head of the esoteric school that he founded in Athens. In accordance with the prevailing traditions of older times, such esoteric wisdom was transmitted orally only. Further, the student would traditionally assume the same name as his teacher. Thus there is a deeper meaning when an author in the 6th century speaks as if he were the pupil of Saint Paul, even if modern theologians feel the need to declare him a counterfeit.

Page 45, "first and fourth stations"
Steiner describes the Christian initiation in several places. See among others CW 94 (lectures of Feb 26, June 1, and July 11, 1906), as well as CW 99 (lecture of June 6, 1907), and CW 103 (lecture of June 30, 1908).

Page 48, "Hegel...to live in pure thinking"
See Steiner's essay on Hegel in CW 20 for an expanded treatment of this statement.

Page 46, "Eduard von Hartmann"
Eduard von Hartmann (1842-1906) was referred to as the famous "Philosopher of the Unconscious." He saw the world as existing between the polarity of will and idea, and consciousness as an accidental side effect of the interaction of the two.

Originally an officer in the Prussian army, he retired from military service because of an illness and took up an intensive study of philosophy. In 1869 his

Philosophie des Unbewussten [Philosophy of the unconscious] appeared and made him famous almost overnight. Of the many other works he wrote, this book remained his most famous. Rudolf Steiner describes a personal impression of von Hartmann, whom he visited in Berlin after corresponding with him over a period of time. This account may be found in Steiner's *Autobiography* (CW 28). Steiner dedicated his *Truth and Science* (CW3) to von Hartmann.

Page 48, "mathesis"
The word "mathesis" is a compound of "math" and the suffix "-ese" meaning "belonging to or originating in."

Page 48, *"Intuitive Thinking as a Spiritual Path"*
Also published as *The Philosophy of Freedom* (CW 4).

Page 49, "Everything...but a parable"
Goethe, *Faust*, Part II, Final Chorus.

Page 49, "three 'Logoi"
In the theosophical literature, the characterization for the divine Trinity (the Three-in-One). Father, Son or Word, and the Holy Spirit are the three Logoi. See Blavatsky, *The Secret Doctrine*, Book I, Part II, Section III.

Page 50, "Even newer scholarship...plant in the head of the human being"
Presumably, Rudolf Steiner has in mind here Gottlieb Haberlandt's "Physiological Plant Anatomy", 1st edition. Compare also Rudolf Steiner's lecture in Berlin on December 8, 1910, "The Spirit in the Plant Realm" (in CW 60), as well as September 28, 1905 (in CW 93a).

Page 50, "kama"
Theosophical designation for the lower astral.

Page 50, "Pythagorean School"
The Pythagorean School was an ancient Greek society of followers of the mathematician/philosopher/mystic Pythagoras of Samos (580-500 B.C.E.).

Page 51, "The Sun intones...rival air"
Goethe, *Faust*, Part I, Prologue in Heaven.

Page 51, "Intoning...spirit ears"
Goethe, *Faust*, Part II, Ariel Scene.

Page 51, "numbers are 1, 3, 7, and 12"
See also the lecture of December 29, 1907 (in CW 101).

Page 51, "German newspaper...have it in hand daily"
The *Reichanzeiger* of October 8, 1796, published an article by Karl Arnold Kortum on the philosopher's stone. This was discovered by Ludwig Kleeberg and published in a footnote in his *Wege und Worte*, 2nd edition, Stuttgart 1961.

Page 52, "Paracelsus once said"
Paracelsus (Theophrastus Bombastus von Hohenheim, 1493-1541) The text reads literally: "Then what do I want to bear witness to with nature: whoever wants to research it must tread upon its books with his feet. A document is explored through its letters. Nature, however, is explored through land and land: a land as frequently as a page. This is the Book of Nature (codex natura), thus must one turn its pages." Quoted according to Sudhoff, *Paracelsus's Complete Works*, Volume 2, "The Fourth Defense." Munich 1924.

Paracelsus (1493-1541) was an alchemist. physician, astrologer, and general esotericist. Born Theophrastus Philippus Aureolus Bombastus von Hohenheim, he took the name Paracelsus later in life, meaning "beside or similar to Celsus," a Roman physician from the first century C.E.

Page 54, "From the might...overcome themselves"
From Goethe's fragment titled "The Mysteries."

Page 55, "This morning we heard"
In a lecture by Annie Besant.

Page 56, "one given by Paracelsus"
Which passage Rudolf Steiner is referring to could not be determined. Possibly related passages include "Concerning the Magnetic force of the 'mumia' in the human being" in the edition by Karl Sudhoff, Volume 14 , (1933):

"Concerning the magnetic force of the 'mumia' in the human being. The sidereal spirit and body is such a magnet and magnetic nature in the human being and is the spirit born out of the stars, as the augurs prove, and such spirit and sidereal body is united with the stars. And thus we test first such magnetic force of the sidereal body in the elemental body of the human being for you. This sidereal body is, in relation to the elemental earthly body of the human being, a spirit and brings also spiritual activities; for as the earthly magnet with its body is a spirit and pulls toward itself, thus also the body and sidereal spirit and spirit in the human being pull toward themselves: this is the microcosmic magnet. The sidereal body and spirit draw to themselves the power of the stars, as we notice with sleepwalkers at the time of the new moon; there the sidereal body-spirit and magnet of the human being act according to the characteristic of the new moon. And as the Moon is attracted through the magnetic force of the innate sidereal body and spirit in the human being, it has a characteristic, in manner and in common, that the precursor of the lunar macrocosm is noticed in the human being in and at the time of the new moon, so that the lunatic raves, roars and is vehement, and such a lunatic speaks in such time like one drunk from hard cider and wine; there is noticed the conventionality, characteristics, and commonalities of such magnetic forces that the human being has with the stars. And notice rightly, the Moon of the great cosmos is a mirror and body in which the sidereal spirit-body and magnet of the human being sees in the night and takes all the dreams, thus ever there proceeds out of the inner in the human being in sleep; hence you have the dreams and the talking in the sleep."

See also Rudolf Steiner's lecture of April 26, 1906 on Paracelsus (in CW 54).

Page 58, "found the connection with the god"
Jean Paul Friedrich Richter (1763-1825) German novelist known for his humor. He is considered part of the Romantic movement.

"I will never forget about the appearance in me, which I have never told anyone, where I stood by the birth of my consciousness of self, of which I can give the time and place. One morning I stood as a very young child in the doorway of the house and saw to the left along the wood pile, as suddenly the inner vision, I am an I, came before me like a bolt of lightning and has remained radiating ever since: there my I saw itself for the first time, and eternally. Deceptions of the memory are hardly thinkable, because no foreign narrative could mix additional things into that which took place only within the 'Holy of Holies' of the human being and whose newness alone gave such ordinary side-circumstances the enduring."

Translated from *Wahrheit aus Jean Pauls Leben, Kindheitsgeschichte von ihm selbst geschrieben,* (3 parts in 2 Volumes, Breslau 1826-1828; 1st volume).

Page 59, "Francis of Assisi"
St. Francis of Assisi (1181-1226), known for his humility and kindness, his living example of holiness inspired the order of Franciscans, monks devoted to poverty and service. The movement grew very rapidly in the 1200s, and Francis is often considered the best-known, even archetypal, saint today.

Page 61, "atman"
In German, the word for breathing is Atmen, and is related through the Indo-European language tree to the Sanskrit Atman.

Page 64, "mineral consciousness...knows the whole solar system"
For more on the various stages of consciousness see, among others, CW 93, lecture of September 26, 1905, and CW 94, lecture of June 10, 1906.

Page 66, "an immense cosmic evolution"
See, among others, CW 13 and CW 104 for a more detailed explication.

Page 67, "natural science...regard to the animal world"
Rudolf Steiner refers to an essay by Theodor Arldt, *Die Atlantisproblem* [The problem of Atlantis] in the magazine *Kosmos: Handweiser für Naturfreunde* [Cosmos: handbook guide for friends of nature], Year Two, 1905, Issue 10.

Page 68, "Nifelheim (Mist-home)"
As mentioned in Snorri Sturluson's "Younger, or Prose, Edda," written around 1220 C.E., which is one of the primary historical sources of ancient Germanic mythology.

Page 69, "with the name 'Rosenkrantz'"
See CW 130 for a lengthier treatment of this topic.

Page 69, "Time is…and all is seed"
Schiller, *The Bride of Messina*, 3rd Act, 5th Scene.

Page 70, "when I spoke about education"
No transcript of this lecture remains. However, the topic was covered in an essay made public shortly before the Congress, "The Education of the Child from the Viewpoint of Spiritual Science" (contained in CW 34, but published as a pamphlet in both English and German, and still in print in both languages). It is the original seed from which the Waldorf Education movement has grown.

Page 70, "If…enter the kingdom of heaven"
Matthew 18:3.

Page 70, "there is blue"
Interesting in this regard is the staging of the first and last Scene of the 3rd Mystery Drama, (CW 14, written in 1912, five years after this lecture). For the 1st Scene—an exoteric mystery space—the directions describe it as completely indigo blue; the last scene—the inside of the temple of the company of Mystics—completely red.

Page 70, "explain these two columns"
See "A Special Note on the Golden Legend and the Two Pillars" in the Appendix.

Page 71, "three seeds"
In the 1957 German edition "a" seed was printed. The editors determined that there was an error in the transcript. Another transcript had "three seeds". In all other printings of the Legend it always says "three seeds". See also "A Special Note on the Golden Legend and the Two Pillars" in the Appendix.

Page 71, "I am Who was…will be"
Exodus 3:14; Revelations 1:8.

Page 71, "Blood is a very special fluid"
Goethe, *Faust*, I, "Study" scene. The statement is made by Mephistopheles.

Page 72, "God breathed…became a living soul"
Genesis 2:7.

Page 78, "twenty-four Elders of the Apocalypse"
Revelations 4:4.

Page 78, *"sixth seal"*
In the congress hall, the 5th and 6th seals were hung in the opposite order (See the illustration of the hall and the explanation lecture on May 21st) from the report Rudolf Steiner printed in the magazine *Lucifer-Gnosis* and in the folio, "Pictures of the Apocalyptic Seals and Columns," that he issued. Mathilde Scholl followed the sequence Rudolf Steiner published in *Lucifer-Gnosis* in her report on the Congress published in August 1907.

Page 78, "eternal feminine"
Goethe, *Faust,* Part II, Final Chorus.

Page 78, "Intoning...born for spirit ears"
Goethe, *Faust,* Part I, Prologue in Heaven; Faust Part II, Ariel Scene.

Page 79, "kama"
Theosophical designation for the lower astral.

Page 79, "counter-space...space in mirror image"
See the second lecture of CW 82.

Page 81, "seven days of the week"
See also CW 262, in a footnote to page 74.

Page 81, "a profane name"
As in not sacred in the sense of mystery wisdom; calling Odin's Day "Mid-Week."

Page 83, "which is the fourth"
The first was1904 in Amsterdam, the second in 1905 in London, the third in 1906 in Paris, and the fourth in 1907 in Munich.

Page 83, "Richard Wagner"
Richard Wagner (1813-83) was a famous composer of what Rudolf Steiner referred to as music dramas rather than operas. Although Rudolf Steiner could not, and did not take any part, in Wagner's anti-Semitism, he recognized his positive spiritual gifts through his art. There were glimmerings of esoteric truths in Wagner's *Parsifal,* and the idea of reincarnation came into his *Sieger.* He made an attempt to unite Shakespeare and Beethoven in his music dramas.

Page 84, "Michelangelo"
Michelangelo di Lodovico Buonarroti Simoni (1475-1564) famous Renaissance sculptor, painter, and poet. Michelangelo sculpted his renowned David (Florence) at age 23. He completed many sculptures, including one of Moses

(Rome), which contains so much living power within that after finishing it, Michelangelo threw a chair at it and yelled "Stand up, damn it!"

He painted the scenes of the Sistine Chapel of the Vatican single-handedly after throwing out his helpers. He used the money paid to him for painting the chapel to pay a debt. This paid-debt went on to finance the Reformation. Michelangelo is less well-known for his sonnets.

Page 84, "Leonardo da Vinci"
Leonardo da Vinci (1452-1519) was an architect, anatomist, sculptor, engineer, inventor, mathematician, musician, and painter. He has been described as the archetype of the "Renaissance man," infinitely curious and equally inventive.

He is widely considered to be one of the greatest painters of all time. He is famous for his *Mona Lisa* and *The Last Supper*, as well as for his drawing of the *Vitruvian Man*. Leonardo da Vinci conceived of ideas vastly ahead of his own time, notably conceptually inventing a helicopter, the use of concentrated solar power, a calculator, a rudimentary theory of plate tectonics, etc. In addition, he greatly advanced the state of knowledge in the fields of anatomy, astronomy, civil engineering, optics, and hydrodynamics.

Page 84, "...can both be clothed in one color"
From "Color Theory. Part VI: Sense-moral Effect of Color." See Volume III of *Goethe's Natural Scientific Writings* with introduction and explanations by Rudolf Steiner. (CW 1).

Page 85, "Grail seal...before the public"
See note for page 35.

Page 85, "fundamental thoughts of Rosicrucianism"
EDN – ICM – PSSR (Ex Deo Nascimur – In Christo Morimur – Per Spiritum Sanctum Reviviscimus).

Page 86, "The Apocalyptic Seals"
This is one of four lectures in a series, held September 13-16, 1907. See CW 101 for the rest of the lectures in this sequence.

Page 87. "regal soul into the heart"
In Plato's *The Republic* courage (Greek *thymos*) is located in the heart, on the basis of a Homeric passage. The courage asserts itself as the middle soul part between the rational and the desires. Likewise in *The Republic*, the human soul is portrayed as a picture of three figures: a colorful, many-headed beast, a lion, and a human. The lion helps the human (= the divine in the human being) with the overcoming of the beast. The lion represents the kingly element.

Page 87, "Paracelsus"
Paracelsus (1493-1541) was an alchemist, physician, astrologer, and general

esotericist. Born Theophrastus Philippus Aureolus Bombastus von Hohenheim, he took the name Paracelsus later in life, meaning "beside or similar to Celsus," a Roman physician from the first century C.E.

Page 88, "In the beginning...a God"
John 1:1.

Page 93, "two statements made by Copernicus"
The three main statements which Copernicus laid at the basis of his world-view are: 1.) The Earth turns around on its own north-south axis every 24 hours. 2.) The Earth moves around the Sun. 3.) Copernicus' third principle (paraphrased) is that not only does such a revolution of the Earth take place around the North-South axis, but that there is also a retrograde movement of the North-South axis round the axis of the Ecliptic. By this means the Earth's axis continuously points to the North celestial pole (the polar star). See the second lecture in CW 323, and also Elisabeth Vreede's, *Anthroposophie und Astronomie* [Anthroposophy and astronomy], Novalis Verlag, Freiburg, 1954.

Page 95, "Symbols and Signs as Effects of Chaos"
The reproduction of this lecture, due to a lack of an exact stenographic transcript, is a summary of more or less fragmentary notes.

Page 95, *"chaos"*
According to Hesiod's *Theogony,* chaos is the immeasurable, empty space that was above all things. Hesiod lived about the time of Homer (700 B.C.) in Boeotia, Greece. Very little is known about his life.

Page 95, "Ginnungagap"
"The Voluspo Song" ("The Seer's Vision") of the *Elder Edda,* Verse 3, reads:

> Of old was the age when Ymir lived;
> Sea nor cool waves nor sand there were;
> Earth had not been, nor heaven above,
> But a yawning gap, and grass nowhere.

In old Icelandic:

> Ár var alda,
> ?ar er ekki var,
> var-a sandr né sær
> né svalar unnir;
> jör? fannsk æva
> né upphiminn,
> gap var ginnunga
> en gras hvergi.

In this 13th Century poem, the seer is remembering the dark primordial space, Ginnungagap (the seventh line of the original), which corresponds to the Greek chaos and the Germanic outer sea, the Okeanus. They have in common an absence of any forms or colors.

Page 95, "In the beginning God...from the darkness"
Genesis 1:1-5.

Page 97, "Comenius...(born in 1592)"
Johann Amos Comenius (1592-1670) is famous for his views on education, but was also significant in the field of natural science. His "Physica" was written in 1632 and was published in 1633 in Leipzig with the title *Physicae ad lumen divinum reformatae Synopsis Philodidacticorum et Theodidactorium censurae exposita.*

Page 97, "Rosicrucian Order ... founded in the fourteenth century"
See CW 130.

Page 97, "Gotthold Lessing"
Gotthold Ephraim Lessing (1729-81) was a German writer, poet, dramatist, philosopher, publicist, and art critic. As such, he was one of the most outstanding representatives of the Enlightenment era. With his plays and his theoretical writings he substantially influenced the development of German literature. He also studied theology and medicine.

Page 98, "Johann Baptist van Helmont"
Johann Baptist van Helmont (1577-1644) was a Flemish chemist, physiologist, and physician. Born into a noble family in Brussels, he was educated in the city of Leuven. After ranging restlessly from one science to another and finding satisfaction in none, Helmont turned to medicine, in which he took his degree in 1599. The next few years he spent travelling throughout Switzerland, Italy, France, and England. Returning to his own country, he was in Antwerp at the time of the great plague in 1605; and having entered into a rich marriage, he settled in 1609 at Vilvoorde, near Brussels, where he occupied himself with chemical experiments and the practice of medicine until his death. In 1630 he was put on trial in the city of Mecheln for being a Rosicrucian.

Page 98, "coin this word and use it"
Helmont, "Daegeraed oft nieuwe opkomst der geneeskunst in verborgen groundt-regelen der natuere", Leiden 1615. After Helmont's death, his son, Franciscus Mercurius van Helmont, did a Latin edition with the title *Ortus Medicinae*, Amsterdam 1648.

Page 99, "Hunc spiritum...gas voco"
The complete sentence reads: "Hunc spiritum, incognitum hactenus, novo

nomine gas voco, qui nec vasis cogi, nec in corpus visibile reduci potest." *Ortus Medicinae,* edition 1652. Basel University Library.

Page 100, "...is but a parable"
Goethe, *Faust,* Part II, Final Chorus.

Page 101, "halitum illum...secretum"
"Halitum illum gas vocavi, non longe a chao veterum secretum" which means: "That breath I have called 'gas'; it is not far different from the 'chaos' of the ancient": The complete quote reads: "Verum quia aqua in vaporem, per frigus delata, alterius sortis, quam vapor, per calorem suscitatus; ideo paradoxi liccutia, in nominis egestate, halitum illum gas vocavi, non longe a chao veterum secretum." (*Ortus Medicinae,* edition 1652, Basel University Library), and translated from the German edition: "Because, however the water/ when it becomes a vapor through the cold/ is a completely different type/ as the vapor/ which is driven into the heights by the warmth; so I have taken the freedom with this unusual matter/ and called this steam / out of a lack of another name gas; because there is no great difference between it/ and between the fundamental-being/ which the ancient called chaos: (In German, we call it a water-spirit.)" *Aufgang der Artzneykunst* [Rise of the art of medicine], Sulzbach 1683, Basel University Library.

Page 101, "interesting scientific connection"
As late as 1935, R. Loewe wrote in his essay, "Gas" for the *Journal for Comparative Language Research in the Field of Indo-Germanic Languages* (Volume 62, Göttingen, 1935): "The (originally neo-Latinate) word 'gas' is known to have been constructed from 'chaos' by the Brussels chemist Johann Baptist van Helmont (1577-1644); it has still not been sufficiently explained just why this scholar chose the word 'chaos' from which to construct the name for the new concept which he discovered."

Page 104, "Goethe, Schiller, Lessing, Herder, and Schelling have written their works"
Johann Wolfgang von Goethe (1749-1832) was a poet, novelist, dramatist, humanist, scientist. As a child, he was home-schooled. His father and private teachers gave him lessons in all the common subjects, especially languages (Latin, Greek, French, English, and Hebrew). Goethe also took lessons in dancing, riding, and fencing. From early on he was interested in drawing, literature, and theater. Each year his family performed the puppet show of *Doktor Faustus* in his childhood home. The theme of this puppet play stayed with him throughout his life and inspired him to write his *Faust* which took Goethe some forty years to complete. Part two could be written only at the end of his life. Already as a child he had a reverent, almost religious feeling toward nature. He set up a little altar in his room on which he placed a candle and stones, plants, and other offerings from nature. However, throughout his life he had a persistent dislike of the church, feeling it to be a mixture of error and power.

Goethe studied law in Leipzig from 1765 to 1768, but much preferred attending the poetry lessons of Christian Fürchtegott Gellert instead. Despite being based on his own ideas, his legal thesis was published uncensored; he wanted to make the legal process more humane. In his first cases, he proceeded too vigorously, was reprimanded, and lost his passion for jurisdiction. This prematurely terminated his legal career after only a few months. In 1770, he anonymously released *Annette*, his first collection of poems. Already at this time, Goethe wrote quite a lot, but he threw away nearly all of these works. He took a position as one of the editors of a literary periodical, but found that he could not make a living at it, and so began to practice law again in 1772 in Wetzlar. At the invitation of Carl August, Grand Duke of Saxe-Weimar-Eisenach, he went, in 1775, to live in Weimar where he held a succession of political offices, even becoming the Duke's chief adviser.

Among the best known of Goethe's works are his dramas *Götz von Berlichingen, Faust I & II, Iphigenia auf Tauris [Iphigenia in Tauris], Egmont, Torquatto Tasso*, and *Reineke Fuchs*; and his novels *The Sorrows of Young Werther* and *Wilhelm Meister*. He also wrote his memoirs *Aus meinem Leben: Dichtung und Wahrheit* (Though published in English as *From My Life: Poetry and Truth*, the last part should read "Fiction and Truth," as he was very aware that one's memories contain a great deal of fiction in them.)

In addition to his literary work, Goethe also contributed significantly to the sciences. In biology, his theory of plant metamorphosis stipulated that all plant formation stems from a modification of the leaf. He also discovered the intermaxillary bones in the human jaw. Goethe considered his *Theory of Colours* to be his most important work. On the recommendation of Julius Schröer, Rudolf Steiner was asked by Joseph Kürschner in 1882 to edit Goethe's scientific writings for *German National Literature*. Steiner's work with these writings led to his own important epistomolgical work, *Theory of Knowledge Implicit in Goethe's World Conception* (CW 2).

Johann Christoph Friedrich von Schiller (1759-1805) was a poet, philosopher, historian, and dramatist. During the last several years of his life (1788–1805), Schiller struck a productive friendship with already famous and influential Johann Wolfgang von Goethe. It is said that Goethe would not have been Goethe without Schiller and that Schiller would not have been Schiller without Goethe. Their relationship had a rocky start, with Schiller attacking Goethe about Goethe's conception of the archetypal plant. Schiller could not accept it as a reality and called it merely an idea. Goethe's response was that he could see his ideas then. They went on to work so closely together that when they co-published a magazine, the readers could not tell which articles had been written by Schiller and which by Goethe. Despite their closeness, they were quite different in temperament and relationship to life. Whereas Goethe was of a watery, phlegmatic temperament, Schiller's was fiery, choleric. Goethe was a romantic, considered by history to be a "lady's man." Schiller led his life according to a very strict view of morality and socio-political ideas, often upsetting others with his views. An example of this was his attempt, as a young man, to seek the favor and assistance of Duke Karl Eugen of Würtemburg for the production of his first play, *Die Räueber* [The robbers], a critique of social corruption and its affirmation of proto-revolutionary republican ideals. Duke Karl Eugen would have nothing of it when Schiller read it aloud for him. It had not helped the situation that Schiller had such a thick Swabian accent that made it difficult to understand and irritating to listen to. Following a remarkable performance of *Die Räueber* in Mannheim, Duke Karl Eugen had Schiller arrested and forbade him from writing anymore plays. This did not deter Schiller from writing plays. He just stayed away from Duke Karl Eugen and Würtemburg.

The early relationship with Eugen had not been so turbulent, however. Schiller's childhood and youth were spent in relative poverty, although he attended both village and Latin schools, and coming to the attention of Karl Eugen, he was allowed to enter the Karlsschule Stuttgart (an elite, extremely strict, military academy founded by Duke Karl Eugen), in 1773, where he eventually studied medicine. In 1780, he obtained a post as regimental doctor in Stuttgart, a job he disliked.

After fleeing Stuttgart and Karl Eugen in 1783, he came, via Leipzig and Dresden, to Weimar, in 1787. In 1789 Schiller was appointed professor of history and philosophy in Jena. He returned to Weimar in 1799, where Goethe convinced him to return to playwriting. Friedrich Schiller went on to write plays that are still performed today. He and Goethe founded the Weimar Theater which became the leading theater in Germany, leading to a dramatic renaissance. He remained in Weimar until his death, at 45 years of age, from tuberculosis. During most of his short life, he suffered from illnesses that he tried to cure himself.

Johann Gotfried Herder (1744-1803) was a poet, critic, theologian, and philosopher. Herder grew up in a poor household, educating himself from his father's Bible and songbook. In 1762 he began his studies at the University of Königsburg, where he became a student of Johann Georg Hamann, who delved back into the German mysticism of Jakob Böhme and others. In 1764, now a clergyman, Herder went to Riga to teach. It was during this period that he produced his first major works, which were literary criticism. By 1770 he went to Straßburg, where he met the young Goethe. This event proved to be a key juncture in the history of German literature, as Goethe was inspired by Herder's literary criticism to develop his own style. This can be seen as the beginning of the Sturm und Drang Movement. In 1771 Herder took a position as head pastor and court preacher at Bückeburg. In 1776 Goethe, now a well-known author, used his influence at the court of Weimar to secure Herder a position as General Superintendent. Towards the end of his career, Herder endorsed the French Revolution, which earned him the enmity of many of his colleagues. At the same time, he and Goethe experienced a personal split.

Page 105, "I described in my introduction"

Steiner is referring to the introduction to the folio " Pictures of the Apocalyptic Seals and Columns" published in 1907. See pages 112-120 in this volume.

Page 109, "Report on the Congress at the Sixth General Meeting of the German Section of the Theosophical Society"
Reprinted from *Mitteilungen für die Mitglieder der Deutschen Sektion der Theosophischen Gesellschaft* [News for the Members of the German Section of the Theosophical Society], edited by Mathilde Scholl, Cologne, No. VI (February 1908).

Page 110, "in the past five years"
Indicated is the span of time since the founding of the German Section with Rudolf Steiner as the General Secretary in October 1902.

Page 113, "the Revelation of John"
See CW 104 and CW 8 for additional material on the Apocalyptic Seals.
Page 113, "The revelation…in the way he has seen it"
Revelations 1:1-3.

Page 113, "made public in this or that modern work"
See Note for page 31. This was a modern work at the time (1907).

Page 114, "And I turned…like the shining Sun"
Revelations 1:12-16.

Page 114, "Among the organs and methods of expression of the human being"
See Note for page 33.

Page 116, "in the course of many incarnations"
See CW 104 and CW 104a.

Page 116, "two pillars…sea…realm of the Earth"
See "A Special Note on the Golden Legend and the Two Pillars" in the Appendix.

Page 117, "mystery of the Holy Grail"
See the note for page 35.

Page 118, "Saturn…Venus conditions"
See CW 13 for greater detail.

Page 120, "not in harmony with them"
In the original, a note from Rudolf Steiner appeared here:

> Unfortunately it was not possible to reproduce the seals here in color. For the Congress they were executed in color. However, it should suffice as a

preview to see them in this form. The Seals for the congress hall were executed by Clara Rettich of Stuttgart, the columns by Mr. Karl Stahl of Munich, according to my indications.

The 1977 German edition was the first to reproduce the seals in color.

Page 121, "Rudolf Steiner pointed to...with the old mystery knowledge"
Referred to are the lectures Rudolf Steiner held by invitation in the winter of 1901/02 in the Theosophical Library in Berlin. These lectures were summarized by Steiner himself and published in the summer of 1902 as the book *Christianity as Mystical Fact* (CW 8). Steiner describes how the meanings of the teachings of Christ are hidden in the Apocalypse of John and are the fulfillment of the old mystery revelation.

Page 122, "Mrs. Besant...obvious choice"
After the death of the Theosophical Society's Co-founder-President Henry Steel Olcott on February 17, 1907, Annie Besant was elected as the new President in May 1907, shortly before the Munich Congress.

Page 122, "mediumistic declarations...Alcott in Adyar"
Besant came under the influence of C.W. Leadbeater and, together with the assistance of several mediums, they began directing the affairs of the Theosophical Society in a way that caused consternation among many longtime Theosophists.

Page 123, "Order of the Star of the East"
The "Order of the Star of the East" was founded in 1910/11 as a separate organization within the Theosophical Society to prepare for the coming of the new "World Leader." An Indian child named Krishnamurti was "discovered" and duly declared the reincarnated Christ. The backlash within the Theosophical Movement (and not just from Germany) was so severe that Besant and Leadbeater quickly backed away from the claim.

Page 123, "in the Ariel scene"
Goethe: *Faust,* Part II, Ariel scene.

Page 123, "wonderful commentaries on Goethe's *Faust*"
See CW 272 and CW 273.

Page 124, "Mathilde Scholl"
Mathilde Scholl (1868-1941). Along with Marie von Sivers (Steiner), she counted as one of Rudolf Steiner's first students of esotericism. Through his personal guidance, she rose to a high degree of development in the early esotericism (that before 1914). Mathilde Scholl's connection with Rudolf Steiner began with her attendance of his lectures in 1901, contained in *Mysticism After*

Modernism (CW 7). She was present at the founding of the German Section of the Theosophical Society on October 20, 1902. Mathilde Scholl is actually to be credited with initiating and developing the Theosophical/Anthroposophical work in the Rheinland area of Germany: Cologne, Düsseldorf, Bonn, and Koblenz. From 1903 she was a member of the Executive Council of the German Section of the Theosophical Society, and from 1905 to 1914 the editor of the journal of the Society, *Mitteilungen für die Mitglieder der Deutschen Sektion der Theosophichen Gesellschaft* [News for the Members of the German Section of the Theosophical Society]. The high point in her life was to work at Rudolf Steiner's side to found the first Anthroposophical Society in December 1912, in Cologne, Germany. She worked tirelessly for the Theosophical Society and then for the Anthroposophical Society. In 1914 she receded more into the background of the work and moved to Dornach. There she devoted herself to inner work, especially to Rudolf Steiner's Mystery Dramas.

Page 124, "From News...(August 1907)"
Here are excerpted those parts of Mathilde Scholl's report that relate to the presentations by Rudolf Steiner and to the arrangement of the congress hall. The whole report appeared in *Mitteilungen für die Mitglieder der Deutschen Sektion der Theosophichen Gesellschaft* [News for the members of the German section of the Theosophical Society], edited by Mathilde Scholl, Cologne, No.V (August 1907).

Page 124, "opened at 10:00 A.M.....of the German Section, Dr. Rudolf Steiner"
There is no transcript of the opening talk or the closing talk by Steiner.

Page 124, "president-founder Colonel Olcott"
Henry Steele Olcott (1832-1907) founded the Theosophical Society in 1875 with William Judge and Helena Blavatsky.

Page 125, "Schelling, Hegel, and Fichte"
See the note for page 40. The note is indicated as: "busts...here before you."

Page 128, "spiritistic experiment"
Spiritism was a movement that started in the mid-1800s. Believers sought to communicate with the spirits of the dead by various means, the most popular of which, at the time of the Munich conference, was the séance. Keeping with the tenor of the times, many within the Theosophical Society sought to take a scientific approach to spiritistic phenomena. Steiner was generally opposed to the practice. See CW 254 for a presentation by Steiner on spiritism.

Page 129, "three seeds"
Compare the note for page 71.

Page 133, "Intoning...horns blew"
Goethe, *Faust*, Part II, Ariel Scene.

Page 134, "kama"
Theosophical designation for the lower astral.

Page 136, "Hans Volkert"
Hans Volkert (1878-?) Munich artist.

Page 136, "Gustave Moreau"
Gustave Moreau (1826-1898) was one of the leading French Symbolists. He was a pupil of Chassérlau and was influenced by his master's exotic Romanticism, but Moreau went far beyond him in his feeling for the bizarre and developed a style that is highly distinctive in subject and technique. His preference was for mystically intense images evoking long-dead civilizations and mythologies, treated with an extraordinary sensuousness, his paint encrusted and jewel-like. Although he had some success at the Salon, he had no need to court this as he had private means, and much of his life was spent in seclusion. In 1892 he became a professor at the Ecole des Beaux-Arts and proved an inspired teacher, bringing out his pupils' individual talents rather than trying to impose ideas on them. His pupils included Marquet and Matisse, but his favorite was Rouault, who became the first curator of the Moreau Museum in Paris (the artist's house), which Moreau left to the nation on his death. The bulk of his work is preserved there.

Page 136, "G.F. Watts"
George Frederick Watts (1817-1904) was a British painter, sometimes considered a Symbolist.

Page 136, "Kalckreuth the Elder"
Eduard Stanislaus Graf von Kalckreuth (1820-1894), was a German Landscape painter. After successfully completing Gymnasium, he attended a cadet institute and then entered, at the age of 20 years, the First Guard Regiment for but a short time. Between 1846-47 he studied at the Academy of Arts in Düsseldorf and was the pupil of, among others, the painter Johann William Schirmer. Friedrich William IV, King of Prussia, appointed Kalckreuth as professor in Wiemar, where he helped with the establishment of the art school there in 1859. In 1860 he became the first director of the art school and, as such, made study trips to Switzerland, France and Italy, from which he brought back numerous sketches. His mountain landscapes originate from these trips. The play of light and form in these paintings give witness to Kalckreuth's great creativity. In 1876 Kalckreuth withdrew into private life, spending the last years of his life in Munich.

Page 136, "Sophie Stinde"
Sophie Stinde (1853-1915), was trained formally as a landscape painter. Along

with Countess Pauline von Kalckreuth she led the work at the main branch in Munich for the German Section of the Theosophical Society. She met Rudolf Steiner in Munich in 1904 and became a student of esotericism. Sophie Stinde became the leader of both the Esoteric School and the Freemasonry and Ritual work. She served on the Executive Council of the German Section from 1904-1913. She and Countess Pauline von Kalckreuth helped prepare the Munich Congress. Sophie Stinde played a large role in bringing about the festival plays in Munich (1907-1913), including the premiers of the Mystery Dramas. She can be considered the creator of the idea of the Goetheanum building, originally thought of as the Johannes-Bau to be built in Munich but later brought to fruition in Dornach.

Page 136, "Haß"
Fritz Hass (1864-?), German painter.

Page 137, "Ludwig Kleeberg"
Ludwig Kleeberg (1886-1972) can be considered the first representative of the student work within the Theosophical Movement, in that he attempted, though unsuccessfully, to bring Theosophical ideas to the students at the universities in Marburg and Munich. He had been fascinated by Buddhism and Brahmanism already as a seventeen-year old. After a long correspondence with Marie von Sivers, he finally met Rudolf Steiner in Munich in 1904. Kleeberg joined the Theosophical Society in 1905. A highlight in his life was his participation in the Munich Congress. His great devotion to documentation is to thank for many lectures and conversations having been written down for posterity, as well as his memoirs, *Wege und Worte* [Ways and Words].

In order not to leave a friend unaccompanied, he left the Theosophical Society in 1911 and joined the Catholic church. In 1918 he rejoined what had in the meantime become the Anthroposophical Society.

Page 137, "who have a profession"
The long weekend in observation of Whitsun was one that almost everyone had off in Europe at that time.

Page 141, "Karl Stockmeyer"
Karl H. W. Stockmeyer (1858-1930), Painter and Theosophist. He had a particular sensibility for Rudolf Steiner's Rosicrucian-artistic intentions. He helped his son, E.A. Karl Stockmeyer, build the model building in Malsch and design and develop the cupola room of the Stuttgart house. He painted two paintings for the dedication of the Stuttgart house. These paintings remained there until WWII broke out, and are now in the Stockmeyer estate in Malsch.

Ernst August Karl Stockmeyer (1886-1963), son of Karl H.W. Stockmeyer and who also went by the name Karl Stockmeyer, studied mathematics, natural science, philosophy, and architecture in Heidelberg and Munich. He was allowed, at age twenty-one, to participate in the Munich Congress and became a member of the Theosophical Society in 1907. His deep inner study of Rudolf Steiner's columns and seals and his questions of Rudolf Steiner about the architectural elements necessary for a building to incorporate these columns led to his designing the model building in Malsch. E.A. Stockmeyer taught mathematics and science in various schools. He also taught philosophy and taught at a teacher training institute in Freiburg. In 1918 Rudolf Steiner and Emil Molt called him to Stuttgart to help found the Waldorf School there. He later assembled a curriculum guide that is still widely used.

Page 142, "obituary...she died a year later"
Published in CW 261.

Page 142, "Max Gümbel-Seiling ... *With Rudolf Steiner in Munich*"
Max Gümbel-Seiling (1879-1964), actor and speech artist, was one of Rudolf Steiner's and Marie Steiner's early students. He played in *The Children of Lucifer* written by Eduouard Schuré, and played Strader in the premieres of the Mystery Dramas. At age 17, he dramatized Wolfram von Eschenbach's *Parzival* for a performance with his classmates. He had wanted to be an actor from the beginning but, at the request of his father, studied architecture. He then studied to become an actor and found success quickly. He met the Theosophical-Anthroposophical Movement and Rudolf Steiner in Munich in 1905 at a lecture being given by Steiner on Goethe. From then on his goal increasingly became to fructify art through Anthroposophy. He became a member of the Theosophical Society in 1908, and then in 1912 he became a member of the Anthroposophical Society. In 1909 he became a personal student of Rudolf Steiner. Gümbel-Seiling participated in the foundation stone laying of the model building in Malsch and gave recitations at Rudolf Steiner's lectures.

In 1924 he participated in the Drama Course in Dornach and worked with Marie Steiner to build up the stage work there, until it became difficult for them to work together any longer.

The German title of his recollections is *Mit Rudolf Steiner in München* (Den Haag, 1945).

Page 143, "twenty-four people present"
Based on the entries in the guestbook and the five members of the Stockmeyer family, the following 41 people were present: Dr. Rudolf Steiner, Marie von Sivers, Gertrud von Tschirsky, Harriet von Vacano, Oskar Grosheintz, Alice Sprengel, Max Gümbel-Seiling, Cecile Peipers, Dr. Felix Peipers, Michael Bauer, Juliane Stössinger, M. Hirter Weber, Martha Welsch, Alice Kinkel, Anna Weißmann, Karl Greber, Toni Völker, Wilhelm Kinkel, Marina Greber, Hugo Harder, Friedrich Schwab, Frau A. Haefliger, Marguerite Gos, Wally Allmendinger, Frieda Weiland, Clara Rettich, Emil Molt, Berta Molt, Emil Schilling, Dr. Trifon Trapesnikoff, Georg Klenk, Maria Frentzel, Helen Weigele, Richard Wiegele, Rudolf Hahn, and M. Hahn.

Page 143, "All above as below"
See the Note for page 42. The note there is given as: "Everything above is as below."

Page 149, "zodiac...over the Saturn column"
See the lecture of July 9, 1921, in CW 205.

Page 149, "syenite"
Syenite is a coarse-grained igneous rock. It is of the same general composition as granite, but with the quartz either absent or present in relatively small amounts. It tends to be gray or pinkish-gray. A different oral source, however, claims that Steiner wanted a "greenish" syenite.

Page 150, "fall and winter of 1908"
Complementing this description by E.A. Karl Stockmeyer is the comment of Rudolf Steiner in his lecture of January 23, 1920, in Dornach: "In 1908 the thought first occurred to me to design the building as a double cupola."

Page 151, "symbolic-ritualistic activities...before World War I"
See CWs 264-266.

Page 151, "*Autobiography*"
CW 28, Chapter 36.

Page 152, "*Mystery Dramas*"
CW 14.

Page 152, "*Truth-Wrought Words*"
CW 40.

Page 152, "Letters to the Members"
In CW 26.

Page 152, "architect Schmid-Curtius"
Dr. Carl Schmid-Curtius (died 1931 in Locarno, Switzerland) was the architect of the first Stuttgart Society house at 70 Landhausstraße. From 1911 to 1914 he was architect for the building project in Munich and later in Dornach. Later he studied medicine, and was active in scientific research.

Page 152, "Imme von Eckhardstein"
Imme von Eckhardstein (1871-1930) was a Munich-based artist, costumer, and set designer. In 1907 she made the costumes for the production of Schuré's *The Sacred Drama of Eleusis,* according to Rudolf Steiner's instructions. She also made the costumes for the premiere performances of Steiner's *Mystery Dramas*

(1910-1913). She worked at the stage of the second Goetheanum starting in 1928. During the construction of the Stuttgart cupola she painted the zodiac in the small cupola. She drew updated, modern zodiacal signs, in accordance with sketches by Rudolf Steiner, for the first edition of his *Calendar of the Soul.* These motifs were the ones used for the Stuttgart cupola. See "Beiträge zur Rudolf Steiners Gesamtausgabe" Volume 37/38 (Spring/Summer 1972).

Page 153, "C. S. Picht"
Carlo Septimus Picht (1887-1954). Born the seventh son (Septimus) of a north German business family, Carlo grew up in northern Italy, where his mother had grown up. During school, he was an accomplished student, wrote poetry, and played music. He wanted to become a musician and medical doctor. His father, instead, guided him into the Prussian officer corps, where he was soon a member of the General Staff. Through his wife, he became acquainted with Anthroposophy during the course of World War I. After the war, he became active in promoting Steiner's ideas. In 1926 he assembled the first systematic overview to Steiner's written works, and in 1934 he was asked by Marie Steiner to work at the Rudolf Steiner Archives. There he was instrumental in producing CW 292, a volume of Steiner's lectures on art history, published along with plates of the paintings under discussion. World War II saw him called back into military service, and he was stationed in Serbia where, at great risk to himself, he saved hundreds of civilians from execution. In 1943 he was relieved of command and discharged from the military, because he belonged to the banned Anthroposophical Society. He returned to his work for the Steiner Archives and, over the next 12 years, assembled CWs 29-33, 38 and 39. He also wrote a book on Rembrandt. He died suddenly in 1954 of a heart attack.

Page 153, "Dr. Friedrich Husemann"
Dr. Friedrich Husemann (1887-1959), physician and psychiatrist, founded Wiesneck Clinc, which was renamed the Friedrich Husemann Clinic after his death. He found Theosophy as a student in Genf in 1909 and met Rudolf Steiner shortly afterward in Berlin. The first book he read by Steiner was *The Philosophy of Freedom*. Husemann then worked through Steiner's foundational books in short order and a few months later held his first Anthroposophical lecture.

Page 153, "the Representative of Humanity"
A wooden sculpture, over 30 feet tall and carved by Rudolf Steiner himself as the centerpiece for the building. It survived the fire that destroyed the building in 1923, because it was not finished and, therefore, had not yet been installed. Today it can be seen in the second Goetheanum.

Page 154, "What should our building...in the individual forms"
CW 286, lecture of June 17, 1914.

Page 154, "Stuttgart Delegates' Meeting in the spring of 1923"
CW 257.

Page 161, "according to Rudolf Steiner's instructions"
From the annual report of the branch in the *Mitteilungen für die Mitglieder der Deutschen Sektion der Theosophischen Gesellschaft* [News for Members of the German Section of the Theosophical Society], Number 10, January 1910.

Page 162, "The branch meeting place…spaces between the windows"
Assya Turgenieff, *Erinnerungen an Rudolf Steiner und die Arbeit am ersten Goetheanum* [Reminiscences of Rudolf Steiner and the work of the first Goetheanum], Stuttgart, 1967.

Page 162, "We have seen…esoteric knowledge in such a space"
CW 133.

Page 162, "lecture of September 12, 1919"
CW 193.

Page 166, "two pictures by Raphael"
Raphael Santi (1483-1520), famous Italian Renaissance painter, worked on two frescos, *The Disputa* and *The School of Athens*, from approximately 1508-1511. According to Herman Grimm's *The Life of Raphael*, the names for these pictures do not originate with Raphael, or even during his lifetime, but were added later. Rudolf Steiner spoke about both pictures again in later lectures (with slides), published in CW 292.

Page 172, "as yet no models for it"
A few years later Rudolf Steiner created this work of art himself. His first attempt was the sculpture called "The Group," the second a painting as the middle motif of the fresco of the small cupola of the first Goetheanum. That these really are the "third picture" Steiner is talking about in this lecture is supported by a lecture at Dornach on September 16, 1916, in CW 171. It was for this reason that William Scott Pyle, in his red chalk drawing, connects Raphael's *Disputa* with his drawing by putting Raphael into the upper right corner. This drawing is the view from the large cupola space into the small cupola space with "The Group" and the middle motif above it, published by the Philosophical-Anthroposophical Verlag in Dornach in 1930 and dedicated to Marie Steiner.

Page 173, "Countess Brockdorff"
Countess Sophie von Brockdorff, Nee von Ahlefeldt, (1848-1906) was connected with the Theosophical Movement in Germany from the beginning, joining the Society in1893, along with her husband, Count Cay Lorenz Brockdorff. Together they directed the Berlin Lodge. They set up a library of Theosophical works in their home that was made available to members of the

Society. Public lectures were held there—Theosophical and other. In 1900 they invited Rudolf Steiner to lecture on Nietzsche and then on Goethe. Rudolf Steiner then held a cycle of lectures that are now titled *Mysticism after Modernism* (CW 7). Another lecture cycle he held there became his second book: *Christianity as Mystical Fact*.

Countess von Brockdorff worked to publish the German edition of the official English periodical of the Theosophical Society, although it came out in 1906 after her death. She also lent financial support and enthusiasm to the launching of Rudolf Steiner's magazine *Lucifer*. It was in the home of the von Brockdorffs that the German Section of the Theosophical Society was founded on October 20, 1902. It was also her husband, Count von Brockdorff, who recommended Rudolf Steiner to become the General Secretary.

Page 173, "same topic in Christiana"
Lectures of May 9-21, 1909, published in CW 104a.

Page 173, "could I make this teaching known in Rome"
Hippolyte Taine (1823-1893). A leading French historian, he was enormously popular during his lifetime. A proponent of sociological positivism, he belonged to the pessimistic school of historians and was among the first to criticize historians for trying to find any sort of sequential progression to events. He held that the human being was the product of heredity, historical conditioning, and environment.

Page 173, "In Düsseldorf"
CW 109/111.

Page 173, "only the cardinals had entered"
The Palazzo del Drago in Rome.

Page 175, "Helena Petrovna Blavatsky"
Helena Petrovna Blavatsky (1831-May 5, 1891) and Henry Steel Olcott (1832-1907) founded the Theosophical Society in New York City in 1875. Later the main headquarters was moved to Adyar, by Madras, in India.

Page 176, "Olcott for the first time"
At the 1902 Theosophical congress in London.

Page 177, "*Isis Unveiled* and *The Secret Doctrine*"
Blavatsky's main books. *Isis Unveiled* was published 1877, and *The Secret Doctrine*, in 1888.

Page 177, "Masters of Wisdom and Harmony of Feelings who inspired her"
With this Rudolf Steiner points to beings which are of great significance for the evolution of humanity. "These lofty beings have already gone the path that the

rest of humanity still has to go. They work now as the great 'teachers of wisdom and the harmony of human feelings'." (From a letter to an unnamed member, Berlin, January 20, 1905.) See also the lectures of August 24, 1911, in CW 129, and December 26, 1909, in CW 117.

Page 178, "Mommsen"

Theodor Mommsen (1817-1903). A German classical scholar and historian, he won the Nobel Prize for literature in 1902 for his historical writings. Tremendously popular during his lifetime, today he has fallen into obscurity except among historians.

Page 178, "Taine"

CW 109/111.

Page 178, "Du Bois-Reymond"

Emil Du Bois-Reymond (1818–1896) German physiologist known for his studies of nerve and muscle action. In 1872 he generated a huge controversy with his *Ignorabimus* proposition (published in *Über die Grenzen des Naturerkennens* [Concerning the limits of Scientific Knowledge]. *Ignorabimus* is short for the Latin ignoramus et ignorabimus meaning "we do not know and will not know," summing up his position on spiritual matters. Steiner was fond of mentioning the ignorabimus proposition in lectures.

Page 178, "Haeckel"

Ernst Heinrich Philipp August Haeckel (1834-1919) was a German zoologist, naturalist, philosopher, physician, professor, and artist. He studied medicine in Berlin but found that the practicing of medicine seemed less worthwhile after having contact with suffering patients. He went on to study and receive his doctorate in zoology at the University of Jena, where he then remained for forty-seven years as professor of comparative anatomy. During this time he made a journey to the Canary Islands where he met Charles Darwin, Thomas Huxley, and Charles Lyell.

Rudolf Steiner had felt no need to meet Haeckel, but when he attended Haeckel's 60th birthday festivities, he was introduced to him at Haeckel's request. In a conversation, Haeckel said to him: "People say that I deny the spirit. I wish they could see how various materials shape themselves through their own forces; then they would perceive 'spirit' in everything that happens in a laboratory retort. Spirit is everywhere." (From CW 28.) Steiner said of this that Haeckel had absolutely no idea what spirit is. He thought the forces of nature were spirit. Steiner dedicated his *Conceptions of the World and of Life in the Nineteenth Century*, later expanded and titled *The Riddles of Philosophy*, to Ernst Haeckel, in spite of the fact that his thinking, and so the content of the book, was so very different from that of Haeckel.

Just when Haeckel had formulated his monism in his talk, "Monism as the Bond between Religion and Science," he heard that Rudolf Steiner was in

Weimar and sent a copy of his talk to him. Steiner returned the favor by sending Haeckel a copy of the magazine containing the talk he had given in Vienna against Haeckel's monism.

Rudolf Steiner said of Ernst Haeckel's work: "Haeckel's research results build, so to speak, the first chapter of Theosophy or spiritual science. One can find one's way into the origin and transformation of the organic forms better when one studies his works than through anything else." (From CW 54). It is a first chapter because, "Haeckel can only see what the senses grasp and how it changes. What is and what changes in this way he can acknowledge as his reality, and he is only satisfied when he is able to comprise the entire human being, including his thought activity, under this concept of being and transformation." (From "Introduction to the 1923 Edition," CW 18) Here spiritual science begins its task of gaining knowledge beyond the threshold or limits of the physical senses.

Haeckel saw the animal as the ancestor the human being, whereas Rudolf Steiner's spiritual research shows that the animal and the human being have the same primordial ancestor, with the evolutionary divergence coming about through the fact that those that could develop upward became human beings, and those that could not separated out and became animals.

Page 180, "from eating too much pork"

Blavatsky presented that in a wonderful way in her *Secret Doctrine*, Volume 3. It says: "...that all the great hierophants in history have died a violent death." First Buddha is named, and a footnote for it reads:

> In the profane history of Gautama Buddha, he dies at the wonderfully high age of 80 years and passes from life into death peacefully and with all the serenity of a great saint, as Barthelemy St. Hilaire describes it. Not so in the esoteric and true explanation, which uncovers the real meaning of the profane and allegorical narrative, which very unpoetically lets the Gautama, the Buddha, die from the effect of too much pork that Tsonda had prepared for him. How someone, who preached that it was a great sin to kill animals and who was a complete vegetarian, could die from eating pork is a question that is never asked by our Orientals, of which some (as now many missionaries in Ceylon do) make fun of the alleged occurrence. The simple truth is that the mentioned rice with pork is purely allegorical. The rice represents the forbidden fruit, like Eve's apple, and means, with the Chinese and Tibetans, theosophical knowledge; and 'pork,' for the Brahman doctrines in which Vischnu in his first Avatar took on the form of a wild boar, in order to raise the Earth onto the surface of the water of the space. Buddha died, therefore, not on pork, but because he made some of the Brahman mysteries public, whereupon he, because he saw that through his disclosure bad effects came over some unworthy human beings, took it upon himself, instead of enjoying the Nirvana, to forsake his earthly form, yet however, to remain in the sphere of the living, in

order to help humanity to progress. Hence his continual reincarnations in the hierarchy of the Dalai and Teschu Lamas, among other good deeds. Thus is the esoteric explanation.

Page 180, "Has anyone ever...especially inspiring"
In Volume 3 of *The Secret Doctrine*, it says in a footnote: "For our part, we have never heard of an ecstasy that thunder and lightning brought and are in difficulty to understand the meaning."

Page 184, "first known date...October 15, 1911"
See the address by Rudolf Steiner in Berlin, on December 15, 1911, in CW 264.

Page 185, "Address at the Laying of the Foundation Stone...January 3, 1911"
There must have been a transcript of Rudolf Steiner's address at that time, as the passage out of the address was placed as a motto on the front of a brochure from October 1911, "To the Members of the Theosophical Society (German Section) and Their Friends Concerning the Johannes Building". As of today, the relevant transcript or notes could not be located and are considered lost.

Page 186, "Carl Schmid-Curtius"
Dr. Carl Schmid-Curtius (died 1931 in Locarno, Switzerland) was the architect of the first Stuttgart Society house at 70 Landhausstraße. From 1911 to 1914 he was architect for the building project in Munich and then in Dornach. Later he studied medicine, and was active in scientific research.

Page 186, "José del Monte"
José del Monte (1875-1950) Stuttgart Member since 1902/03 and from 1911-1937 the Chairman of the Building Association of the Association of the Stuttgart Branches for the construction of the Stuttgart house, 70 Landhausstraße. In 1920 he was co-founder and first Chairman of the "Eurythmy Association," which built and furnished the Stuttgart Eurythmy School. He was the nephew of Adolf Arenson.

Page 187, "Adolf Arenson"
Adolf Arenson (1855-1936), businessman and composer. By 1895 he composed five operas but wrote his last one already in 1901. He joined the Theosophical Society in Stuttgart in 1902/03. Upon hearing Rudolf Steiner speak at a delegates' meeting in Berlin in 1903, he immediately invited him to come to Stuttgart to lecture. Arenson became a member of the Executive Council of the German Section of the Theosophical Society in 1904. At that time he became a personal student of Rudolf Steiner. Together with Dr. Carl Unger, he lead the Stuttgart Main Branch, later called the Rudolf Steiner Branch. Adolf Arenson supported Marie von Sivers in her publishing of Steiner's works. Out of this work the idea was born for his *Arenson Leitfaden*, a topic-guide through fifty of Steiner's lecture cycles. Adolf Arenson was one of the official lecturers on Theosophy.

Page 189, "of our dear friend"
The pharmacist Ernst Heim, a member of the Arenson-Unger Branch. In 1910 he donated the significant sum of 50,000 Marks to make possible the work of erecting the Society building in Stuttgart.

Page 191, "about a similar building"
At the Festival Plays in the summer of 1910 the plan to build a central building was made known. Because of difficulties on the side of the building authority, this building plan was moved to Dornach in the spring of 1913.

Page 192, "Hölderlin...'One in all'"
Johann Christian Friedrich Hölderlin (1770-1843). At the age of 14 Hölderlin already had started to write poems, which were read by his friends from school and teachers. In 1788 he entered the University of Tübingen, where he studied theology and obtained a master's degree. During this period he became friends with Friedrich Wilhelm Hegel and shared with him a great admiration of the French Revolution. In 1793 he was introduced to Friedrich von Schiller, who published some of his poems. He worked as a private tutor in Waltershausen, but the turning point in his life was when he took a post in a house of a wealthy Frankfurt banker Jakob Gontard. Hölderlin had a painful, but platonic, love affair with his employer's wife whom he called 'Diotima' in his poems. Their happiness was short-lived and was ended by the husband. Hölderin spent the last 36 years of his life under the shadow of insanity, largely because of the tragic end of this impossible love. He lived his last years in a carpenter's house in Tübingen. During the periods, when he regained enough sanity to write, he translated, among other things, Sophocles's tragedies.

Hölderlin was not directly affiliated with either of the two major literary movements of his time, Weimar Classicism or Romanticism, but his thought has elements in common with both. Hölderlin shared the classicists' love of noble simplicity and quiet greatness and added to it his mystical sense of nature with elements of pantheism and Christian images. Like William Blake and W.B. Yeats, he explored cosmology and history. His was an attempt to find meaning in an uncertain world. Hölderlin also played an important role in the development of philosophy from Kant to Hegel, and hence in the formation of German Idealism.

Page 192, "Oetinger"
Friedrich Christoph Oetinger (1702-82) was an influential German theologian. Already as a young student in the Evangelical seminary in Tübingen, Oetinger found the writings of Jakob Böhme, which he studied from then on. His high esteem for the Bible was decidedly influenced by Johann Albrecht Bengel. After his studies at the seminary, he traveled to Frankfurt where he was introduced to the Kabbala. In Herrnhut he became acquainted with the work of Count Nikolaus Ludwig von Zinzendorf. In 1731 he was Repetent in the Tübingen seminary. This was followed by a short time as instructor in Halle. After serving

as pastor in various locations, he was made the pastor in Murrhardt in 1766, where he also served as ducal counselor and district representative. Oetinger influenced many poets and thinkers: Wieland, Herder, Goethe, Schiller, Hölderlin, Hegel, Schelling, Kerner, Mörike, and Hesse.

Page 192, "of local significance here"
The evangelical Theosophist Friedrich Christoph Oetinger describes Völker, a farmer from Thüringen, who lived in the first half of the 18th century in Großrudestedt, north of Ehrfurt, in his autobiography and letters. Völker must have been an extraordinary human being; he made a deep impression upon Oetinger, who stayed with him twice for extended periods. Völker had the inner sight and taught Oetinger extensively. For further details, see the essay by C.S. Picht, "Marcus Völker" in the magazine *Die Drei*, 8th year, 1927, Volume VIII.

Page 192, "great philosophers...spiritual substance of this region"
Georg Wilhelm Friedrich Hegel (1770-1831) and Friedrich Wilhelm Joseph Schelling (1775-1854), towering figures in the German Idealist school of philosophy. See note for page 40.

Page 192, "...winged instrument is the word"
Friedrich Schiller. In *The Homage of the Arts: A Lyrical Play* wrote:

> No bond holds me, no barrier chains me,
> Freely I swing forth through all spaces.
> An immeasurable realm is the thought,
> And my winged tool is the Word.

Page 193, "You, Spirit of the Cosmos...dedicated to you"
Words of Solomon formed by Rudolf Steiner based on 1 Kings 8: 12-53 and 2 Chronicles 6.

Page 194, "Masters of Wisdom and Harmony of Feelings"
See the note for page 177.

Page 196, "to outfit the mystery performances"
At the annual summer conferences in Munich, mystery dramas were performed, starting with the Congress of 1907. From 1910-1913 Rudolf Steiner wrote four Mystery Dramas that were premiered there.

Page 200, "symbolic figures in this space"
See the photographs of the column hall in the Stuttgart house in the color section at the back of this book.

Page 201, "kamaloca"
Our every action, thought, and feeling has a spiritual counterpart engraved into

the spiritual world. For the first three days after death our life experiences are spread out before us in a panorama. Following that, we actually go through the spiritual counterpart of all of our experiences between life and death but in reverse order—from death back to birth. In this process, we live through what others have experienced through our actions. We experience with bitter pain the harm we have done, and with burning thirst the passions we did not overcome, until such time as we have realized sufficiently the worthlessness of these passions for the spiritual world. The length of this period of kamaloca equals approximately one-third of the time spent between birth and death on Earth.

Page 201, "two pictures...by our friend Stockmeyer"
Two paintings by Karl H.W. Stockmeyer hung in the space until the house had to be given up in 1935; today they are in the Stockmeyer estate in Malsch.

Page 202, "form-shape forces of the physical body"
See CW 131.

Page 205, *"How to Know Higher Worlds"*
CW 9.

Page 207, "Karlsruhe lecture cycle"
CW 131.

Page 210, "should not be used for other beings"
Steiner is referring to the idea propagated in the Theosophical Society at that time that a young Indian boy, Krishnamurti, was the reincarnation of Christ. Rudolf Steiner sternly rejected this as "esoteric nonsense," which also further led to the separation of the Anthroposophical Movement from the Theosophical Society.

Page 211, "H. P. Blavatsky"
Helena Petrovna Blavatsky (1831-1891), co-founder of the Theosophical Society and author of *Isis Unveiled* (1877) and *The Secret Doctrine* (1888). See her biographical sketch in the Appendix.

Page 211, "cannot be discussed now"
See CW 254, where Steiner does discuss the reason.

Page 211, "never be thought...in a physical body"
It could not be determined where Blavatsky stated this.

Page 212, "have opened quite differently since 1899"
According to Steiner, in 1899 the Kali Yuga, or 3000 years of spiritual darkness, came to an end. See, among others, CW 116, lecture of February 2, 1910.

Page 213, "I am with you...end of the world"
Matthew 28:20.

Page 215, "the *Mitteilungen*"
The *Mitteilungen für die Mitglieder der Deutschen Sektion der Theosophischen Gesellschaft* [News for members of the German section of the Theosophical Society].

Page 216, "institute of Theosophical spiritual striving"
From its inception, Rudolf Steiner had conceived of a free institute together with the central building, and starting in 1913/14, the first building in Dornach was called "The Free High School for Spiritual Science". Yet Rudolf Steiner formally founded it only at the turn of 1923/24. See CW 260a.

Page 217, "What lofty thanks be given to one"
This is a free rendering by Steiner. Goethe's actual words: Which lofty thanks is to be said to the one / Who brought us afresh to the book / That to all searching, all complaining / A grandiose end has made. Zahme Xenien VIII, dated Weimar, July 23, 1824.

Page 219, "Concerning the Unity of Temple...Goetheanum Building-Idea"
This essay was written in 1957 in connection with the completion of the great hall in the second Goetheanum building.

Page 219, "in the magazine *Lucifer-Gnosis*"
Reprinted in CW 11.

Page 219, "ritual...with a group of members"
See CW 28, chapter 36.

Page 220, "ritual...after Rudolf Steiner's death"
Marie Steiner, who along with Rudolf Steiner led the ritual part of the Esoteric School before World War I, arranged a festival on March 30, 1926, in memory of Rudolf Steiner's death date, which she fashioned in the sense mentioned.

Page 220, "Mr. Aisenpreis"
Ernst Aisenpreis (1884-1949) was the lead architect during the construction of both the first and second Goetheanum buildings. Stockmeyer is refering to an entry Ernst Aisenpreis made in a notebook—which was mentioned by Assya Turgenieff in her essay, "What Has Happened to the Goetheanum Building?"— in which Rudolf Steiner said to him that he intended to set up the "Group" in front of a background formed in wood in the stage space of the second Goetheanum. Later, however, Rudolf Steiner considered a different arrangement.

Page 220, "called the reverse ritual in 1923"
See CW 257, lecture of March 3, 1923.

Page 220, "karma lectures of 1924, on April 27th"
CW 236.

Page 229, "Hermann Ranzenberger"
Hermann Ranzenberger (1891-1967) was an architect who was asked by Rudolf Steiner to come from Stuttgart to Dornach to work on the Goetheanum being built there. He was one of several architects who worked on the first and second Goetheanum buildings. After the completion of the second building in 1928, he continued working in Dornach as an independent architect.

Page 244, "Church Father Origen of Alexandria"
Origen of Alexandria (185-254 C.E.) is considered among the greatest Christian theologians. His *On First Principles* is one of the seminal works of Christian Neo-Platonism.

Page 245, "Gospel of Nicodemus"
The Gospel of Nicodemus is part of the apocryphal New Testament, or those contemporary or nearly contemporary books about the life of Jesus that did not make it into the official New Testament when it was canonically fixed in the 4th Century A.D. Its provenance is difficult to determine; fragments in Greek date to the 4th Century, while there are references to portions as early as the 2nd Century. The name was assigned only in the 13th Century. The text was published in German in 1853. Today it can be found in any collection of Ante-Nicene Church writings.

Page 245, "lecture on May 29, 1905, in Berlin"
CW 93.

Page 245, "lecture of June 29, 1907, in Kassel"
CW 100.

Page 248, "The human being enters...in it I will live"
CW 169.

Page 248, "lecture in Dornach, on December 29, 1918"
CW 187.

Page 248, "lecture in Berlin on June 20, 1916"
CW 169.

RUDOLF STEINER'S COLLECTED WORKS

The German Edition of Rudolf Steiner's Collected Works (the Gesamtausgabe [GA] published by Rudolf Steiner Verlag, Dornach, Switzerland) presently runs to over 354 titles, organized either by type of work (written or spoken), chronology, audience (public or other), or subject (education, art, etc.). For ease of comparison, the Collected Works in English [CW] follows the German organization exactly. A complete listing of the CWs follows with literal translations of the German titles. Other than in the case of the books published in his lifetime, titles were rarely given by Rudolf Steiner himself, and were often provided by the editors of the German editions. The titles in English are not necessarily the same as the German; and, indeed, over the past seventy-five years have frequently been different, with the same book sometimes appearing under different titles.

For ease of identification and to avoid confusion, we suggest that readers looking for a title should do so by CW number. Because the work of creating the Collected Works of Rudolf Steiner is an ongoing process, with new titles being published every year, we have not indicated in this listing which books are presently available. To find out what titles in the Collected Works are currently in print, please check our website at www.steinerbooks.org, or write to SteinerBooks 610 Main Street, Great Barrington, MA 01230:

Written Work

CW 1	Goethe: Natural-Scientific Writings, Introduction, with Footnotes and Explanations in the text by Rudolf Steiner
CW 2	Outlines of an Epistemology of the Goethean World View, with Special Consideration of Schiller
CW 3	Truth and Science
CW 4	The Philosophy of Freedom
CW 4a	Documents to "The Philosophy of Freedom"
CW 5	Friedrich Nietzsche, A Fighter against His Own Time
CW 6	Goethe's Worldview
CW 6a	Now in CW 30
CW 7	Mysticism at the Dawn of Modern Spiritual Life and Its Relationship with Modern Worldviews
CW 8	Christianity as Mystical Fact and the Mysteries of Antiquity
CW 9	Theosophy: An Introduction into Supersensible World Knowledge and Human Purpose
CW 10	How Does One Attain Knowledge of Higher Worlds?
CW 11	From the Akasha-Chronicle
CW 12	Levels of Higher Knowledge

CW 13	Occult Science in Outline
CW 14	Four Mystery Dramas
CW 15	The Spiritual Guidance of the Individual and Humanity
CW 16	A Way to Human Self-Knowledge: Eight Meditations
CW 17	The Threshold of the Spiritual World. Aphoristic Comments
CW 18	The Riddles of Philosophy in Their History, Presented as an Outline
CW 19	Contained in CW 24
CW 20	The Riddles of the Human Being: Articulated and Unarticulated in the Thinking, Views and Opinions of a Series of German and Austrian Personalities
CW 21	The Riddles of the Soul
CW 22	Goethe's Spiritual Nature And Its Revelation In "Faust" and through the "Fairy Tale of the Snake and the Lily"
CW 23	The Central Points of the Social Question in the Necessities of Life in the Present and the Future
CW 24	Essays Concerning the Threefold Division of the Social Organism and the Period 1915-1921
CW 25	Cosmology, Religion and Philosophy
CW 26	Anthroposophical Leading Thoughts
CW 27	Fundamentals for Expansion of the Art of Healing according to Spiritual-Scientific Insights
CW 28	The Course of My Life
CW 29	Collected Essays on Dramaturgy, 1889-1900
CW 30	Methodical Foundations of Anthroposophy: Collected Essays on Philosophy, Natural Science, Aesthetics and Psychology, 1884-1901
CW 31	Collected Essays on Culture and Current Events, 1887-1901
CW 32	Collected Essays on Literature, 1884-1902
CW 33	Biographies and Biographical Sketches, 1894-1905
CW 34	Lucifer-Gnosis: Foundational Essays on Anthroposophy and Reports from the Periodicals "Lucifer" and "Lucifer-Gnosis," 1903-1908
CW 35	Philosophy and Anthroposophy: Collected Essays, 1904-1923
CW 36	The Goetheanum-Idea in the Middle of the Cultural Crisis of the Present: Collected Essays from the Periodical "Das Goetheanum," 1921-1925
CW 37	Now in CWs 260a and 251
CW 38	Letters, Vol. 1: 1881-1890
CW 39	Letters, Vol. 2: 1890-1925
CW 40	Truth-Wrought Words
CW 40a	Sayings, Poems and Mantras; Supplementary Volume
CW 42	Now in CWs 264-266

CW 43 Stage Adaptations
CW 44 On the Four Mystery Dramas. Sketches, Fragments and Paralipomena on the Four Mystery Dramas
CW 45 Anthroposophy: A Fragment from the Year 1910

Public Lectures

CW 51 On Philosophy, History and Literature
CW 52 Spiritual Teachings Concerning the Soul and Observation of the World
CW 53 The Origin and Goal of the Human Being
CW 54 The Riddles of the World and Anthroposophy
CW 55 Knowledge of the Supersensible in Our Times and Its Meaning for Life Today
CW 56 Knowledge of the Soul and of the Spirit
CW 57 Where and How Does One Find the Spirit?
CW 58 The Metamorphoses of the Soul Life. Paths of Soul Experiences: Part One
CW 59 The Metamorphoses of the Soul Life. Paths of Soul Experiences: Part Two
CW 60 The Answers of Spiritual Science to the Biggest Questions of Existence
CW 61 Human History in the Light of Spiritual Research
CW 62 Results of Spiritual Research
CW 63 Spiritual Science as a Treasure for Life
CW 64 Out of Destiny-Burdened Times
CW 65 Out of Central European Spiritual Life
CW 66 Spirit and Matter, Life and Death
CW 67 The Eternal in the Human Soul. Immortality and Freedom
CW 68 Public lectures in various cities, 1906-1918
CW 69 Public lectures in various cities, 1906-1918
CW 70 Public lectures in various cities, 1906-1918
CW 71 Public lectures in various cities, 1906-1918
CW 72 Freedom – Immortality – Social Life
CW 73 The Supplementing of the Modern Sciences through Anthroposophy
CW 73a Specialized Fields of Knowledge and Anthroposophy
CW 74 The Philosophy of Thomas Aquinas
CW 75 Public lectures in various cities, 1906-1918
CW 76 The Fructifying Effect of Anthroposophy on Specialized Fields
CW 77a The Task of Anthroposophy in Relation to Science and Life: The Darmstadt College Course
CW 77b Art and Anthroposophy. The Goetheanum-Impulse

CW 78	Anthroposophy, Its Roots of Knowledge and Fruits for Life
CW 79	The Reality of the Higher Worlds
CW 80	Public lectures in various cities, 1922
CW 81	Renewal-Impulses for Culture and Science–Berlin College Course
CW 82	So that the Human Being Can Become a Complete Human Being
CW 83	Western and Eastern World-Contrast. Paths to Understanding It through Anthroposophy
CW 84	What Did the Goetheanum Intend and What Should Anthroposophy Do?

Lectures to the Members of the Anthroposophical Society

CW 88	Concerning the Astral World and Devachan
CW 89	Consciousness–Life–Form. Fundamental Principles of a Spiritual-Scientific Cosmology
CW 90	Participant Notes from the Lectures during the Years 1903-1905
CW 91	Participant Notes from the Lectures during the Years 1903-1905
CW 92	The Occult Truths of Ancient Myths and Sagas
CW 93	The Temple Legend and the Golden Legend
CW 93a	Fundamentals of Esotericism
CW 94	Cosmogony. Popular Occultism. The Gospel of John. The Theosophy in the Gospel of John
CW 95	At the Gates of Theosophy
CW 96	Origin-Impulses of Spiritual Science. Christian Esotericism in the Light of New Spirit-Knowledge
CW 97	The Christian Mystery
CW 98	Nature Beings and Spirit Beings – Their Effects in Our Visible World
CW 99	The Theosophy of the Rosicrucians
CW 100	Human Development and Christ-Knowledge
CW 101	Myths and Legends. Occult Signs and Symbols
CW 102	The Working into Human Beings by Spiritual Beings
CW 103	The Gospel of John
CW 104	The Apocalypse of John
CW 104a	From the Picture-Script of the Apocalypse of John
CW 105	Universe, Earth, the Human Being: Their Being and Development, as well as Their Reflection in the Connection between Egyptian Mythology and Modern Culture
CW 106	Egyptian Myths and Mysteries in Relation to the Active Spiritual Forces of the Present
CW 107	Spiritual-Scientific Knowledge of the Human Being
CW 108	Answering the Questions of Life and the World through Anthroposophy

CW 109	The Principle of Spiritual Economy in Connection with the Question of Reincarnation. An Aspect of the Spiritual Guidance of Humanity
CW 110	The Spiritual Hierarchies and Their Reflection in the Physical World. Zodiac, Planets and Cosmos
CW 111	Contained in 109
CW 112	The Gospel of John in Relation to the Three Other Gospels, Especially the Gospel of Luke
CW 113	The Orient in the Light of the Occident. The Children of Lucifer and the Brothers of Christ
CW 114	The Gospel of Luke
CW 115	Anthroposophy – Psychosophy – Pneumatosophy
CW 116	The Christ-Impulse and the Development of "I"- Consciousness
CW 117	The Deeper Secrets of the Development of Humanity in Light of the Gospels
CW 118	The Event of the Christ-Appearance in the Etheric World
CW 119	Macrocosm and Microcosm. The Large World and the Small World. Soul-Questions, Life-Questions, Spirit-Questions
CW 120	The Revelation of Karma
CW 121	The Mission of Individual Folk-Souls in Connection with Germanic-Nordic Mythology
CW 122	The Secrets of the Biblical Creation-Story. The Six-Day Work in the First Book of Moses
CW 123	The Gospel of Matthew
CW 124	Excursus in the Area of the Gospel of Mark
CW 125	Paths and Goals of the Spiritual Human Being. Life Questions in the Light of Spiritual Science
CW 126	Occult History. Esoteric Observations of the Karmic Relationships of Personalities and Events of World History
CW 127	The Mission of the New Spiritual Revelation. The Christ-Event as the Middle-Point of Earth Evolution
CW 128	An Occult Physiology
CW 129	Wonders of the World, Trials of the Soul, and Revelations of the Spirit
CW 130	Esoteric Christianity and the Spiritual Guidance of Humanity
CW 131	From Jesus to Christ
CW 132	Evolution from the View Point of the Truth
CW 133	The Earthly and the Cosmic Human Being
CW 134	The World of the Senses and the World of the Spirit
CW 135	Reincarnation and Karma and their Meaning for the Culture of the Present
CW 136	The Spiritual Beings in Celestial Bodies and the Realms of Nature

CW 137	The Human Being in the Light of Occultism, Theosophy and Philosophy
CW 138	On Initiation. On Eternity and the Passing Moment. On the Light of the Spirit and the Darkness of Life
CW 139	The Gospel of Mark
CW 140	Occult Investigation into the Life between Death and New Birth. The Living Interaction between Life and Death
CW 141	Life between Death and New Birth in Relationship to Cosmic Facts
CW 142	The Bhagavad Gita and the Letters of Paul
CW 143	Experiences of the Supersensible. Three Paths of the Soul to Christ
CW 144	The Mysteries of the East and of Christianity
CW 145	What Significance Does Occult Development of the Human Being Have for His Sheaths–Physical Body, Etheric Body, Astral Body, and Self?
CW 146	The Occult Foundations of the Bhagavad Gita
CW 147	The Secrets of the Threshold
CW 148	Out of Research in the Akasha: The Fifth Gospel
CW 149	Christ and the Spiritual World. Concerning the Search for the Holy Grail
CW 150	The World of the Spirit and Its Extension into Physical Existence; The Influence of the Dead in the World of the Living
CW 151	Human Thought and Cosmic Thought
CW 152	Preliminary Stages to the Mystery of Golgotha
CW 153	The Inner Being of the Human Being and Life Between Death and New Birth
CW 154	How does One Gain an Understanding of the Spiritual World? The Flowing in of Spiritual Impulses from out of the World of the Deceased
CW 155	Christ and the Human Soul. Concerning the Meaning of Life. Theosophical Morality. Anthroposophy and Christianity
CW 156	Occult Reading and Occult Hearing
CW 157	Human Destinies and the Destiny of Peoples
CW 157a	The Formation of Destiny and the Life after Death
CW 158	The Connection Between the Human Being and the Elemental World. Kalevala – Olaf Asteson – The Russian People – The World as the Result of the Influences of Equilibrium
CW 159	The Mystery of Death. The Nature and Significance of Middle Europe and the European Folk Spirits
CW 160	In CW 159
CW 161	Paths of Spiritual Knowledge and the Renewal of the Artistic Worldview
CW 162	Questions of Art and Life in Light of Spiritual Science

CW 163 Coincidence, Necessity and Providence. Imaginative Knowledge and the Processes after Death

CW 164 The Value of Thinking for a Knowledge That Satisfies the Human Being. The Relationship of Spiritual Science to Natural Science

CW 165 The Spiritual Unification of Humanity through the Christ-Impulse

CW 166 Necessity and Freedom in the Events of the World and in Human Action

CW 167 The Present and the Past in the Human Spirit

CW 168 The Connection between the Living and the Dead

CW 169 World-being and Selfhood

CW 170 The Riddle of the Human Being. The Spiritual Background of Human History. Cosmic and Human History, Vol. 1

CW 171 Inner Development-Impulses of Humanity. Goethe and the Crisis of the 19th Century. Cosmic and Human History, Vol. 2

CW 172 The Karma of the Vocation of the Human Being in Connection with Goethe's Life. Cosmic and Human History, Vol. 3

CW 173 Contemporary-Historical Considerations: The Karma of Untruthfulness, Part One. Cosmic and Human History, Vol. 4

CW 174 Contemporary-Historical Considerations: The Karma of Untruthfulness, Part Two. Cosmic and Human History, Vol. 5

CW 174a Middle Europe between East and West. Cosmic and Human History, Vol. 6

CW 174b The Spiritual Background of the First World War. Cosmic and Human History, Vol. 7

CW 175 Building Stones for an Understanding of the Mystery of Golgotha. Cosmic and Human Metamorphoses

CW 176 Truths of Evolution of the Individual and Humanity. The Karma of Materialism

CW 177 The Spiritual Background of the Outer World. The Fall of the Spirits of Darkness. Spiritual Beings and Their Effects, Vol. 1

CW 178 Individual Spiritual Beings and their Influence in the Soul of the Human Being. Spiritual Beings and their Effects, Vol. 2

CW 179 Spiritual Beings and Their Effects. Historical Necessity and Freedom. The Influences on Destiny from out of the World of the Dead. Spiritual Beings and Their Effects, Vol. 3

CW 180 Mystery Truths and Christmas Impulses. Ancient Myths and their Meaning. Spiritual Beings and Their Effects, Vol. 4

CW 181 Earthly Death and Cosmic Life. Anthroposophical Gifts for Life. Necessities of Consciousness for the Present and the Future.

CW 182 Death as Transformation of Life

CW 183 The Science of the Development of the Human Being

CW 184 The Polarity of Duration and Development in Human Life. The Cosmic Pre-History of Humanity

CW 185	Historical Symptomology
CW 185a	Historical-Developmental Foundations for Forming a Social Judgment
CW 186	The Fundamental Social Demands of Our Time–In Changed Situations
CW 187	How Can Humanity Find the Christ Again? The Threefold Shadow-Existence of our Time and the New Christ-Light
CW 188	Goetheanism, a Transformation-Impulse and Resurrection-Thought. Science of the Human Being and Science of Sociology
CW 189	The Social Question as a Question of Consciousness. The Spiritual Background of the Social Question, Vol. 1
CW 190	Impulses of the Past and the Future in Social Occurrences. The Spiritual Background of the Social Question, Vol. 2
CW 191	Social Understanding from Spiritual-Scientific Cognition. The Spiritual Background of the Social Question, Vol. 3
CW 192	Spiritual-Scientific Treatment of Social and Pedagogical Questions
CW 193	The Inner Aspect of the Social Riddle. Luciferic Past and Ahrimanic Future
CW 194	The Mission of Michael. The Revelation of the Actual Mysteries of the Human Being
CW 195	Cosmic New Year and the New Year Idea
CW 196	Spiritual and Social Transformations in the Development of Humanity
CW 197	Polarities in the Development of Humanity: West and East Materialism and Mysticism Knowledge and Belief
CW 198	Healing Factors for the Social Organism
CW 199	Spiritual Science as Knowledge of the Foundational Impulses of Social Formation
CW 200	The New Spirituality and the Christ-Experience of the 20th Century
CW 201	The Correspondences Between Microcosm and Macrocosm. The Human Being – A Hieroglyph of the Universe. The Human Being in Relationship with the Cosmos: 1
CW 202	The Bridge between the World-Spirituality and the Physical Aspect of the Human Being. The Search for the New Isis, the Divine Sophia. The Human Being in Relationship with the Cosmos: 2
CW 203	The Responsibility of Human Beings for the Development of the World through their Spiritual Connection with the Planet Earth and the World of the Stars. The Human Being in Relationship with the Cosmos: 3
CW 204	Perspectives of the Development of Humanity. The Materialistic Knowledge-Impulse and the Task of Anthroposophy. The Human Being in Relationship with the Cosmos: 4

CW 205 Human Development, World-Soul, and World-Spirit. Part One: The Human Being as a Being of Body and Soul in Relationship to the World. The Human Being in Relationship with the Cosmos: 5

CW 206 Human Development, World-Soul, and World-Spirit. Part Two: The Human Being as a Spiritual Being in the Process of Historical Development. The Human Being in Relationship with the Cosmos: 6

CW 207 Anthroposophy as Cosmosophy. Part One: Characteristic Features of the Human Being in the Earthly and the Cosmic Realms. The Human Being in Relationship with the Cosmos: 7

CW 208 Anthroposophy as Cosmosophy. Part Two: The Forming of the Human Being as the Result of Cosmic Influence. The Human Being in Relationship with the Cosmos: 8

CW 209 Nordic and Central European Spiritual Impulses. The Festival of the Appearance of Christ. The Human Being in Relationship with the Cosmos: 9

CW 210 Old and New Methods of Initiation. Drama and Poetry in the Change of Consciousness in the Modern Age

CW 211 The Sun Mystery and the Mystery of Death and Resurrection. Exoteric and Esoteric Christianity

CW 212 Human Soul Life and Spiritual Striving in Connection with World and Earth Development

CW 213 Human Questions and World Answers

CW 214 The Mystery of the Trinity: The Human Being in Relationship to the Spiritual World in the Course of Time

CW 215 Philosophy, Cosmology, and Religion in Anthroposophy

CW 216 The Fundamental Impulses of the World-Historical Development of Humanity

CW 217 Spiritually Active Forces in the Coexistence of the Older and Younger Generations. Pedagogical Course for Youth

CW 217a Youth's Cognitive Task

CW 218 Spiritual Connections in the Forming of the Human Organism

CW 219 The Relationship of the World of the Stars to the Human Being, and of the Human Being to the World of the Stars. The Spiritual Communion of Humanity

CW 220 Living Knowledge of Nature. Intellectual Fall and Spiritual Redemption

CW 221 Earth-Knowing and Heaven-Insight

CW 222 The Imparting of Impulses to World-Historical Events through Spiritual Powers

CW 223 The Cycle of the Year as Breathing Process of the Earth and the Four Great Festival-Seasons. Anthroposophy and Human Heart (Gemüt)

CW 224	The Human Soul and its Connection with Divine-Spiritual Individualities. The Internalization of the Festivals of the Year
CW 225	Three Perspectives of Anthroposophy. Cultural Phenomena observed from a Spiritual-Scientific Perspective
CW 226	Human Being, Human Destiny, and World Development
CW 227	Initiation-Knowledge
CW 228	Science of Initiation and Knowledge of the Stars. The Human Being in the Past, the Present, and the Future from the Viewpoint of the Development of Consciousness
CW 229	The Experiencing of the Course of the Year in Four Cosmic Imaginations
CW 230	The Human Being as Harmony of the Creative, Building, and Formative World-Word
CW 231	The Supersensible Human Being, Understood Anthroposophically
CW 232	The Forming of the Mysteries
CW 233	World History Illuminated by Anthroposophy and as the Foundation for Knowledge of the Human Spirit
CW 233a	Mystery Sites of the Middle Ages: Rosicrucianism and the Modern Initiation-Principle. The Festival of Easter as Part of the History of the Mysteries of Humanity
CW 234	Anthroposophy. A Summary after 21 Years
CW 235	Esoteric Observations of Karmic Relationships in 6 Volumes, Vol. 1
CW 236	Esoteric Observations of Karmic Relationships in 6 Volumes, Vol. 2
CW 237	Esoteric Observations of Karmic Relationships in 6 Volumes, Vol. 3: The Karmic Relationships of the Anthroposophical Movement
CW 238	Esoteric Observations of Karmic Relationships in 6 Volumes, Vol. 4: The Spiritual Life of the Present in Relationship to the Anthroposoph-ical Movement
CW 239	Esoteric Observations of Karmic Relationships in 6 Volumes, Vol. 5
CW 240	Esoteric Observations of Karmic Relationships in 6 Volumes, Vol. 6
CW 243	The Consciousness of the Initiate
CW 245	Instructions for an Esoteric Schooling
CW 250	The Building-Up of the Anthroposophical Society. From the Beginning to the Outbreak of the First World War
CW 251	The History of the Goetheanum Building-Association
CW 252	Life in the Anthroposophical Society from the First World War to the Burning of the First Goetheanum
CW 253	The Problems of Living Together in the Anthroposophical Society. On the Dornach Crisis of 1915. With Highlights on Swedenborg's Clairvoyance, the Views of Freudian Psychoanalysts, and the Concept of Love in Relation to Mysticism

CW 254 The Occult Movement in the 19th Century and Its Relationship to World Culture. Significant Points from the Exoteric Cultural Life around the Middle of the 19th Century
CW 255 Rudolf Steiner during the First World War
CW 255a Anthroposophy and the Reformation of Society. On the History of the Threefold Movement
CW 255b Anthroposophy and Its Opponents, 1919-1921
CW 256 How Can the Anthroposophical Movement Be Financed?
CW 256a Futurum, Inc. / International Laboratories, Inc.
CW 256b The Coming Day, Inc.
CW 257 Anthroposophical Community-Building
CW 258 The History of and Conditions for the Anthroposophical Movement in Relationship to the Anthroposophical Society. A Stimulus to Self-Contemplation
CW 259 The Year of Destiny 1923 in the History of the Anthroposophical Society. From the Burning of the Goetheanum to the Christmas Conference
CW 260 The Christmas Conference for the Founding of the General Anthroposophical Society
CW 260a The Constitution of the General Anthroposophical Society and the School for Spiritual Science. The Rebuilding of the Goetheanum
CW 261 Our Dead. Addresses, Words of Remembrance, and Meditative Verses, 1906-1924
CW 262 Rudolf Steiner and Marie Steiner-von Sivers: Correspondence and Documents, 1901-1925
CW 263/1 Rudolf Steiner and Edith Maryon: Correspondence: Letters, Verses, Sketches, 1912-1924
CW 264 On the History and the Contents of the First Section of the Esoteric School from 1904 to 1914. Letters, Newsletters, Documents, Lectures
CW 265 On the History and Out of the Contents of the Ritual-Knowledge Section of the Esoteric School from 1904 to 1914. Documents, and Lectures from the Years 1906 to 1914, as well as on New Approaches to Ritual-Knowledge Work in the Years 1921-1924
CW 266/1 From the Contents of the Esoteric Lessons. Volume 1: 1904-1909. Notes from Memory of Participants. Meditation texts from the notes of Rudolf Steiner
CW 266/2 From the Contents of the Esoteric Lessons. Volume 2: 1910-1912. Notes from Memory of Participants
CW 266/3 From the Contents of the Esoteric Lessons. Volume 3: 1913, 1914 and 1920-1923. Notes from Memory of Participants. Meditation texts from the notes of Rudolf Steiner

CW 267 Soul-Exercises: Vol. 1: Exercises with Word and Image Meditations for the Methodological Development of Higher Powers of Knowledge, 1904-1924
CW 268 Soul-Exercises: Vol. 2: Mantric Verses, 1903-1925
CW 269 Ritual Texts for the Celebration of the Free Christian Religious Instruction. The Collected Verses for Teachers and Students of the Waldorf School
CW 270 Esoteric Instructions for the First Class of the School for Spiritual Science at the Goetheanum 1924, 4 Volumes
CW 271 Art and Knowledge of Art. Foundations of a New Aesthetic
CW 272 Spiritual-Scientific Commentary on Goethe's "Faust" in Two Volumes. Vol. 1: Faust, the Striving Human Being
CW 273 Spiritual-Scientific Commentary on Goethe's "Faust" in Two Volumes. Vol. 2: The Faust-Problem
CW 274 Addresses for the Christmas Plays from the Old Folk Traditions
CW 275 Art in the Light of Mystery-Wisdom
CW 276 The Artistic in Its Mission in the World. The Genius of Language. The World of the Self-Revealing Radiant Appearances – Anthroposophy and Art. Anthroposophy and Poetry
CW 277 Eurythmy. The Revelation of the Speaking Soul
CW 277a The Origin and Development of Eurythmy
CW 278 Eurythmy as Visible Song
CW 279 Eurythmy as Visible Speech
CW 280 The Method and Nature of Speech Formation
CW 281 The Art of Recitation and Declamation
CW 282 Speech Formation and Dramatic Art
CW 283 The Nature of Things Musical and the Experience of Tone in the Human Being
CW284/285 Images of Occult Seals and Pillars. The Munich Congress of Whitsun 1907 and Its Consequences
CW 286 Paths to a New Style of Architecture. "And the Building Becomes Human"
CW 287 The Building at Dornach as a Symbol of Historical Becoming and an Artistic Transformation Impulse
CW 288 Style-Forms in the Living Organic
CW 289 The Building-Idea of the Goetheanum: Lectures with Slides from the Years 1920-1921
CW 290 The Building-Idea of the Goetheanum: Lectures with Slides from the Years 1920-1921
CW 291 The Nature of Colors
CW 291a Knowledge of Colors. Supplementary Volume to "The Nature of Colors"
CW 292 Art History as Image of Inner Spiritual Impulses

CW 293 General Knowledge of the Human Being as the Foundation of Pedagogy
CW 294 The Art of Education, Methodology and Didactics
CW 295 The Art of Education: Seminar Discussions and Lectures on Lesson Planning
CW 296 The Question of Education as a Social Question
CW 297 The Idea and Practice of the Waldorf School
CW 297a Education for Life: Self-Education and the Practice of Pedagogy
CW 298 Rudolf Steiner in the Waldorf School
CW 299 Spiritual-Scientific Observations on Speech
CW 300a Conferences with the Teachers of the Free Waldorf School in Stuttgart, 1919 to 1924, in 3 Volumes, Vol. 1
CW 300b Conferences with the Teachers of the Free Waldorf School in Stuttgart, 1919 to 1924, in 3 Volumes, Vol. 2
CW 300c Conferences with the Teachers of the Free Waldorf School in Stuttgart, 1919 to 1924, in 3 Volumes, Vol. 3
CW 301 The Renewal of the Pedagogical-Didactical Art through Spiritual Science
CW 302 Knowledge of the Human Being and the Forming of Class Lessons
CW 302a Education and Teaching out of a Knowledge of the Human Being
CW 303 The Healthy Development of the Human Being
CW 304 Methods of Education and Teaching Based on Anthroposophy
CW 304a Anthroposophical Knowledge of the Human Being and Pedagogy
CW 305 The Soul-Spiritual Foundational Forces of the Art of Education. Spiritual Values in Education and Social Life
CW 306 Pedagogical Praxis from the Viewpoint of a Spiritual-Scientific Knowledge of the Human Being. The Education of the Child and Young Human Beings
CW 307 The Spiritual Life of the Present and Education
CW 308 The Method of Teaching and the Life-Requirements for Teaching
CW 309 Anthroposophical Pedagogy and Its Prerequisites
CW 310 The Pedagogical Value of a Knowledge of the Human Being and the Cultural Value of Pedagogy
CW 311 The Art of Education Out of an Understanding of the Being of Humanity
CW 312 Spiritual Science and Medicine
CW 313 Spiritual-Scientific Viewpoints on Therapy
CW 314 Physiology and Therapy Based on Spiritual Science
CW 315 Curative Eurythmy
CW 316 Meditative Observations and Instructions for a Deepening of the Art of Healing
CW 317 The Curative Education Course
CW 318 The Working Together of Doctors and Pastors

CW 319	Anthroposophical Knowledge of the Human Being and Medicine
CW 320	Spiritual-Scientific Impulses for the Development of Physics 1: The First Natural-Scientific Course: Light, Color, Tone, Mass, Electricity, Magnetism
CW 321	Spiritual-Scientific Impulses for the Development of Physics 2: The Second Natural-Scientific Course: Warmth at the Border of Positive and Negative Materiality
CW 322	The Borders of the Knowledge of Nature
CW 323	The Relationship of the various Natural-Scientific Fields to Astronomy
CW 324	Nature Observation, Mathematics, and Scientific Experimentation and Results from the Viewpoint of Anthroposophy
CW 324a	The Fourth Dimension in Mathematics and Reality
CW 325	Natural Science and the World-Historical Development of Humanity since Ancient Times
CW 326	The Moment of the Coming Into Being of Natural Science in World History and Its Development Since Then
CW 327	Spiritual-Scientific Foundations for Success in Farming. The Agricultural Course
CW 328	The Social Question
CW 329	The Liberation of the Human Being as the Foundation for a New Social Form
CW 330	The Renewal of the Social Organism
CW 331	Work-Council and Socialization
CW 332	The Alliance for Threefolding and the Total Reform of Society. The Council on Culture and the Liberation of the Spiritual Life
CW 332a	The Social Future
CW 333	Freedom of Thought and Social Forces
CW 334	From the Unified State to the Threefold Social Organism
CW 335	The Crisis of the Present and the Path to Healthy Thinking
CW 336	The Great Questions of the Times and Anthroposophical Spiritual Knowledge
CW 337a	Social Ideas, Social Reality, Social Practice, Vol. 1: Question-and-Answer Evenings and Study Evenings of the Alliance for the Threefold Social Organism in Stuttgart, 1919-1920
CW 337b	Social Ideas, Social Realities, Social Practice, Vol. 2: Discussion Evenings of the Swiss Alliance for the Threefold Social Organism
CW 338	How Does One Work on Behalf of the Impulse for the Threefold Social Organism?
CW 339	Anthroposophy, Threefold Social Organism, and the Art of Public Speaking
CW 340	The National-Economics Course. The Tasks of a New Science of Economics, Volume 1

CW 341 The National-Economics Seminar. The Tasks of a New Science of Economics, Volume 2

CW 342 Lectures and Courses on Christian Religious Work, Vol. 1: Anthroposophical Foundations for a Renewed Christian Religious Working

CW 343 Lectures and Courses on Christian Religious Work, Vol. 2: Spiritual Knowledge – Religious Feeling – Cultic Doing

CW 344 Lectures and Courses on Christian Religious Work, Vol. 3: Lectures at the Founding of the Christian Community

CW 345 Lectures and Courses on Christian Religious Work, Vol. 4: Concerning the Nature of the Working Word

CW 346 Lectures and Courses on Christian Religious Work, Vol. 5: The Apocalypse and the Working of the Priest

CW 347 The Knowledge of the Nature of the Human Being According to Body, Soul and Spirit. On Earlier Conditions of the Earth

CW 348 On Health and Illness. Foundations of a Spiritual-Scientific Doctrine of the Senses

CW 349 On the Life of Human Being and of the Earth. On the Nature of Christianity

CW 350 Rhythms in the Cosmos and in the Human Being. How Does One Come To See the Spiritual World?

CW 351 The Human Being and the World. The Influence of the Spirit in Nature. On the Nature of Bees

CW 352 Nature and the Human Being Observed Spiritual-Scientifically

CW 353 The History of Humanity and the World-Views of the Folk Cultures

CW 354 The Creation of the World and the Human Being. Life on Earth and the Influence of the Stars

SIGNIFICANT EVENTS IN THE LIFE OF RUDOLF STEINER

1829: June 23: birth of Johann Steiner (1829-1910)—Rudolf Steiner's father—in Geras, Lower Austria.

1834: May 8: birth of Franciska Blie (1834-1918)—Rudolf Steiner's mother—in Horn, Lower Austria. "My father and mother were both children of the glorious Lower Austrian forest district north of the Danube."

1860: May 16: marriage of Johann Steiner and Franciska Blie.

1861: February 25: birth of *Rudolf Joseph Lorenz Steiner* in Kraljevec, Croatia, near the border with Hungary, where Johann Steiner works as a telegrapher for the South Austria Railroad. Rudolf Steiner is baptized two days later, February 27, the date usually given as his birthday.

1862: Summer: the family moves to Mödling, Lower Austria.

1863: The family moves to Pottschach, Lower Austria, near the Styrian border, where Johann Steiner becomes stationmaster. "The view stretched to the mountains...majestic peaks in the distance and the sweet charm of nature in the immediate surroundings."

1864: November 15: birth of Rudolf Steiner's sister, Leopoldine (d. November 1, 1927). She will become a seamstress and live with her parents for the rest of her life.

1866: July 28: birth of Rudolf Steiner's deaf-mute brother, Gustav (d. May 1, 1941).

1867: Rudolf Steiner enters the village school. Following a disagreement between his father and the schoolmaster, whose wife falsely accused the boy of causing a commotion, Rudolf Steiner is taken out of school and taught at home.

1868: A critical experience. Unknown to the family, an aunt dies in a distant town. Sitting in the station waiting room, Rudolf Steiner sees her "form," which speaks to him, asking for help. "Beginning with this experience, a new soul life began in the boy, one in which not only the outer trees and mountains spoke to him, but also the worlds that lay behind them. From this moment on, the boy began to live with the spirits of nature...."

1869: The family moves to the peaceful, rural village of Neudorfl, near Wiener-Neustadt in present-day Hungary. Rudolf Steiner attends the village school. Because of the "unorthodoxy" of his writing and spelling, he has to do "extra lessons."

1870: Through a book lent to him by his tutor, he discovers geometry: "To grasp something purely in the spirit brought me inner happiness. I know that I first learned happiness through geometry." The same tutor allows him to draw, while other students still struggle with their reading and writing. "An artistic element" thus enters his education.

1871: Though his parents are not religious, Rudolf Steiner becomes a "church child," a favorite of the priest, who was "an exceptional character." "Up to the age of ten or eleven, among those I came to know, he was far and away the most significant." Among other things, he introduces Steiner to Copernican, heliocentric cosmology. As an altar boy, Rudolf Steiner serves at Masses, funerals, and Corpus Christi processions. At year's end, after an incident in which he escapes a thrashing, his father forbids him to go to church.

1872: Rudolf Steiner transfers to grammar school in Wiener-Neustadt, a five-mile walk from home, which must be done in all weathers.

1873-75: Through his teachers and on his own, Rudolf Steiner has many wonderful experiences with science and mathematics. Outside school, he teaches himself analytic geometry, trigonometry, differential equations, and calculus.

1876: Rudolf Steiner begins tutoring other students. He learns bookbinding from his father. He also teaches himself stenography.

1877: Rudolf Steiner discovers Kant's *Critique of Pure Reason*, which he reads and rereads. He also discovers and reads von Rotteck's *World History*.

1878: He studies extensively in contemporary psychology and philosophy.

1879: Rudolf Steiner graduates from high school with honors. His father is transferred to Inzersdorf, near Vienna. He uses his first visit to Vienna "to purchase a great number of philosophy books"— Kant, Fichte, Schelling, and Hegel, as well as numerous histories of philosophy. His aim: to find a path from the "I" to nature.

October 1879-1883: Rudolf Steiner attends the Technical College in Vienna—to study mathematics, chemistry, physics, mineralogy, botany, zoology, biology, geology, and mechanics—with a scholarship. He also attends lectures in history and literature, while avidly reading philosophy on his own. His two favorite professors are Karl Julius Schröer (German language and literature) and Edmund Reitlinger (physics). He also audits lectures by Robert Zimmerman on aesthetics and Franz Brentano on philosophy. During this year he begins his friendship with Moritz Zitter (1861-1921), who will help support him financially when he is in Berlin.

1880: Rudolf Steiner attends lectures on Schiller and Goethe by Karl Julius Schröer, who becomes his mentor. Also "through a remarkable combination of circumstances," he meets Felix Koguzki, an "herb gatherer" and healer, who could "see deeply into the secrets of nature." Rudolf Steiner will meet and study with this "emissary of the Master" throughout his time in Vienna.

1881: January: "… I didn't sleep a wink. I was busy with philosophical problems until about 12:30 a.m. Then, finally, I threw myself down on my couch. All my striving during the previous year had been to research whether the following statement by Schelling was true or not: *Within everyone dwells a secret, marvelous capacity to draw back from the stream of time—out of the self clothed in all that comes to us from outside—into our innermost being and there, in the immutable form of the Eternal, to look into ourselves.* I believe, and I am still quite certain of it, that I discovered this capacity in myself; I had long had an inkling of it. Now the whole of idealist philosophy stood before me in modified form. What's a sleepless night compared to that!"

Rudolf Steiner begins communicating with leading thinkers of the day, who send him books in return, which he reads eagerly.

July: "I am not one of those who dives into the day like an animal in human form. I pursue a quite specific goal, an idealistic aim—knowledge of the truth! This cannot be done offhandedly. It requires the greatest striving in the world, free of all egotism, and equally of all resignation."

August: Steiner puts down on paper for the first time thoughts for a "Philosophy of Freedom." "The striving for the absolute: this human yearning is freedom." He also seeks to outline a "peasant philosophy," describing what the worldview of a "peasant"—one who lives close to the earth and the old ways—really is.

1881-1882: Felix Koguzki, the herb gatherer, reveals himself to be the envoy of another, higher initiatory personality, who instructs Rudolf Steiner to penetrate Fichte's philosophy and to master modern scientific thinking as a preparation for right entry into the spirit. This "Master" also teaches him the double (evolutionary and involutionary) nature of time.

1882: Through the offices of Karl Julius Schröer, Rudolf Steiner is asked by Joseph Kurschner to edit Goethe's scientific works for the *Deutschen National-Literatur* edition. He writes "A Possible Critique of Atomistic Concepts" and sends it to Friedrich Theodore Vischer.

1883: Rudolf Steiner completes his college studies and begins work on the Goethe project.

1884: First volume of Goethe's *Scientific Writings* (CW 1) appears (March). He lectures on Goethe and Lessing, and Goethe's approach to science. In July, he enters the household of Ladislaus and Pauline Specht as tutor to the four Specht boys. He will live there until 1890. At this time, he meets Josef Breuer ((1842-1925), the coauthor with Sigmund Freud of *Studies in Hysteria*, who is the Specht family doctor.

1885: While continuing to edit Goethe's writings, Rudolf Steiner reads deeply in contemporary philosophy (Edouard von Hartmann, Johannes Volkelt, and Richard Wahle, among others).

1886: May: Rudolf Steiner sends Kurschner the manuscript of *Outlines of Goethe's Theory of Knowledge* (CW 2), which appears in October, and which he sends out widely. He also meets the poet Marie Eugenie Delle Grazie and writes "Nature and Our Ideals" for her. He attends her salon, where he meets many priests, theologians, and philosophers, who will become his friends. Meanwhile, the director of the Goethe Archive in Weimar requests his collaboration with the *Sophien* edition of Goethe's works, particularly the writings on color.

1887: At the beginning of the year, Rudolf Steiner is very sick. As the year progresses and his health improves, he becomes increasingly "a man of letters," lecturing, writing essays, and taking part in Austrian cultural life. In August-September, the second volume of Goethe's *Scientific Writings* appears.

1888: January-July: Rudolf Steiner assumes editorship of the "German Weekly" (*Deutsche Wochenschrift*). He begins lecturing more intensively, giving, for example, a lecture titled "Goethe as Father of a New Aesthetics." He meets and becomes soul friends with Friedrich Eckstein (1861-1939), a vegetarian, philosopher of symbolism, alchemist, and musician, who will introduce him to various spiritual currents (including Theosophy) and with whom he will meditate and interpret esoteric and alchemical texts.

1889: Rudolf Steiner first reads Nietzsche (*Beyond Good and Evil*). He encounters Theosophy again and learns of Madame Blavatsky in the Theosophical circle around Marie Lang (1858-1934). Here he also meets well-known figures of Austrian life, as well as esoteric figures like the occultist Franz Hartman and Karl Leinigen-Billigen (translator of C.G. Harrison's *The Transcendental Universe*.) During this period, Steiner first reads A.P. Sinnett's *Esoteric Buddhism* and Mabel Collins's *Light on the Path*. He also begins traveling, visiting Budapest, Weimar, and Berlin (where he meets philosopher Edouard von Hartman).

1890: Rudolf Steiner finishes volume 3 of Goethe's scientific writings. He begins his doctoral dissertation, which will become *Truth and Science* (CW 3). He also meets the poet and feminist Rosa Mayreder (1858-1938), with whom he can exchange his most intimate thoughts. In September, Rudolf Steiner moves to Weimar to work in the Goethe-Schiller Archive.

1891: Volume 3 of the Kurschner edition of Goethe appears. Meanwhile, Rudolf Steiner edits Goethe's studies in mineralogy and scientific writings for the *Sophien* edition. He meets Ludwig Laistner of the Cotta Publishing Company, who asks for a book on the basic question of metaphysics. From this will result, ultimately, *The Philosophy of Freedom* (CW 4), which will be published not by Cotta but by Emil Felber. In October, Rudolf Steiner takes the oral exam for a doctorate in philosophy, mathematics, and mechanics at Rostock University, receiving his doctorate on the twenty-sixth. In November, he gives his first lecture on Goethe's "Fairy Tale" in Vienna.

1892: Rudolf Steiner continues work at the Goethe-Schiller Archive and on his *Philosophy of Freedom*. *Truth and Science*, his doctoral dissertation, is published. Steiner undertakes to write introductions to books on Schopenhauer and Jean Paul for Cotta. At year's end, he finds lodging with Anna Eunike, née Schulz (1853-1911), a widow with four daughters and a son. He also develops a friendship with Otto Erich Hartleben (1864-1905) with whom he shares literary interests.

1893: Rudolf Steiner begins his habit of producing many reviews and articles. In March, he gives a lecture titled "Hypnotism, with Reference to Spiritism." In September, volume 4 of the Kurschner edition is completed. In November, *The Philosophy of Freedom* appears. This year, too, he meets John Henry Mackay (1864-1933), the anarchist, and Max Stirner, a scholar and biographer.

1894: Rudolf Steiner meets Elisabeth Förster Nietzsche, the philosopher's sister, and begins to read Nietzsche in earnest, beginning with the as yet unpublished *Antichrist*. He also meets Ernst Haeckel (1834-1919). In the fall, he begins to write *Nietzsche, A Fighter against His Time* (CW 5).

1895: May, *Nietzsche, A Fighter against His Time* appears.

1896: January 22: Rudolf Steiner sees Friedrich Nietzsche for the first and only time. Moves between the Nietzsche and the Goethe-Schiller Archives, where he completes his work before year's end. He falls out with Elisabeth Förster Nietzsche, thus ending his association with the Nietzsche Archive.

1897: Rudolf Steiner finishes the manuscript of *Goethe's Worldview* (CW 6). He moves to Berlin with Anna Eunike and begins editorship of the *Magazin fur Literatur*. From now on, Steiner will write countless reviews, literary and philosophical articles, and so on. He begins lecturing at the "Free Literary Society." In September, he attends the Zionist Congress in Basel. He sides with Dreyfus in the Dreyfus affair.

1898: Rudolf Steiner is very active as an editor in the political, artistic, and theatrical life of Berlin. He becomes friendly with John Henry Mackay and poet Ludwig Jacobowski (1868-1900). He joins Jacobowski's circle of writers, artists, and scientists—"The Coming Ones" (*Die Kommenden*)—and contributes lectures to the group until 1903. He also lectures at the "League for College Pedagogy." He writes an article for Goethe's sesquicentennial, "Goethe's Secret Revelation," on the "Fairy Tale of the Green Snake and the Beautiful Lily."

1888-89: "This was a trying time for my soul as I looked at Christianity. . . . I was able to progress only by contemplating, by means of spiritual perception, the evolution of Christianity . . . . Conscious knowledge of real Christianity began to dawn in me around the turn of the century. This seed continued to develop. My soul trial occurred shortly before the beginning of the twentieth century. It was decisive for my soul's development that I stood spiritually before the Mystery of Golgotha in a deep and solemn celebration of knowledge."

1899: Rudolf Steiner begins teaching and giving lectures and lecture cycles at the Workers' College, founded by Wilhelm Liebknecht (1826-1900). He will continue to do so until 1904. Writes: *Literature and Spiritual Life in the Nineteenth Century; Individualism in Philosophy; Haeckel and His Opponents; Poetry in the Present;* and begins what will become (fifteen years later). *The Riddles of Philosophy* (CW 18). He also meets many artists and writers, including Käthe Kollwitz, Stefan

Zweig, and Rainer Maria Rilke. On October 31, he marries Anna Eunike.

1900: "I thought that the turn of the century must bring humanity a new light. It seemed to me that the separation of human thinking and willing from the spirit had peaked. A turn or reversal of direction in human evolution seemed to me a necessity." Rudolf Steiner finishes *World and Life Views in the Nineteenth Century* (the second part of what will become *The Riddles of Philosophy*) and dedicates it to Ernst Haeckel. It is published in March. He continues lecturing at *Die Kommenden*, whose leadership he assumes after the death of Jacobowski. Also, he gives the Gutenberg Jubilee lecture before 7,000 typesetters and printers. In September, Rudolf Steiner is invited by Count and Countess Brockdorff to lecture in the Theosophical Library. His first lecture is on Nietzsche. His second lecture is titled "Goethe's Secret Revelation." October 6, he begins a lecture cycle on the mystics that will become *Mystics after Modernism* (CW 7). November-December: "Marie von Sivers appears in the audience...." Also in November, Steiner gives his first lecture at the Giordano Bruno Bund (where he will continue to lecture until May, 1905). He speaks on Bruno and modern Rome, focusing on the importance of the philosophy of Thomas Aquinas as monism.

1901: In continual financial straits, Rudolf Steiner's early friends Moritz Zitter and Rosa Mayreder help support him. In October, he begins the lecture cycle *Christianity as Mystical Fact* (CW 8) at the Theosophical Library. In November, he gives his first "Theosophical lecture" on Goethe's "Fairy Tale" in Hamburg at the invitation of Wilhelm Hubbe-Schleiden. He also attends a tea to celebrate the founding of the Theosophical Society at Count and Countess Brockdorff's. He gives a lecture cycle, "From Buddha to Christ," for the circle of the *Kommenden*. November 17, Marie von Sivers asks Rudolf Steiner if Theosophy does not need a Western-Christian spiritual movement (to complement Theosophy's Eastern emphasis). "The question was posed. Now, following spiritual laws, I could begin to give an answer...." In December, Rudolf Steiner writes his first article for a Theosophical publication. At year's end, the Brockdorffs and possibly Wilhelm Hubbe-Schleiden ask Rudolf Steiner to join the Theosophical Society and undertake the leadership of the German section. Rudolf Steiner agrees, on the condition that Marie von Sivers (then in Italy) work with him.

1902: Beginning in January, Rudolf Steiner attends the opening of the Workers' School in Spandau with Rosa Luxemberg (1870-1919). January 17, Rudolf Steiner joins the Theosophical Society. In April, he is asked to become general secretary of the German Section of the Theosophical Society, and works on preparations for its founding. In July, he visits London for a Theosophical congress. He meets Bertram

Keightly, G.R.S. Mead, A.P. Sinnett, and Annie Besant, among others. In September, *Christianity as Mystical Fact* appears. In October, Rudolf Steiner gives his first public lecture on Theosophy ("Monism and Theosophy") to about three hundred people at the Giordano Bruno Bund. On October 19-21, the German Section of the Theosophical Society has its first meeting; Rudolf Steiner is the general secretary, and Annie Besant attends. Steiner lectures on practical karma studies. On October 23, Annie Besant inducts Rudolf Steiner into the Esoteric School of the Theosophical Society. On October 25, Steiner begins a weekly series of lectures: "The Field of Theosophy." During this year, Rudolf Steiner also first meets Ita Wegman (1876-1943), who will become his close collaborator in his final years.

1903: Rudolf Steiner holds about 300 lectures and seminars. In May, the first issue of the periodical *Luzifer* appears. In June, Rudolf Steiner visits London for the first meeting of the Federation of the European Sections of the Theosophical Society, where he meets Colonel Olcott. He begins to write *Theosophy* (CW 9).

1904: Rudolf Steiner continues lecturing at the Workers' College and elsewhere (about 90 lectures), while lecturing intensively all over Germany among Theosophists (about a 140 lectures). In February, he meets Carl Unger (1878-1929), who will become a member of the board of the Anthroposophical Society (1913). In March, he meets Michael Bauer (1871-1929), a Christian mystic, who will also be on the board. In May, *Theosophy* appears, with the dedication: "To the spirit of Giordano Bruno." Rudolf Steiner and Marie von Sivers visit London for meetings with Annie Besant. June: Rudolf Steiner and Marie von Sivers attend the meeting of the Federation of European Sections of the Theosophical Society in Amsterdam. In July, Steiner begins the articles in *Luzifer-Gnosis* that will become *How to Know Higher Worlds* (CW 10) and *Cosmic Memory* (CW 11). In September, Annie Besant visits Germany. In December, Steiner lectures on Freemasonry. He mentions the High Grade Masonry derived from John Yarker and represented by Theodore Reuss and Karl Kellner as a blank slate "into which a good image could be placed."

1905: This year, Steiner ends his non-Theosophical lecturing activity. Supported by Marie von Sivers, his Theosophical lecturing—both in public and in the Theosophical Society—increases significantly: "The German Theosophical Movement is of exceptional importance." Steiner recommends reading, among others, Fichte, Jacob Boehme, and Angelus Silesius. He begins to introduce Christian themes into Theosophy. He also begins to work with doctors (Felix Peipers and Ludwig Noll). In July, he is in London for the Federation of European Sections, where he attends a lecture by Annie Besant: "I have seldom seen Mrs. Besant speak in so inward and heartfelt a manner...." "Through Mrs. Besant I have found the way to H.P. Blavatsky."

September to October, he gives a course of thirty-one lectures for a small group of esoteric students. In October, the annual meeting of the German Section of the Theosophical Society, which still remains very small, takes place. Rudolf Steiner reports membership has risen from 121 to 377 members. In November, seeking to establish esoteric "continuity," Rudolf Steiner and Marie von Sivers participate in a "Memphis-Misraim" Masonic ceremony. They pay forty-five marks for membership. "Yesterday, you saw how little remains of former esoteric institutions." "We are dealing only with a 'framework'... for the present, nothing lies behind it. The occult powers have completely withdrawn."

1906: Expansion of Theosophical work. Rudolf Steiner gives about 245 lectures, only 44 of which take place in Berlin. Cycles are given in Paris, Leipzig, Stuttgart, and Munich. Esoteric work also intensifies. Rudolf Steiner begins writing *An Outline of Esoteric Science* (CW 13). In January, Rudolf Steiner receives permission (a patent) from the Great Orient of the Scottish A & A Thirty-Three Degree Rite of the Order of the Ancient Freemasons of the Memphis-Misraim Rite to direct a chapter under the name "Mystica Aeterna." This will become the "Cognitive Cultic Section" (also called "Misraim Service") of the Esoteric School. (See: *From the History and Contents of the Cognitive Cultic Section* (CW 264). During this time, Steiner also meets Albert Schweitzer. In May, he is in Paris, where he visits Edouard Schuré. Many Russians attend his lectures (including Konstantin Balmont, Dimitri Mereszkovski, Zinaida Hippius, and Maximilian Woloshin). He attends the General Meeting of the European Federation of the Theosophical Society, at which Col. Olcott is present for the last time. He spends the year's end in Venice and Rome, where he writes and works on his translation of H.P. Blavatsky's *Key to Theosophy*.

1907: Further expansion of the German Theosophical Movement according to the Rosicrucian directive to "introduce spirit into the world"—in education, in social questions, in art, and in science. In February, Col. Olcott dies in Adyar. Before he dies, Olcott indicates that "the Masters" wish Annie Besant to succeed him: much politicking ensues. Rudolf Steiner supports Besant's candidacy. April-May: preparations for the Congress of the Federation of European Sections of the Theosophical Society—the great, watershed Whitsun "Munich Congress," attended by Annie Besant and others. Steiner decides to separate Eastern and Western (Christian-Rosicrucian) esoteric schools. He takes his esoteric school out of the Theosophical Society (Besant and Rudolf Steiner are "in harmony" on this). Steiner makes his first lecture tours to Austria and Hungary. That summer, he is in Italy. In September, he visits Edouard Schuré, who will write the introduction to the French edition of *Christianity as Mystical Fact* in Barr, Alsace. Rudolf Steiner writes the autobiographical statement known as the "Barr Document." In *Luzifer–Gnosis*, "The Education of the Child" appears.

1908: The movement grows (membership: 1150). Lecturing expands. Steiner makes his first extended lecture tour to Holland and Scandinavia, as well as visits to Naples and Sicily. Themes: St. John's Gospel, the Apocalypse, Egypt, science, philosophy, and logic. *Luzifer-Gnosis* ceases publication. In Berlin, Marie von Sivers (with Johanna Mücke (1864-1949) forms the *Philosophisch-Theosophisch* (after 1915 *Philosophisch-Anthroposophisch*) *Verlag* to publish Steiner's work. Steiner gives lecture cycles titled *The Gospel of St. John* (CW 103) and *The Apocalypse* (104).

1909: *An Outline of Esoteric Science* appears. Lecturing and travel continues. Rudolf Steiner's spiritual research expands to include the polarity of Lucifer and Ahriman; the work of great individualities in history; the Maitreya Buddha and the Bodhisattvas; spiritual economy (CW 109); the work of the spiritual hierarchies in heaven and on Earth (CW 110). He also deepens and intensifies his research into the Gospels, giving lectures on the Gospel of St. Luke (CW 114) with the first mention of two Jesus children. Meets and becomes friends with Christian Morgenstern (1871-1914). In April, he lays the foundation stone for the Malsch model—the building that will lead to the first Goetheanum. In May, the International Congress of the Federation of European Sections of the Theosophical Society takes place in Budapest. Rudolf Steiner receives the Subba Row medal for *How to Know Higher Worlds*. During this time, Charles W. Leadbeater discovers Jiddu Krishnamurti (1895-1986) and proclaims him the future "world teacher," the bearer of the Maitreya Buddha and the "reappearing Christ." In October, Steiner delivers seminal lectures on "anthroposophy," which he will try, unsuccessfully, to rework over the next years into the unfinished work, *Anthroposophy (A Fragment)* (CW 45).

1910: New themes: *The Reappearance of Christ in the Etheric* (CW 118); *The Fifth Gospel; The Mission of Folk Souls* (CW 121); *Occult History* (CW 126); the evolving development of etheric cognitive capacities. Rudolf Steiner continues his Gospel research with *The Gospel of St. Matthew* (CW 123). In January, his father dies. In April, he takes a month-long trip to Italy, including Rome, Monte Cassino, and Sicily. He also visits Scandinavia again. July-August, he writes the first mystery drama, *The Portal of Initiation* (CW 14). In November, he gives "psychosophy" lectures. In December, he submits "On the Psychological Foundations and Epistemological Framework of Theosophy" to the International Philosophical Congress in Bologna.

1911: The crisis in the Theosophical Society deepens. In January, "The Order of the Rising Sun," which will soon become "The Order of the Star in the East," is founded for the coming world teacher, Krishnamurti. At the same time, Marie von Sivers, Rudolf Steiner's coworker, falls ill. Fewer lectures are given, but important new ground is broken. In Prague, in March, Steiner meets Franz Kafka (1883-1924) and Hugo Bergmann (1883-1975). In April, he delivers his paper to the

Philosophical Congress. He writes the second mystery drama, *The Soul's Probation* (CW 14). Also, while Marie von Sivers is convalescing, Rudolf Steiner begins work on *Calendar 1912/1913*, which will contain the "Calendar of the Soul" meditations. On March 19, Anna (Eunike) Steiner dies. In September, Rudolf Steiner visits Einsiedeln, birthplace of Paracelsus. In December, Friedrich Rittelmeyer, future founder of the Christian Community, meets Rudolf Steiner. The *Johannes-Bauverein*, the "building committee," which would lead to the first Goetheanum (first planned for Munich), is also founded, and a preliminary committee for the founding of an independent association is created that, in the following year, will become the Anthroposophical Society. Important lecture cycles include *Occult Physiology* (CW 128); *Wonders of the World* (CW 129); *From Jesus to Christ* (CW 131). Other themes: esoteric Christianity; Christian Rosenkreutz; the spiritual guidance of humanity; the sense world and the world of the spirit.

1912: Despite the ongoing, now increasing crisis in the Theosophical Society, much is accomplished: *Calendar 1912/1913* is published; eurythmy is created; both the third mystery drama, *The Guardian of the Threshold* (CW 14) and *A Way of Self-Knowledge* (CW 16) are written. New (or renewed) themes included life between death and rebirth and karma and reincarnation. Other lecture cycles: *Spiritual Beings in the Heavenly Bodies and the Kingdoms of Nature* (CW 136); *The Human Being in the Light of Occultism, Theosophy, and Philosophy* (CW 137); *The Gospel of St. Mark* (CW 139); and *The Bhagavad Gita and the Epistles of Paul* (CW 142). On May 8, Rudolf Steiner celebrates White Lotus Day, H.P. Blavatsky's death day, which he had faithfully observed for the past decade, for the last time. In August, Rudolf Steiner suggests the "independent association" be called the "Anthroposophical Society." In September, the first eurythmy course takes place. In October, Rudolf Steiner declines recognition of a Theosophical Society lodge dedicated to the Star of the East and decides to expel all Theosophical Society members belonging to the order. Also, with Marie von Sivers, he first visits Dornach, near Basel, Switzerland, and they stand on the hill where the Goetheanum will be. In November, a Theosophical Society lodge is opened by direct mandate from Adyar (Annie Besant). In December, a meeting of the German section occurs at which it is decided that belonging to the Order of the Star of the East is incompatible with membership in the Theosophical Society. December 28: informal founding of the Anthroposophical Society in Berlin.

1913: Expulsion of the German section from the Theosophical Society. February 2-3: Foundation meeting of the Anthroposophical Society. Board members include: Marie von Sivers, Michael Bauer, and Carl Unger. September 20: Laying of the foundation stone for the *Johannes Bau* (Goetheanum) in Dornach. Building begins immediately. The third mystery drama, *The Soul's Awakening* (CW 14), is completed.

Also: *The Threshold of the Spiritual World* (CW 147). Lecture cycles include: *The Bhagavad Gita and the Epistles of Paul* and *The Esoteric Meaning of the Bhagavad Gita* (CW 146), which the Russian philosopher Nikolai Berdyaev attends; *The Mysteries of the East and of Christianity* (CW 144); *The Effects of Esoteric Development* (CW 145); and *The Fifth Gospel* (CW 148). In May, Rudolf Steiner is in London and Paris, where anthroposophical work continues.

1914: Building continues on the *Johannes Bau* (Goetheanum) in Dornach, with artists and coworkers from seventeen nations. The general assembly of the Anthroposophical Society takes place. In May, Rudolf Steiner visits Paris, as well as Chartres Cathedral. June 28: assassination in Sarajevo ("Now the catastrophe has happened!"). August 1: War is declared. Rudolf Steiner returns to Germany from Dornach—he will travel back and forth. He writes the last chapter of *The Riddles of Philosophy*. Lecture cycles include: *Human and Cosmic Thought* (CW 151); *Inner Being of Humanity between Death and a New Birth* (CW 153); *Occult Reading and Occult Hearing* (CW 156). December 24: marriage of Rudolf Steiner and Marie von Sivers.

1915: Building continues. Life after death becomes a major theme, also art. Writes: *Thoughts during a Time of War* (CW 24). Lectures include: *The Secret of Death* (CW 159); *The Uniting of Humanity through the Christ Impulse* (CW 165).

1916: Rudolf Steiner begins work with Edith Maryon (1872-1924) on the sculpture "The Representative of Humanity" ("The Group"—Christ, Lucifer, and Ahriman). He also works with the alchemist Alexander von Bernus on the quarterly *Das Reich*. He writes *The Riddle of Humanity* (CW 20). Lectures include: *Necessity and Freedom in World History and Human Action* (CW 166); *Past and Present in the Human Spirit* (CW 167); *The Karma of Vocation* (CW 172); *The Karma of Untruthfulness* (CW 173).

1917: Russian Revolution. The U.S. enters the war. Building continues. Rudolf Steiner delineates the idea of the "threefold nature of the human being" (in a public lecture March 15) and the "threefold nature of the social organism" (hammered out in May-June with the help of Otto von Lerchenfeld and Ludwig Polzer-Hoditz in the form of two documents titled *Memoranda*, which were distributed in high places). August-September: Rudolf Steiner writes *The Riddles of the Soul* (CW 20). Also: commentary on "The Chemical Wedding of Christian Rosenkreutz" for Alexander Bernus (*Das Reich*). Lectures include: *The Karma of Materialism* (CW 176); *The Spiritual Background of the Outer World: The Fall of the Spirits of Darkness* (CW 177).

1918: March 18: peace treaty of Brest-Litovsk—"Now everything will truly enter chaos! What is needed is cultural renewal." June: Rudolf Steiner visits Karlstein (Grail) Castle outside Prague. Lecture cycle: *From Symptom to Reality in Modern History* (CW 185). In mid-November,

Emil Molt, of the Waldorf-Astoria Cigarette Company, has the idea of founding a school for his workers' children.

1919: Focus on the threefold social organism: tireless travel, countless lectures, meetings, and publications. At the same time, a new public stage of Anthroposophy emerges as cultural renewal begins. The coming years will see initiatives in pedagogy, medicine, pharmacology, and agriculture. January 27: threefold meeting: " We must first of all, with the money we have, found free schools that can bring people what they need." February: first public eurythmy performance in Zurich. Also: "Appeal to the German People" (CW 24), circulated March 6 as a newspaper insert. In April, *Toward Social Renewal* (CW 23)—"perhaps the most widely read of all books on politics appearing since the war"—appears. Rudolf Steiner is asked to undertake the "direction and leadership" of the school founded by the Waldorf-Astoria Company. Rudolf Steiner begins to talk about the "renewal" of education. May 30: a building is selected and purchased for the future Waldorf School. August-September, Rudolf Steiner gives a lecture course for Waldorf teachers, *The Foundations of Human Experience (Study of Man)* (CW 293). September 7: Opening of the first Waldorf School. December (into January): first science course, the *Light Course* (CW 320).

1920: The Waldorf School flourishes. New threefold initiatives. Founding of limited companies *Der Kommenden Tag* and *Futurum A.G.* to infuse spiritual values into the economic realm. Rudolf Steiner also focuses on the sciences. Lectures: *Introducing Anthroposophical Medicine* (CW 312); *The Warmth Course* (CW 321); *The Boundaries of Natural Science* (CW 322); *The Redemption of Thinking* (CW 74). February: Johannes Werner Klein—later a cofounder of the Christian Community—asks Rudolf Steiner about the possibility of a "religious renewal," a "Johannine church." In March, Rudolf Steiner gives the first course for doctors and medical students. In April, a divinity student asks Rudolf Steiner a second time about the possibility of religious renewal. September 27-October 16: anthroposophical "university course." December: lectures titled *The Search for the New Isis* (CW 202).

1921: Rudolf Steiner continues his intensive work on cultural renewal, including the uphill battle for the threefold social order. "University" arts, scientific, theological, and medical courses include: *The Astronomy Course* (CW 323); *Observation, Mathematics, and Scientific Experiment* (CW 324); the *Second Medical Course* (CW 313); *Color*. In June and September-October, Rudolf Steiner also gives the first two "priests' courses" (CW 342 and 343). The "youth movement" gains momentum. Magazines are founded: *Die Drei* (January), and—under the editorship of Albert Steffen (1884-1963)—the weekly, *Das Goetheanum* (August). In February-March, Rudolf Steiner takes his first trip outside Germany since the war (Holland). On April 7, Steiner receives a letter regarding "religious renewal," and May 22-23, he agrees to address the question in a practical way. In June, the Klinical-Therapeutic Institute opens in Arlesheim under the direction of Dr. Ita Wegman. In August, the Chemical-Pharmaceutical Laboratory opens in Arlesheim (Oskar Schmiedel and Ita Wegman, directors). The Clinical Therapeutic Institute is inaugurated in Stuttgart (Dr. Ludwig Noll, director); also the Research Laboratory in Dornach (Ehrenfried Pfeiffer and Gunther Wachsmuth, directors). In November-December, Rudolf Steiner visits Norway.

1922: The first half of the year involves very active public lecturing (thousands attend); in the second half, Rudolf Steiner begins to withdraw and turn toward the Society—"The Society is asleep." It is "too weak" to do what is asked of it. The businesses—*Die Kommenden Tag* and *Futura A.G.*—fail. In January, with the help of an agent, Steiner undertakes a twelve-city German tour, accompanied by eurythmy performances. In two weeks he speaks to more than 2,000 people. In April, he gives a "university course" in The Hague. He also visits England. In June, he is in Vienna for the East-West Congress. In August-September, he is back in England for the Oxford Conference on Education. Returning to Dornach, he gives the lectures *Philosophy, Cosmology, and Religion* (CW 215), and gives the third priest's course (CW 344). On September 16, The Christian Community is founded. In October-November, Steiner is in Holland and England. He also speaks to the youth: *The Youth Course* (CW 217). In December, Steiner gives lectures titled *The Origins of Natural Science* (CW 326), and *Humanity and the World of Stars: The Spiritual Communion of Humanity* (CW 219). December 31: Fire at the Goetheanum, which is destroyed.

1923: Despite the fire, Rudolf Steiner continues his work unabated. A very hard year. Internal dispersion, dissension, and apathy abound. There is conflict—between old and new visions—within the society. A wake-up call is needed, and Rudolf Steiner responds with renewed lecturing vitality. His focus: the spiritual context of human life; initiation science; the course of the year; and community building. As a foundation for an artistic school, he creates a series of pastel sketches. Lecture cycles: *The Anthroposophical Movement; Initiation Science* (CW 227) (in England at the Penmaenmawr Summer School); *The Four Seasons and the Archangels* (CW 229); *Harmony of the Creative Word* (CW 230); *The Supersensible Human* (CW 231), given in Holland for the founding of the Dutch society. On November 10, in response to the failed Hitler-Ludendorf putsch in Munich, Steiner closes his Berlin residence and moves the *Philosophisch-Anthroposophisch Verlag* (Press) to Dornach. On December 9, Steiner begins the serialization of his *Autobiography: The Course of My Life* (CW 28) in *Das Goetheanum*. It will continue to appear weekly, without a break, until his death. Late December-early January: Rudolf Steiner refounds the Anthroposophical Society (about 12,000 members internationally) and takes over its leadership. The new board members are: Marie Steiner, Ita Wegman, Albert Steffen, Elizabeth Vreede, and Guenther Wachsmuth. (See *The Christmas Meeting for the Founding of the General Anthroposophical Society* (CW 260). Accompanying lectures: *Mystery Knowledge and Mystery Centers* (CW 232); *World History in the Light of Anthroposophy* (CW 233). December 25: the Foundation Stone is laid (in the hearts of members) in the form of the "Foundation Stone Meditation."

1924: January 1: having founded the Anthroposophical Society and taken over its leadership, Rudolf Steiner has the task of "reforming" it. The process begins with a weekly newssheet ("What's Happening in the Anthroposophical Society") in which Rudolf Steiner's "Letters to Members" and "Anthroposophical Leading Thoughts" appear (CW 26). The next step is the creation of a new esoteric class, the "first class" of the "University of Spiritual Science" (which was to have been followed, had Rudolf Steiner lived longer, by two more advanced classes). Then comes a new language for Anthroposophy—practical, phenomenological, and direct; and Rudolf Steiner creates the model for the second Goetheanum. He begins the series of extensive "karma" lectures (CW 235-40); and finally, responding to needs, he creates two new initiatives: biodynamic agriculture and curative education. After the middle of the year, rumors begin to circulate regarding Steiner's health. Lectures: January-February, *Anthroposophy* (CW 234); February: *Tone Eurythmy* (CW 278); June: *The Agriculture Course* (CW 327); June-July: Speech [?] Eurythmy (CW 279); *Curative Education* (CW 317); August: (England, "Second International Summer School"), *Initiation Consciousness: True and False Paths in Spiritual Investigation* (CW 243); September: *Pastoral Medicine* (CW 318). On September 26, for the first time, Rudolf Steiner cancels a lecture. On September 28, he gives his last lecture. On September 29, he withdraws to his studio in the carpenter's shop; now he is definitively ill. Cared for by Ita Wegman, he continues working, however, and writing the weekly installments of his *Autobiography* and *Letters to the Members/Leading Thoughts* (CW 26).

1925: Rudolf Steiner, while continuing to work, continues to weaken. He finishes *Extending Practical Medicine* (CW 27) with Ita Wegman.

On March 30, around ten in the morning, Rudolf Steiner dies.

INDEX

FACSIMILE REPRODUCTIONS,

PHOTOGRAPHS,

AND PLATES

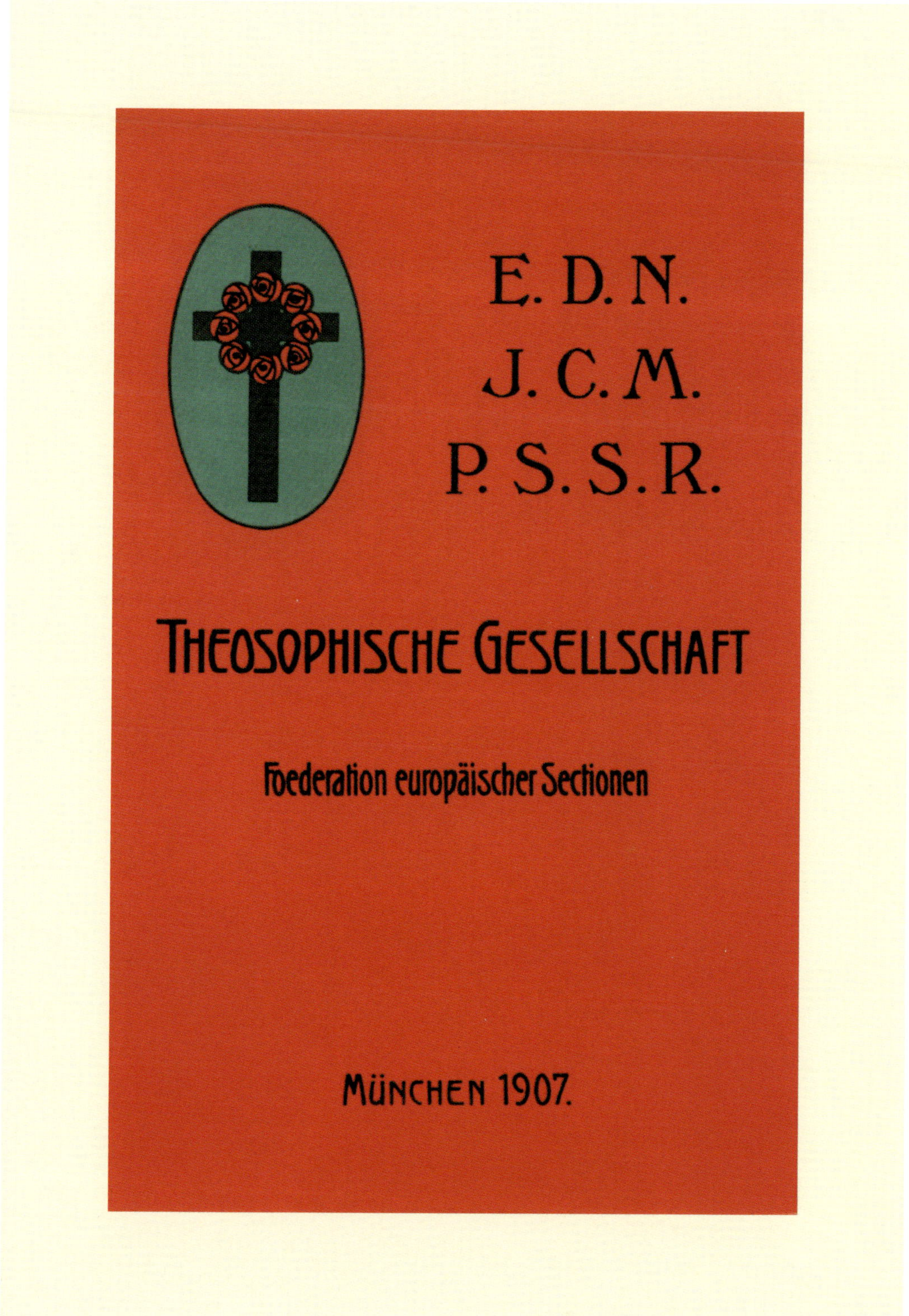

E. D. N.
J. C. M.
P. S. S. R.

THEOSOPHISCHE GESELLSCHAFT

Foederation europäischer Sectionen

MÜNCHEN 1907.

Cover of the program brochure for the Munich Congress, Whitsun 1907

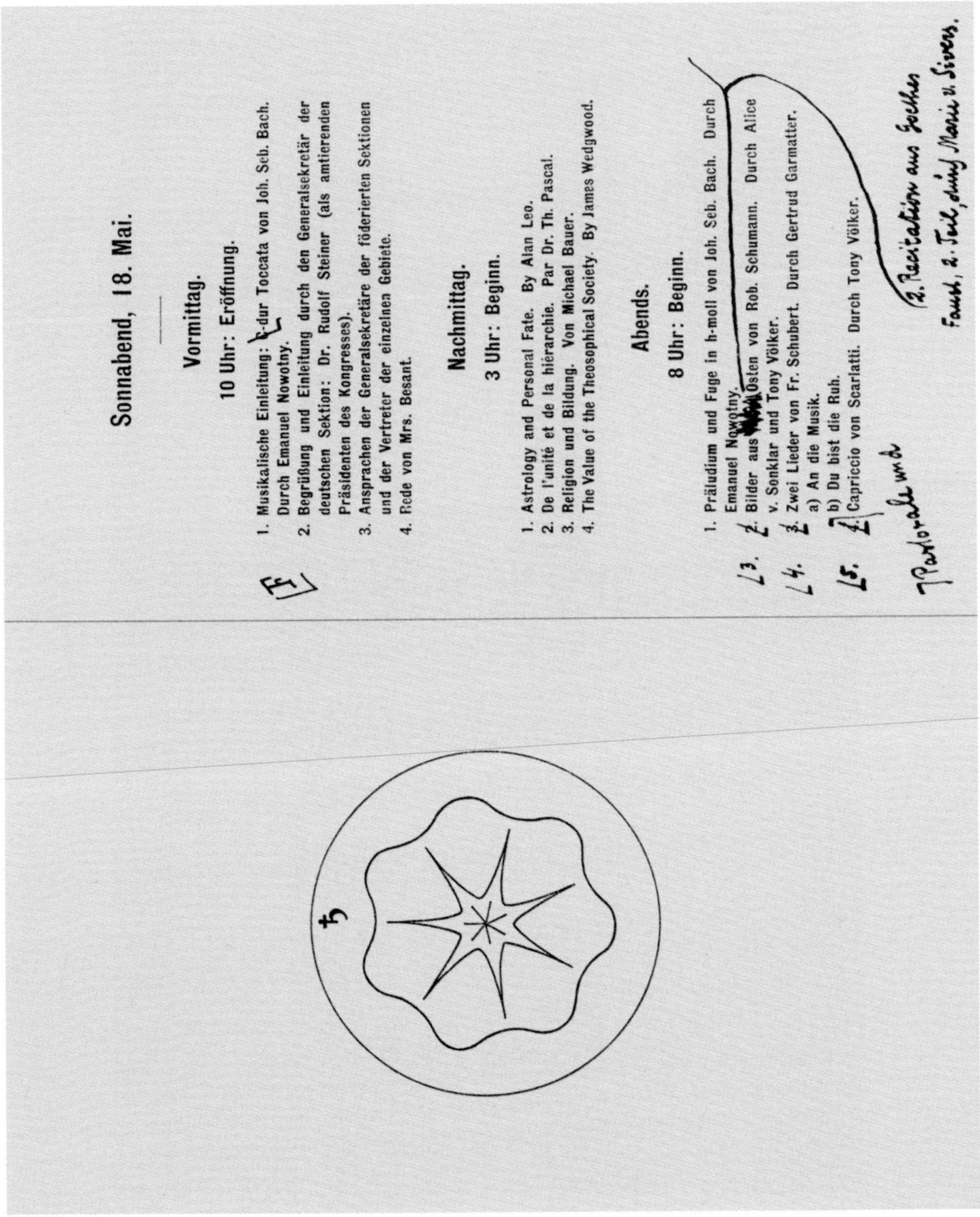

Sonnabend, 18. Mai.

Vormittag.

10 Uhr: Eröffnung.

1. Musikalische Einleitung: C-dur Toccata von Joh. Seb. Bach. Durch Emanuel Nowotny.
2. Begrüßung und Einleitung durch den Generalsekretär der deutschen Sektion: Dr. Rudolf Steiner (als amtierenden Präsidenten des Kongresses).
3. Ansprachen der Generalsekretäre der föderierten Sektionen und der Vertreter der einzelnen Gebiete.
4. Rede von Mrs. Besant.

Nachmittag.

3 Uhr: Beginn.

1. Astrology and Personal Fate. By Alan Leo.
2. De l'unité et de la hiérarchie. Par Dr. Th. Pascal.
3. Religion und Bildung. Von Michael Bauer.
4. The Value of the Theosophical Society. By James Wedgwood.

Abends.

8 Uhr: Beginn.

1. Präludium und Fuge in h-moll von Joh. Seb. Bach. Durch Emanuel Nowotny.
2. Bilder aus Osten von Rob. Schumann. Durch Alice v. Sonklar und Tony Völker.
3. Zwei Lieder von Fr. Schubert. Durch Gertrud Garmatter.
   a) An die Musik.
   b) Du bist die Ruh.
4. Capriccio von Scarlatti. Durch Tony Völker.

2. Recitation aus Goethes Faust, 2. Teil, durch Marie v. Sivers.

Pastorale und

Pages of the program brochure (with handwritten corrections by Rudolf Steiner)

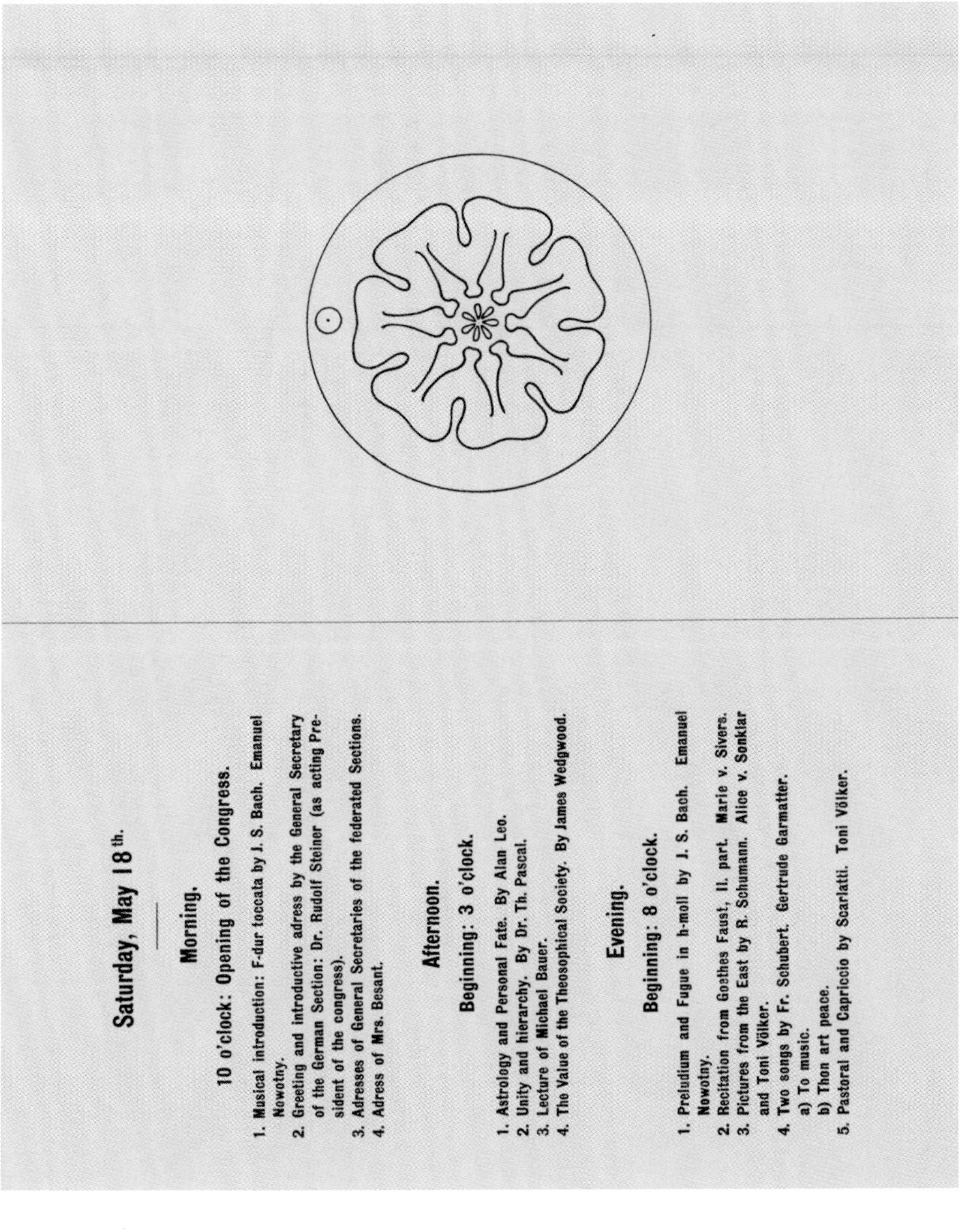

Saturday, May 18 th.

Morning.

10 o'clock: Opening of the Congress.

1. Musical introduction: F-dur toccata by J. S. Bach. Emanuel Nowotny.
2. Greeting and introductive adress by the General Secretary of the German Section: Dr. Rudolf Steiner (as acting President of the congress).
3. Adresses of General Secretaries of the federated Sections.
4. Adress of Mrs. Besant.

Afternoon.

Beginning: 3 o'clock.

1. Astrology and Personal Fate. By Alan Leo.
2. Unity and hierarchy. By Dr. Th. Pascal.
3. Lecture of Michael Bauer.
4. The Value of the Theosophical Society. By James Wedgwood.

Evening.

Beginning: 8 o'clock.

1. Preludium and Fugue in h-moll by J. S. Bach. Emanuel Nowotny.
2. Recitation from Goethes Faust, II. part. Marie v. Sivers.
3. Pictures from the East by R. Schumann. Alice v. Sonklar and Toni Völker.
4. Two songs by Fr. Schubert. Gertrude Garmatter.
   a) To music.
   b) Thon art peace.
5. Pastoral and Capriccio by Scarlatti. Toni Völker.

Pages of the program brochure

Sonntag, 19. Mai.

Vormittag.

10 Uhr: Beginn.

1. Trio in Es-dur von Joh. Brahms (1. Satz). Durch Johanna Fritsch, Marika v. Gumppenberg, Hermann Tuckermann.
2. A vision of Hades. By G. R. S. Mead.
3. Theosophie in Russland. Von Anna Kamensky.
4. Die Einweihung des Rosenkreuzers. Von Dr. Rudolf Steiner.

Nachmittag.

5 Uhr: Beginn.

Das heilige Drama von Eleusis. ⌈Mysterium von Eduard Schuré. Musik von Bernhard Stavenhagen.

Nachher: Geselliges Zusammensein. Ein Buffet ist aufgestellt während der Zwischenakte des Dramas und während des geselligen Zusammenseins.

⌈(Aus dem Französischen).

Sunday, May 19th.

Morning.

Beginning: 10 o'clock.

1. Trio in Es-dur by J. Brahms (1. composition). J. Fritsch, M. v. Gumppenberg, H. Tuckermann.
2. A vision of Hades. By G. R. S. Mead.
3. Theosophy in Russia. By Anna Kamensky.
4. The Initiation of the Rosicrucian. By Dr. Rudolf Steiner.

Afternoon.

Beginning: 5 o'clock.

The Sacred Drama of Eleusis. (Translated from the french.) A Mystery-play by Edouard Schuré. Music by Bernhard Stavenhagen.

Afterwards Social meeting.

A Buffet will be opened during the intervals of the drama and during the social meeting.

Pages of the program brochure

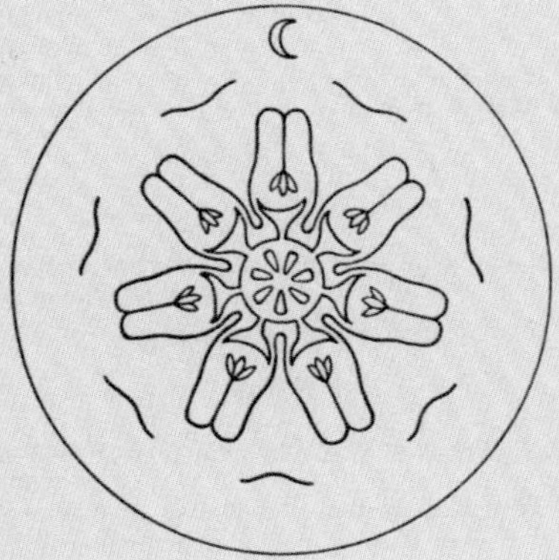

Montag, 20. Mai.

Vormittag.

10 Uhr: Beginn.

1. Rezitation. Von Richard Jürgas.
2. a) Gebet. b) Verborgenheit. c) Jesuskind. Von Hugo Wolf. Durch Elisabeth Lauser.
3. Vortrag von Mrs. Besant.
4. Absolute and relative truths. By Arvid Knös.
5. Die Wege der theosophischen Weltanschauung. Von Dr. Carl Unger.
6. Die occulte Grundlage der Siegfriedsage. Von Elise Wolfram.

Nachmittag.

3½ Uhr: Beginn.

1. Vortrag von Bailly.
2. Planetenentwickelung und Menschheitsentwickelung. Von Dr. Rudolf Steiner.

Abends.

8 Uhr: Beginn.

1. Sonate in g-moll. Von L. van Beethoven. (Adagio, Allegro, Rondo). Durch Chr. Döbereiner (Violoncell) und Elfride Schunk (Klavier).
2. Zwei Lieder. Durch Gertrud Garmatter.
   a) Weylas Gesang. Von Hugo Wolf.
   b) Frühlingsglaube. Von Franz Schubert.
3. Soli für Viola da Gamba mit Klavier. Durch Chr. Döbereiner und Elfride Schunk.
   a) Adagio. Von G. Fr. Händel.
   b) Aria con variazione. Von A. Kühnel (comp. 1645).
   (Die Viola da Gamba [vom Ende des 15. bis zum Ende des 18. Jahrhunderts allgemein gebräuchlich] ist mit sechs bis sieben Saiten in der Stimmung (A), D, G, c, e, a, d bezogen. Mitte des 18. Jahrhunderts wurde sie durch das voller klingende viersaitige Violoncell verdrängt.)

Pages of the program brochure

Monday, May 20th.

Morning.

Beginning: 10 o'clock.

1. Recitation. By Richard Jürgas.
2. a) Prayer. b) Retirement. c) The sleeping child Jesus. By Hugo Wolf. Elisabeth Lauser.
3. Lecture of Mrs. Besant.
4. Absolute and relative truths. By Arvid Knös.
5. The means for theosophical World-conception. By Dr. Carl Unger.
6. The occult basis of the myth of Siegfried. By Elise Wolfram.

Afternoon.

Beginning: 3½ o'clock.

1. Lecture of Mr. Bailly.
2. Planetary and Human Evolution. By Dr. Rudolf Steiner.

Evening.

Beginning: 8 o'clock.

1. Sonata in g-moll. By L. van Beethoven. (Adagio, Allegro, Rondo). Chr. Döbereiner (violoncell) and Elfriede Schunk (piano).
2. Two songs. Gertrude Garmatter.
   a) Song of Weyla. By Hugo Wolf.
   b) Belief in Spring. By Fr. Schubert.
3. Soli for Viola da Gamba with piano. Chr. Döbereiner and Elfride Schunk.
   a) Adagio. By G. Fr. Händel.
   b) Aria con variazione. By A. Kühnel (composed in 1645).
   (The Viola da Gamba [generally used from the end of the 15th century till the end of the 18th century] is strung with six or seven strings in the tune (A), D, G, c, e, a, d. In the middle of the 18th century it was removed by the four-stringed violoncell sounding fuller.)

Between 1., 2., 3. members are kindly invited for tea.

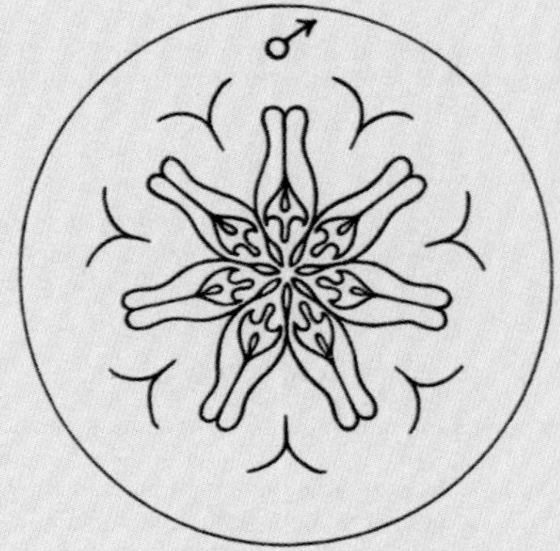

Pages of the program brochure

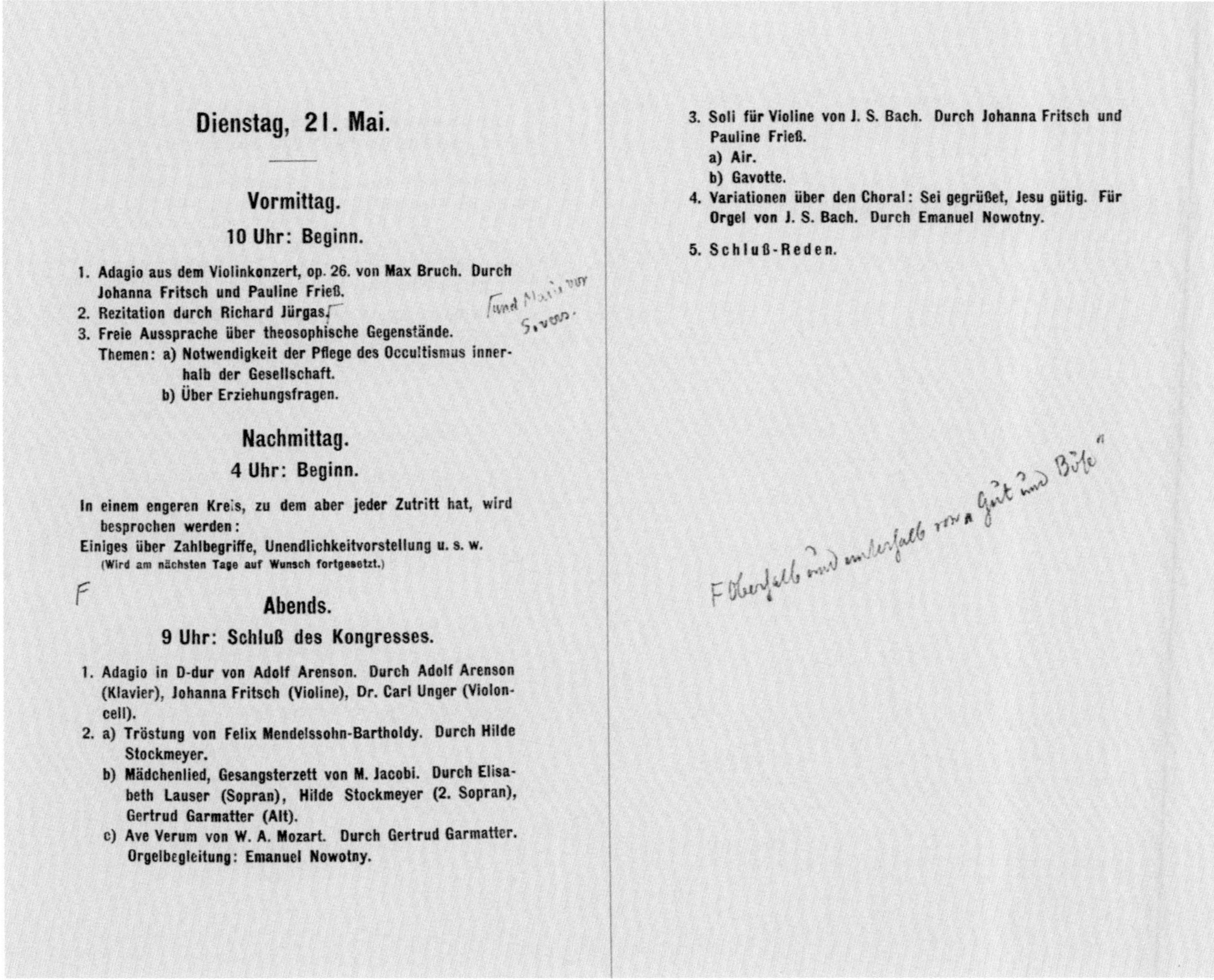

Dienstag, 21. Mai.

Vormittag.

10 Uhr: Beginn.

1. Adagio aus dem Violinkonzert, op. 26. von Max Bruch. Durch Johanna Fritsch und Pauline Frieß.
2. Rezitation durch Richard Jürgas.
3. Freie Aussprache über theosophische Gegenstände.
   Themen: a) Notwendigkeit der Pflege des Occultismus innerhalb der Gesellschaft.
   b) Über Erziehungsfragen.

Nachmittag.

4 Uhr: Beginn.

In einem engeren Kreis, zu dem aber jeder Zutritt hat, wird besprochen werden:
Einiges über Zahlbegriffe, Unendlichkeitvorstellung u. s. w.
(Wird am nächsten Tage auf Wunsch fortgesetzt.)

Abends.

9 Uhr: Schluß des Kongresses.

1. Adagio in D-dur von Adolf Arenson. Durch Adolf Arenson (Klavier), Johanna Fritsch (Violine), Dr. Carl Unger (Violoncell).
2. a) Tröstung von Felix Mendelssohn-Bartholdy. Durch Hilde Stockmeyer.
   b) Mädchenlied, Gesangsterzett von M. Jacobi. Durch Elisabeth Lauser (Sopran), Hilde Stockmeyer (2. Sopran), Gertrud Garmatter (Alt).
   c) Ave Verum von W. A. Mozart. Durch Gertrud Garmatter. Orgelbegleitung: Emanuel Nowotny.
3. Soli für Violine von J. S. Bach. Durch Johanna Fritsch und Pauline Frieß.
   a) Air.
   b) Gavotte.
4. Variationen über den Choral: Sei gegrüßet, Jesu gütig. Für Orgel von J. S. Bach. Durch Emanuel Nowotny.
5. Schluß-Reden.

Pages of the program brochure

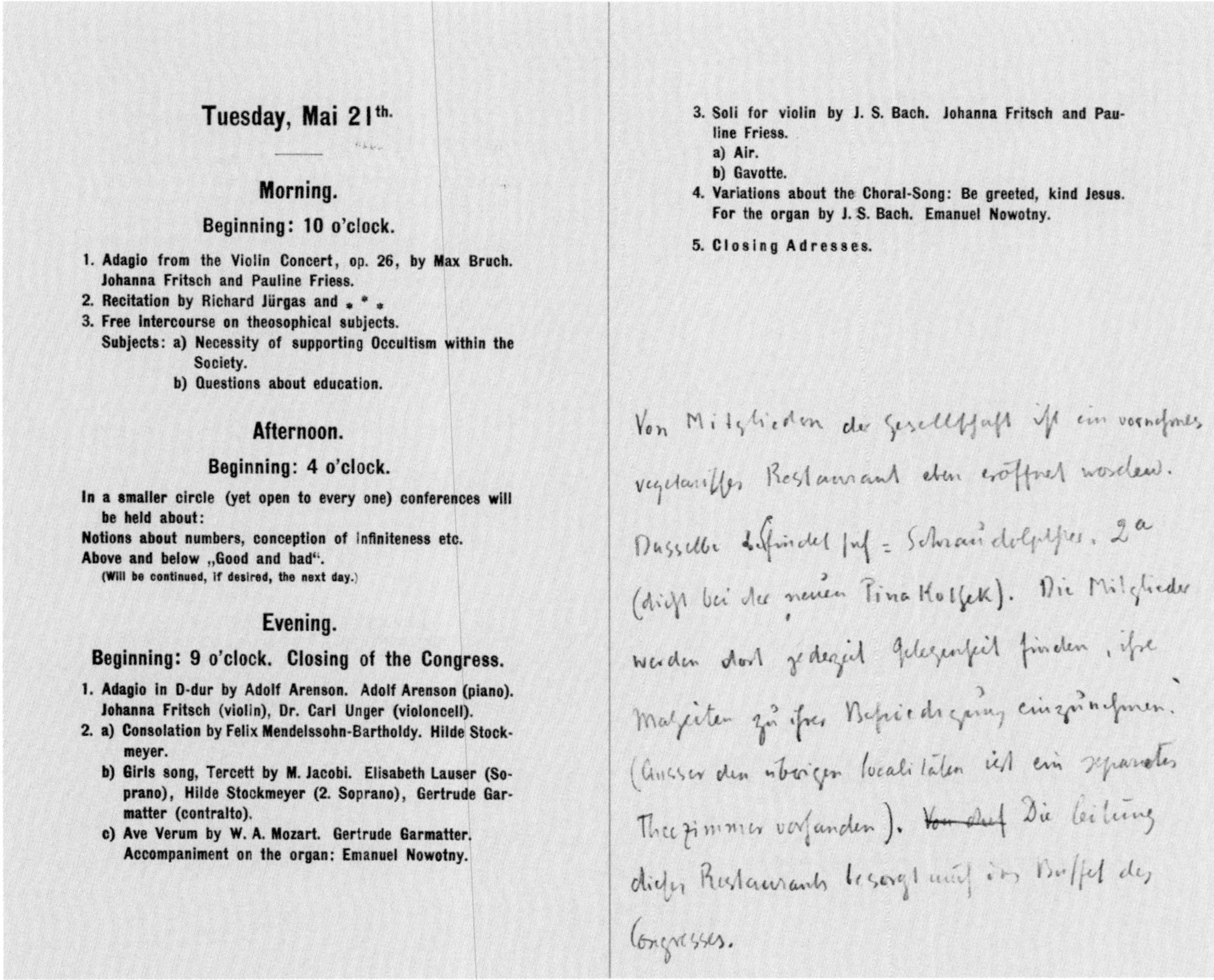

Tuesday, Mai 21th.

Morning.

Beginning: 10 o'clock.

1. Adagio from the Violin Concert, op. 26, by Max Bruch. Johanna Fritsch and Pauline Friess.
2. Recitation by Richard Jürgas and * * *
3. Free intercourse on theosophical subjects.
   Subjects: a) Necessity of supporting Occultism within the Society.
   b) Questions about education.

Afternoon.

Beginning: 4 o'clock.

In a smaller circle (yet open to every one) conferences will be held about:
Notions about numbers, conception of infiniteness etc.
Above and below „Good and bad".
(Will be continued, if desired, the next day.)

Evening.

Beginning: 9 o'clock. Closing of the Congress.

1. Adagio in D-dur by Adolf Arenson. Adolf Arenson (piano). Johanna Fritsch (violin), Dr. Carl Unger (violoncell).
2. a) Consolation by Felix Mendelssohn-Bartholdy. Hilde Stockmeyer.
   b) Girls song, Tercett by M. Jacobi. Elisabeth Lauser (Soprano), Hilde Stockmeyer (2. Soprano), Gertrude Garmatter (contralto).
   c) Ave Verum by W. A. Mozart. Gertrude Garmatter. Accompaniment on the organ: Emanuel Nowotny.
3. Soli for violin by J. S. Bach. Johanna Fritsch and Pauline Friess.
   a) Air.
   b) Gavotte.
4. Variations about the Choral-Song: Be greeted, kind Jesus. For the organ by J. S. Bach. Emanuel Nowotny.
5. Closing Adresses.

Von Mitgliedern der Gesellschaft ist ein vornehmes vegetarisches Restaurant eben eröffnet worden. Dasselbe befindet sich = Schraudolphstr. 2a (dicht bei der neuen Pinakothek). Die Mitglieder werden dort jederzeit Gelegenheit finden, ihre Mahlzeiten zu ihrer Befriedigung einzunehmen. (Ausser den übrigen Localitäten ist ein separates Theezimmer vorhanden). ~~Von dort~~ Die Leitung dieses Restaurants besorgt auch das Buffet des Congresses.

Pages of the program brochure

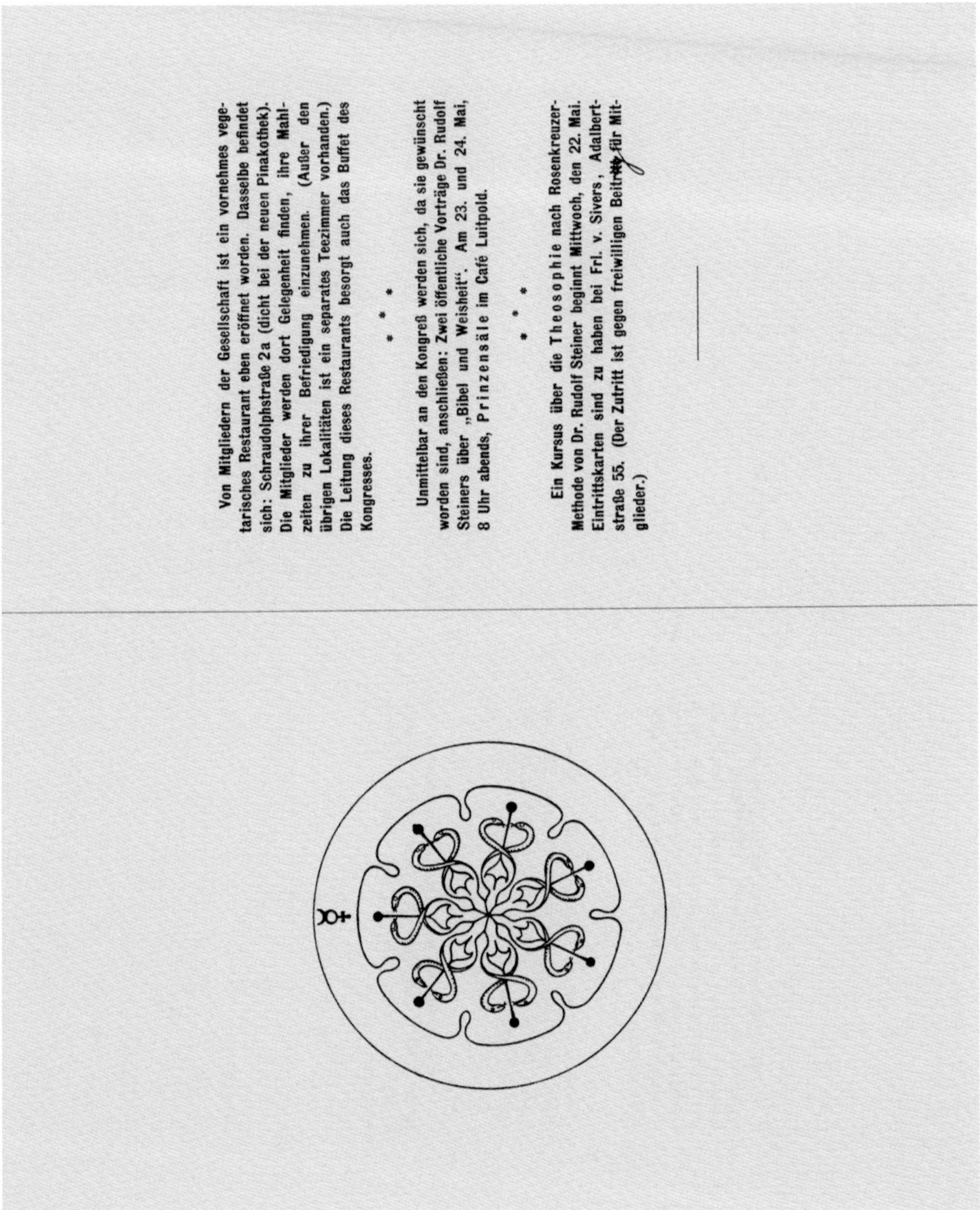

Von Mitgliedern der Gesellschaft ist ein vornehmes vegetarisches Restaurant eben eröffnet worden. Dasselbe befindet sich: Schraudolphstraße 2a (dicht bei der neuen Pinakothek). Die Mitglieder werden dort Gelegenheit finden, ihre Mahlzeiten zu ihrer Befriedigung einzunehmen. (Außer den übrigen Lokalitäten ist ein separates Teezimmer vorhanden.) Die Leitung dieses Restaurants besorgt auch das Buffet des Kongresses.

* * *

Unmittelbar an den Kongreß werden sich, da sie gewünscht worden sind, anschließen: Zwei öffentliche Vorträge Dr. Rudolf Steiners über „Bibel und Weisheit". Am 23. und 24. Mai, 8 Uhr abends, Prinzensäle im Café Luitpold.

* * *

Ein Kursus über die Theosophie nach Rosenkreuzer-Methode von Dr. Rudolf Steiner beginnt Mittwoch, den 22. Mai. Eintrittskarten sind zu haben bei Frl. v. Sivers, Adalbertstraße 55. (Der Zutritt ist gegen freiwilligen Beitrag für Mitglieder.)

Pages of the program brochure

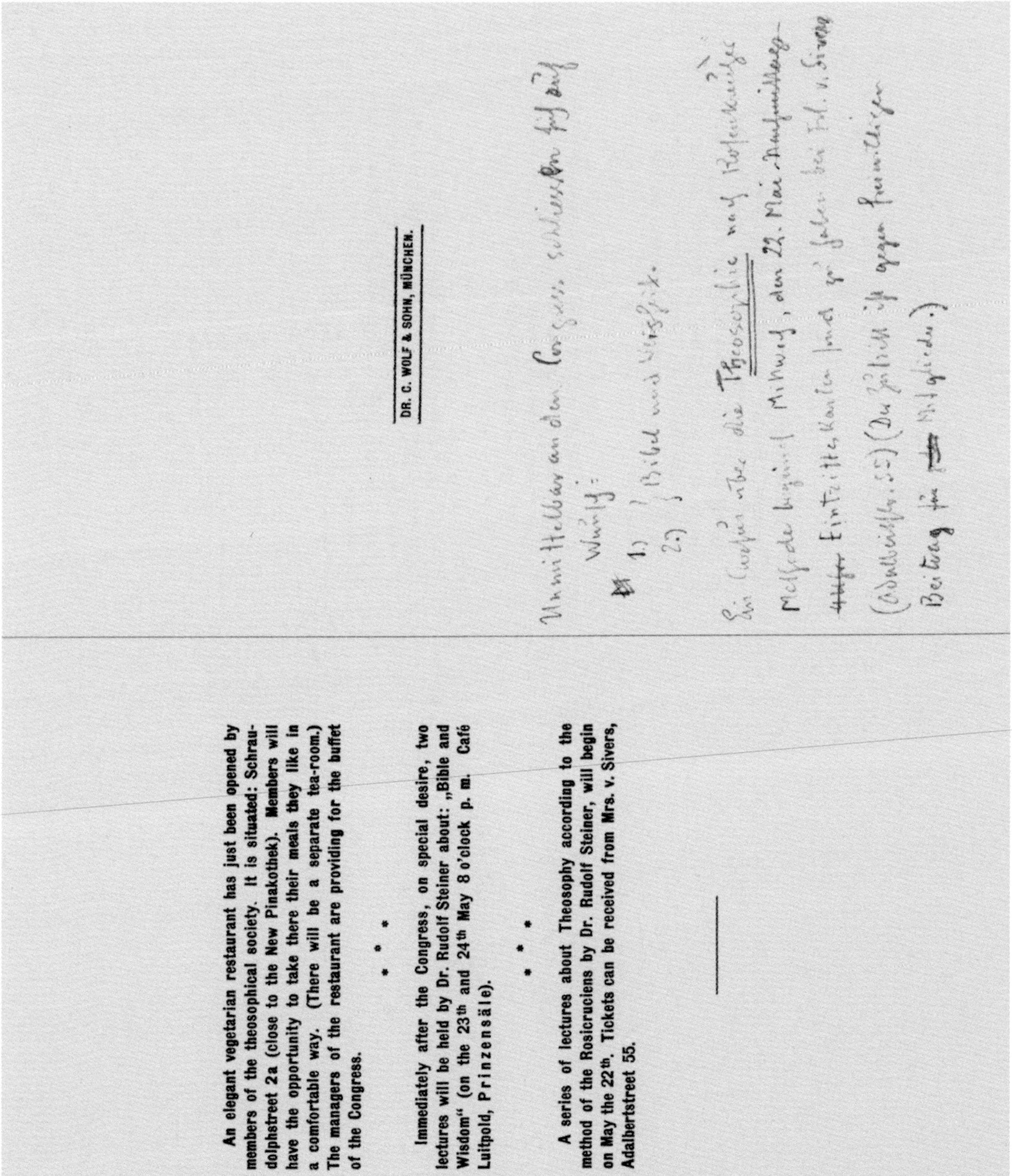

An elegant vegetarian restaurant has just been opened by members of the theosophical society. It is situated: Schraudolphstreet 2a (close to the New Pinakothek). Members will have the opportunity to take there their meals they like in a comfortable way. (There will be a separate tea-room.) The managers of the restaurant are providing for the buffet of the Congress.

* * *

Immediately after the Congress, on special desire, two lectures will be held by Dr. Rudolf Steiner about: „Bible and Wisdom" (on the 23th and 24th May 8 o'clock p. m. Café Luitpold, Prinzensäle).

* * *

A series of lectures about Theosophy according to the method of the Rosicrucians by Dr. Rudolf Steiner, will begin on May the 22th. Tickets can be received from Mrs. v. Sivers, Adalbertstreet 55.

DR. C. WOLF & SOHN, MÜNCHEN.

Pages of the program brochure

18.

Eröffnung: Waldweben: Orgel — (durch Arenson besorgen lassen):

abends: Trio (Violine, Clavier, Waldhorn): Brahms. —

Recitation: Faust-2. Teil: Sivers.

Prometheus: Jürgas.

19.

20.

Recitation am Jordan: — Jürgas

Hamerling: — ?

abends: Clavierspiel: Elspermann

Marika.

~~Frl. Lauf~~ Frl. Völcker

21.

Laufer. Arenson.: Requiem: Cello-Solo (Dr. Unger).

Fritz Brandenburger.

Melchior Lechter.

Peipers: Köpfe

Hegel

Novalis —

Schelling

Fichte.

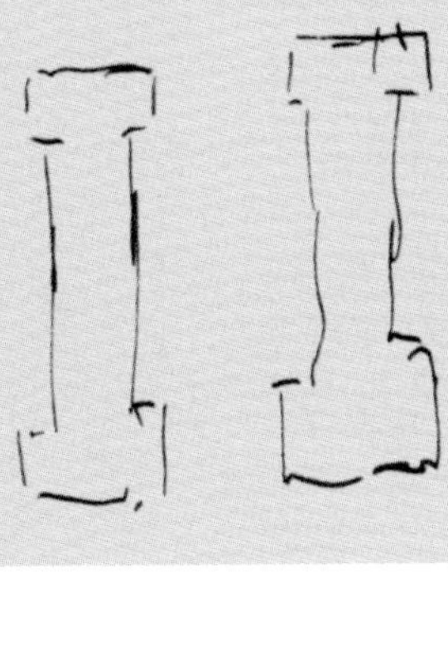

Notes for the congress program by Rudolf Steiner

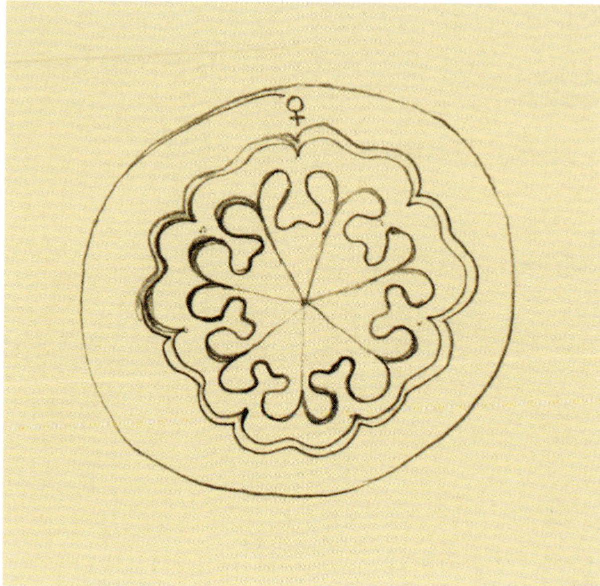

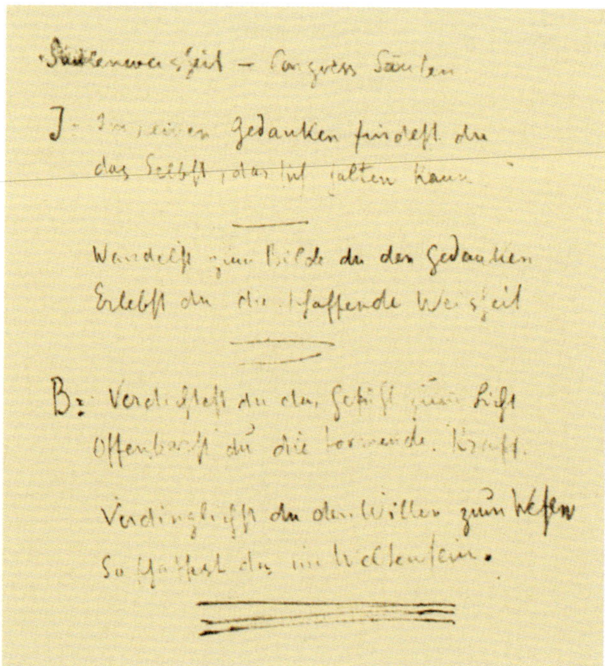

Säulenweisheit – Congress Säulen

J: Im reinen Gedanken findest du
das Selbst, das sich halten kann.

Wandelst zum Bilde du den Gedanken
Erlebst du die schaffende Weisheit

B: Verdichtest du das Gefühl zum Licht
Offenbarst du die formende Kraft.

Verdinglichst du den Willen zum Wesen
So schaffest du im Weltensein.

ABOVE: Sketch by Rudolf Steiner for the seventh planetary seal [Venus]
BELOW: The four sayings of the pillar wisdom. (from a notebook)

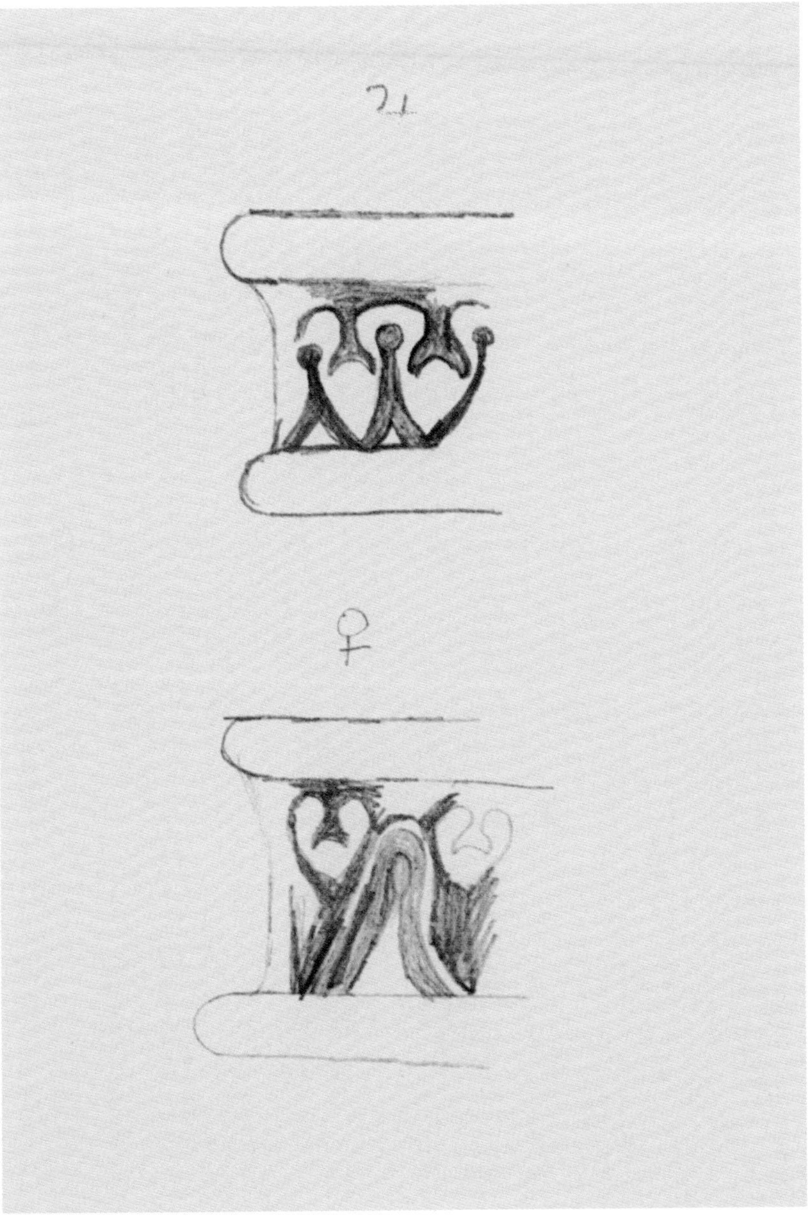

Rudolf Steiner's design for the Jupiter and Venus capitals of the painted columns in the Munich Congress hall (from a 1907 notebook)

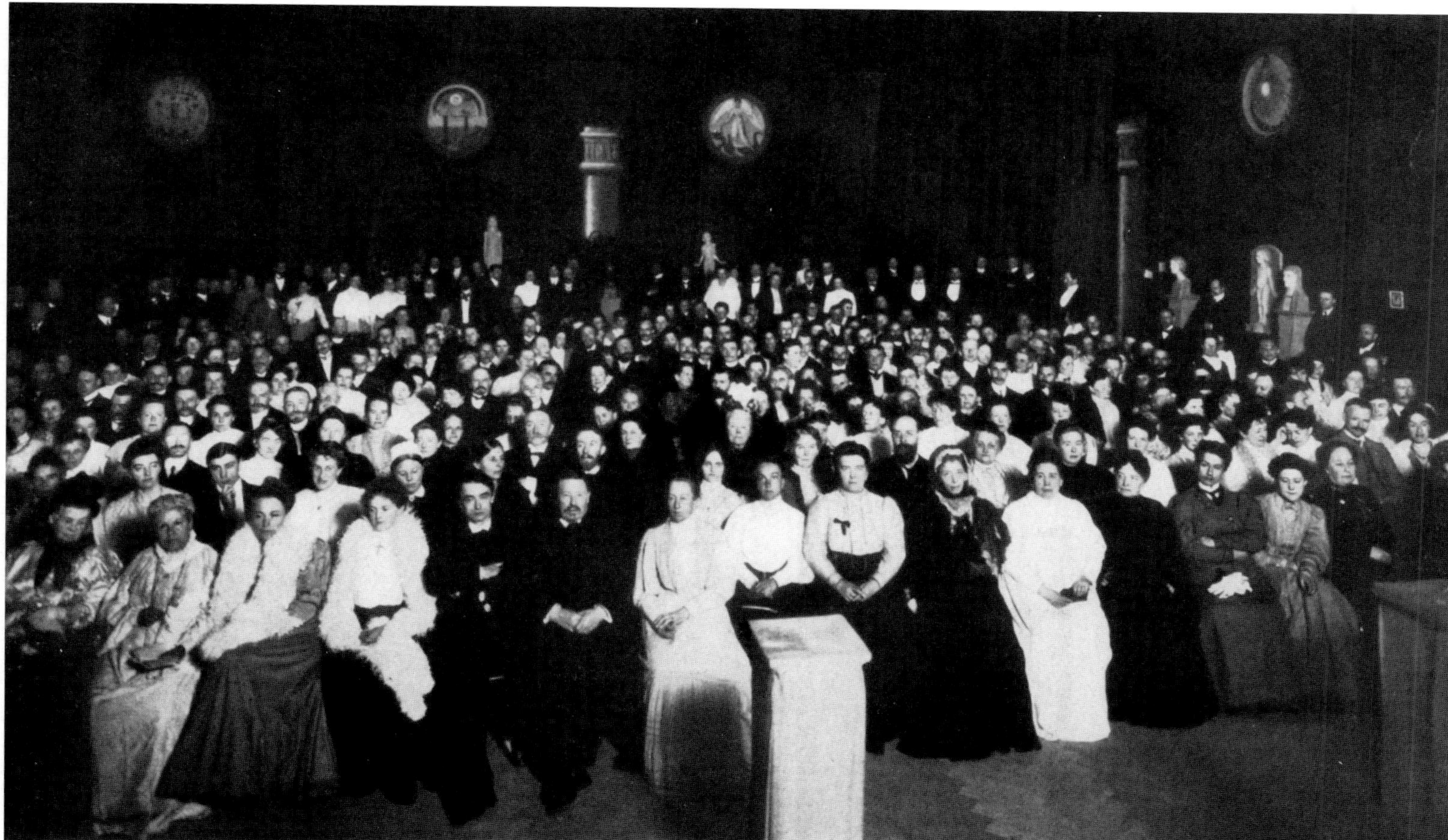

The Munich Congress hall with the painted seals and columns (May 21, 1907)

IN THE FIRST ROW, FROM LEFT: 2. Annie Besant 4. Marie von Sivers (Marie Steiner) 5. Rudolf Steiner 7. Sophie Stinde

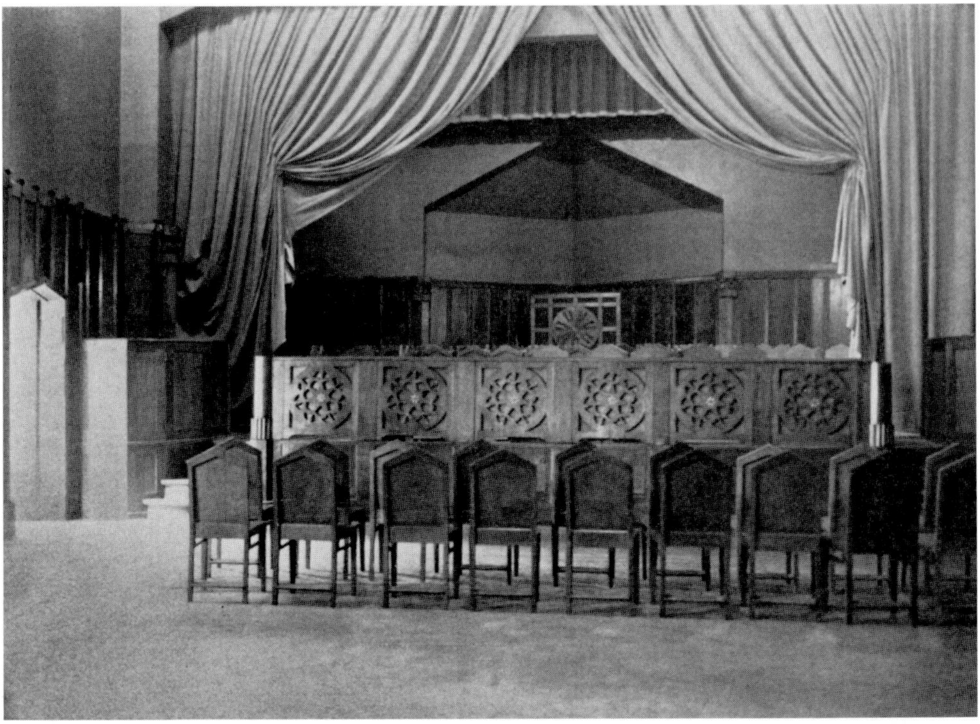

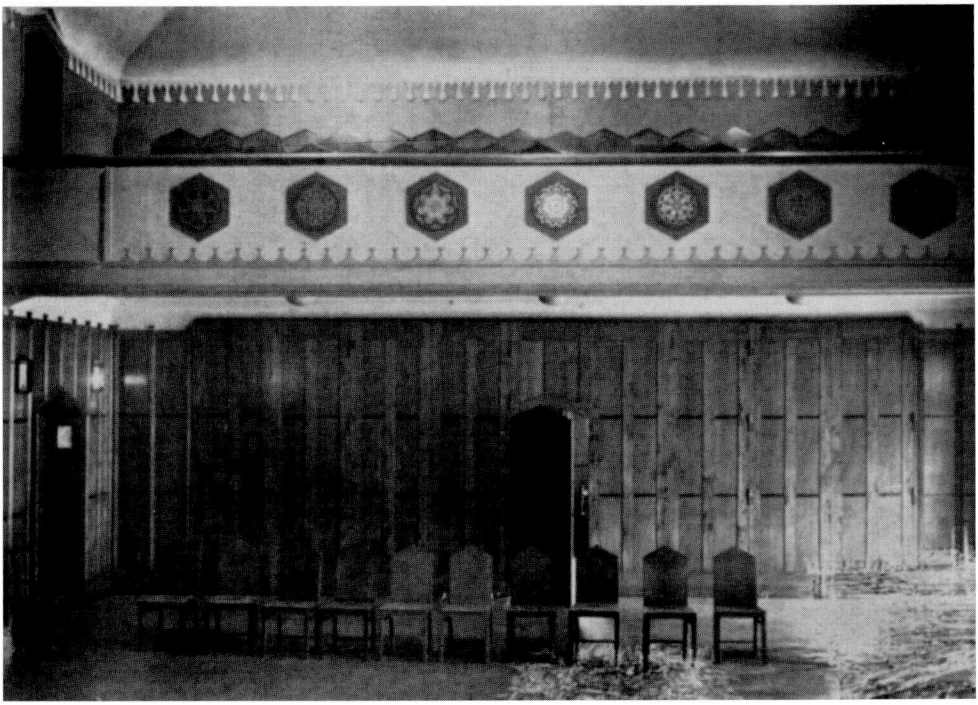

The main hall of the Stuttgart house (1935)
ABOVE: View toward the stage. BELOW: View toward the emporium with the planetary seals

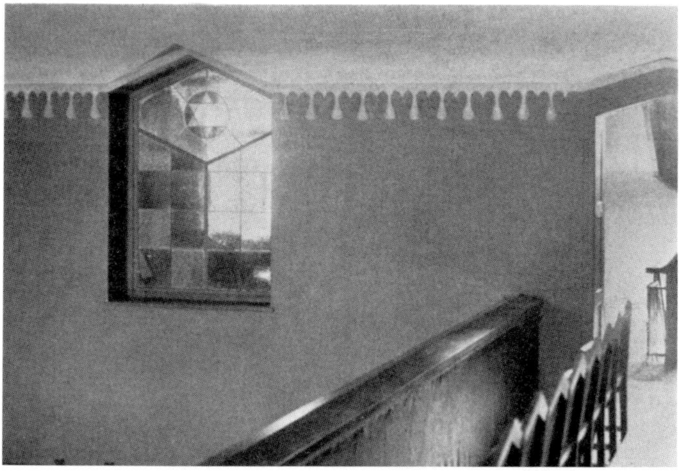

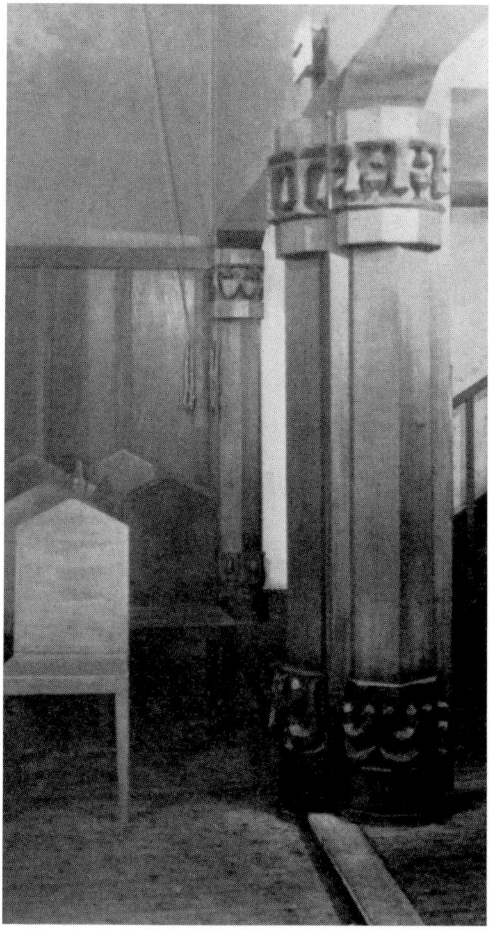

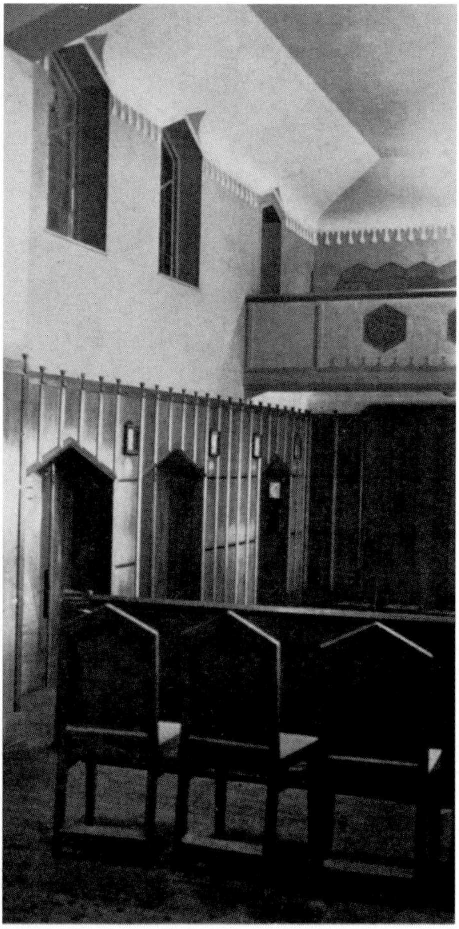

Individual views of the main hall of the Stuttgart house (1935)

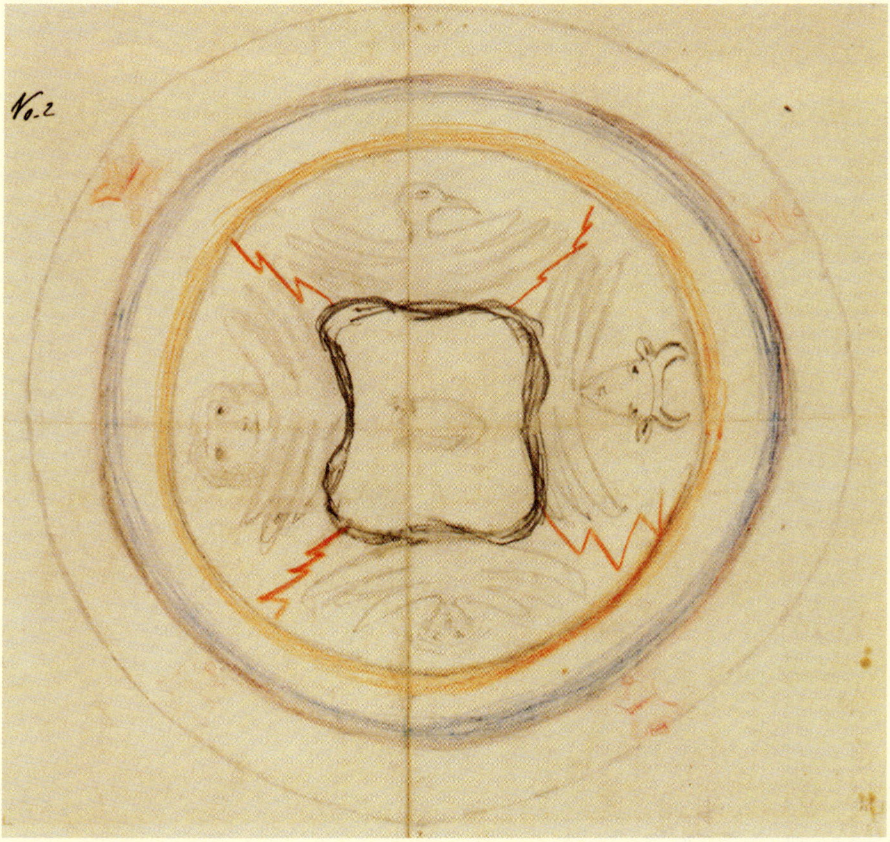

PLATE 1 : Rudolf Steiner's sketch for the second seal

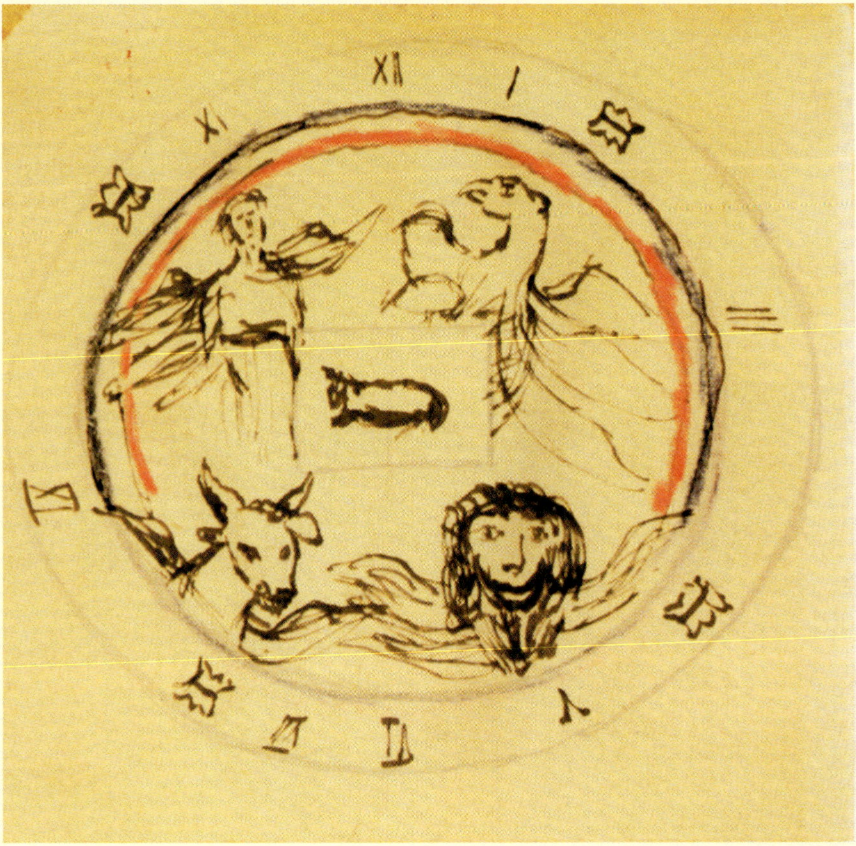

PLATE 2 : Additional sketch for the second seal

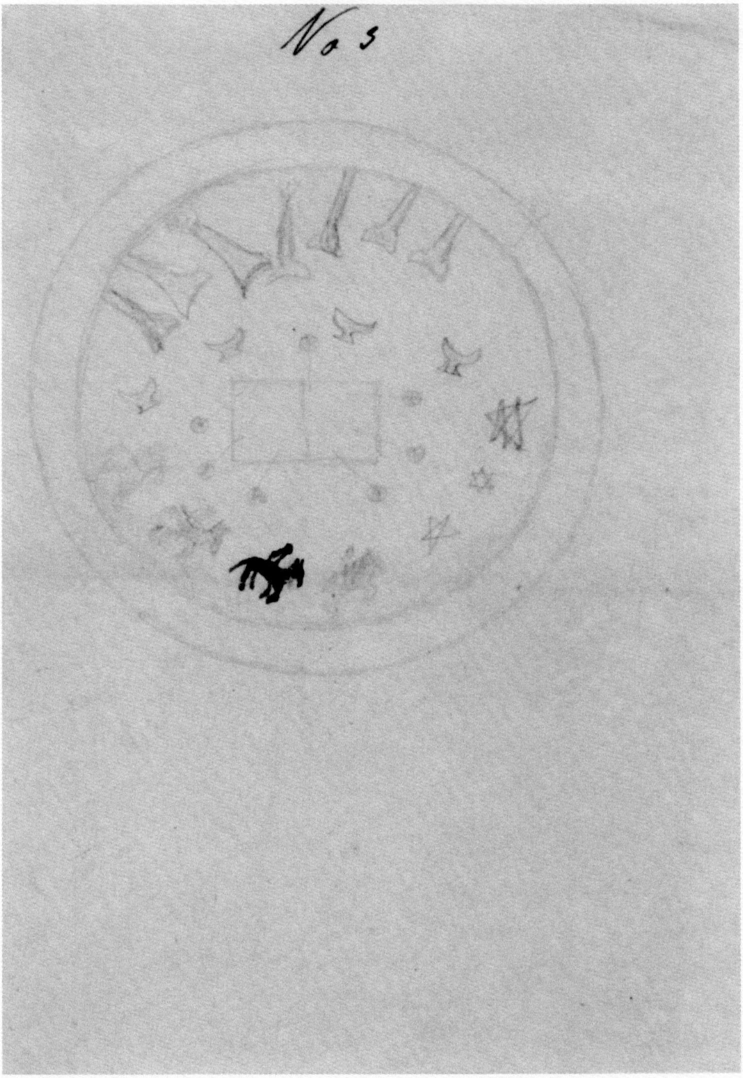

PLATE 3 : Rudolf Steiner's sketch for the third seal

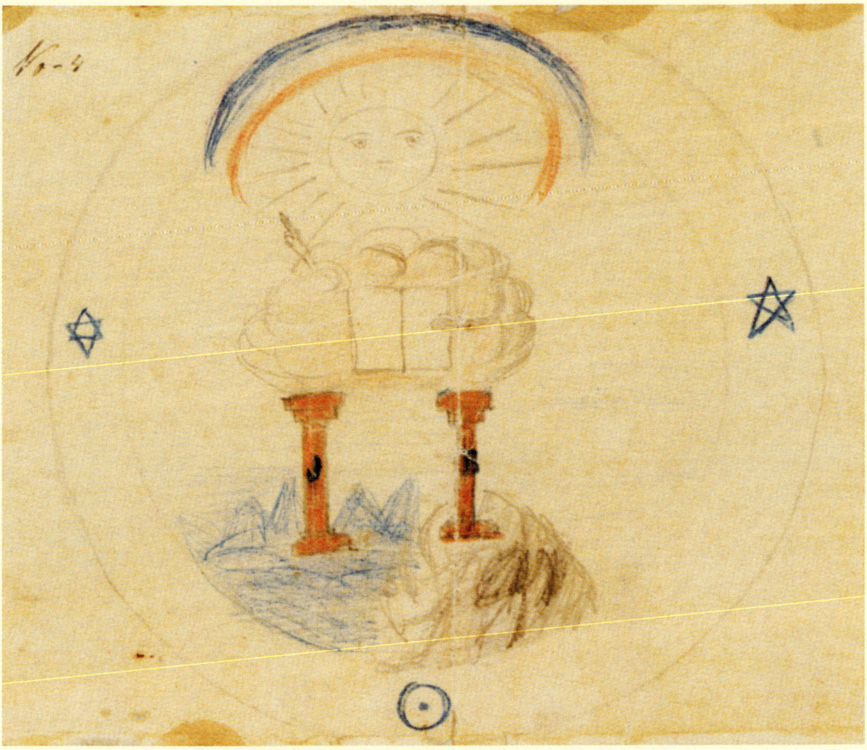

PLATE 4 : Rudolf Steiner's sketch for the fourth seal

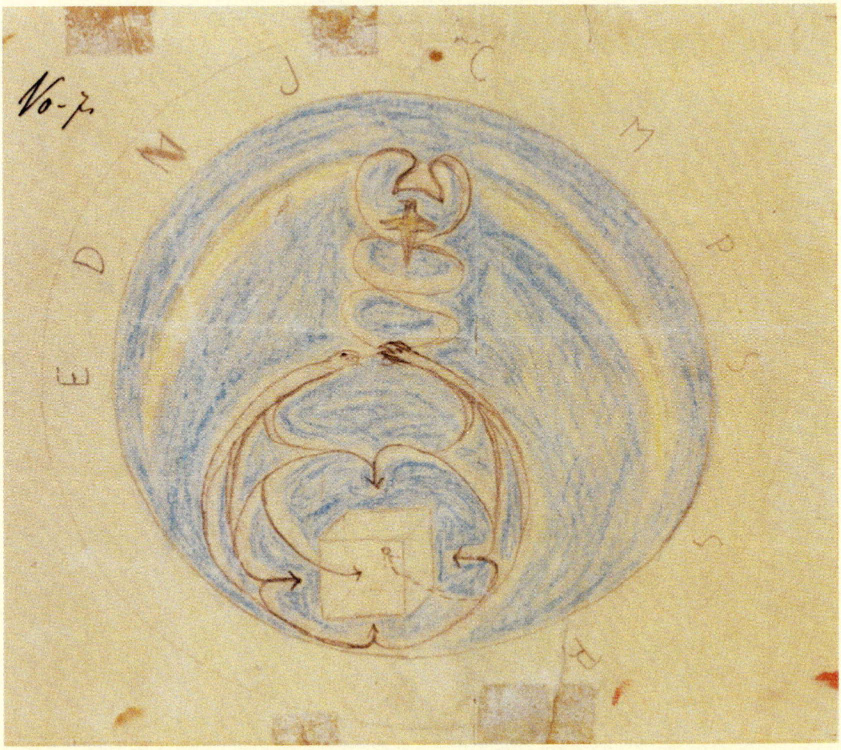

PLATE 5 : Rudolf Steiner's sketch for the seventh seal

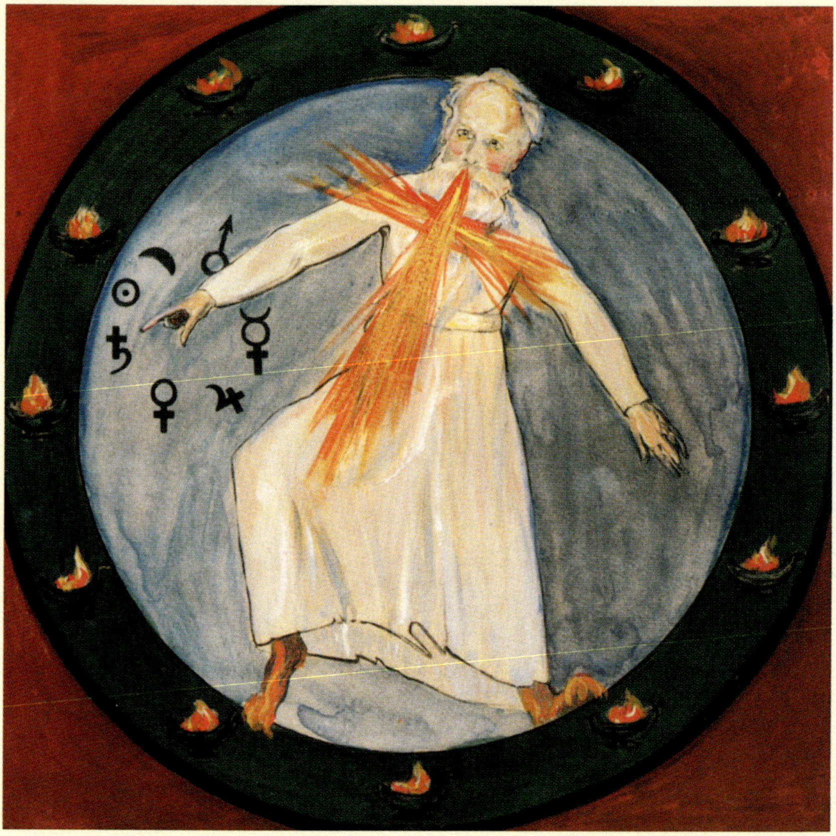

PLATE 6 : First seal (painted by Clara Rettich, 1907)

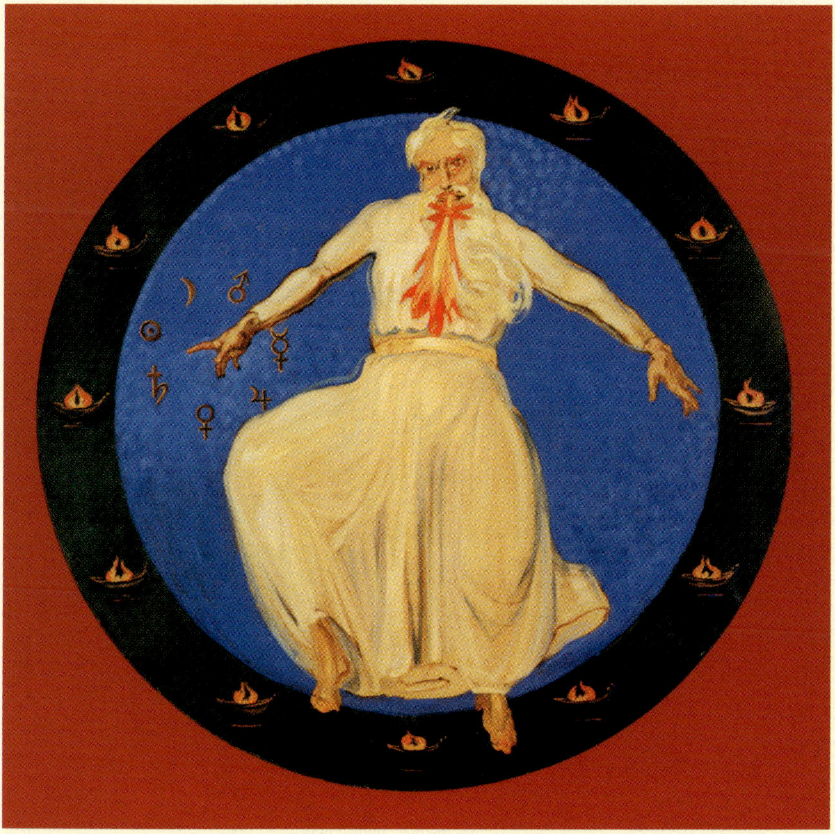

PLATE 7 : First seal (painted Clara Rettich, Stuttgart, 1911)

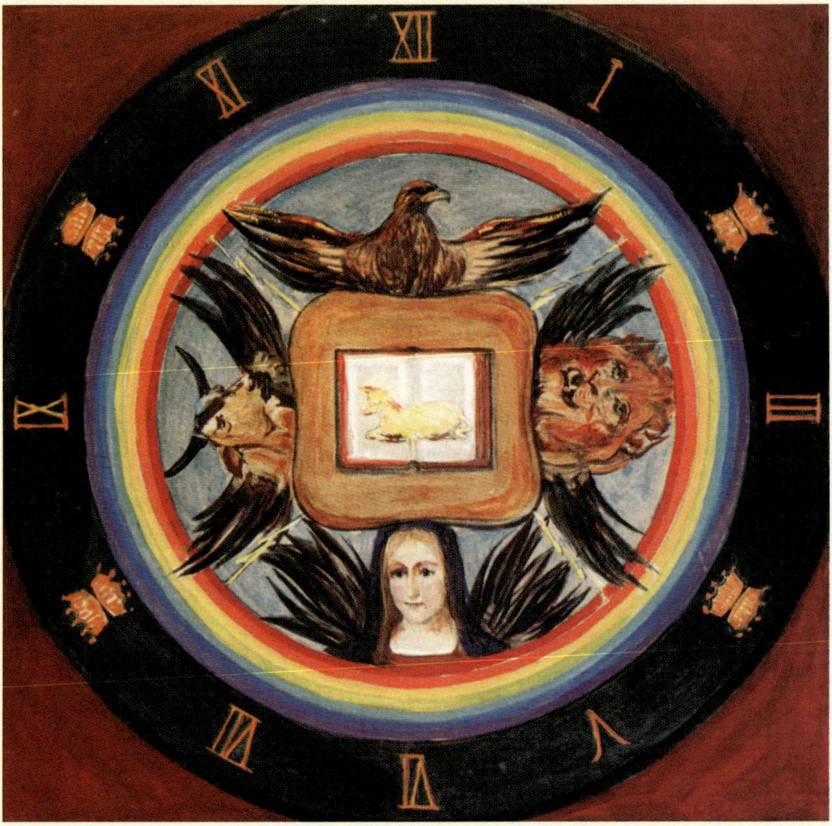

PLATE 8 : Second seal (painted by Clara Rettich, 1907)

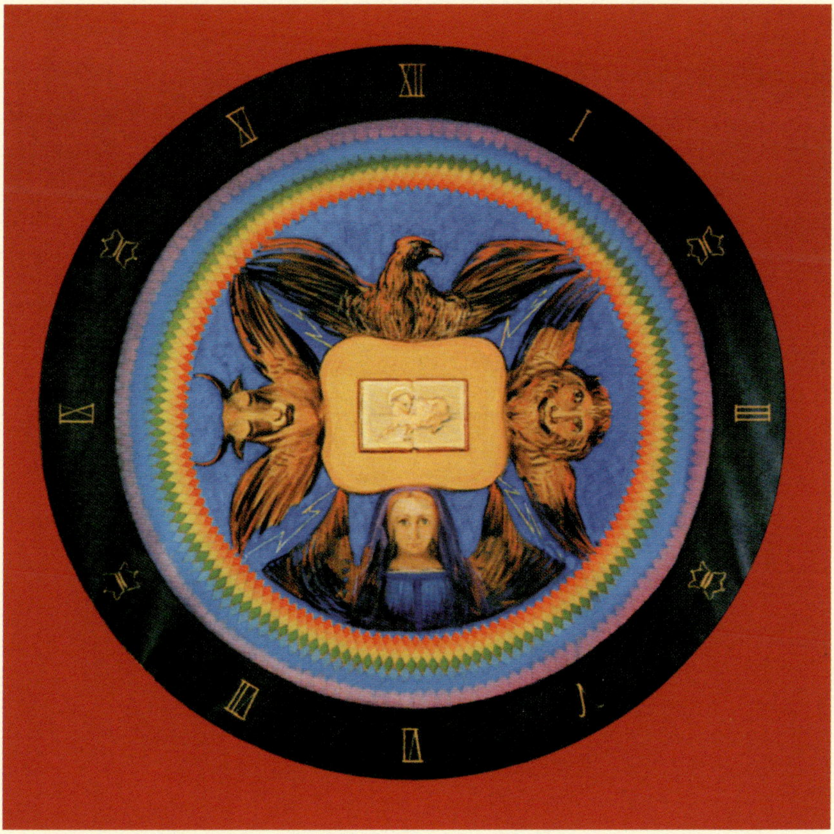

PLATE 9 : Second seal (painted by Clara Rettich, Stuttgart, 1911)

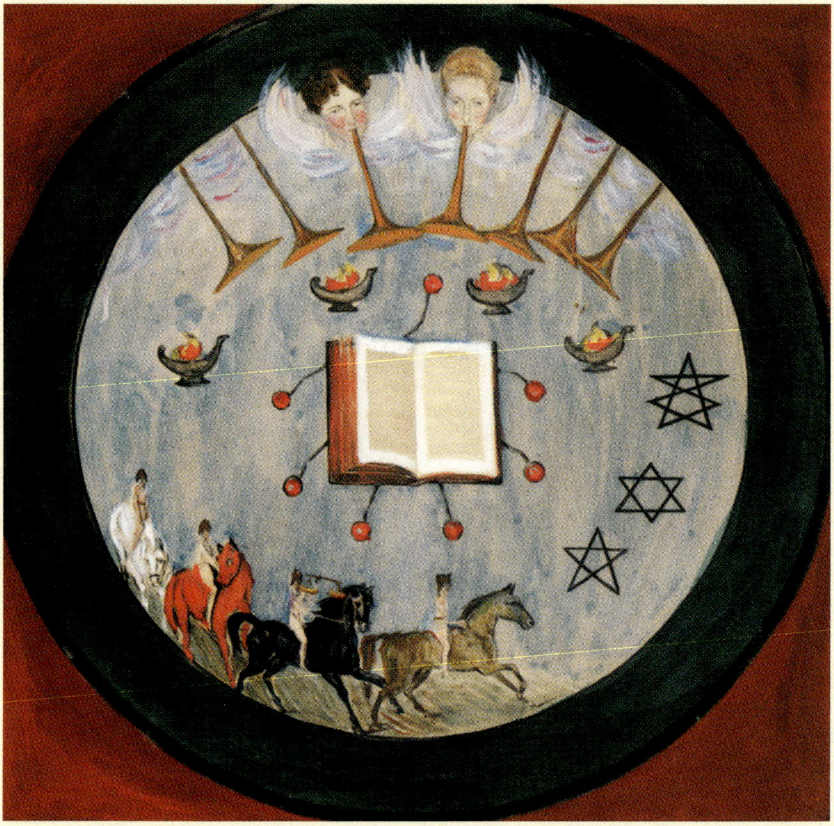

PLATE 10 : Third seal (painted by Clara Rettich, Stuttgart, 1907)

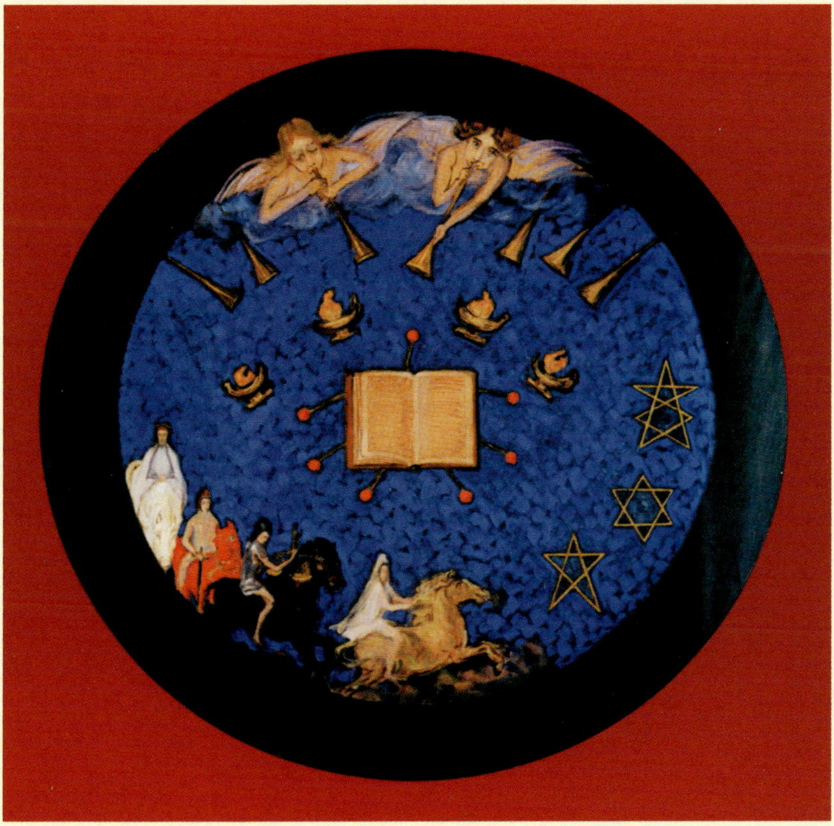

PLATE 11 : Third seal (painted by Clara Rettich, Stuttgart, 1911)

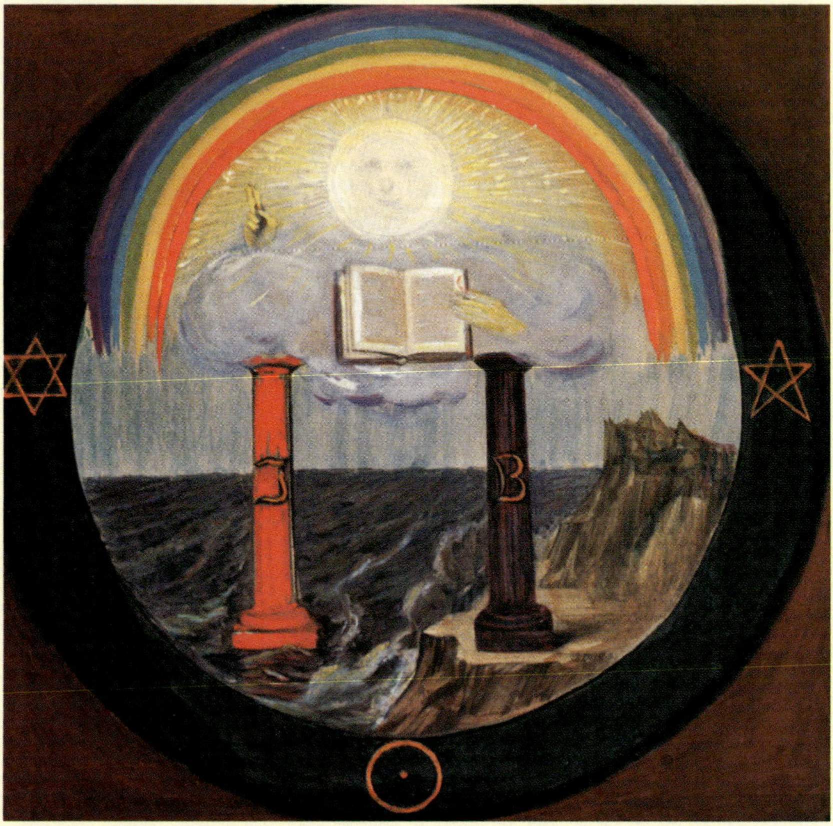

PLATE 12 : Fourth seal (painted by Clara Rettich, 1907)

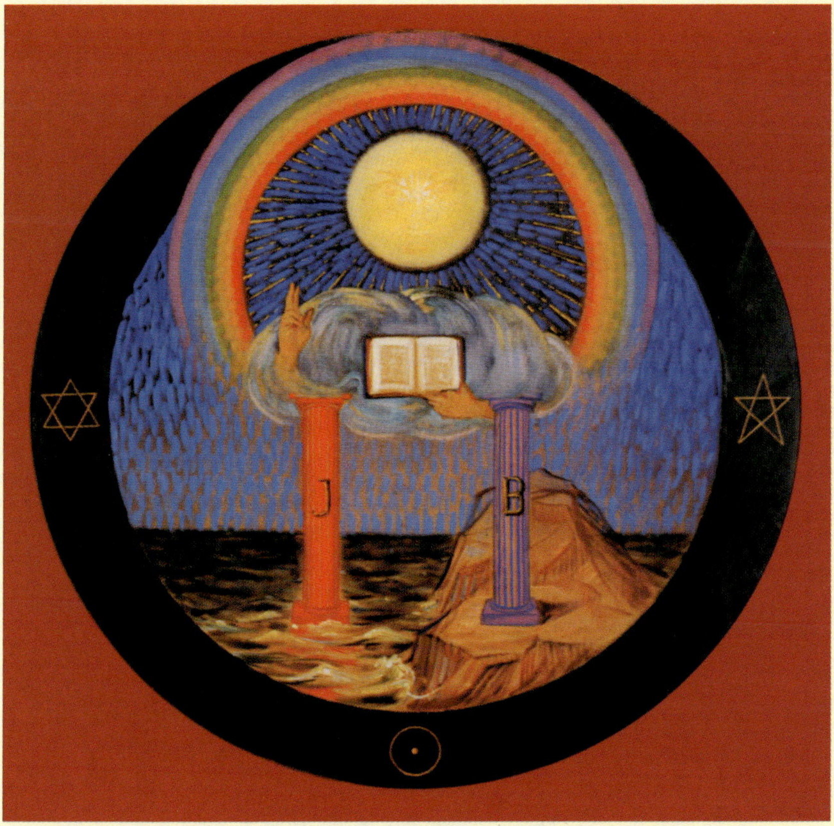

PLATE 13 : Fourth seal (painted by Clara Rettich, Stuttgart, 1911)

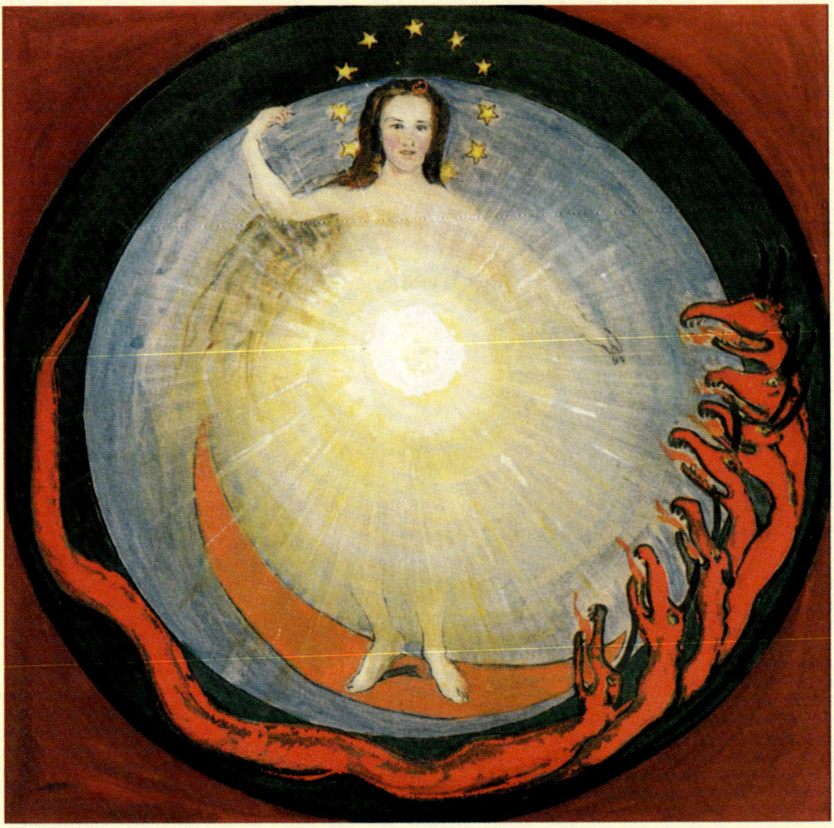

PLATE 14 : Fifth seal (painted by Clara Rettich, 1907)

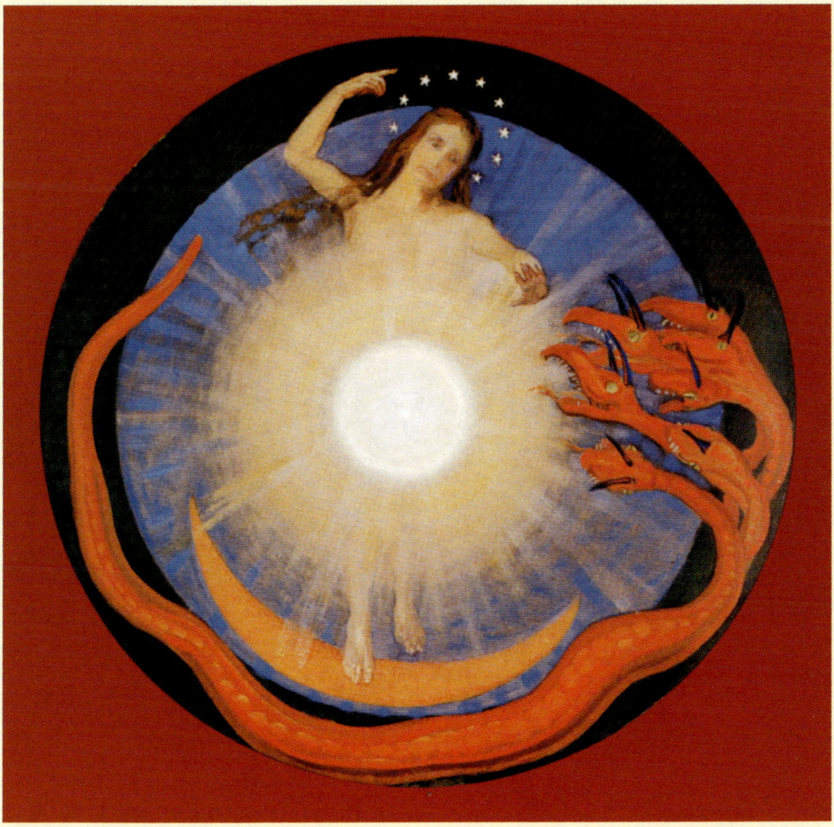

PLATE 15 : Fifth seal (painted by Clara Rettich, Stuttgart, 1911)

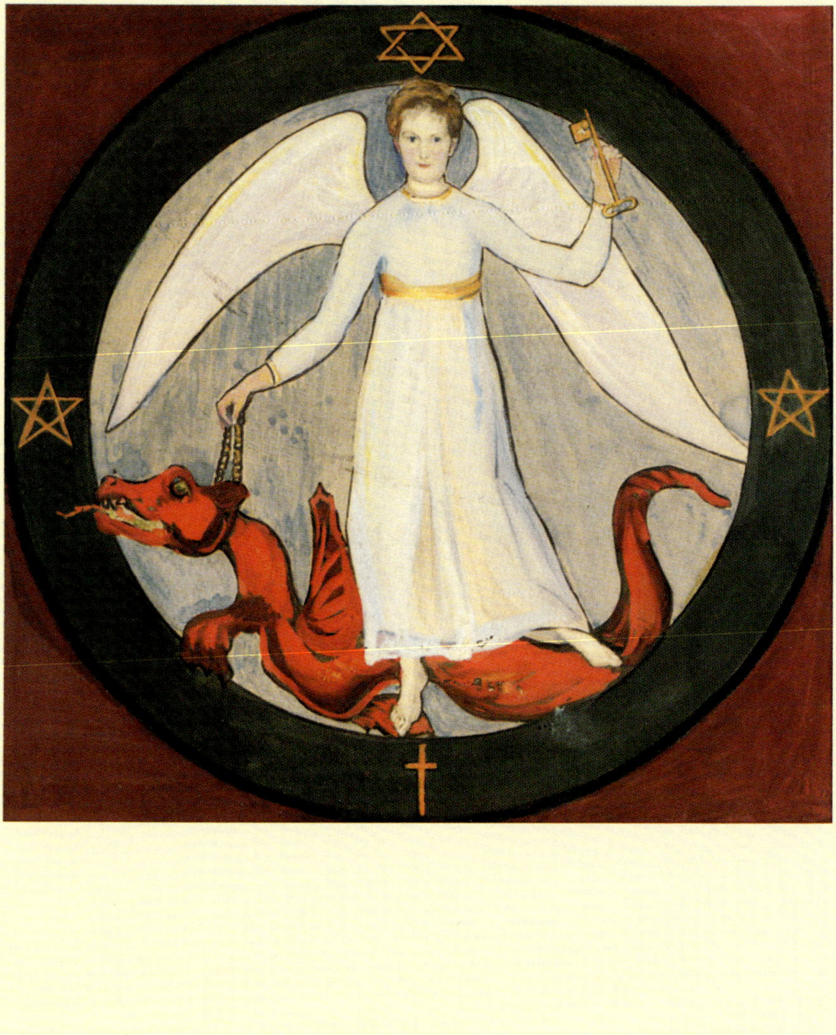

PLATE 16 : Sixth seal (painted by Clara Rettich, 1907)

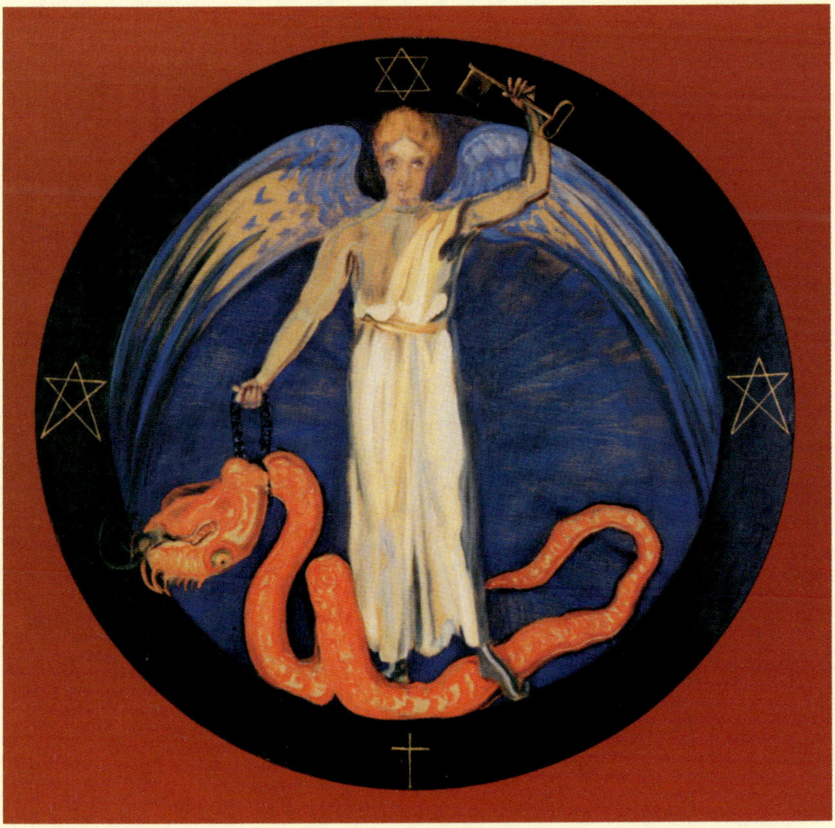

PLATE 17 : Sixth seal (painted by Clara Rettich, Stuttgart, 1911)

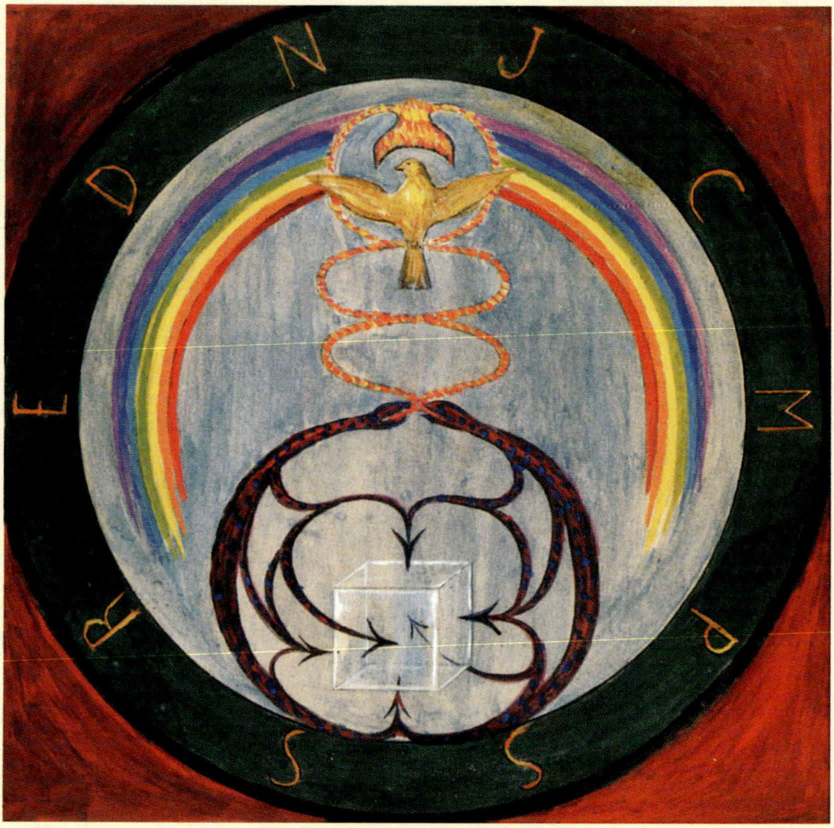

PLATE 18 : Seventh seal (painted by Clara Rettich, 1907)

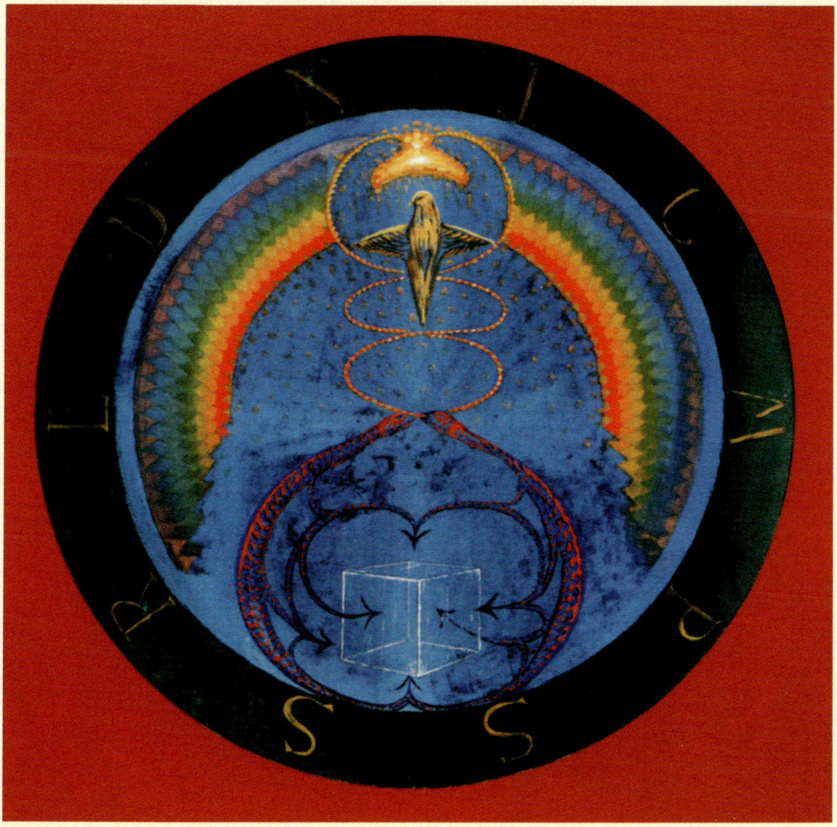

PLATE 19 : Seventh seal (painted by Clara Rettich, Stuttgart, 1911)

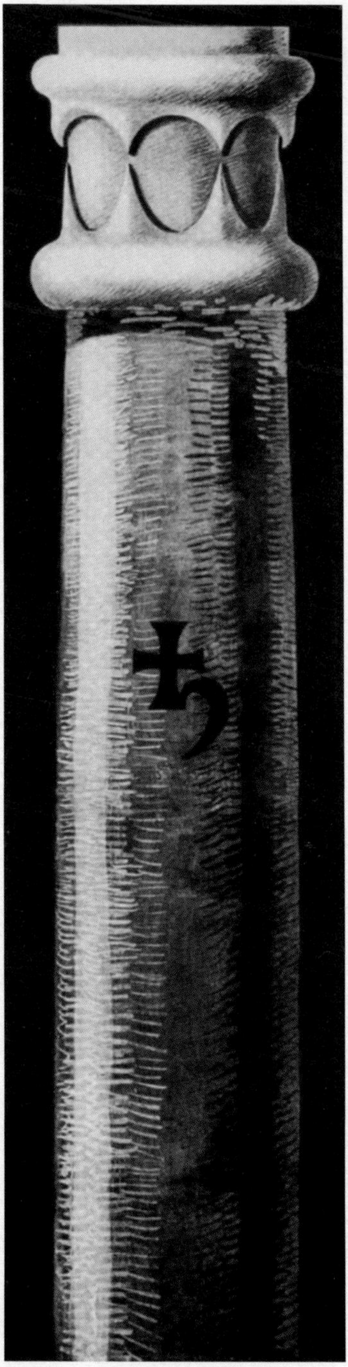

PLATE 20 : First column [Saturn] (painted by Karl Stahl)

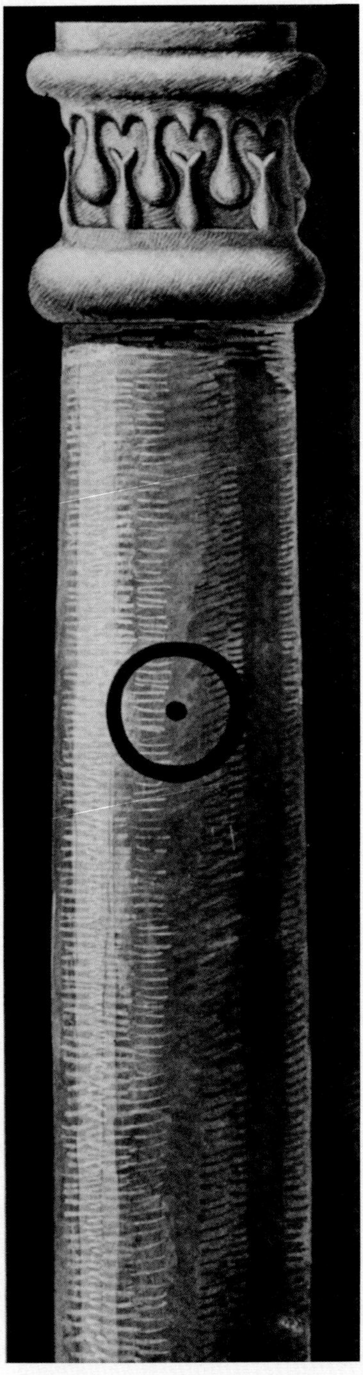

PLATE 21 : Second column [Sun] (painted by Karl Stahl)

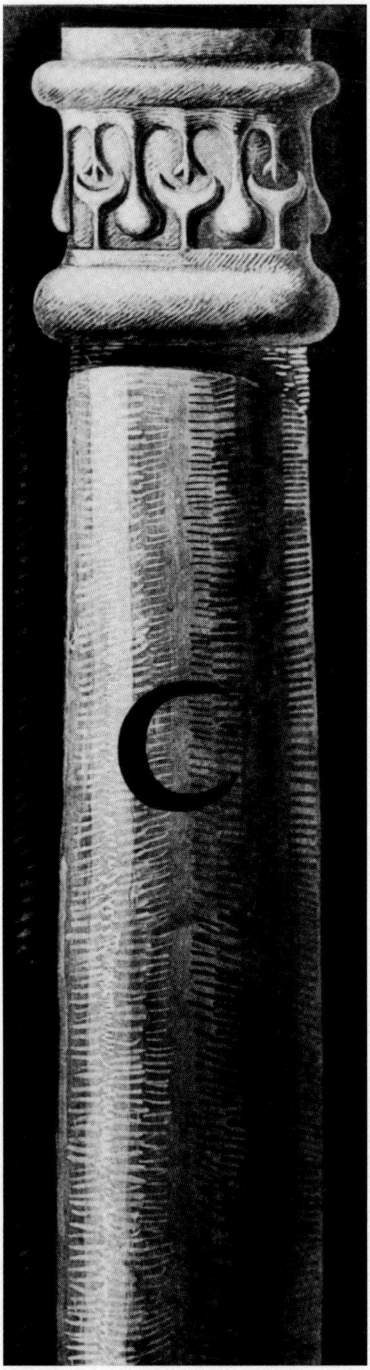

PLATE 22 : Third column [Moon] (painted by Karl Stahl)

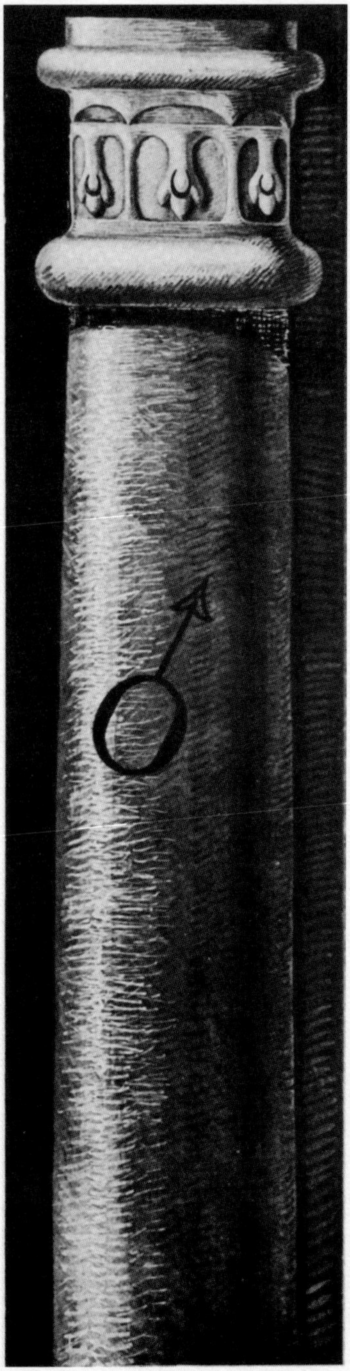

PLATE 23 : Fourth column [Mars] (painted by Karl Stahl)

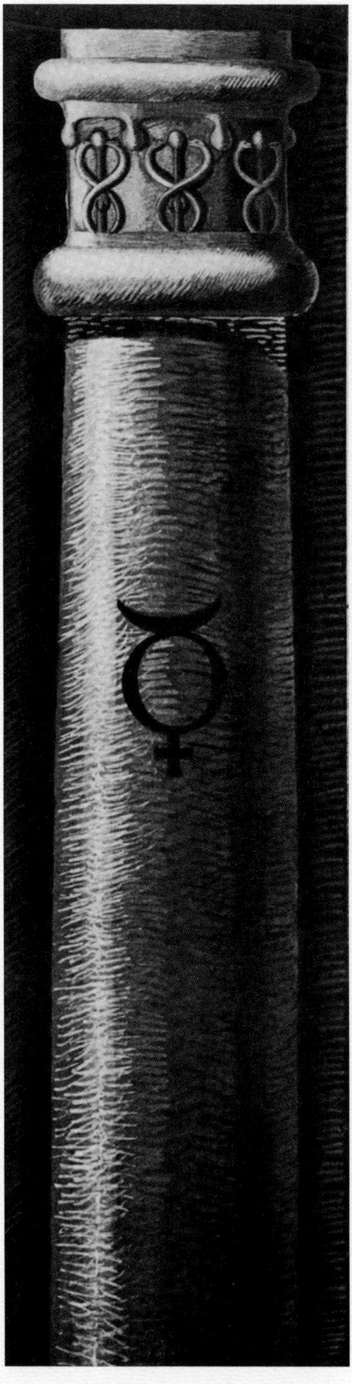

PLATE 24 : Fifth column [Mercury] (painted by Karl Stahl)

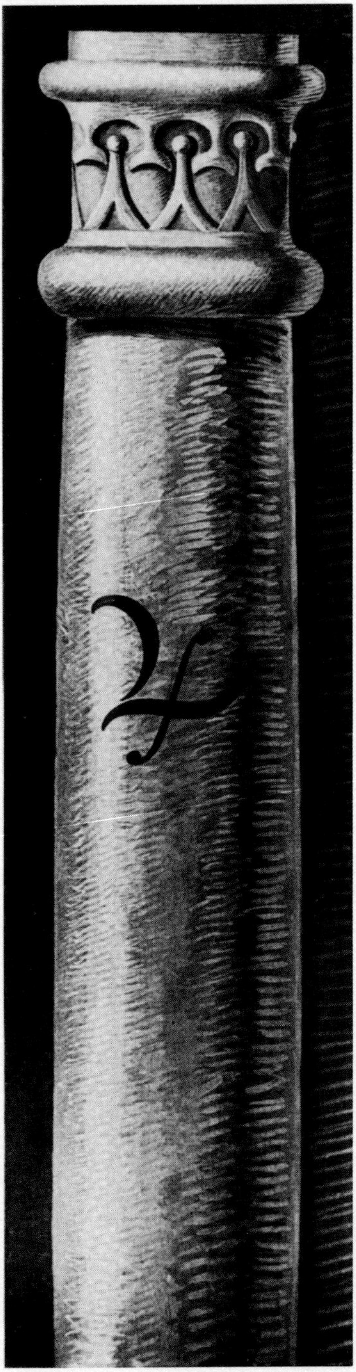

PLATE 25 : Sixth column [Jupiter] (painted by Karl Stahl)

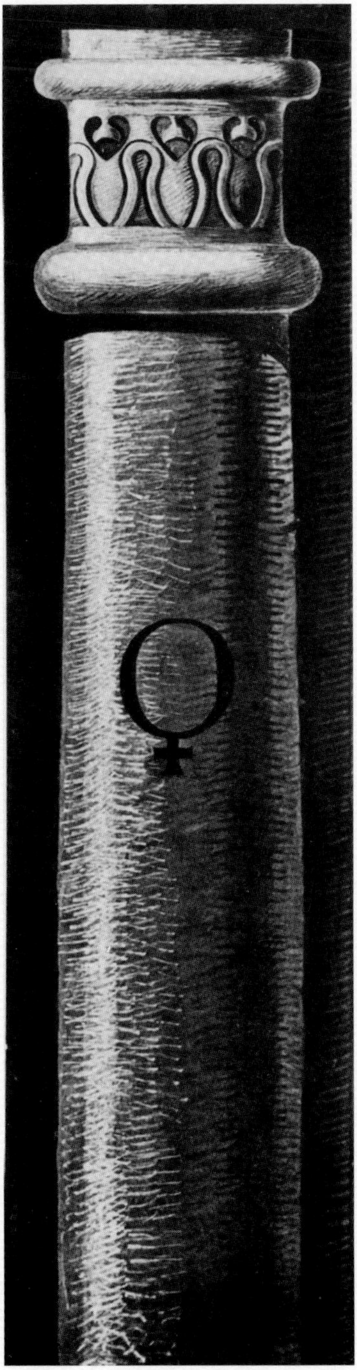

PLATE 26 : Seventh column [Venus] (painted by Karl Stahl)

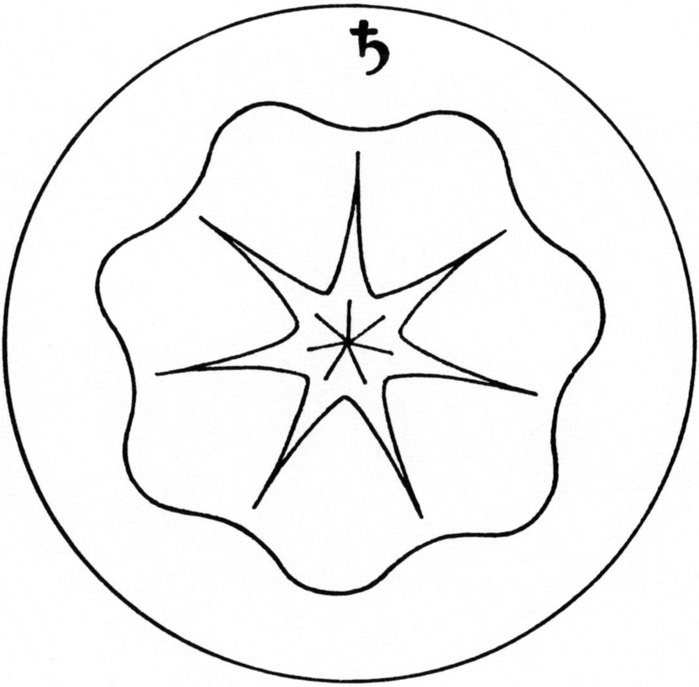

PLATE 27 : First planetary seal [Saturn]

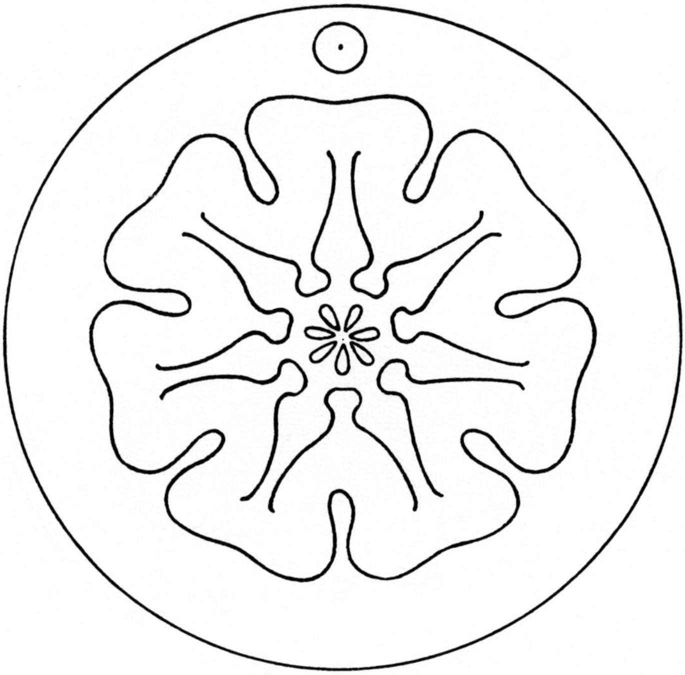

PLATE 28 : Second planetary seal [Sun]

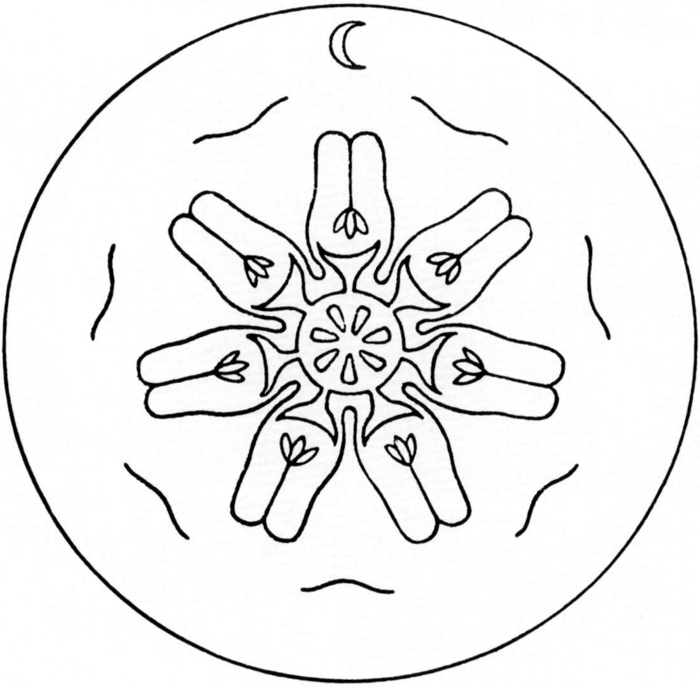

PLATE 29 : Third planetary seal [Moon]

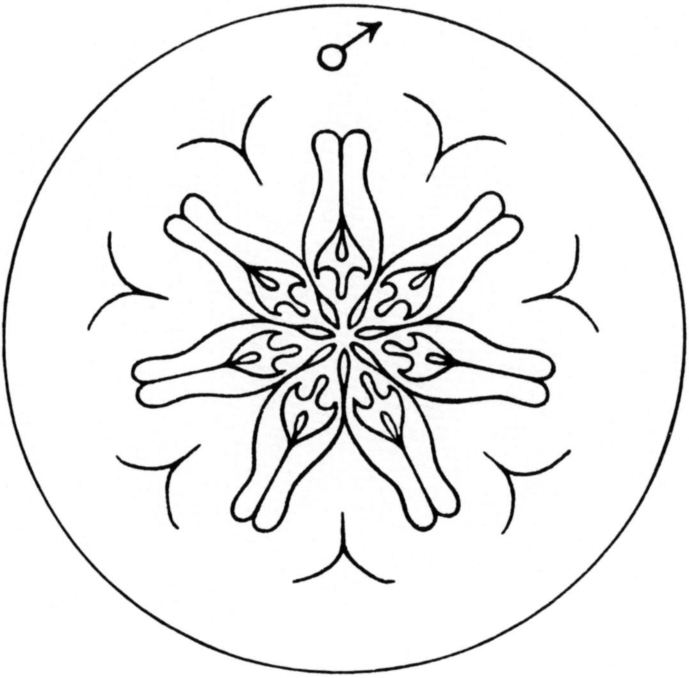

PLATE 30 : Fourth planetary seal [Mars]

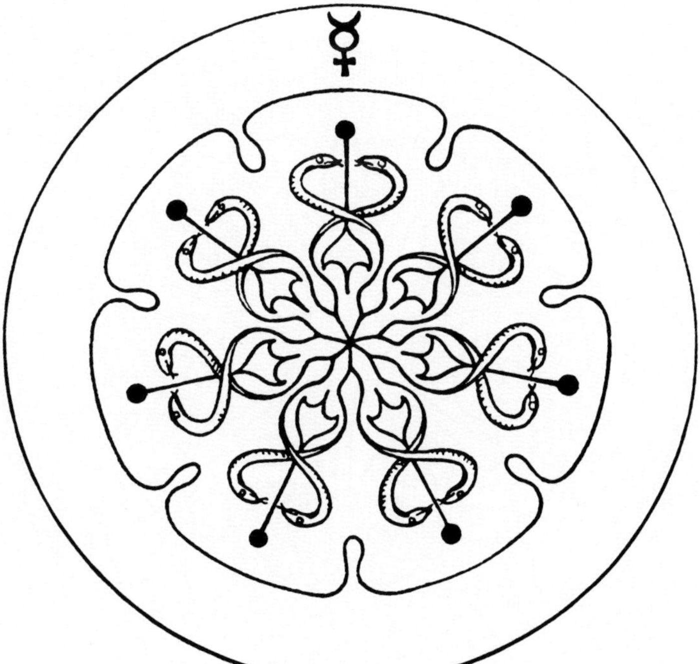

PLATE 31 : Fifth planetary seal [Mercury]

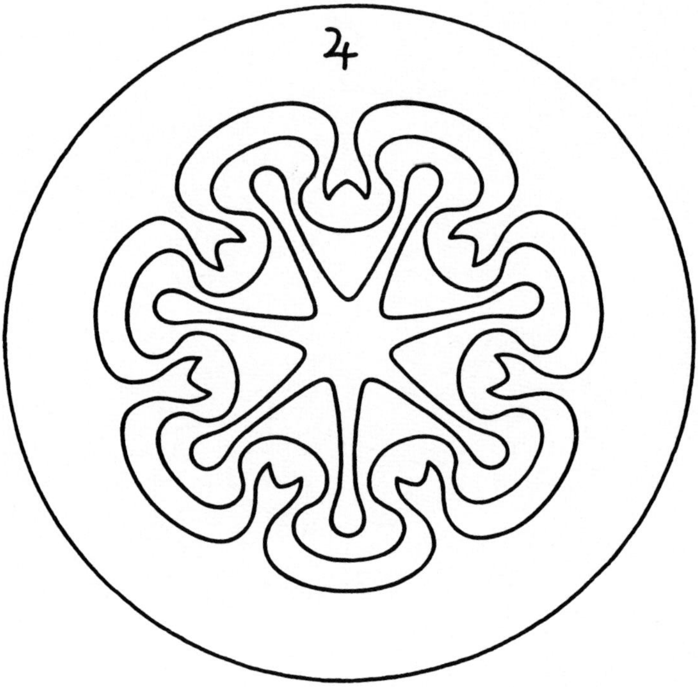

PLATE 32 : Sixth planetary seal [Jupiter]

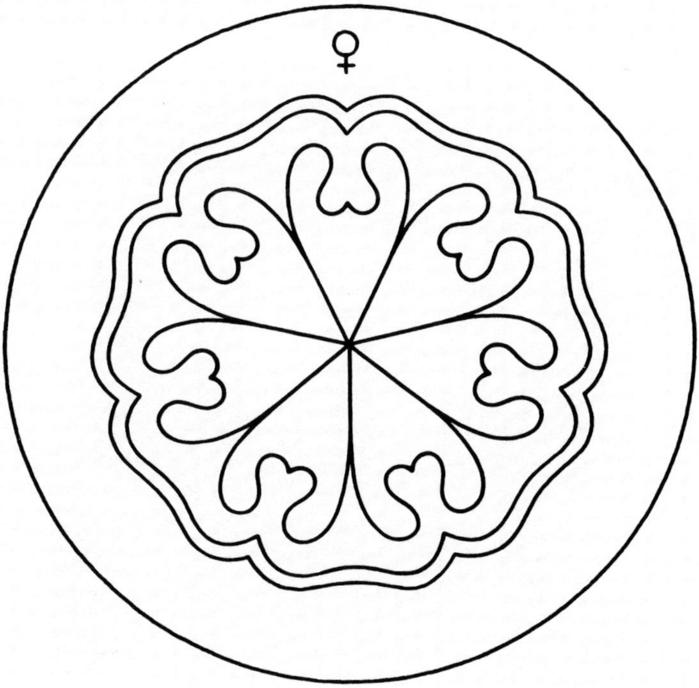

PLATE 33 : Seventh planetary seal [Venus]

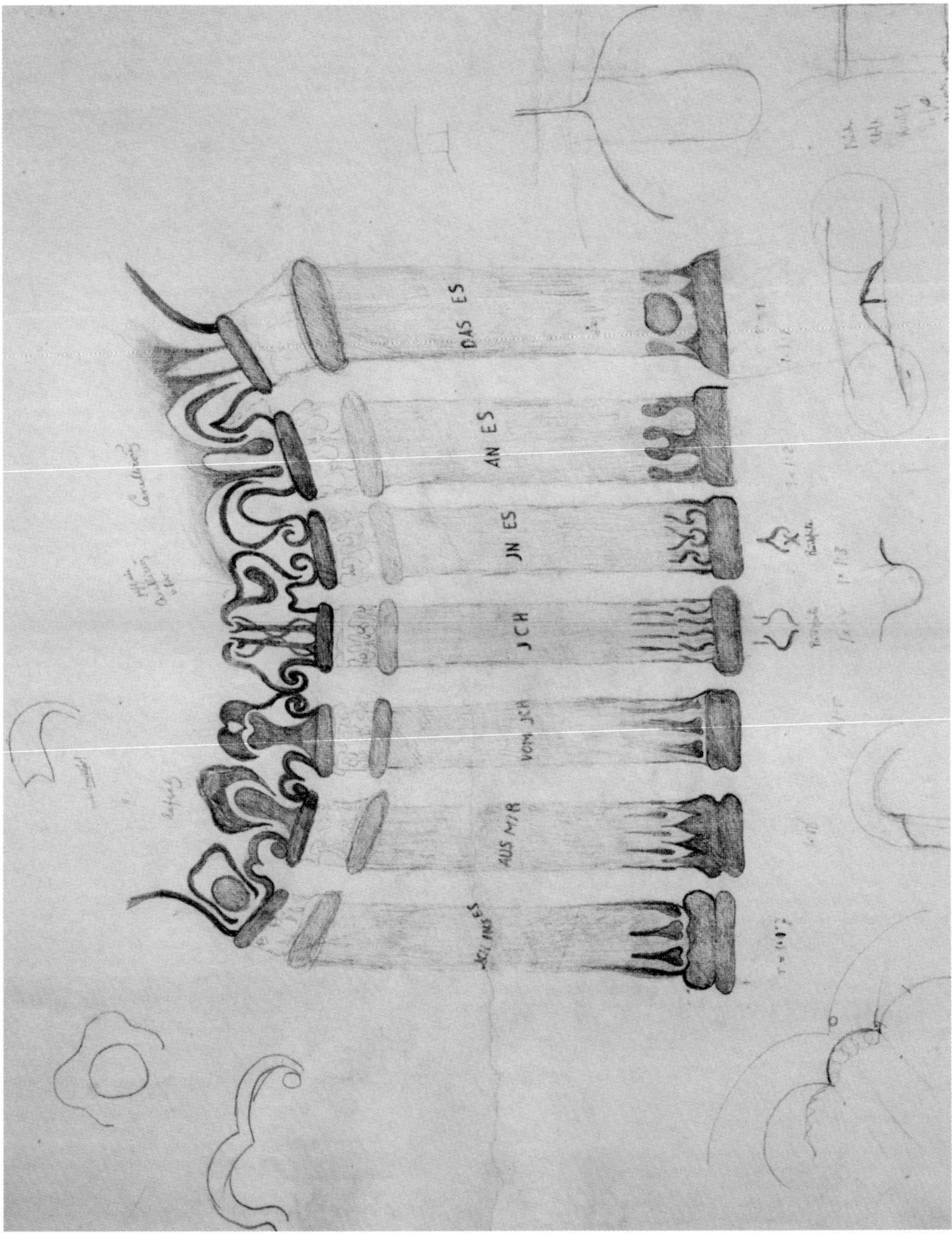

PLATE 34 : Rudolf Steiner's sketch for the columns and architrave of the large cupola room of the first Goetheanum

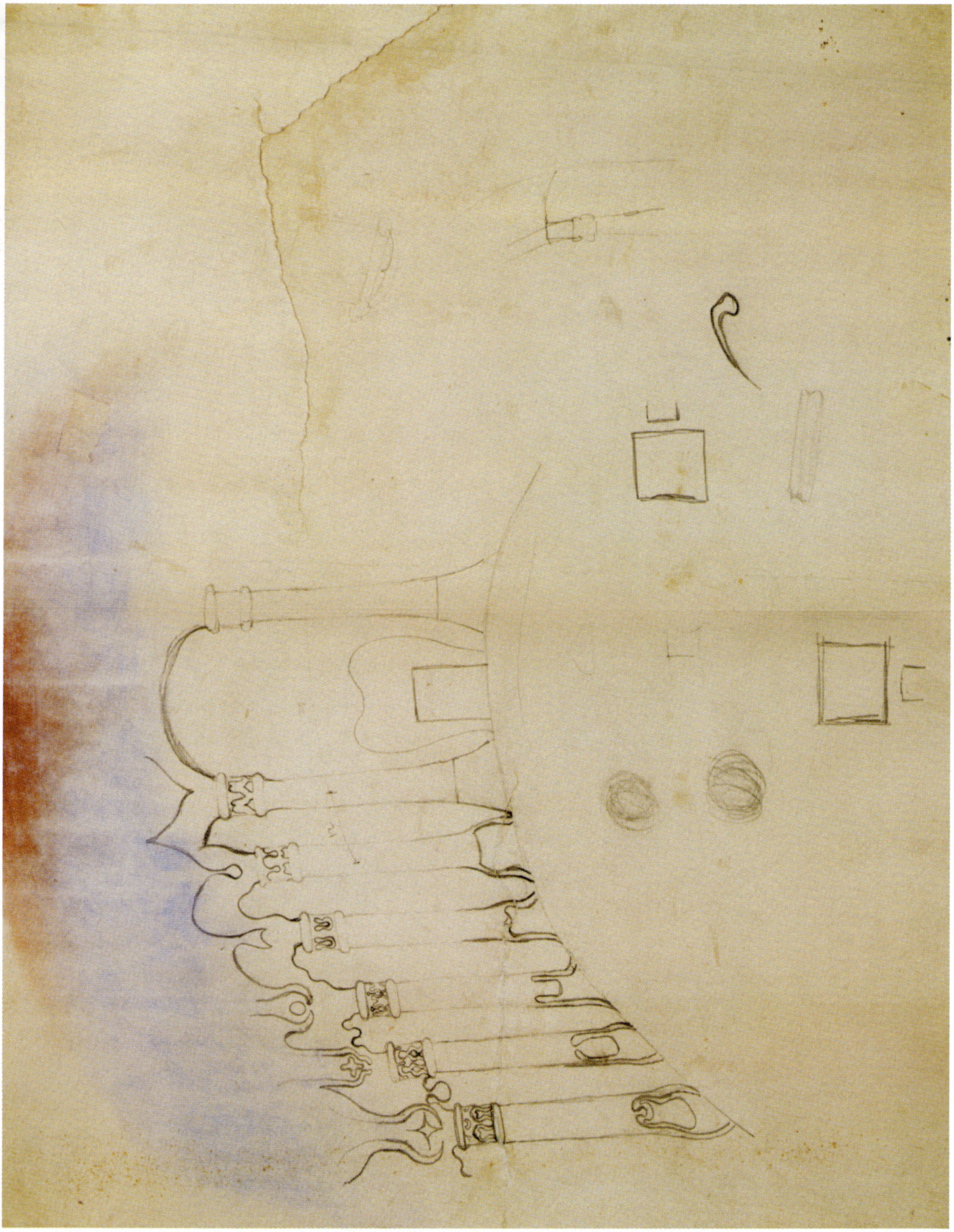

PLATE 35 : Rudolf Steiner's sketch for the columns and architrave of the small cupola room of the first Goetheanum

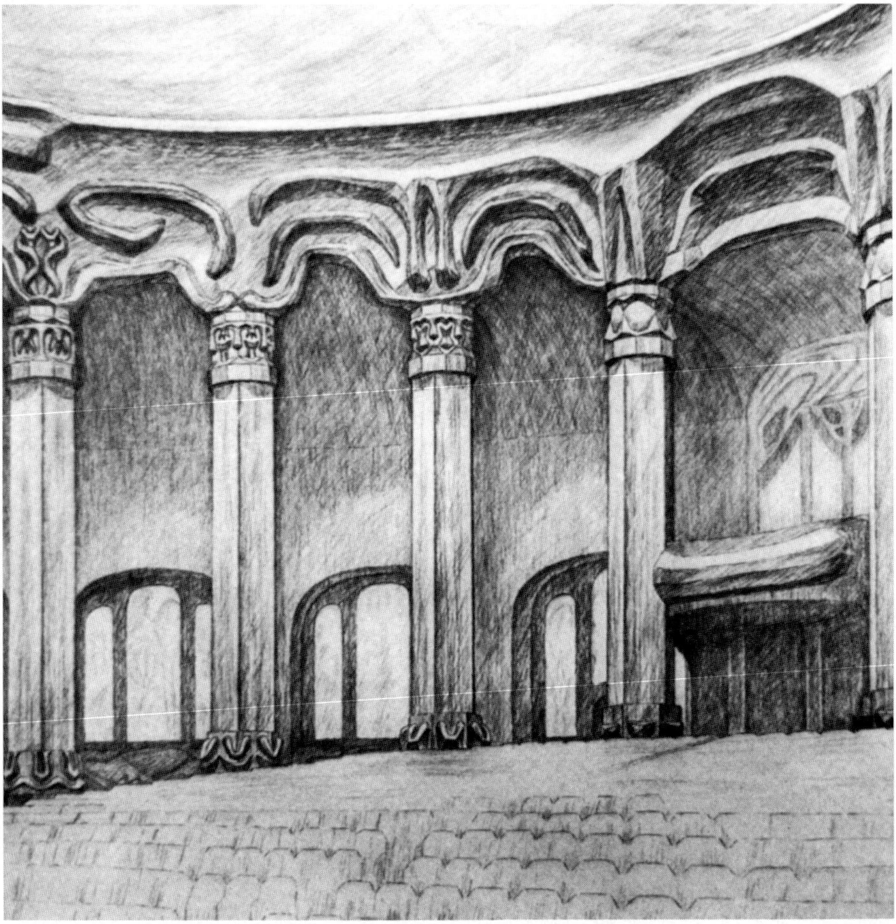

PLATE 36 : Large cupola room of the first Goetheanum: first through fourth columns (drawing by Friedrich Bergmann)

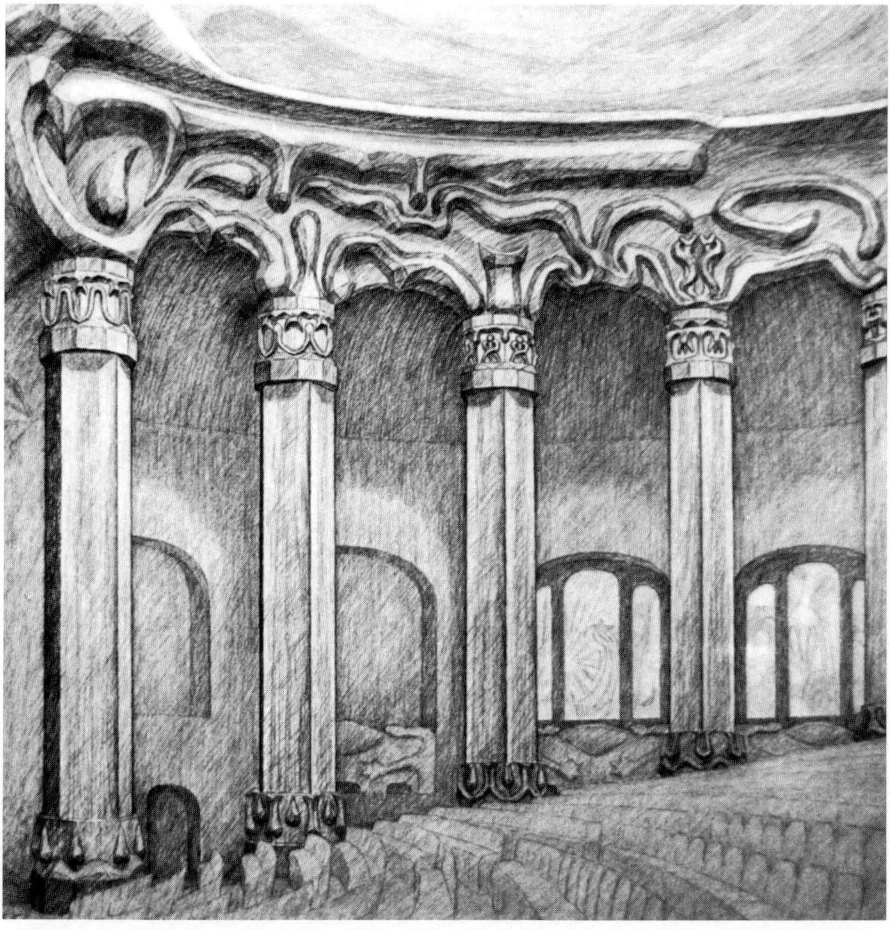

PLATE 37 : Large cupola room of the first Goetheanum: fourth through seventh columns (drawing by Friedrich Bergmann)

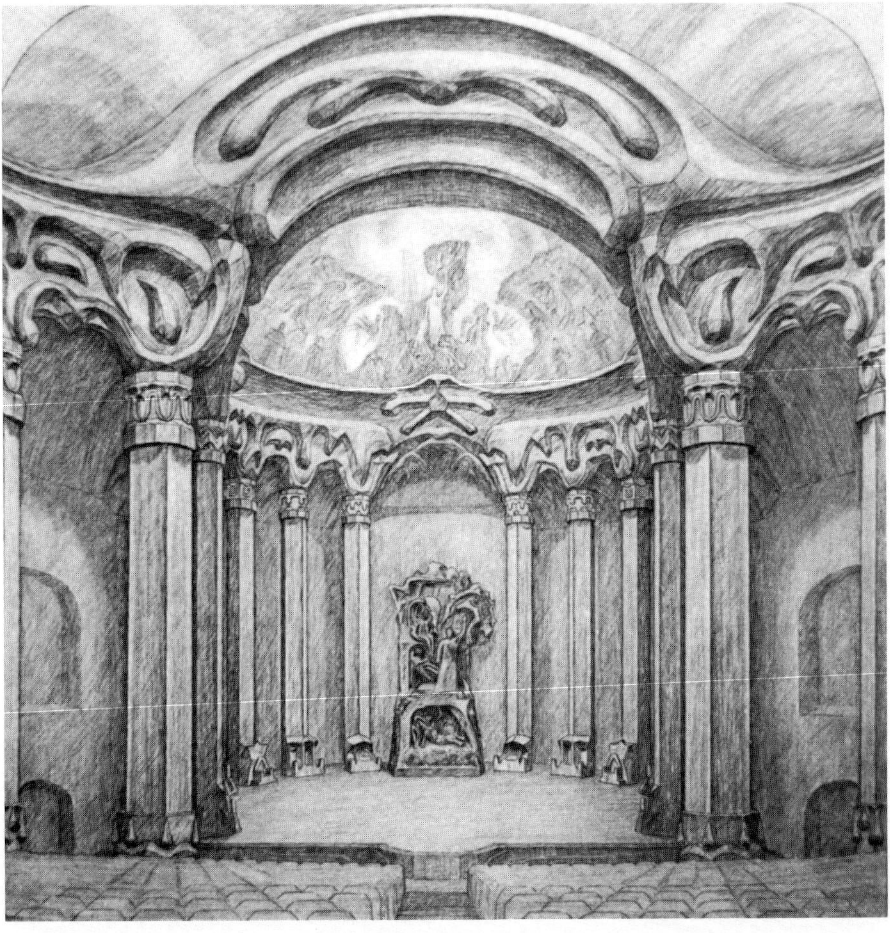

PLATE 38 : View from the auditorium into the small cupola room of the first Goetheanum (drawing by Friedrich Bergmann)